THE FINAL QUEST

ELFQUEST®

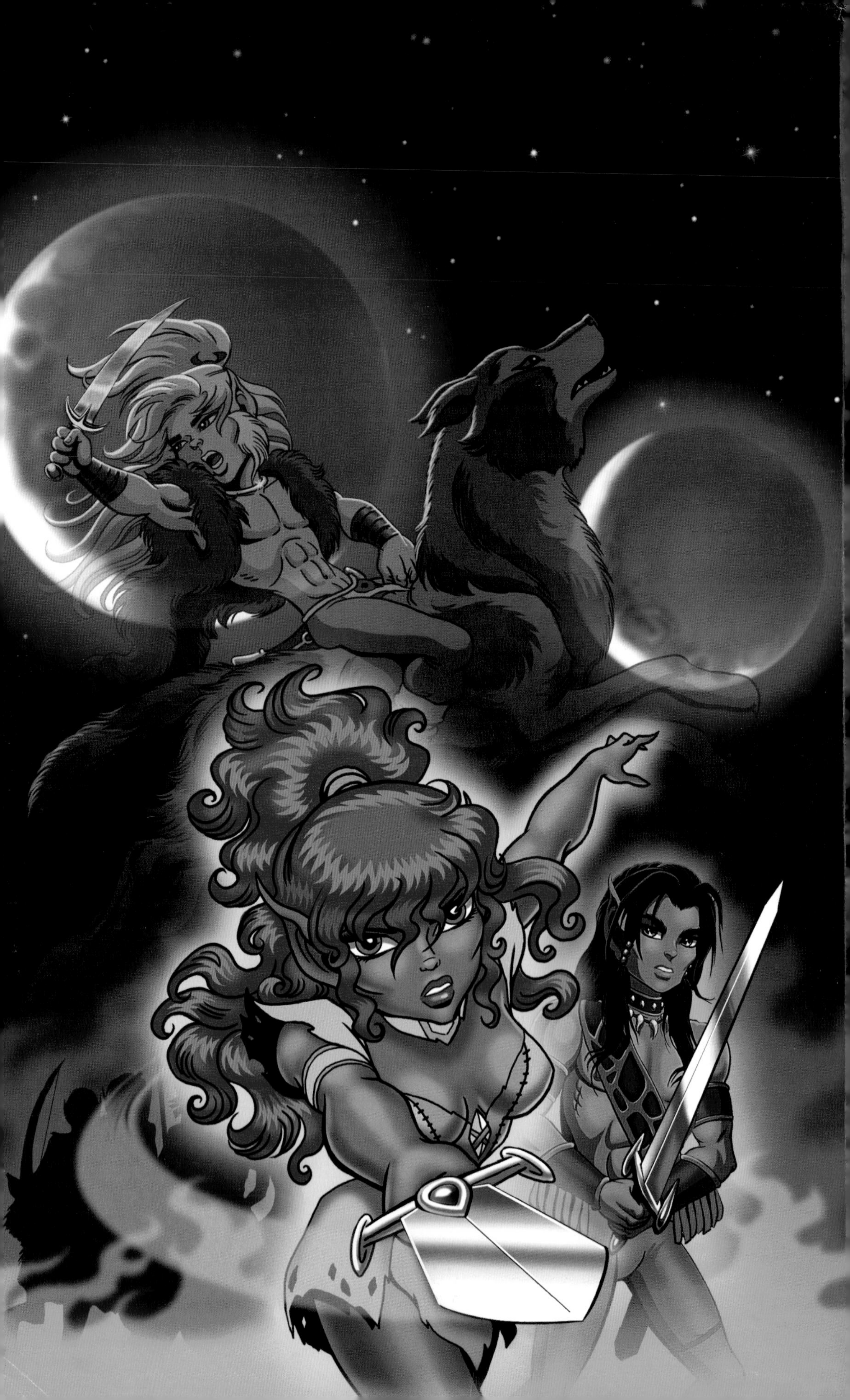

THE **FINAL QUEST**

ELFQUEST®

VOLUME ONE

BY WENDY AND RICHARD PINI

COLORS BY
SONNY STRAIT

LETTERS BY
NATE PIEKOS OF BLAMBOT®

DARK HORSE BOOKS

President & Publisher MIKE RICHARDSON

Editor SIERRA HAHN

Assistant Editor SPENCER CUSHING

Digital Production ALLYSON HALLER

Designer TINA ALESSI

Special thanks to Allyson Willsey.

NEIL HANKERSON Executive Vice President · TOM WEDDLE Chief Financial Officer · RANDY STRADLEY Vice President of Publishing
MICHAEL MARTENS Vice President of Book Trade Sales · SCOTT ALLIE Editor in Chief · MATT PARKINSON Vice President of Marketing
DAVID SCROGGY Vice President of Product Development · DALE LaFOUNTAIN Vice President of Information Technology
DARLENE VOGEL Senior Director of Print, Design, and Production · KEN LIZZI General Counsel · DAVEY ESTRADA Editorial Director
CHRIS WARNER Senior Books Editor · DIANA SCHUTZ Executive Editor · CARY GRAZZINI Director of Print and Development
LIA RIBACCHI Art Director · CARA NIECE Director of Scheduling · MARK BERNARDI Director of Digital Publishing

Published by Dark Horse Books
A division of Dark Horse Comics, Inc.
10956 SE Main Street
Milwaukie, OR 97222

First edition: April 2015
ISBN 978-1-61655-409-5
Convention exclusive edition: April 2015
ISBN 978-1-61655-862-8
1 3 5 7 9 10 8 6 4 2
Printed in China

International Licensing: (503) 905-2377
Comic Shop Locator Service: (888) 266-4226

LIBRARY OF CONGRESS CATALOGING-IN-PUBLICATION DATA

Pini, Wendy.
 Elfquest : the final quest / by Wendy and Richard Pini ; colors by Sonny Strait ; letters by Nate Piekos of Blambot. – First edition.
   volumes cm
 Summary: "The Palace of the High Ones is changing the elves. Cutter's daughter Ember and her tribe must fight off the
tyrant Angrif Djun"– Provided by publisher.
 ISBN 978-1-61655-409-5 (v. 1 : paperback)
 1. Elves–Comic books, strips, etc. 2. Graphic novels. I. Pini, Richard. II. Title.

 PN6728.E45 P5639 2015
 741.5'973–dc23

         2014046866

This volume collects and reprints the comic books ElfQuest: The Final Quest Special *and* The Final Quest #1–#6.

FOR GENERATIONS, the elves sought
refuge from a primitive, savage world.
After much strife they found it in the Palace
of the High Ones. In this sanctuary, Chief
Cutter and his Wolfriders avoid nature's
wrath and the threat of an ever-expanding
human population. And yet comfort comes at
a price as certain elves begin to lose the skills
that once aided them in battle and allowed
them to survive the harshest circumstances.
The magical palace's influence may lead
to their undoing when the Wolfriders start
upon the ultimate quest for survival!

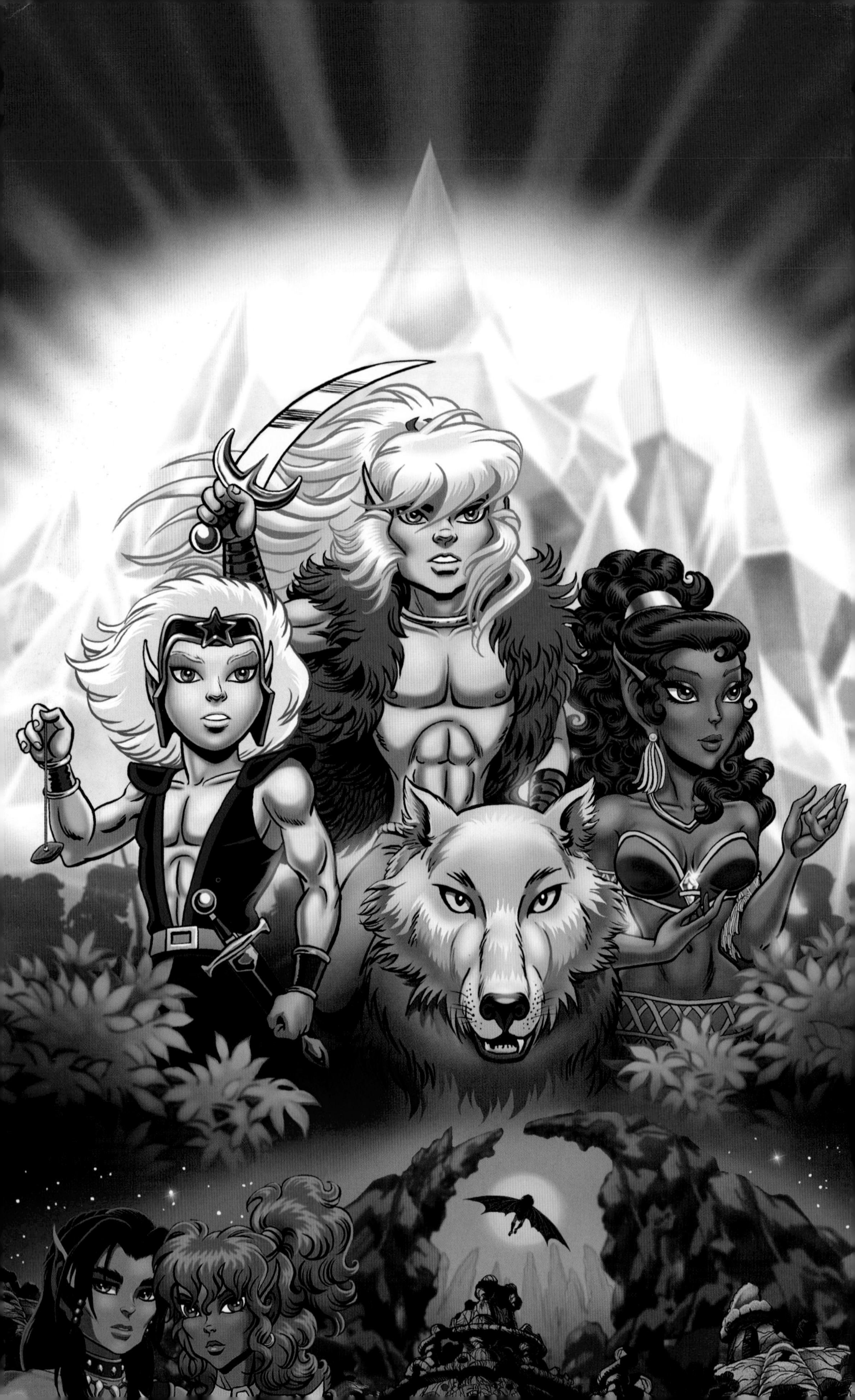

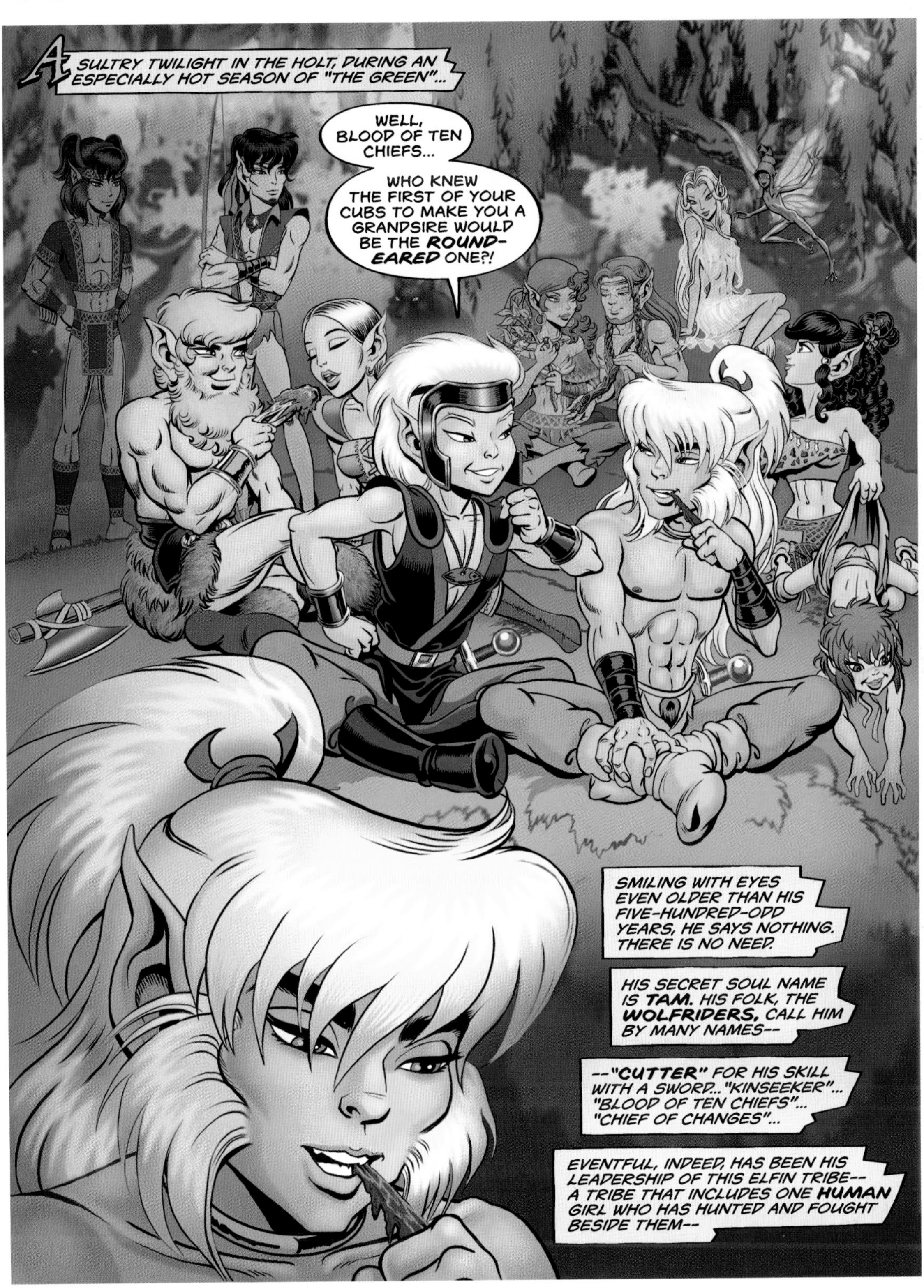
A SULTRY TWILIGHT IN THE HOLT, DURING AN ESPECIALLY HOT SEASON OF "THE GREEN"...
WELL, BLOOD OF TEN CHIEFS...
WHO KNEW THE FIRST OF YOUR CUBS TO MAKE YOU A GRANDSIRE WOULD BE THE **ROUND-EARED** ONE?!
SMILING WITH EYES EVEN OLDER THAN HIS FIVE-HUNDRED-ODD YEARS, HE SAYS NOTHING. THERE IS NO NEED.
HIS SECRET SOUL NAME IS **TAM.** HIS FOLK, THE **WOLFRIDERS,** CALL HIM BY MANY NAMES--
--**"CUTTER"** FOR HIS SKILL WITH A SWORD... "KINSEEKER"... "BLOOD OF TEN CHIEFS"... "CHIEF OF CHANGES"...
EVENTFUL, INDEED, HAS BEEN HIS LEADERSHIP OF THIS ELFIN TRIBE-- A TRIBE THAT INCLUDES ONE **HUMAN** GIRL WHO HAS HUNTED AND FOUGHT BESIDE THEM--

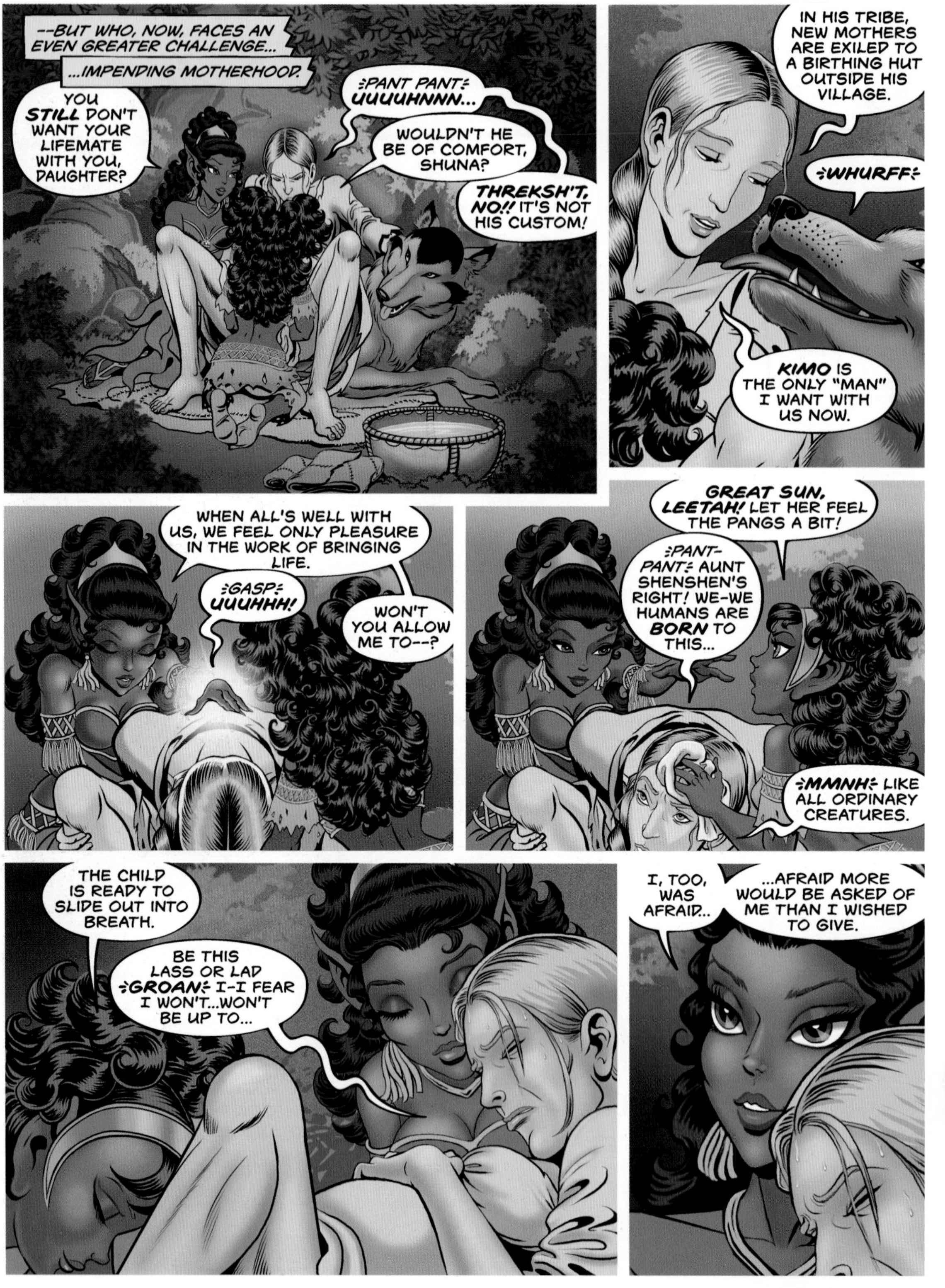
--BUT WHO, NOW, FACES AN EVEN GREATER CHALLENGE...
...IMPENDING MOTHERHOOD.
YOU STILL DON'T WANT YOUR LIFEMATE WITH YOU, DAUGHTER?
PANT PANT UUUUHNNN...
WOULDN'T HE BE OF COMFORT, SHUNA?
THREKSH'T, NO!! IT'S NOT HIS CUSTOM!
IN HIS TRIBE, NEW MOTHERS ARE EXILED TO A BIRTHING HUT OUTSIDE HIS VILLAGE.
WHURFF
KIMO IS THE ONLY "MAN" I WANT WITH US NOW.
WHEN ALL'S WELL WITH US, WE FEEL ONLY PLEASURE IN THE WORK OF BRINGING LIFE.
GASP UUUHHH!
WON'T YOU ALLOW ME TO--?
GREAT SUN, LEETAH! LET HER FEEL THE PANGS A BIT!
PANT-PANT AUNT SHENSHEN'S RIGHT! WE-WE HUMANS ARE BORN TO THIS...
MMNH LIKE ALL ORDINARY CREATURES.
THE CHILD IS READY TO SLIDE OUT INTO BREATH.
BE THIS LASS OR LAD GROAN I-I FEAR I WON'T...WON'T BE UP TO...
I, TOO, WAS AFRAID...
...AFRAID MORE WOULD BE ASKED OF ME THAN I WISHED TO GIVE.

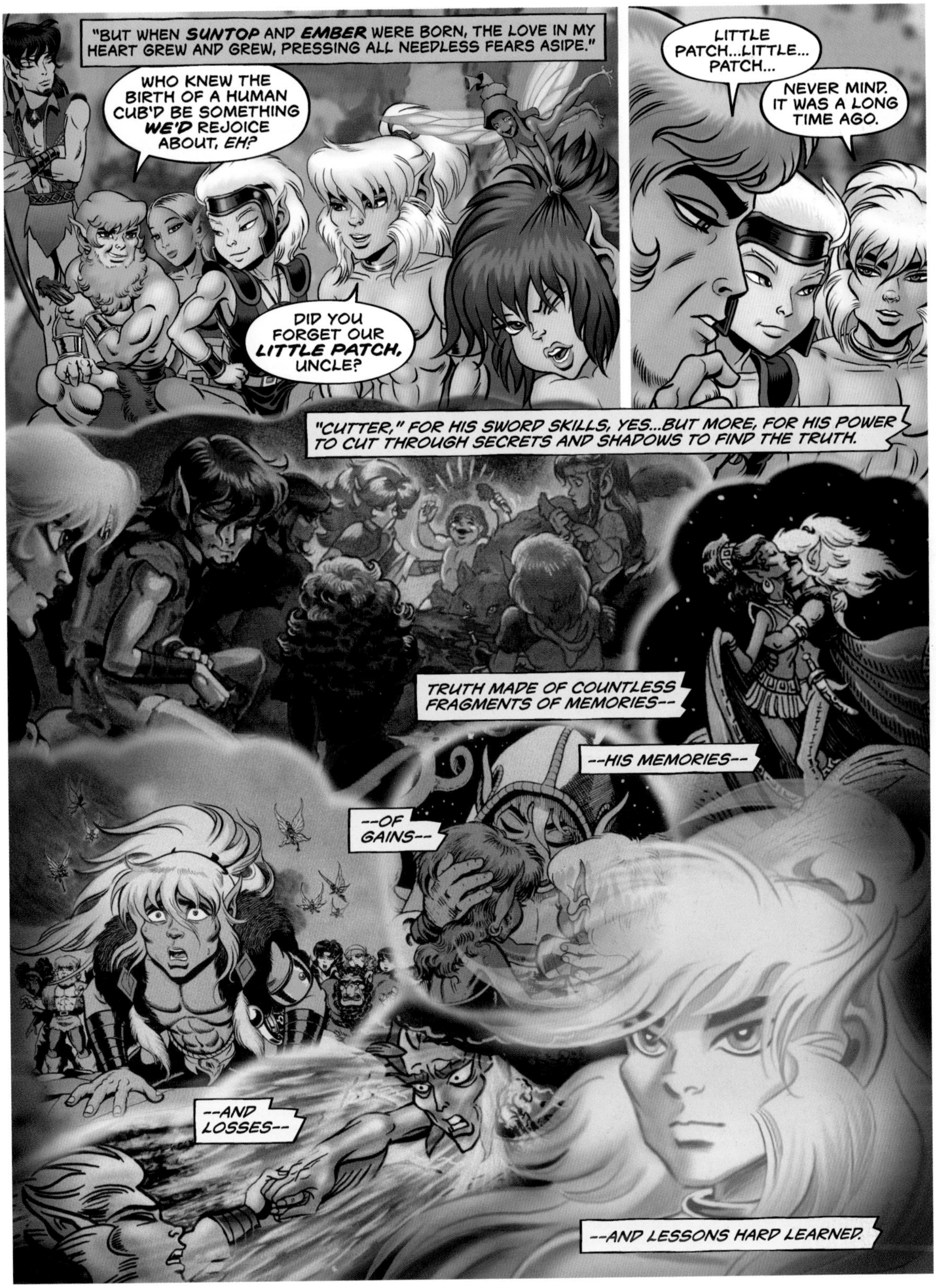
"BUT WHEN SUNTOP AND EMBER WERE BORN, THE LOVE IN MY HEART GREW AND GREW, PRESSING ALL NEEDLESS FEARS ASIDE."
WHO KNEW THE BIRTH OF A HUMAN CUB'D BE SOMETHING WE'D REJOICE ABOUT, EH?
DID YOU FORGET OUR LITTLE PATCH, UNCLE?
LITTLE PATCH...LITTLE... PATCH...
NEVER MIND. IT WAS A LONG TIME AGO.
"CUTTER," FOR HIS SWORD SKILLS, YES...BUT MORE, FOR HIS POWER TO CUT THROUGH SECRETS AND SHADOWS TO FIND THE TRUTH.
TRUTH MADE OF COUNTLESS FRAGMENTS OF MEMORIES--
--HIS MEMORIES--
--OF GAINS--
--AND LOSSES--
--AND LESSONS HARD LEARNED.

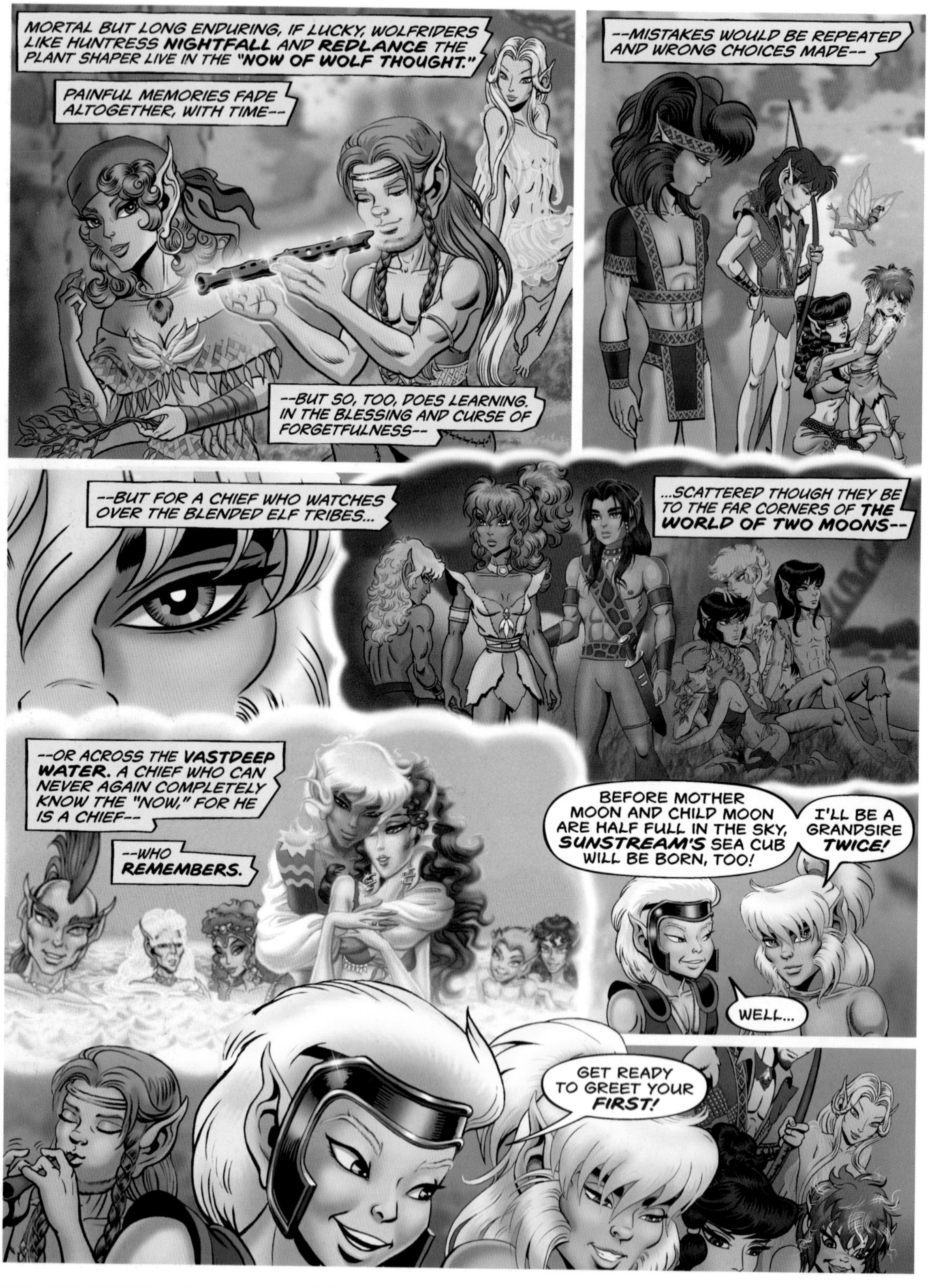
MORTAL BUT LONG ENDURING, IF LUCKY, WOLFRIDERS LIKE HUNTRESS NIGHTFALL AND REDLANCE THE PLANT SHAPER LIVE IN THE "NOW OF WOLF THOUGHT."
PAINFUL MEMORIES FADE ALTOGETHER, WITH TIME--
--BUT SO, TOO, DOES LEARNING. IN THE BLESSING AND CURSE OF FORGETFULNESS--
--MISTAKES WOULD BE REPEATED AND WRONG CHOICES MADE--
--BUT FOR A CHIEF WHO WATCHES OVER THE BLENDED ELF TRIBES...
...SCATTERED THOUGH THEY BE TO THE FAR CORNERS OF THE WORLD OF TWO MOONS--
--OR ACROSS THE VASTDEEP WATER. A CHIEF WHO CAN NEVER AGAIN COMPLETELY KNOW THE "NOW," FOR HE IS A CHIEF--
--WHO REMEMBERS.
BEFORE MOTHER MOON AND CHILD MOON ARE HALF FULL IN THE SKY, SUNSTREAM'S SEA CUB WILL BE BORN, TOO!
I'LL BE A GRANDSIRE TWICE!
WELL...
GET READY TO GREET YOUR FIRST!

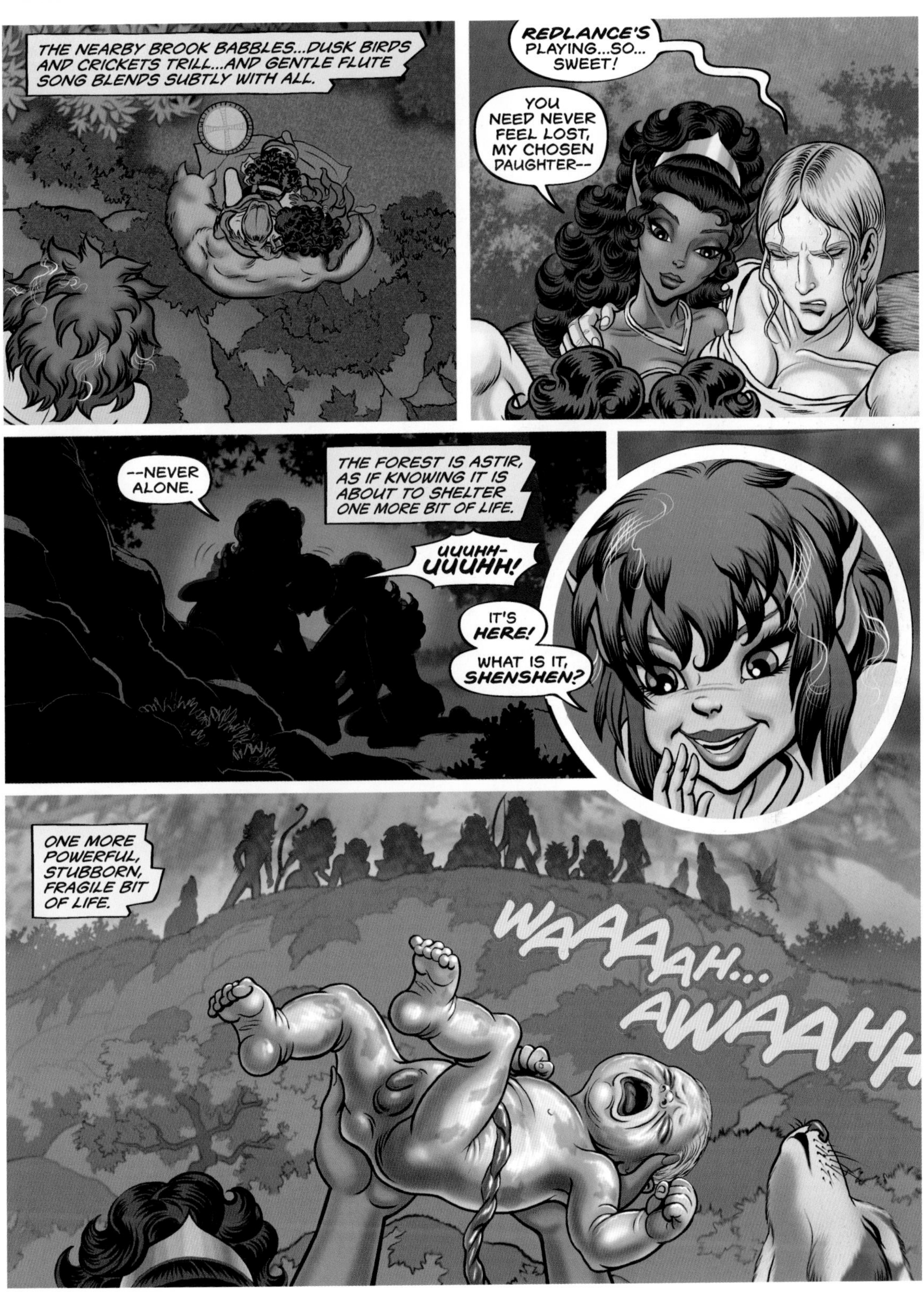
THE NEARBY BROOK BABBLES...DUSK BIRDS AND CRICKETS TRILL...AND GENTLE FLUTE SONG BLENDS SUBTLY WITH ALL.
REDLANCE'S PLAYING...SO... SWEET!
YOU NEED NEVER FEEL LOST, MY CHOSEN DAUGHTER--
--NEVER ALONE.
THE FOREST IS ASTIR, AS IF KNOWING IT IS ABOUT TO SHELTER ONE MORE BIT OF LIFE.
UUUHH-UUUHH!
IT'S HERE!
WHAT IS IT, SHENSHEN?
ONE MORE POWERFUL, STUBBORN, FRAGILE BIT OF LIFE.
WAAAAH... AWAAHH

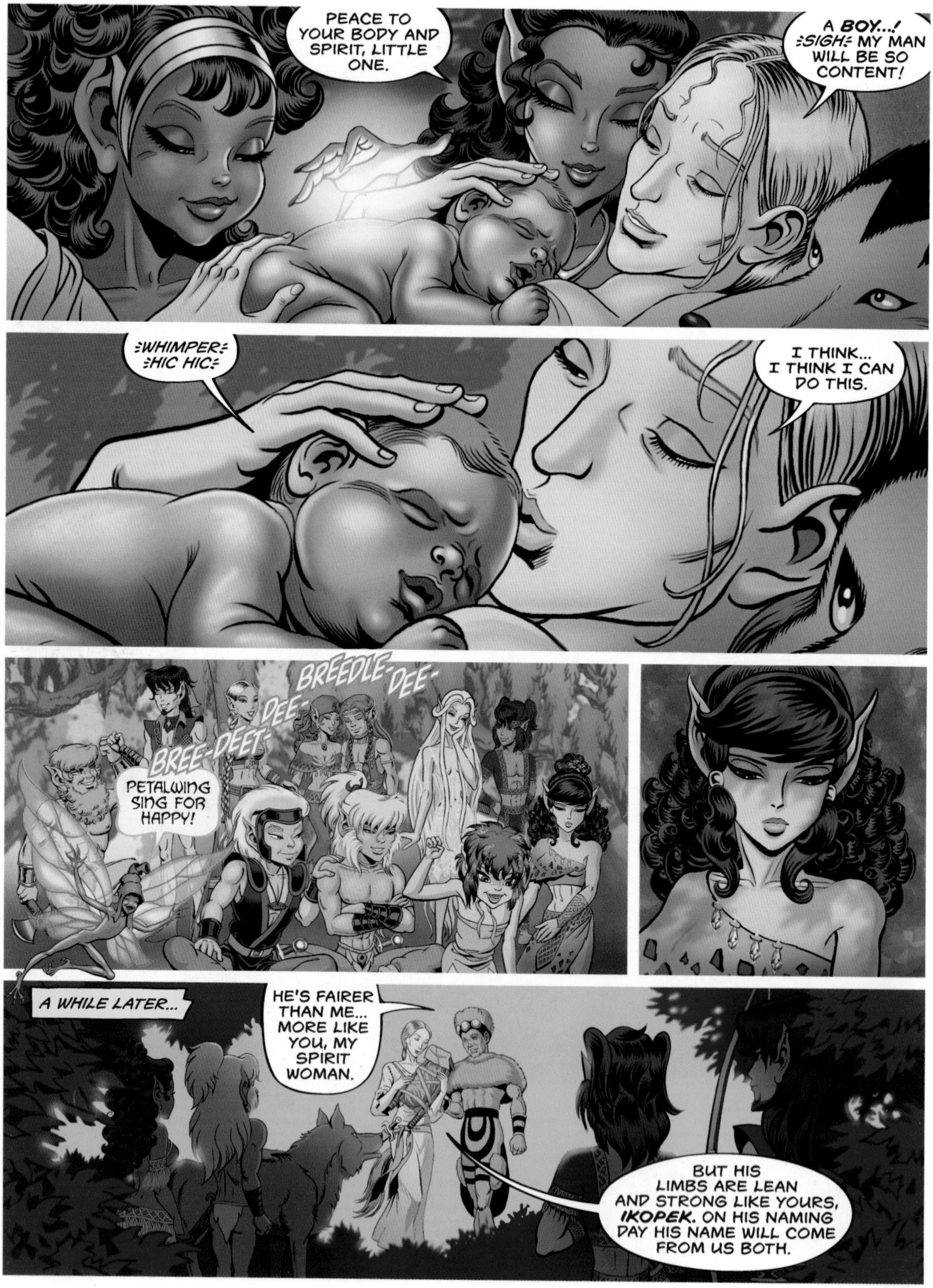
PEACE TO YOUR BODY AND SPIRIT, LITTLE ONE.
A BOY...! ≶SIGH≶ MY MAN WILL BE SO CONTENT!
≶WHIMPER≶ ≶HIC HIC≶
I THINK... I THINK I CAN DO THIS.
BREE-DEET-DEE-BREEDLE-DEE-
PETALWING SING FOR HAPPY!
A WHILE LATER...
HE'S FAIRER THAN ME... MORE LIKE YOU, MY SPIRIT WOMAN.
BUT HIS LIMBS ARE LEAN AND STRONG LIKE YOURS, IKOPEK. ON HIS NAMING DAY HIS NAME WILL COME FROM US BOTH.

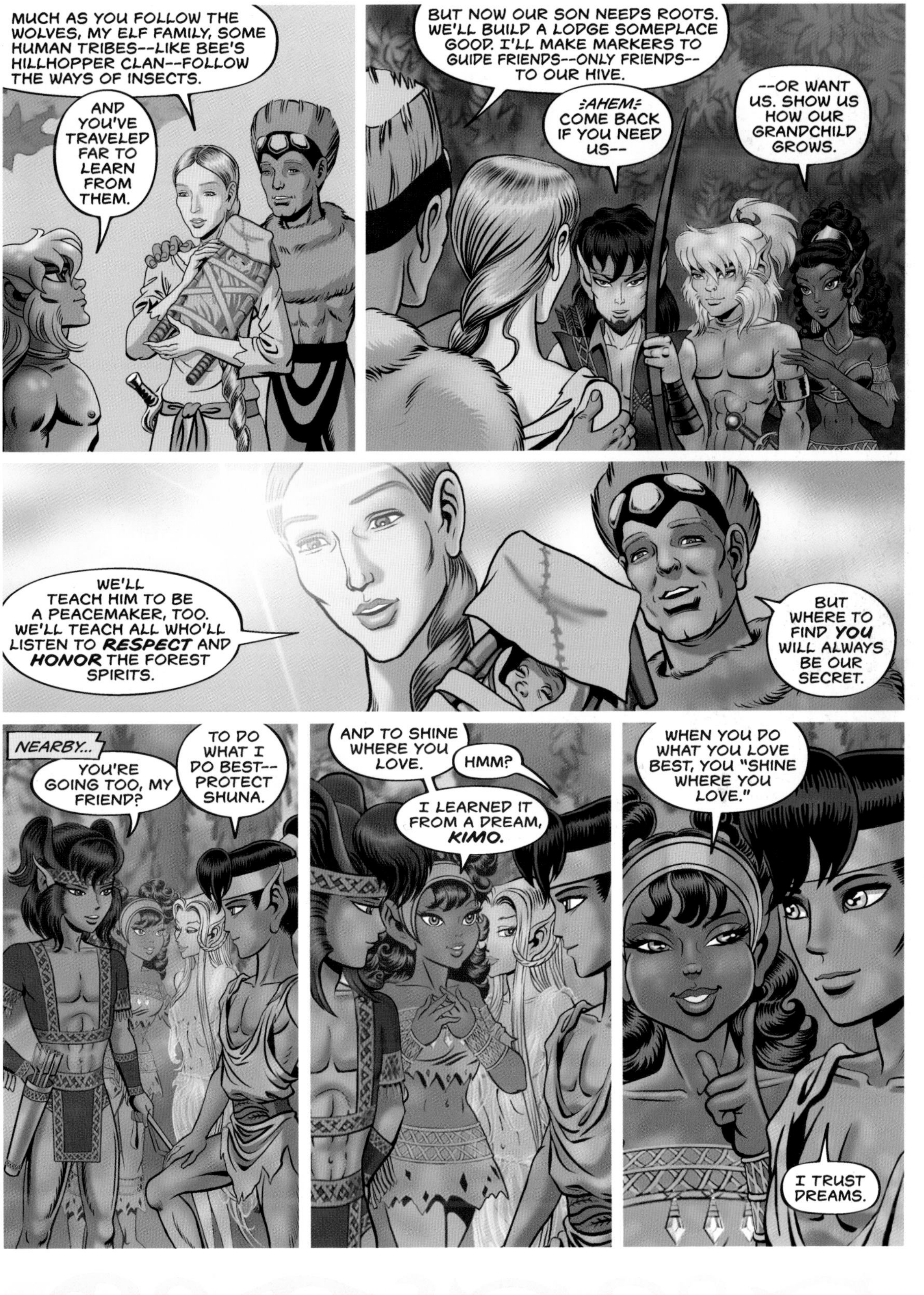
MUCH AS YOU FOLLOW THE WOLVES, MY ELF FAMILY, SOME HUMAN TRIBES--LIKE BEE'S HILLHOPPER CLAN--FOLLOW THE WAYS OF INSECTS.
AND YOU'VE TRAVELED FAR TO LEARN FROM THEM.
BUT NOW OUR SON NEEDS ROOTS. WE'LL BUILD A LODGE SOMEPLACE GOOD. I'LL MAKE MARKERS TO GUIDE FRIENDS--ONLY FRIENDS--TO OUR HIVE.
AHEM COME BACK IF YOU NEED US--
--OR WANT US. SHOW US HOW OUR GRANDCHILD GROWS.
WE'LL TEACH HIM TO BE A PEACEMAKER, TOO. WE'LL TEACH ALL WHO'LL LISTEN TO RESPECT AND HONOR THE FOREST SPIRITS.
BUT WHERE TO FIND YOU WILL ALWAYS BE OUR SECRET.
NEARBY...
YOU'RE GOING TOO, MY FRIEND?
TO DO WHAT I DO BEST--PROTECT SHUNA.
AND TO SHINE WHERE YOU LOVE.
HMM?
I LEARNED IT FROM A DREAM, KIMO.
WHEN YOU DO WHAT YOU LOVE BEST, YOU "SHINE WHERE YOU LOVE."
I TRUST DREAMS.

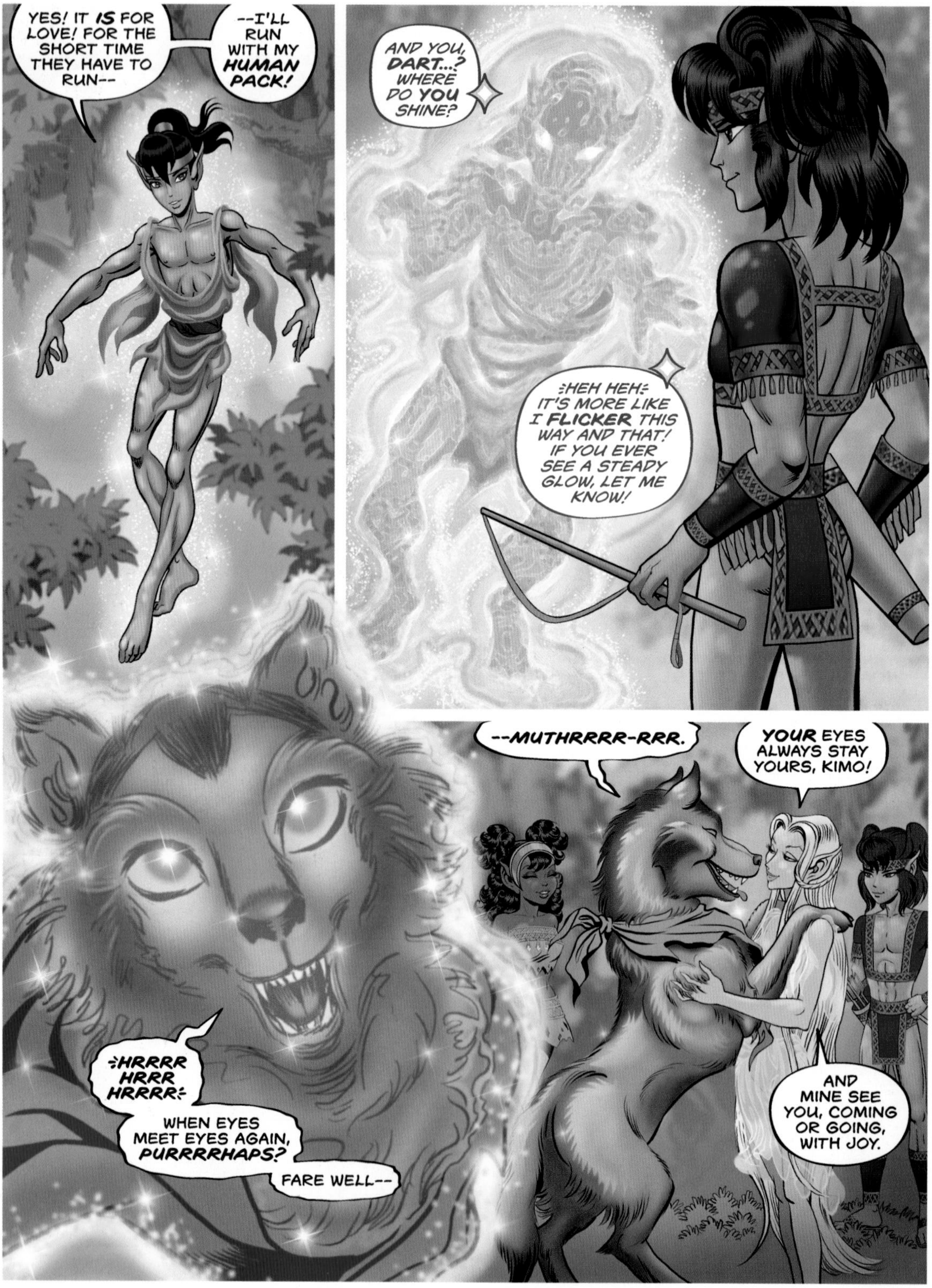
YES! IT IS FOR LOVE! FOR THE SHORT TIME THEY HAVE TO RUN--
--I'LL RUN WITH MY HUMAN PACK!
AND YOU, DART...? WHERE DO YOU SHINE?
HEH HEH IT'S MORE LIKE I FLICKER THIS WAY AND THAT! IF YOU EVER SEE A STEADY GLOW, LET ME KNOW!
HRRRR HRRR HRRRR
WHEN EYES MEET EYES AGAIN, PURRRRHAPS?
FARE WELL--
--MUTHRRRR-RRR.
YOUR EYES ALWAYS STAY YOURS, KIMO!
AND MINE SEE YOU, COMING OR GOING, WITH JOY.

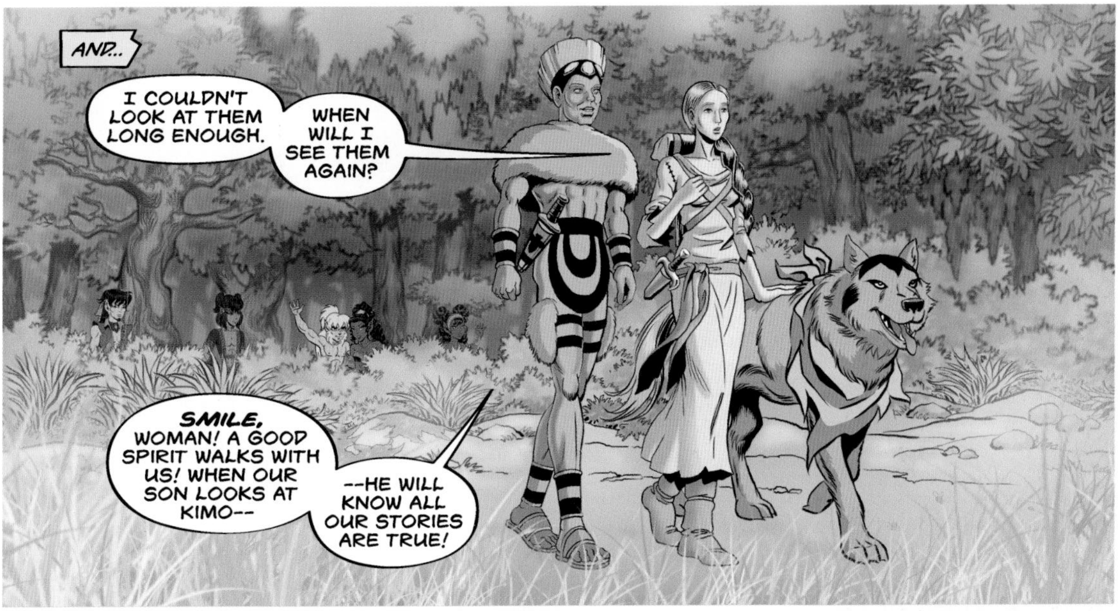
AND...
I COULDN'T LOOK AT THEM LONG ENOUGH.
WHEN WILL I SEE THEM AGAIN?
SMILE, WOMAN! A GOOD SPIRIT WALKS WITH US! WHEN OUR SON LOOKS AT KIMO--
--HE WILL KNOW ALL OUR STORIES ARE TRUE!

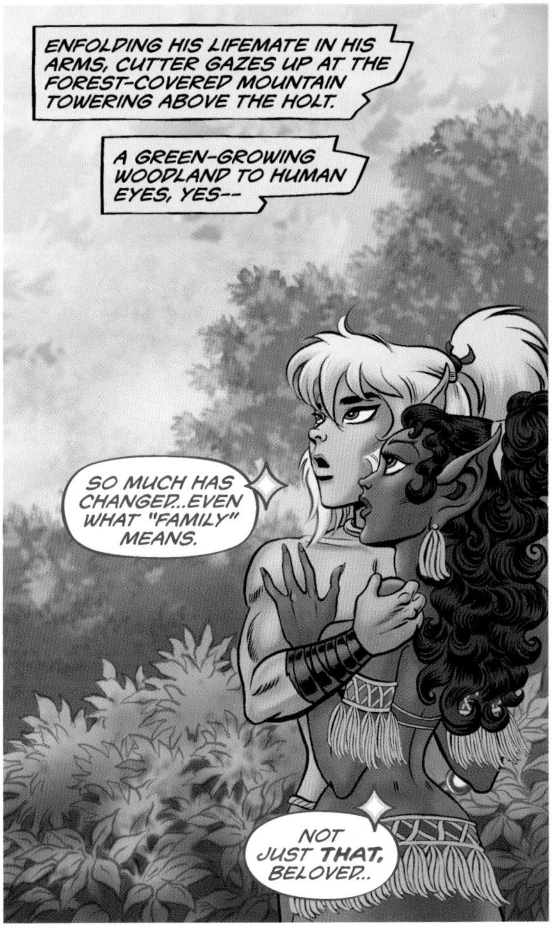
ENFOLDING HIS LIFEMATE IN HIS ARMS, CUTTER GAZES UP AT THE FOREST-COVERED MOUNTAIN TOWERING ABOVE THE HOLT.
A GREEN-GROWING WOODLAND TO HUMAN EYES, YES--
SO MUCH HAS CHANGED...EVEN WHAT "FAMILY" MEANS.
NOT JUST THAT, BELOVED...

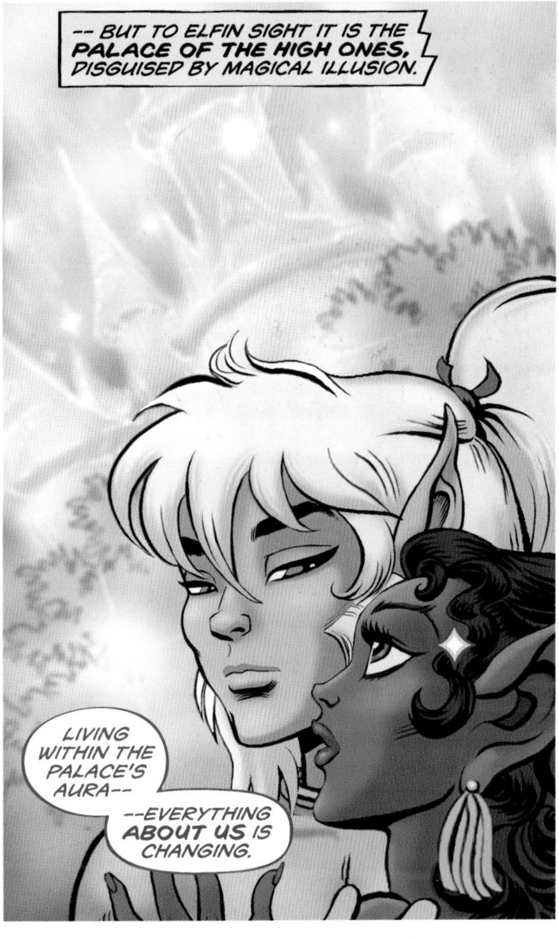
-- BUT TO ELFIN SIGHT IT IS THE PALACE OF THE HIGH ONES, DISGUISED BY MAGICAL ILLUSION.
LIVING WITHIN THE PALACE'S AURA--
--EVERYTHING ABOUT US IS CHANGING.

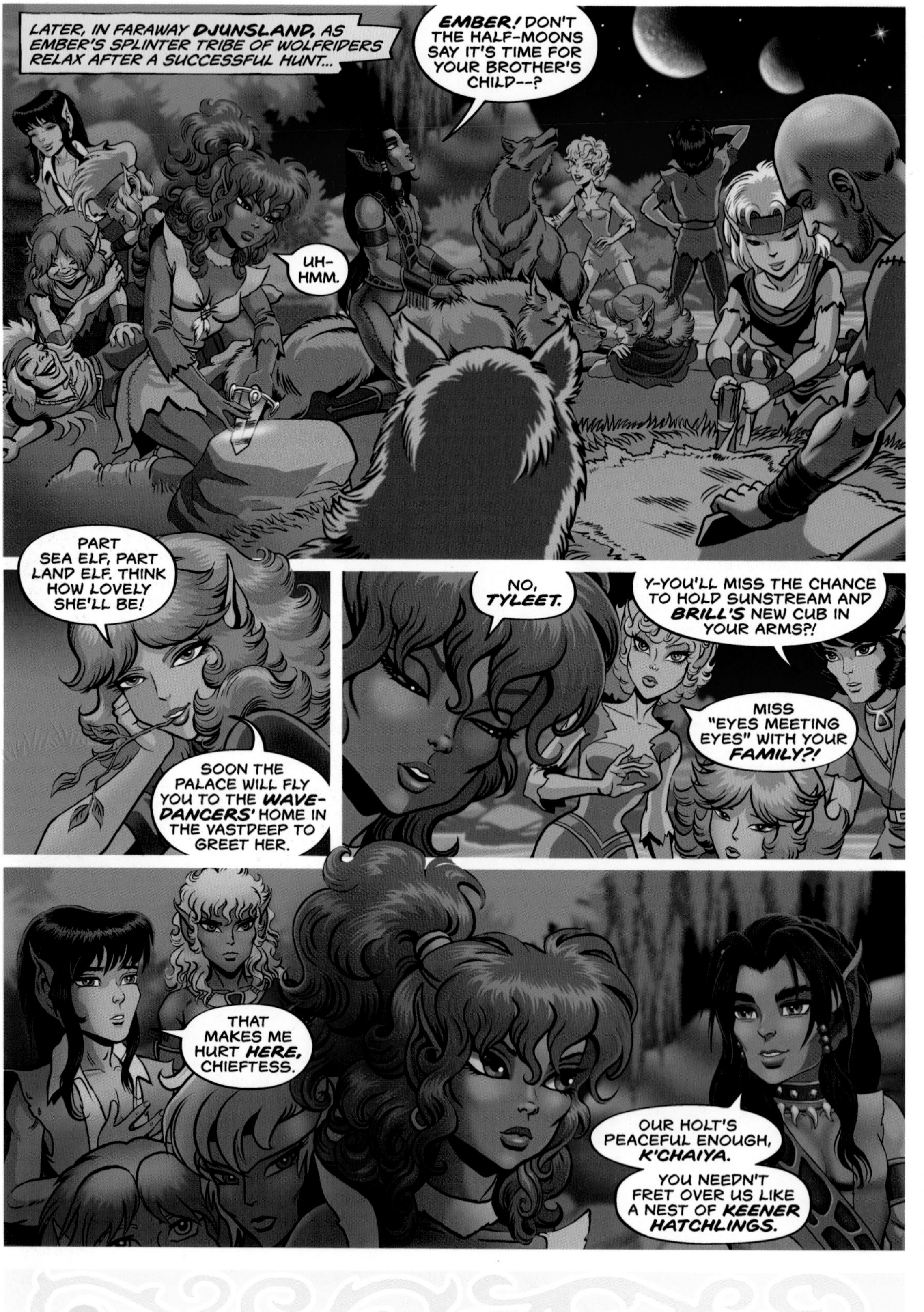
LATER, IN FARAWAY DJUNSLAND, AS EMBER'S SPLINTER TRIBE OF WOLFRIDERS RELAX AFTER A SUCCESSFUL HUNT...
EMBER! DON'T THE HALF-MOONS SAY IT'S TIME FOR YOUR BROTHER'S CHILD--?
UH-HMM.
PART SEA ELF, PART LAND ELF. THINK HOW LOVELY SHE'LL BE!
SOON THE PALACE WILL FLY YOU TO THE WAVE-DANCERS' HOME IN THE VASTDEEP TO GREET HER.
NO, TYLEET.
Y-YOU'LL MISS THE CHANCE TO HOLD SUNSTREAM AND BRILL'S NEW CUB IN YOUR ARMS?!
MISS "EYES MEETING EYES" WITH YOUR FAMILY?!
THAT MAKES ME HURT HERE, CHIEFTESS.
OUR HOLT'S PEACEFUL ENOUGH, K'CHAIYA.
YOU NEEDN'T FRET OVER US LIKE A NEST OF KEENER HATCHLINGS.

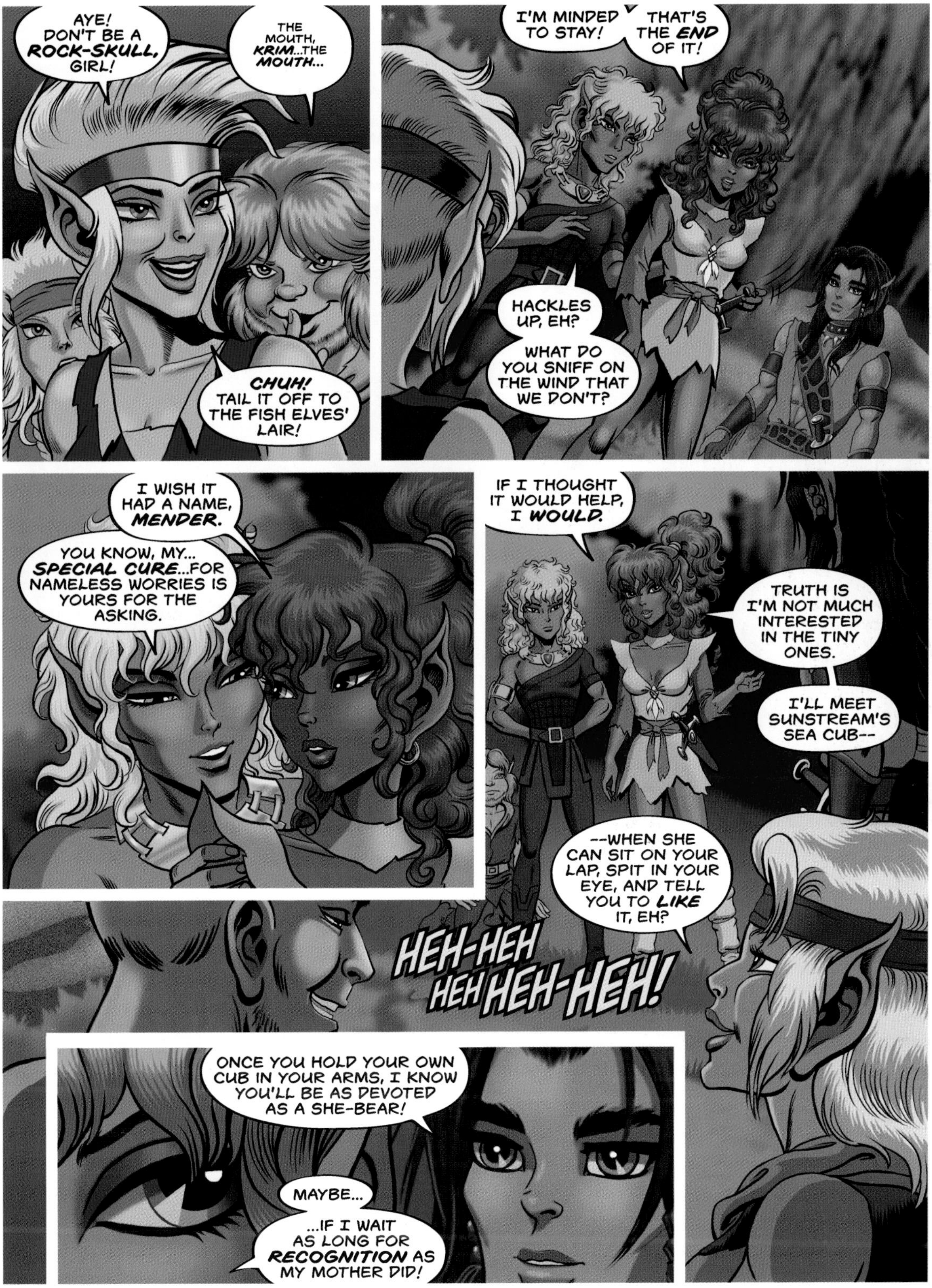
AYE! DON'T BE A ROCK-SKULL, GIRL!
THE MOUTH, KRIM...THE MOUTH...
CHUH! TAIL IT OFF TO THE FISH ELVES' LAIR!
I'M MINDED TO STAY!
THAT'S THE END OF IT!
HACKLES UP, EH?
WHAT DO YOU SNIFF ON THE WIND THAT WE DON'T?
I WISH IT HAD A NAME, MENDER.
YOU KNOW, MY... SPECIAL CURE...FOR NAMELESS WORRIES IS YOURS FOR THE ASKING.
IF I THOUGHT IT WOULD HELP, I WOULD.
TRUTH IS I'M NOT MUCH INTERESTED IN THE TINY ONES.
I'LL MEET SUNSTREAM'S SEA CUB--
--WHEN SHE CAN SIT ON YOUR LAP, SPIT IN YOUR EYE, AND TELL YOU TO LIKE IT, EH?
HEH-HEH HEH HEH-HEH!
ONCE YOU HOLD YOUR OWN CUB IN YOUR ARMS, I KNOW YOU'LL BE AS DEVOTED AS A SHE-BEAR!
MAYBE...
...IF I WAIT AS LONG FOR RECOGNITION AS MY MOTHER DID!

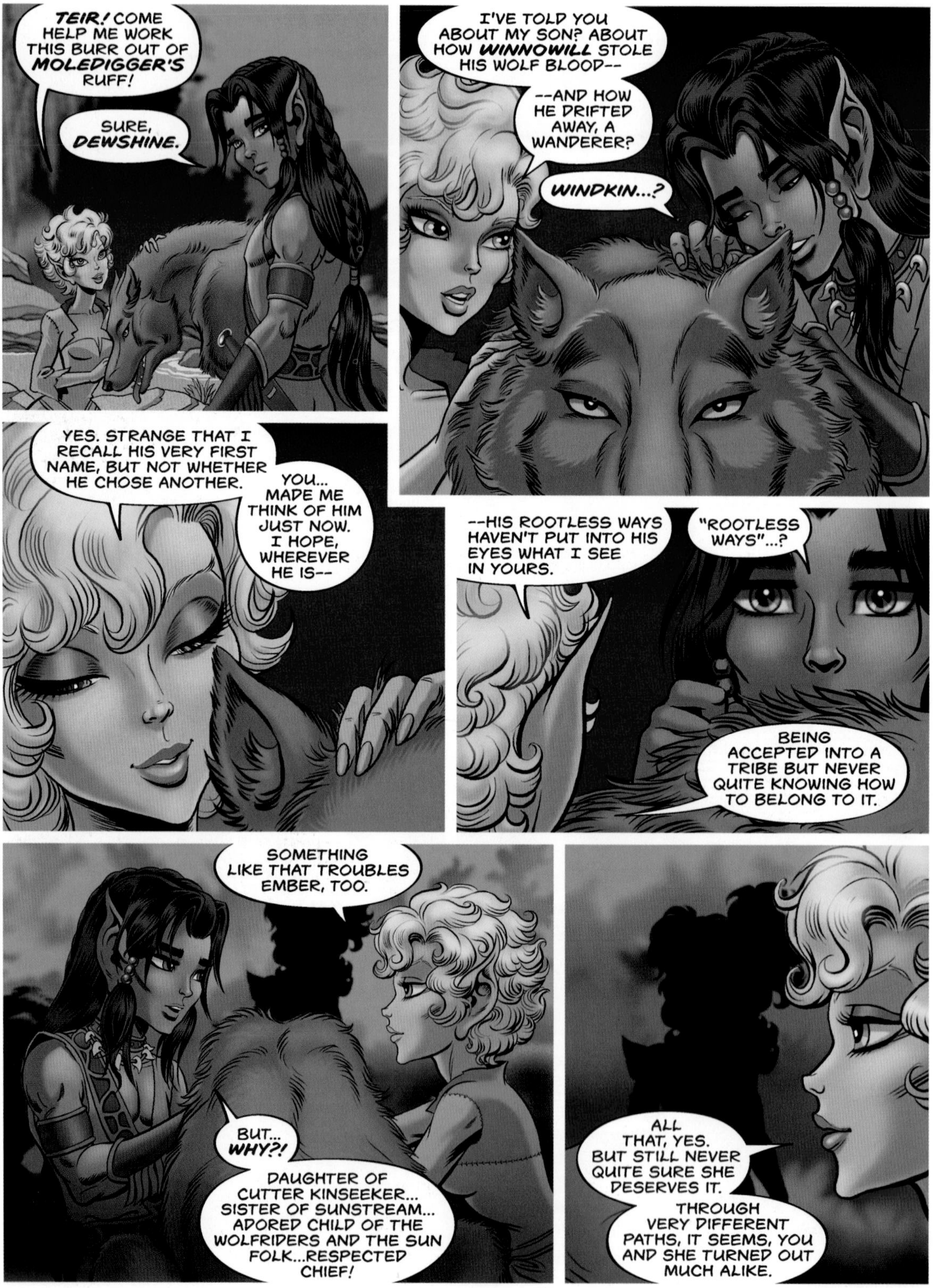
TEIR! COME HELP ME WORK THIS BURR OUT OF MOLEDIGGER'S RUFF!
SURE, DEWSHINE.
I'VE TOLD YOU ABOUT MY SON? ABOUT HOW WINNOWILL STOLE HIS WOLF BLOOD--
--AND HOW HE DRIFTED AWAY, A WANDERER?
WINDKIN...?
YES. STRANGE THAT I RECALL HIS VERY FIRST NAME, BUT NOT WHETHER HE CHOSE ANOTHER.
YOU... MADE ME THINK OF HIM JUST NOW. I HOPE, WHEREVER HE IS--
--HIS ROOTLESS WAYS HAVEN'T PUT INTO HIS EYES WHAT I SEE IN YOURS.
"ROOTLESS WAYS"...?
BEING ACCEPTED INTO A TRIBE BUT NEVER QUITE KNOWING HOW TO BELONG TO IT.
SOMETHING LIKE THAT TROUBLES EMBER, TOO.
BUT... WHY?!
DAUGHTER OF CUTTER KINSEEKER... SISTER OF SUNSTREAM... ADORED CHILD OF THE WOLFRIDERS AND THE SUN FOLK...RESPECTED CHIEF!
ALL THAT, YES. BUT STILL NEVER QUITE SURE SHE DESERVES IT.
THROUGH VERY DIFFERENT PATHS, IT SEEMS, YOU AND SHE TURNED OUT MUCH ALIKE.

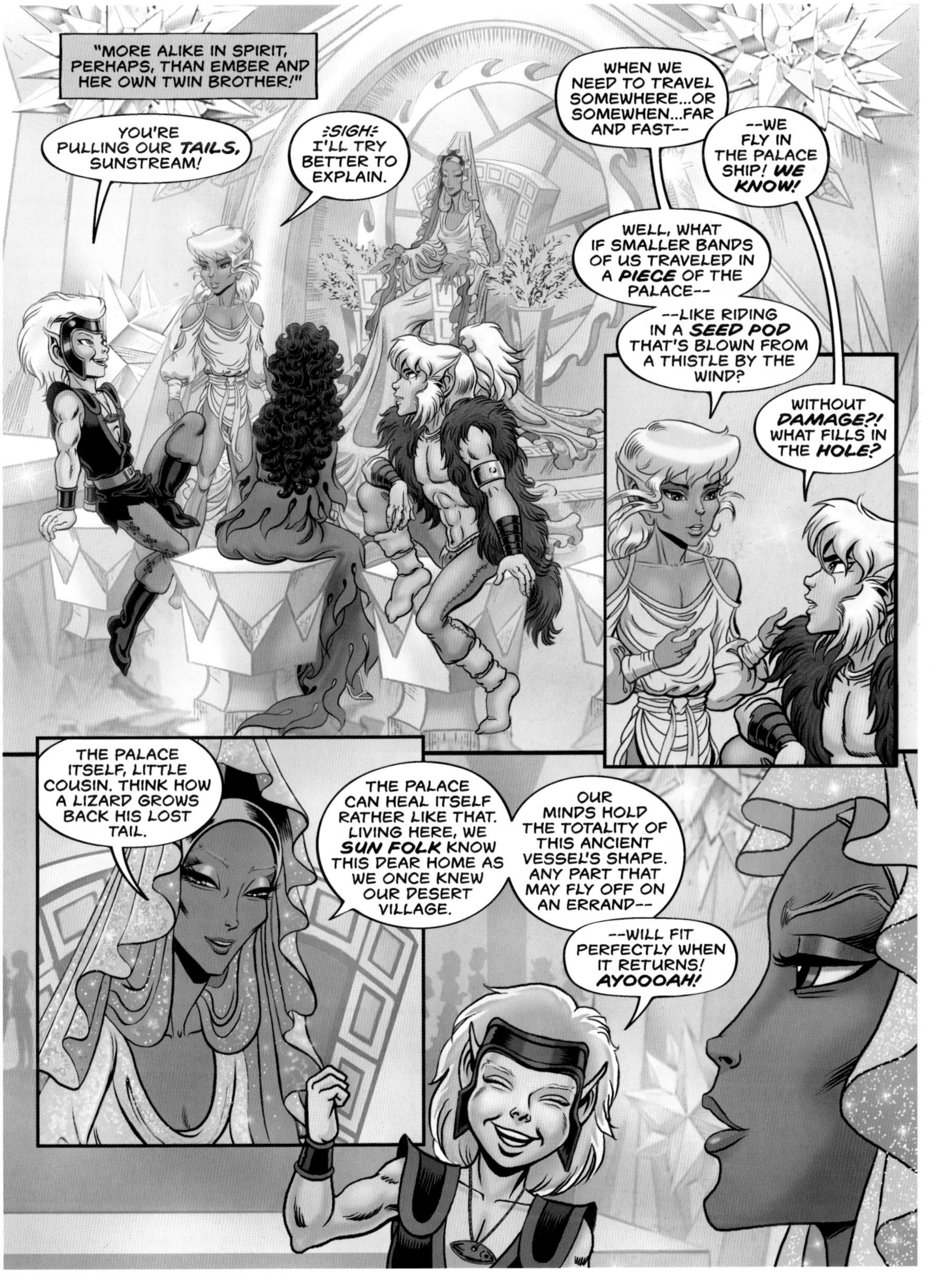
"MORE ALIKE IN SPIRIT, PERHAPS, THAN EMBER AND HER OWN TWIN BROTHER!"
YOU'RE PULLING OUR TAILS, SUNSTREAM!
:SIGH: I'LL TRY BETTER TO EXPLAIN.
WHEN WE NEED TO TRAVEL SOMEWHERE...OR SOMEWHEN...FAR AND FAST--
--WE FLY IN THE PALACE SHIP! WE KNOW!
WELL, WHAT IF SMALLER BANDS OF US TRAVELED IN A PIECE OF THE PALACE--
--LIKE RIDING IN A SEED POD THAT'S BLOWN FROM A THISTLE BY THE WIND?
WITHOUT DAMAGE?! WHAT FILLS IN THE HOLE?
THE PALACE ITSELF, LITTLE COUSIN. THINK HOW A LIZARD GROWS BACK HIS LOST TAIL.
THE PALACE CAN HEAL ITSELF RATHER LIKE THAT. LIVING HERE, WE SUN FOLK KNOW THIS DEAR HOME AS WE ONCE KNEW OUR DESERT VILLAGE.
OUR MINDS HOLD THE TOTALITY OF THIS ANCIENT VESSEL'S SHAPE. ANY PART THAT MAY FLY OFF ON AN ERRAND--
--WILL FIT PERFECTLY WHEN IT RETURNS! AYOOOAH!

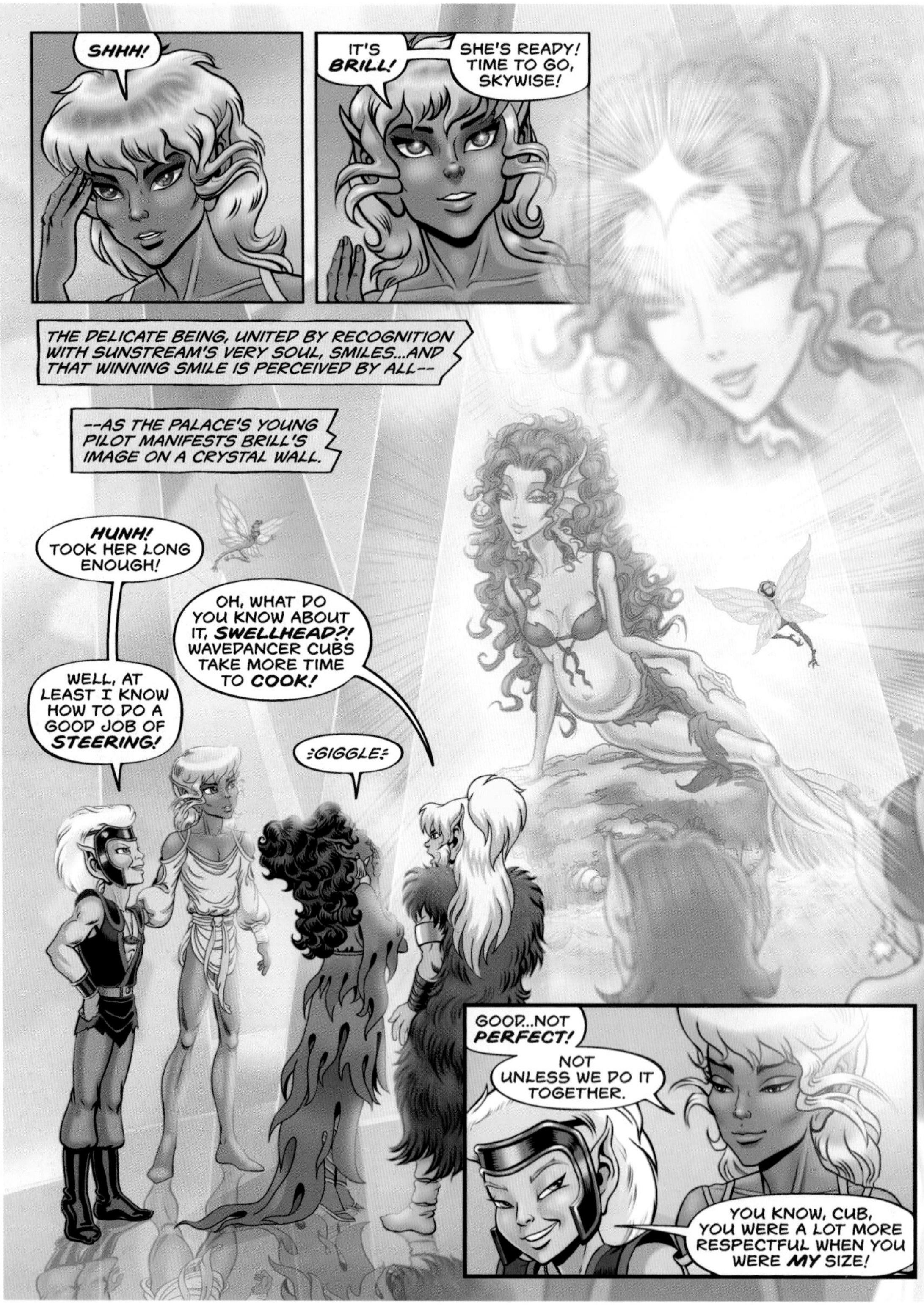
SHHH!
IT'S BRILL!
SHE'S READY! TIME TO GO, SKYWISE!
THE DELICATE BEING, UNITED BY RECOGNITION WITH SUNSTREAM'S VERY SOUL, SMILES...AND THAT WINNING SMILE IS PERCEIVED BY ALL--
--AS THE PALACE'S YOUNG PILOT MANIFESTS BRILL'S IMAGE ON A CRYSTAL WALL.
HUNH! TOOK HER LONG ENOUGH!
OH, WHAT DO YOU KNOW ABOUT IT, SWELLHEAD?! WAVEDANCER CUBS TAKE MORE TIME TO COOK!
WELL, AT LEAST I KNOW HOW TO DO A GOOD JOB OF STEERING!
=GIGGLE=
GOOD...NOT PERFECT!
NOT UNLESS WE DO IT TOGETHER.
YOU KNOW, CUB, YOU WERE A LOT MORE RESPECTFUL WHEN YOU WERE MY SIZE!

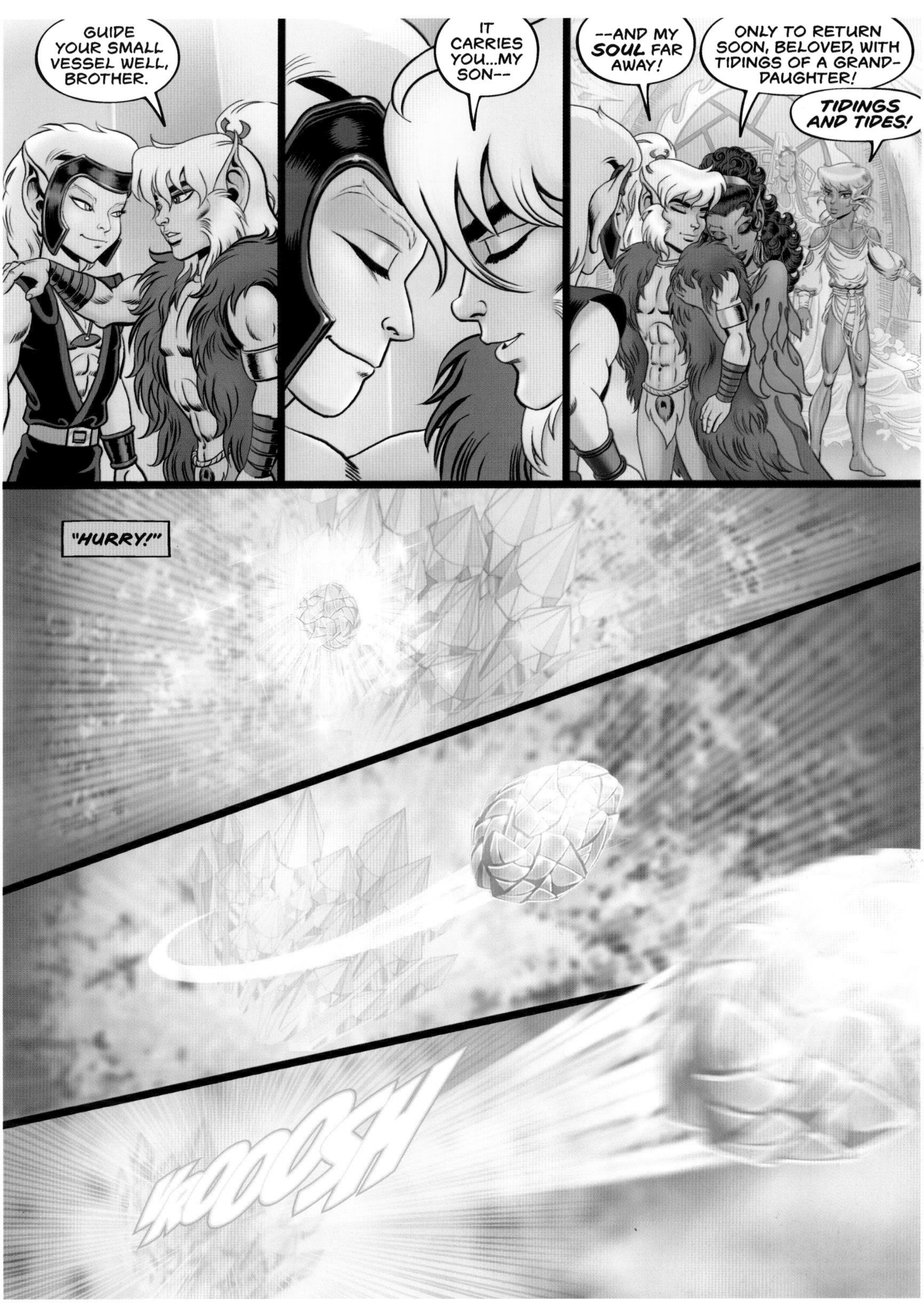
GUIDE YOUR SMALL VESSEL WELL, BROTHER.
IT CARRIES YOU...MY SON--
--AND MY SOUL FAR AWAY!
ONLY TO RETURN SOON, BELOVED, WITH TIDINGS OF A GRAND-DAUGHTER!
TIDINGS AND TIDES!
"HURRY!"
VROOOSH

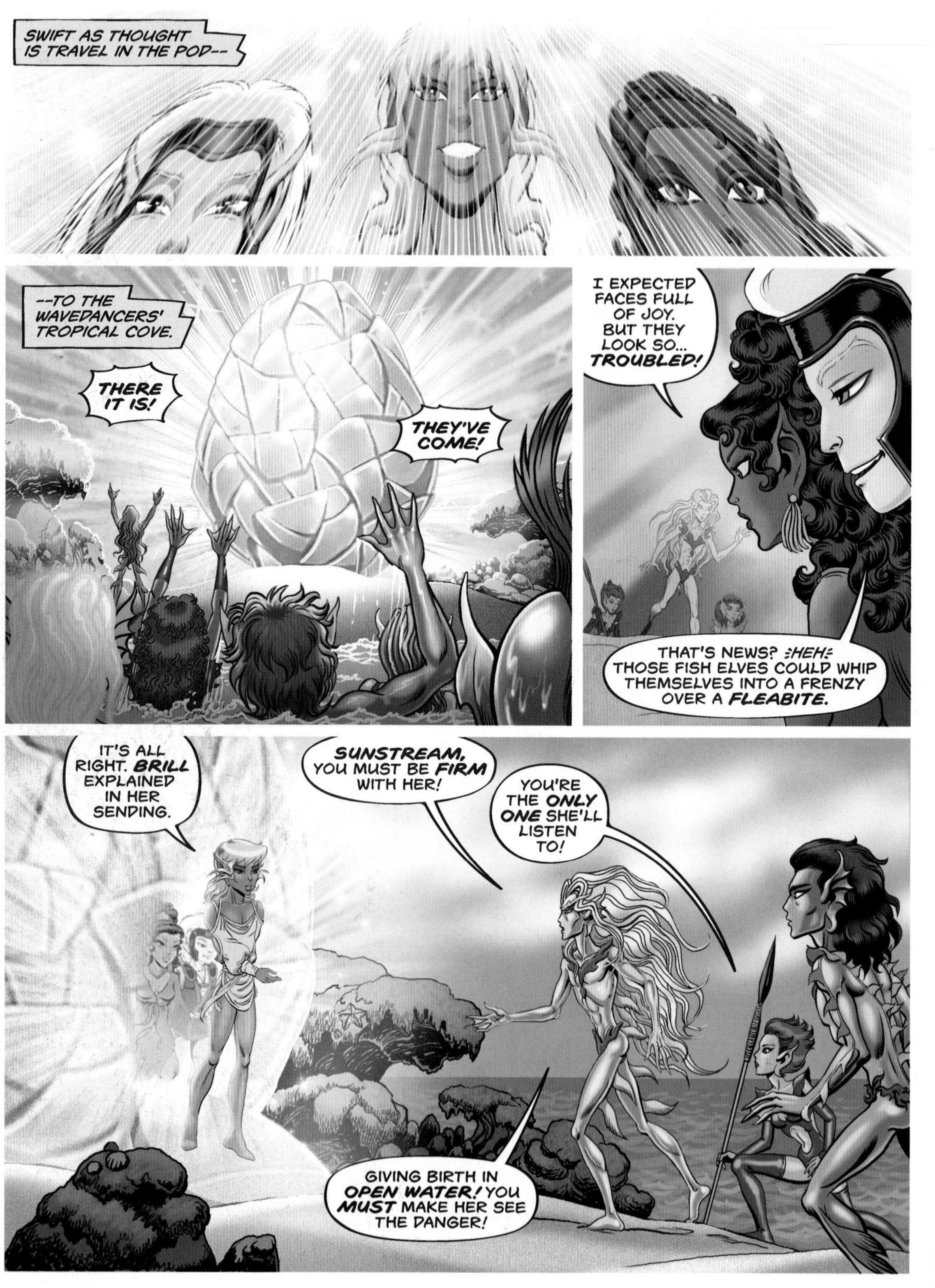
SWIFT AS THOUGHT IS TRAVEL IN THE POD--
--TO THE WAVEDANCERS' TROPICAL COVE.
THERE IT IS!
THEY'VE COME!
I EXPECTED FACES FULL OF JOY. BUT THEY LOOK SO... TROUBLED!
THAT'S NEWS? HEH THOSE FISH ELVES COULD WHIP THEMSELVES INTO A FRENZY OVER A FLEABITE.
IT'S ALL RIGHT. BRILL EXPLAINED IN HER SENDING.
SUNSTREAM, YOU MUST BE FIRM WITH HER!
YOU'RE THE ONLY ONE SHE'LL LISTEN TO!
GIVING BIRTH IN OPEN WATER! YOU MUST MAKE HER SEE THE DANGER!

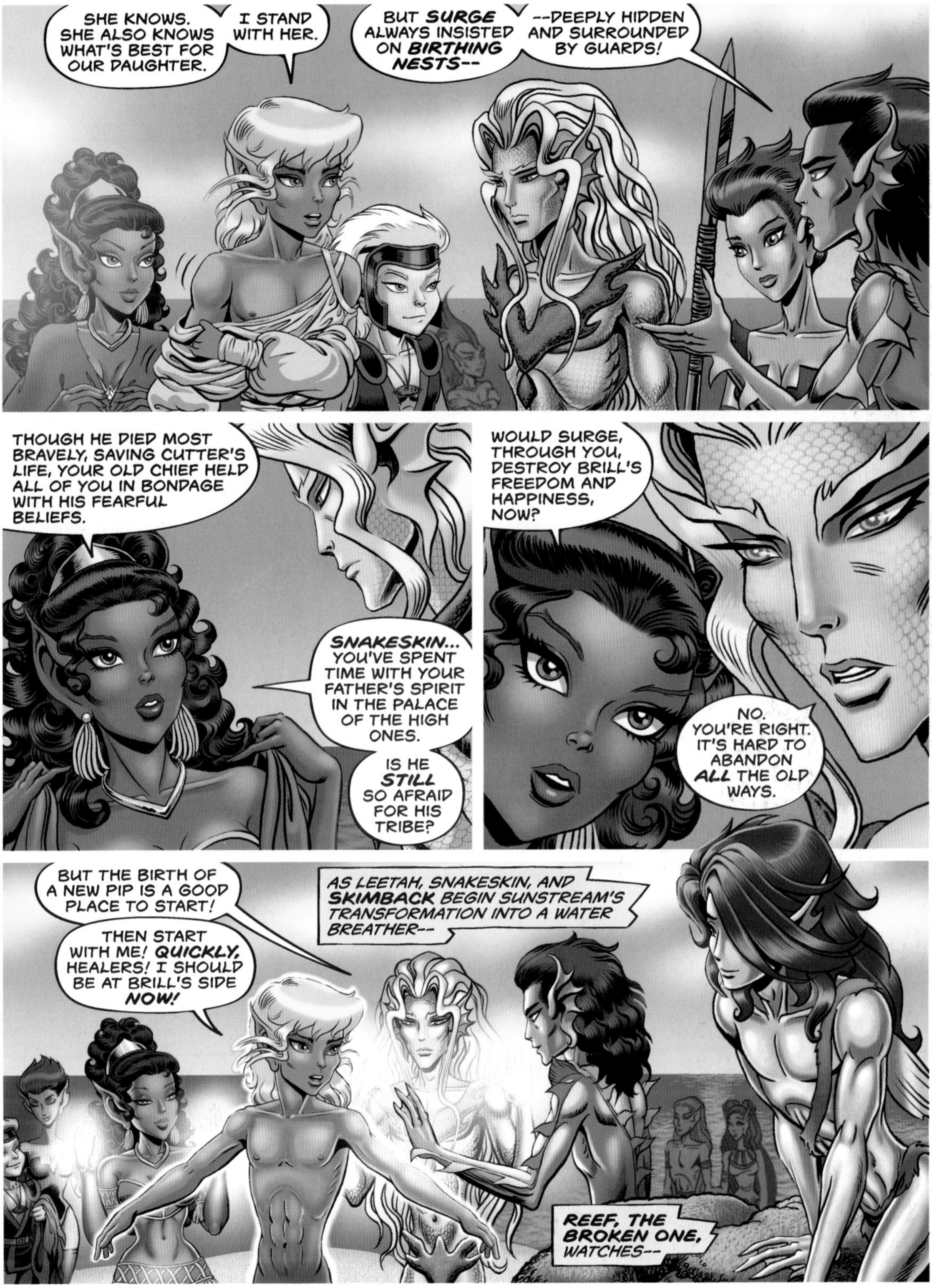
SHE KNOWS. SHE ALSO KNOWS WHAT'S BEST FOR OUR DAUGHTER.
I STAND WITH HER.
BUT SURGE ALWAYS INSISTED ON BIRTHING NESTS--
--DEEPLY HIDDEN AND SURROUNDED BY GUARDS!
THOUGH HE DIED MOST BRAVELY, SAVING CUTTER'S LIFE, YOUR OLD CHIEF HELD ALL OF YOU IN BONDAGE WITH HIS FEARFUL BELIEFS.
SNAKESKIN... YOU'VE SPENT TIME WITH YOUR FATHER'S SPIRIT IN THE PALACE OF THE HIGH ONES.
IS HE STILL SO AFRAID FOR HIS TRIBE?
WOULD SURGE, THROUGH YOU, DESTROY BRILL'S FREEDOM AND HAPPINESS, NOW?
NO. YOU'RE RIGHT. IT'S HARD TO ABANDON ALL THE OLD WAYS.
BUT THE BIRTH OF A NEW PIP IS A GOOD PLACE TO START!
THEN START WITH ME! QUICKLY, HEALERS! I SHOULD BE AT BRILL'S SIDE NOW!
AS LEETAH, SNAKESKIN, AND SKIMBACK BEGIN SUNSTREAM'S TRANSFORMATION INTO A WATER BREATHER--
REEF, THE BROKEN ONE, WATCHES--

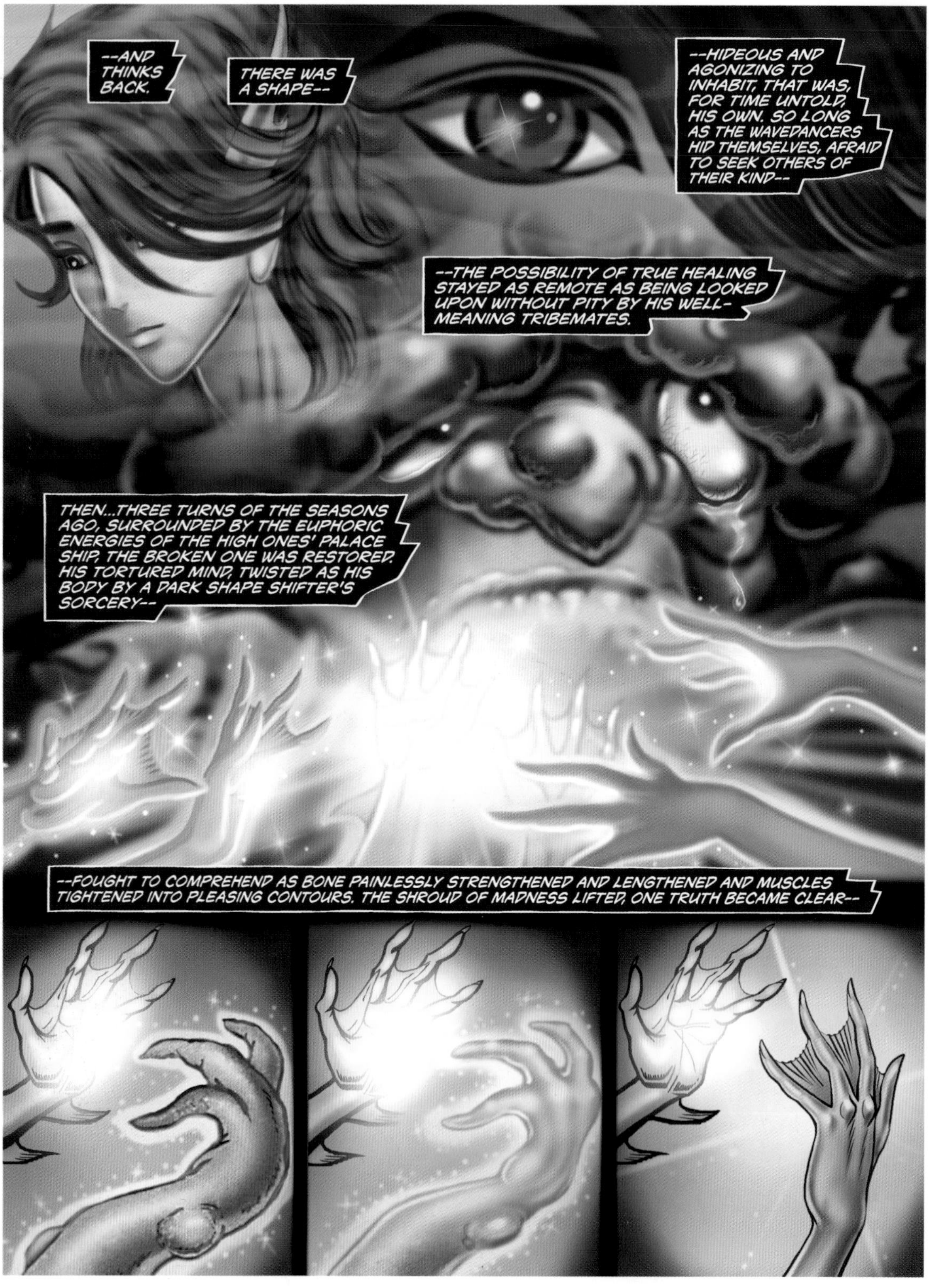
--AND THINKS BACK.
THERE WAS A SHAPE--
--HIDEOUS AND AGONIZING TO INHABIT, THAT WAS, FOR TIME UNTOLD, HIS OWN. SO LONG AS THE WAVEDANCERS HID THEMSELVES, AFRAID TO SEEK OTHERS OF THEIR KIND--
--THE POSSIBILITY OF TRUE HEALING STAYED AS REMOTE AS BEING LOOKED UPON WITHOUT PITY BY HIS WELL-MEANING TRIBEMATES.
THEN...THREE TURNS OF THE SEASONS AGO, SURROUNDED BY THE EUPHORIC ENERGIES OF THE HIGH ONES' PALACE SHIP, THE BROKEN ONE WAS RESTORED. HIS TORTURED MIND, TWISTED AS HIS BODY BY A DARK SHAPE SHIFTER'S SORCERY--
--FOUGHT TO COMPREHEND AS BONE PAINLESSLY STRENGTHENED AND LENGTHENED AND MUSCLES TIGHTENED INTO PLEASING CONTOURS. THE SHROUD OF MADNESS LIFTED, ONE TRUTH BECAME CLEAR--

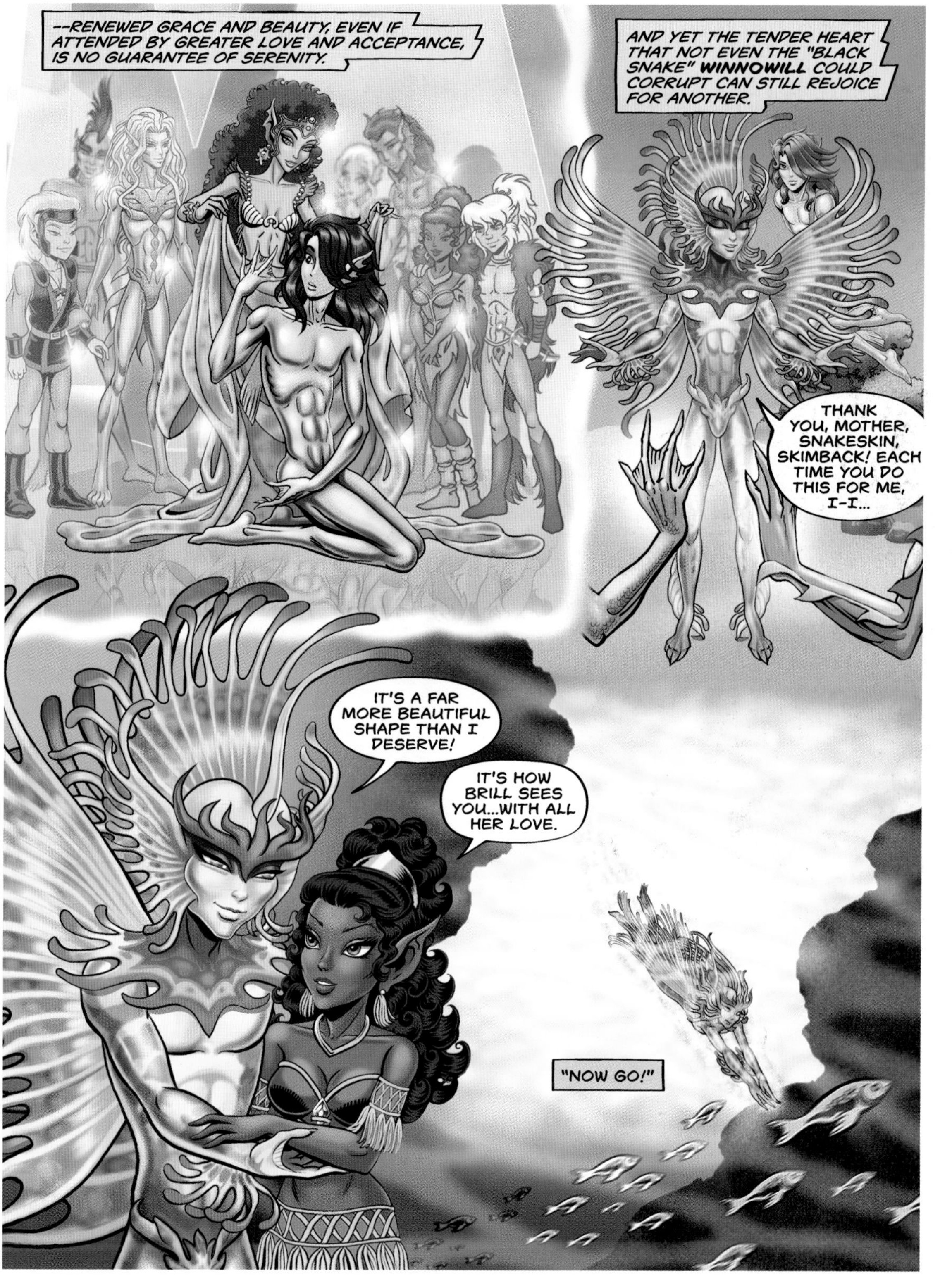
--RENEWED GRACE AND BEAUTY, EVEN IF ATTENDED BY GREATER LOVE AND ACCEPTANCE, IS NO GUARANTEE OF SERENITY.
AND YET THE TENDER HEART THAT NOT EVEN THE "BLACK SNAKE" WINNOWILL COULD CORRUPT CAN STILL REJOICE FOR ANOTHER.
THANK YOU, MOTHER, SNAKESKIN, SKIMBACK! EACH TIME YOU DO THIS FOR ME, I-I...
IT'S A FAR MORE BEAUTIFUL SHAPE THAN I DESERVE!
IT'S HOW BRILL SEES YOU...WITH ALL HER LOVE.
"NOW GO!"

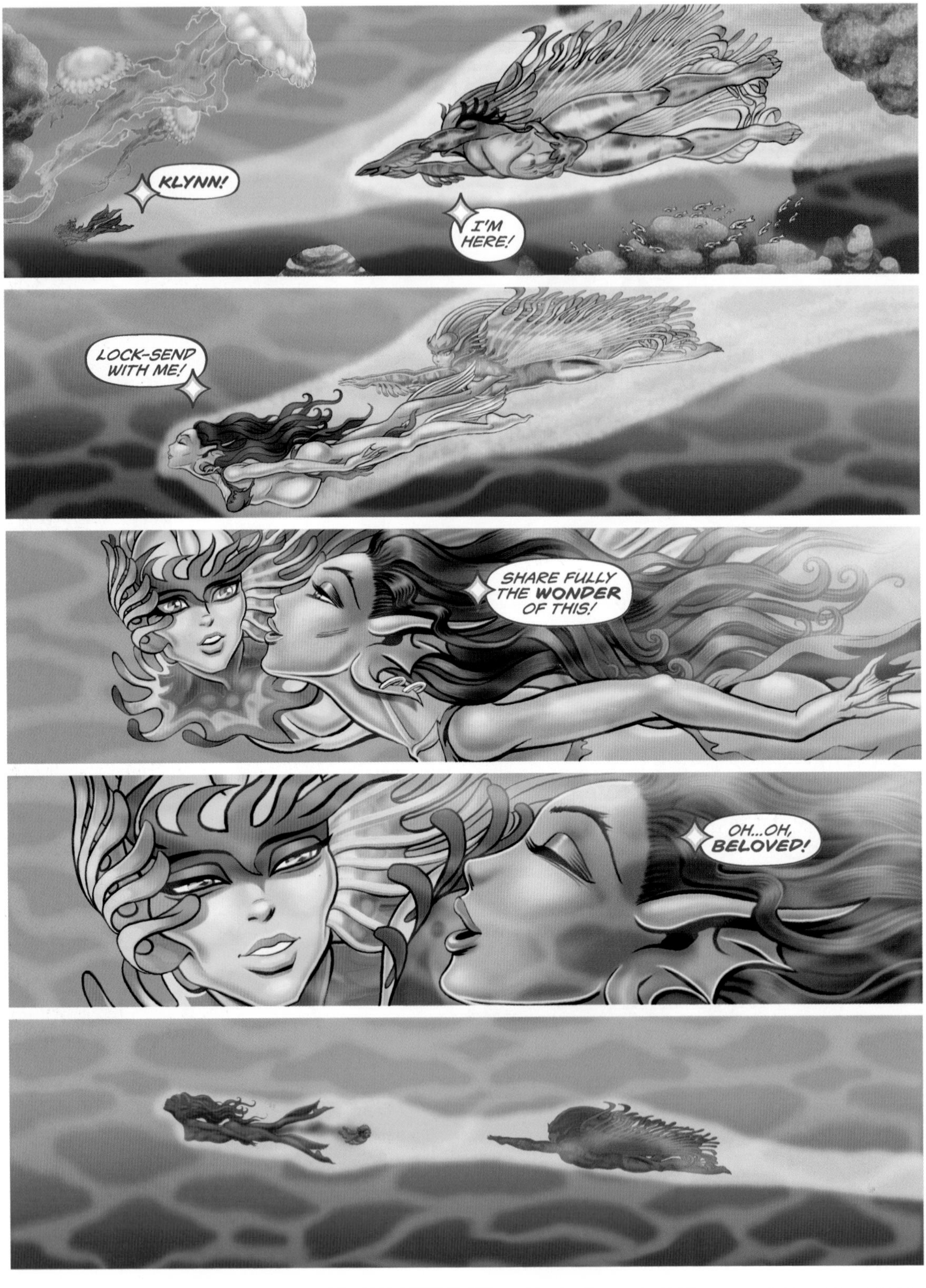
KLYNN!
I'M HERE!
LOCK-SEND WITH ME!
SHARE FULLY THE **WONDER** OF THIS!
OH...OH, **BELOVED!**

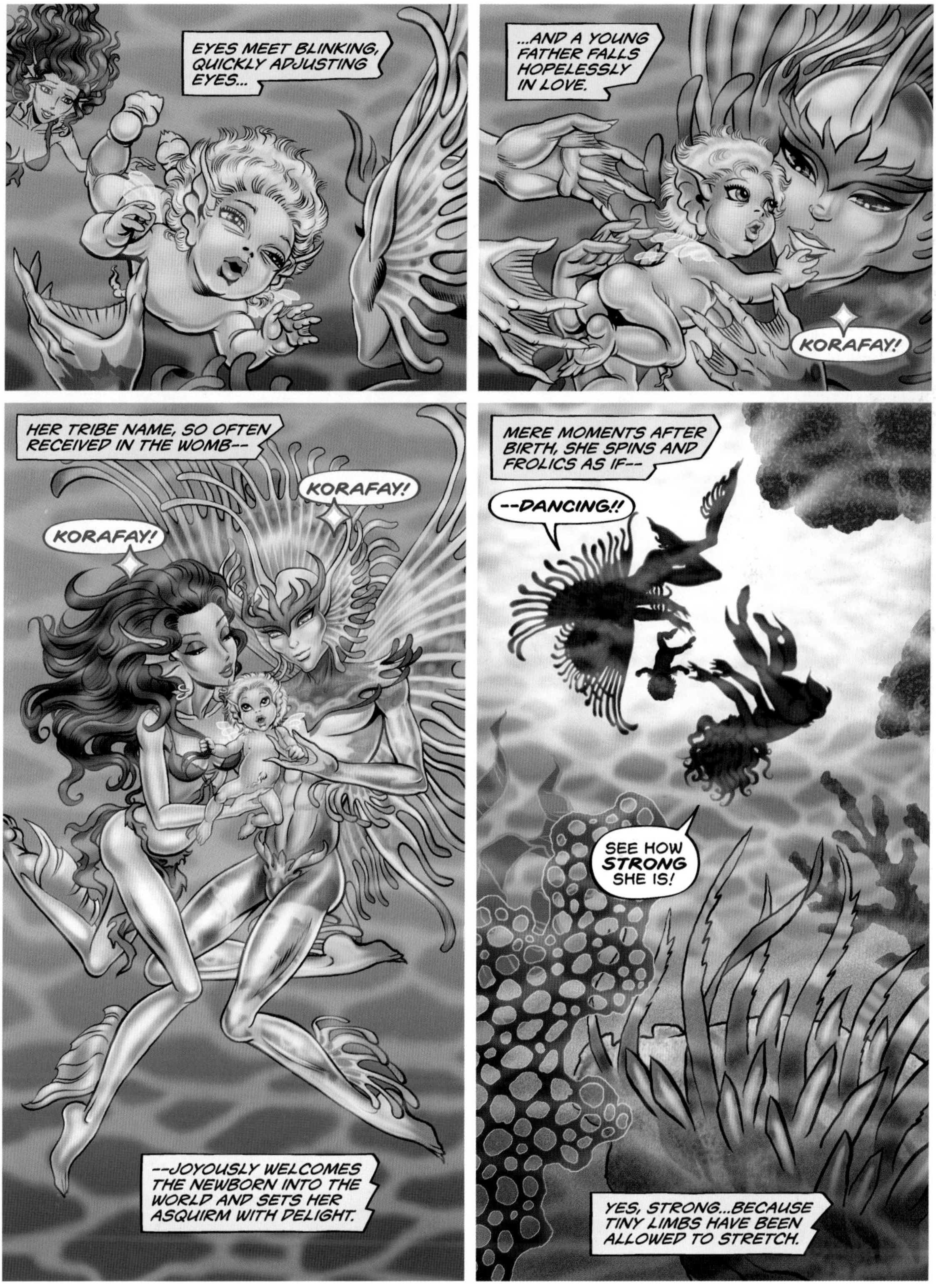
EYES MEET BLINKING, QUICKLY ADJUSTING EYES...
...AND A YOUNG FATHER FALLS HOPELESSLY IN LOVE.
KORAFAY!
HER TRIBE NAME, SO OFTEN RECEIVED IN THE WOMB--
KORAFAY!
KORAFAY!
--JOYOUSLY WELCOMES THE NEWBORN INTO THE WORLD AND SETS HER ASQUIRM WITH DELIGHT.
MERE MOMENTS AFTER BIRTH, SHE SPINS AND FROLICS AS IF--
--DANCING!!
SEE HOW STRONG SHE IS!
YES, STRONG...BECAUSE TINY LIMBS HAVE BEEN ALLOWED TO STRETCH.

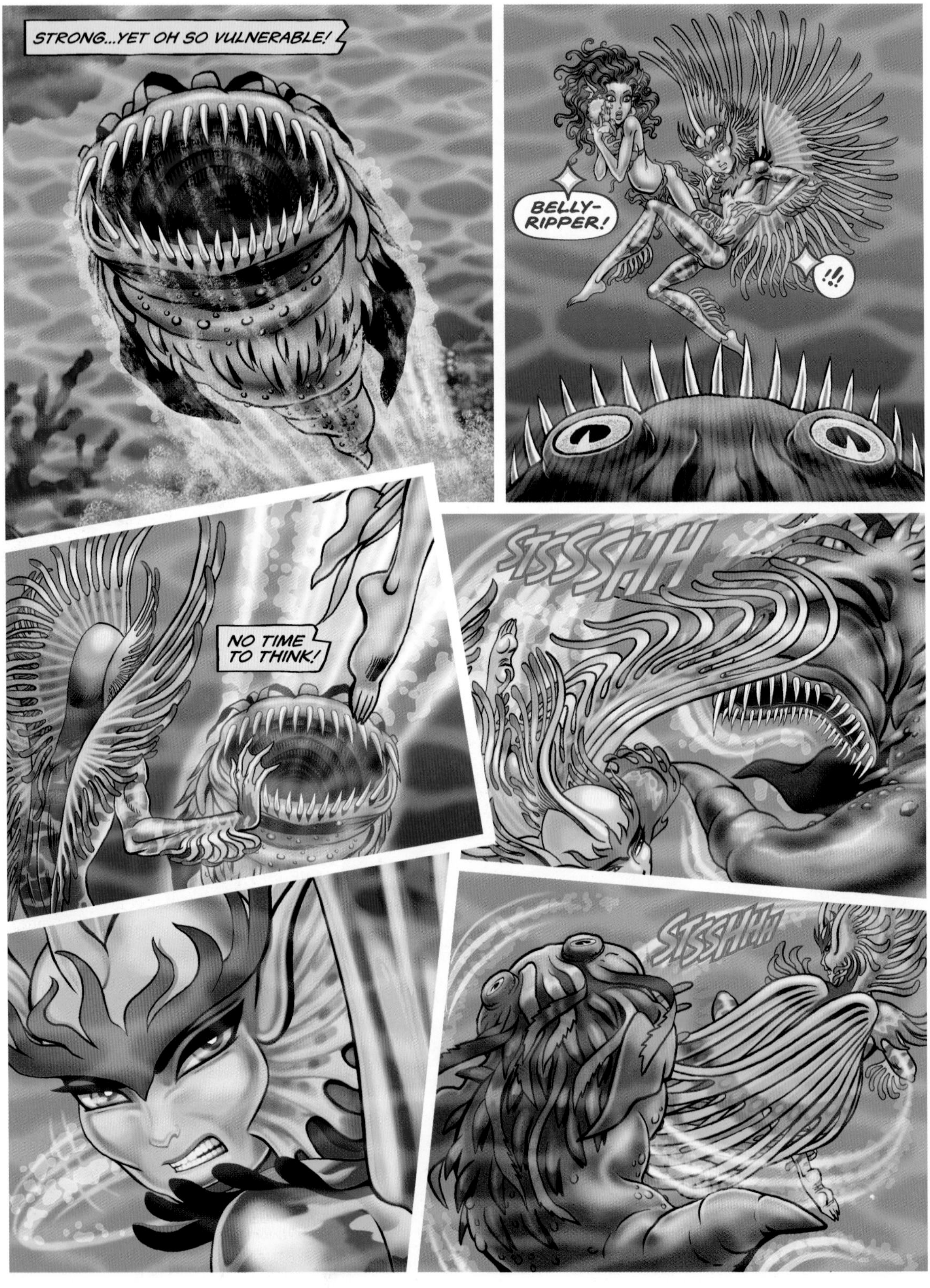
STRONG...YET OH SO VULNERABLE!
BELLY-RIPPER!
!!!
NO TIME TO THINK!
STSSSHH
STSSHHH

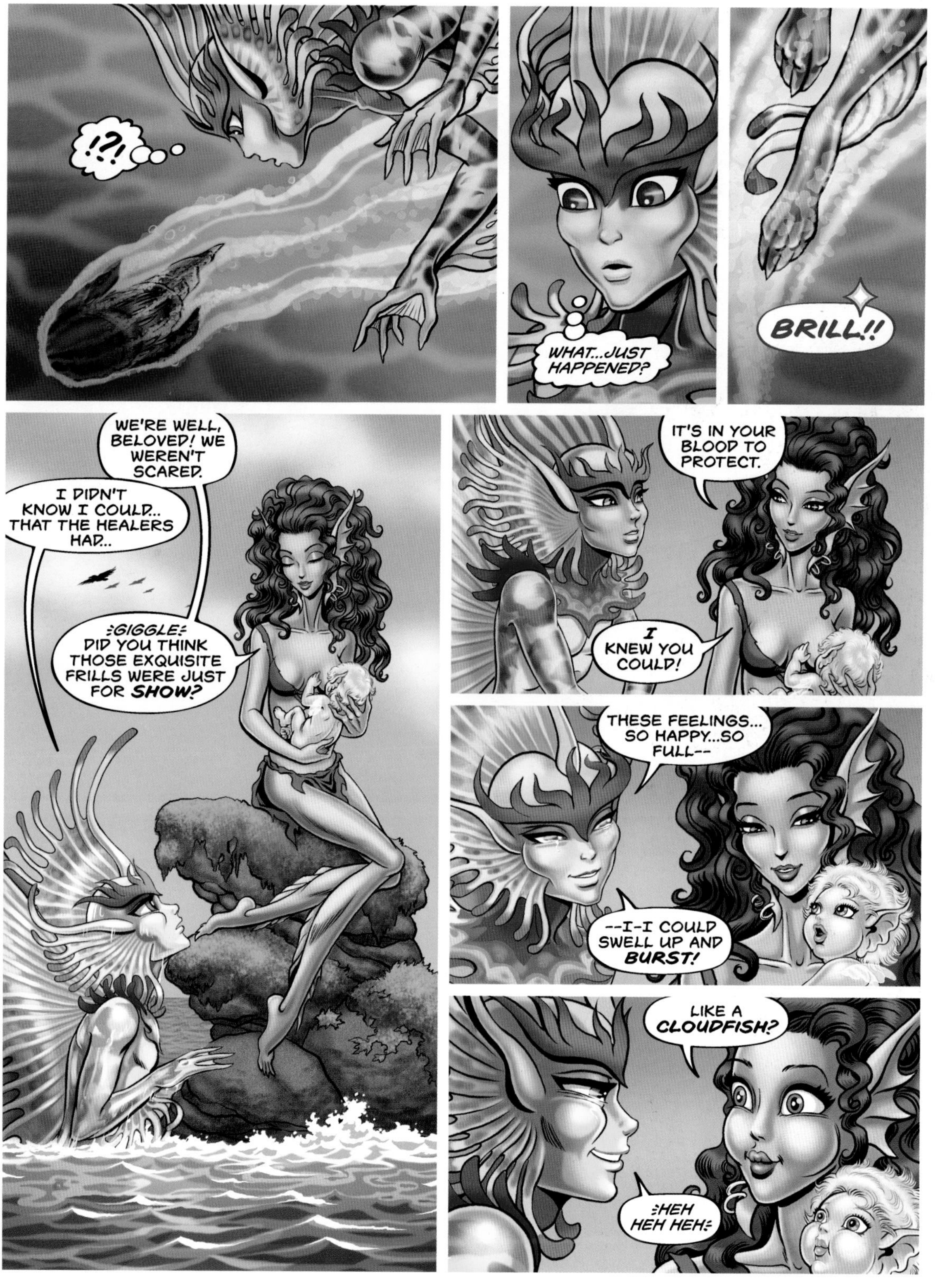

!?!
WHAT...JUST HAPPENED?
BRILL!!
WE'RE WELL, BELOVED! WE WEREN'T SCARED.
I DIDN'T KNOW I COULD... THAT THE HEALERS HAD...
GIGGLE
DID YOU THINK THOSE EXQUISITE FRILLS WERE JUST FOR SHOW?
IT'S IN YOUR BLOOD TO PROTECT.
I KNEW YOU COULD!
THESE FEELINGS... SO HAPPY...SO FULL--
--I-I COULD SWELL UP AND BURST!
LIKE A CLOUDFISH?
HEH HEH HEH

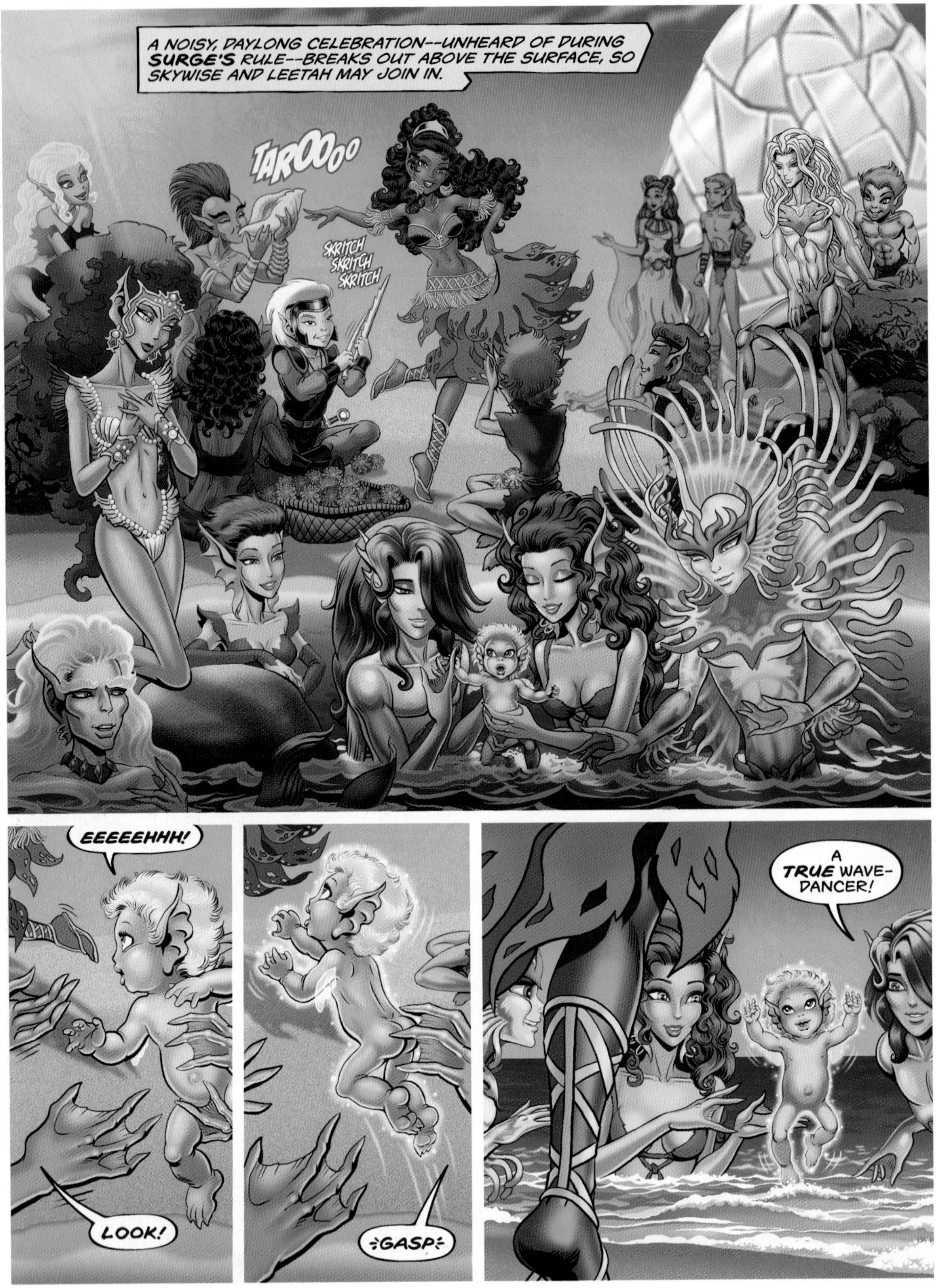
A NOISY, DAYLONG CELEBRATION--UNHEARD OF DURING SURGE'S RULE--BREAKS OUT ABOVE THE SURFACE, SO SKYWISE AND LEETAH MAY JOIN IN.
TAROOOO
SKRITCH SKRITCH SKRITCH
EEEEEHHH!
LOOK!
GASP
A TRUE WAVE-DANCER!

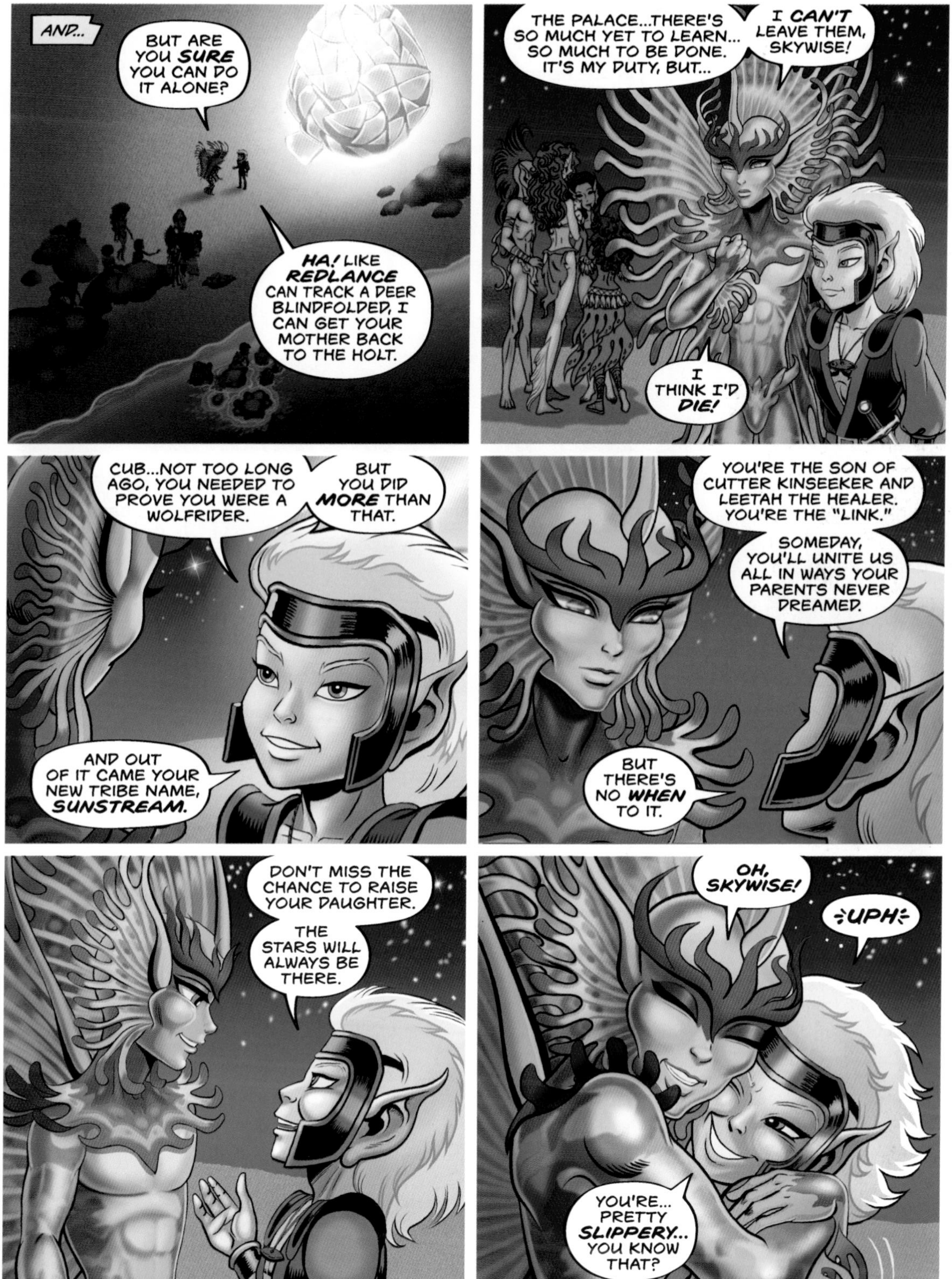
AND...
BUT ARE YOU SURE YOU CAN DO IT ALONE?
HA! LIKE REDLANCE CAN TRACK A DEER BLINDFOLDED, I CAN GET YOUR MOTHER BACK TO THE HOLT.
THE PALACE...THERE'S SO MUCH YET TO LEARN... SO MUCH TO BE DONE. IT'S MY DUTY, BUT...
I CAN'T LEAVE THEM, SKYWISE!
I THINK I'D DIE!
CUB...NOT TOO LONG AGO, YOU NEEDED TO PROVE YOU WERE A WOLFRIDER.
BUT YOU DID MORE THAN THAT.
AND OUT OF IT CAME YOUR NEW TRIBE NAME, SUNSTREAM.
YOU'RE THE SON OF CUTTER KINSEEKER AND LEETAH THE HEALER. YOU'RE THE "LINK."
SOMEDAY, YOU'LL UNITE US ALL IN WAYS YOUR PARENTS NEVER DREAMED.
BUT THERE'S NO WHEN TO IT.
DON'T MISS THE CHANCE TO RAISE YOUR DAUGHTER.
THE STARS WILL ALWAYS BE THERE.
OH, SKYWISE!
UPH
YOU'RE... PRETTY SLIPPERY... YOU KNOW THAT?

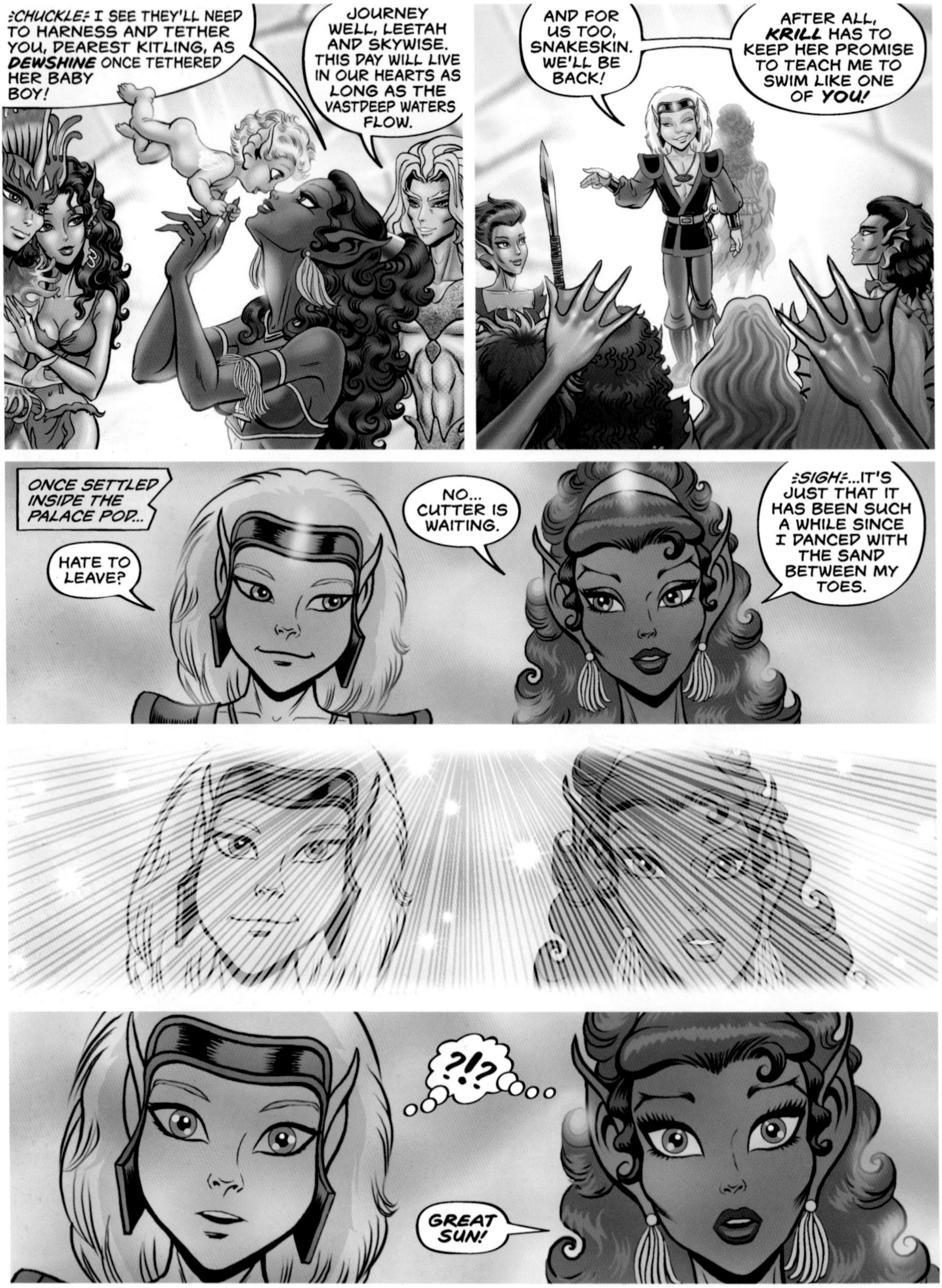

:CHUCKLE: I SEE THEY'LL NEED TO HARNESS AND TETHER YOU, DEAREST KITLING, AS DEWSHINE ONCE TETHERED HER BABY BOY!
JOURNEY WELL, LEETAH AND SKYWISE. THIS DAY WILL LIVE IN OUR HEARTS AS LONG AS THE VASTDEEP WATERS FLOW.
AND FOR US TOO, SNAKESKIN. WE'LL BE BACK!
AFTER ALL, KRILL HAS TO KEEP HER PROMISE TO TEACH ME TO SWIM LIKE ONE OF YOU!
ONCE SETTLED INSIDE THE PALACE POD...
HATE TO LEAVE?
NO... CUTTER IS WAITING.
:SIGH:...IT'S JUST THAT IT HAS BEEN SUCH A WHILE SINCE I DANCED WITH THE SAND BETWEEN MY TOES.
?!?
GREAT SUN!

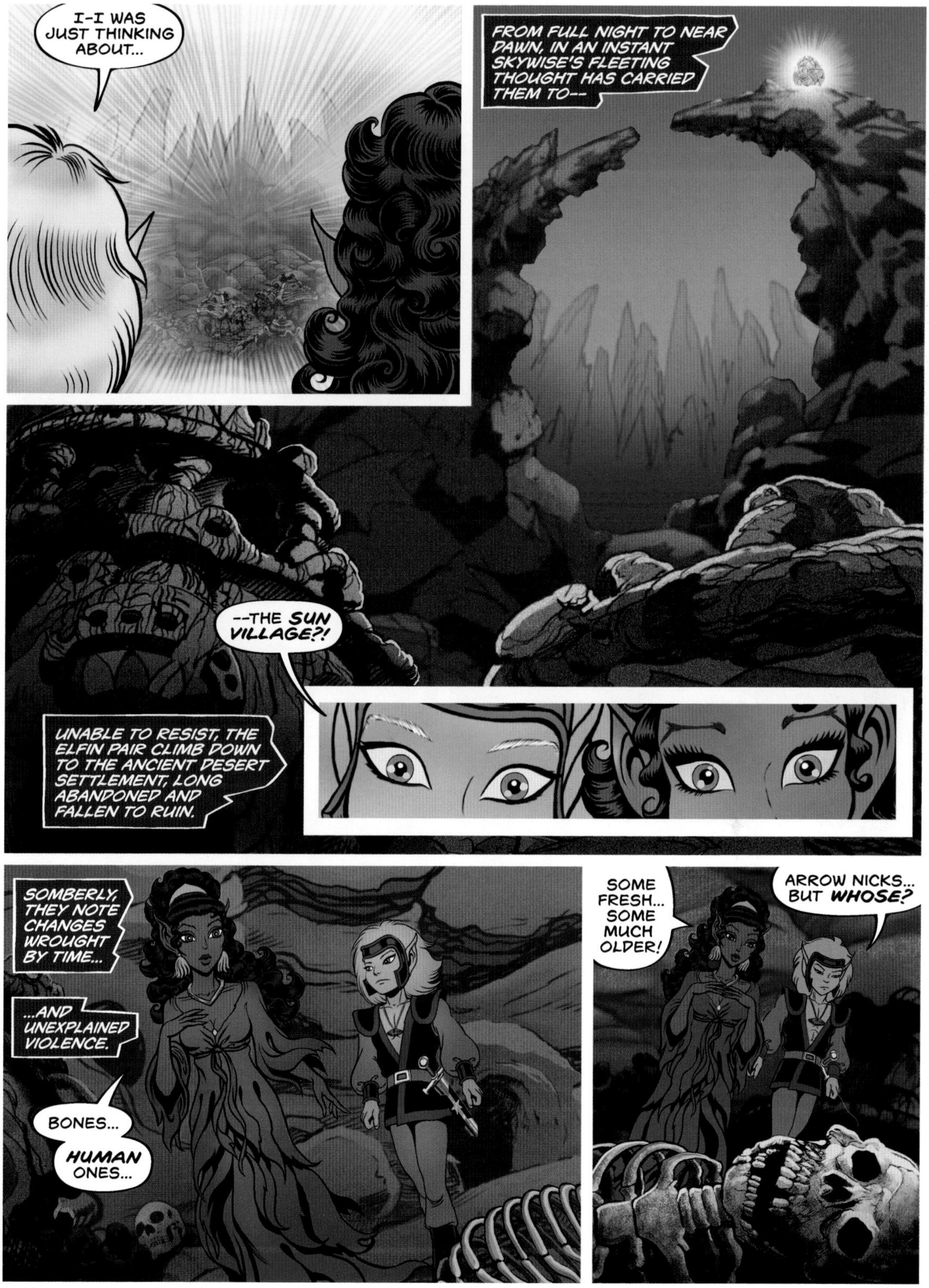

I-I WAS JUST THINKING ABOUT...
FROM FULL NIGHT TO NEAR DAWN, IN AN INSTANT SKYWISE'S FLEETING THOUGHT HAS CARRIED THEM TO--
--THE **SUN VILLAGE?!**
UNABLE TO RESIST, THE ELFIN PAIR CLIMB DOWN TO THE ANCIENT DESERT SETTLEMENT, LONG ABANDONED AND FALLEN TO RUIN.
SOMBERLY, THEY NOTE CHANGES WROUGHT BY TIME...
...AND UNEXPLAINED VIOLENCE.
BONES... **HUMAN** ONES...
SOME FRESH... SOME MUCH OLDER!
ARROW NICKS... BUT **WHOSE?**

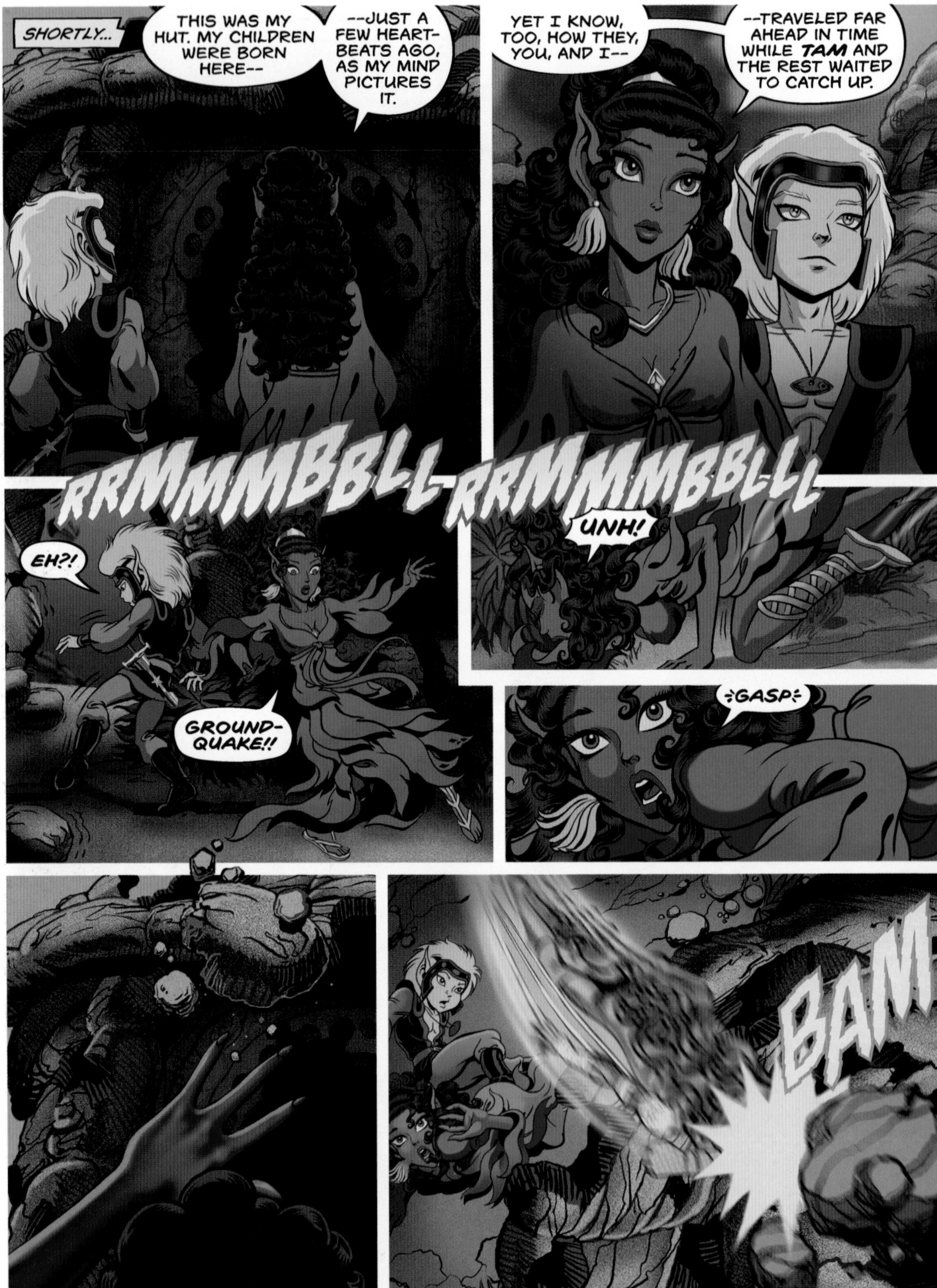
SHORTLY...
THIS WAS MY HUT. MY CHILDREN WERE BORN HERE--
--JUST A FEW HEART-BEATS AGO, AS MY MIND PICTURES IT.
YET I KNOW, TOO, HOW THEY, YOU, AND I--
--TRAVELED FAR AHEAD IN TIME WHILE TAM AND THE REST WAITED TO CATCH UP.
RRMMMMBBLLL RRMMMMBBLLL
EH?!
GROUND-QUAKE!!
UNH!
GASP
BAM

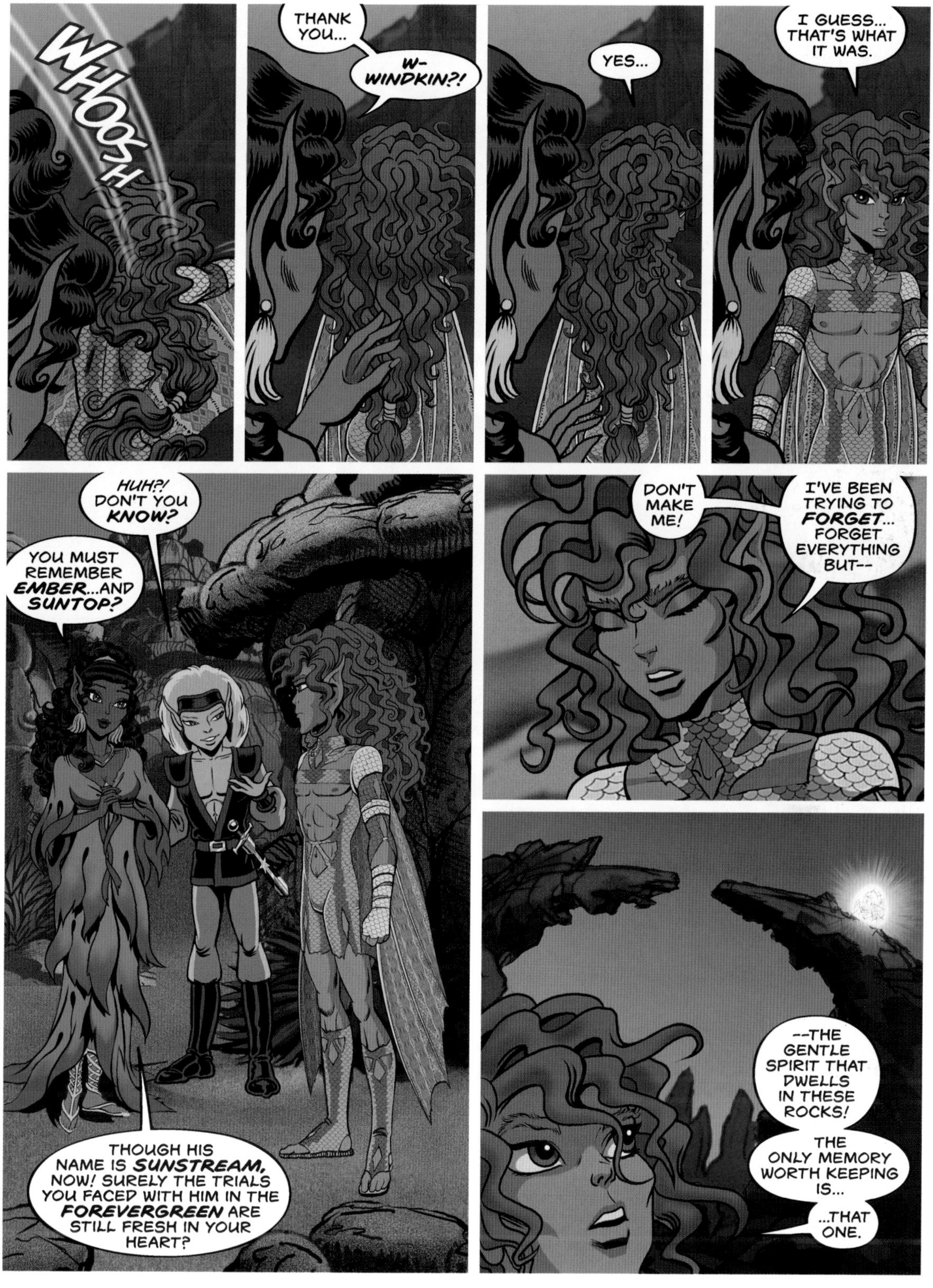
WHOOOSH
THANK YOU...
W-WINDKIN?!
YES...
I GUESS... THAT'S WHAT IT WAS.
HUH?! DON'T YOU KNOW?
YOU MUST REMEMBER EMBER...AND SUNTOP?
THOUGH HIS NAME IS SUNSTREAM, NOW! SURELY THE TRIALS YOU FACED WITH HIM IN THE FOREVERGREEN ARE STILL FRESH IN YOUR HEART?
DON'T MAKE ME!
I'VE BEEN TRYING TO FORGET... FORGET EVERYTHING BUT--
--THE GENTLE SPIRIT THAT DWELLS IN THESE ROCKS!
THE ONLY MEMORY WORTH KEEPING IS...
...THAT ONE.

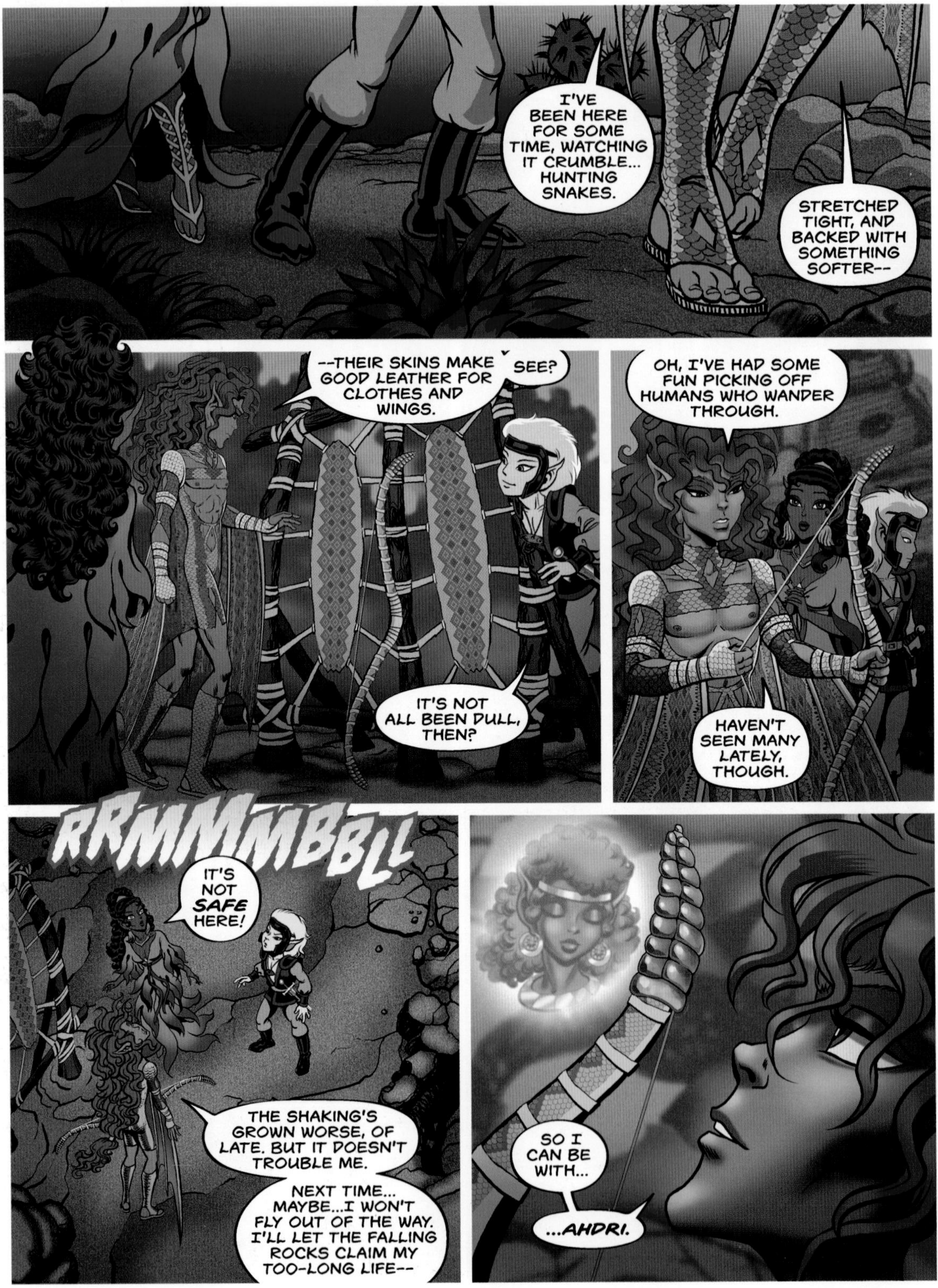
I'VE BEEN HERE FOR SOME TIME, WATCHING IT CRUMBLE... HUNTING SNAKES.
STRETCHED TIGHT, AND BACKED WITH SOMETHING SOFTER--
--THEIR SKINS MAKE GOOD LEATHER FOR CLOTHES AND WINGS.
SEE?
IT'S NOT ALL BEEN DULL, THEN?
OH, I'VE HAD SOME FUN PICKING OFF HUMANS WHO WANDER THROUGH.
HAVEN'T SEEN MANY LATELY, THOUGH.
RRMMMBBLL
IT'S NOT *SAFE* HERE!
THE SHAKING'S GROWN WORSE, OF LATE. BUT IT DOESN'T TROUBLE ME.
NEXT TIME... MAYBE...I WON'T FLY OUT OF THE WAY. I'LL LET THE FALLING ROCKS CLAIM MY TOO-LONG LIFE--
SO I CAN BE WITH...
...*AHDRI.*

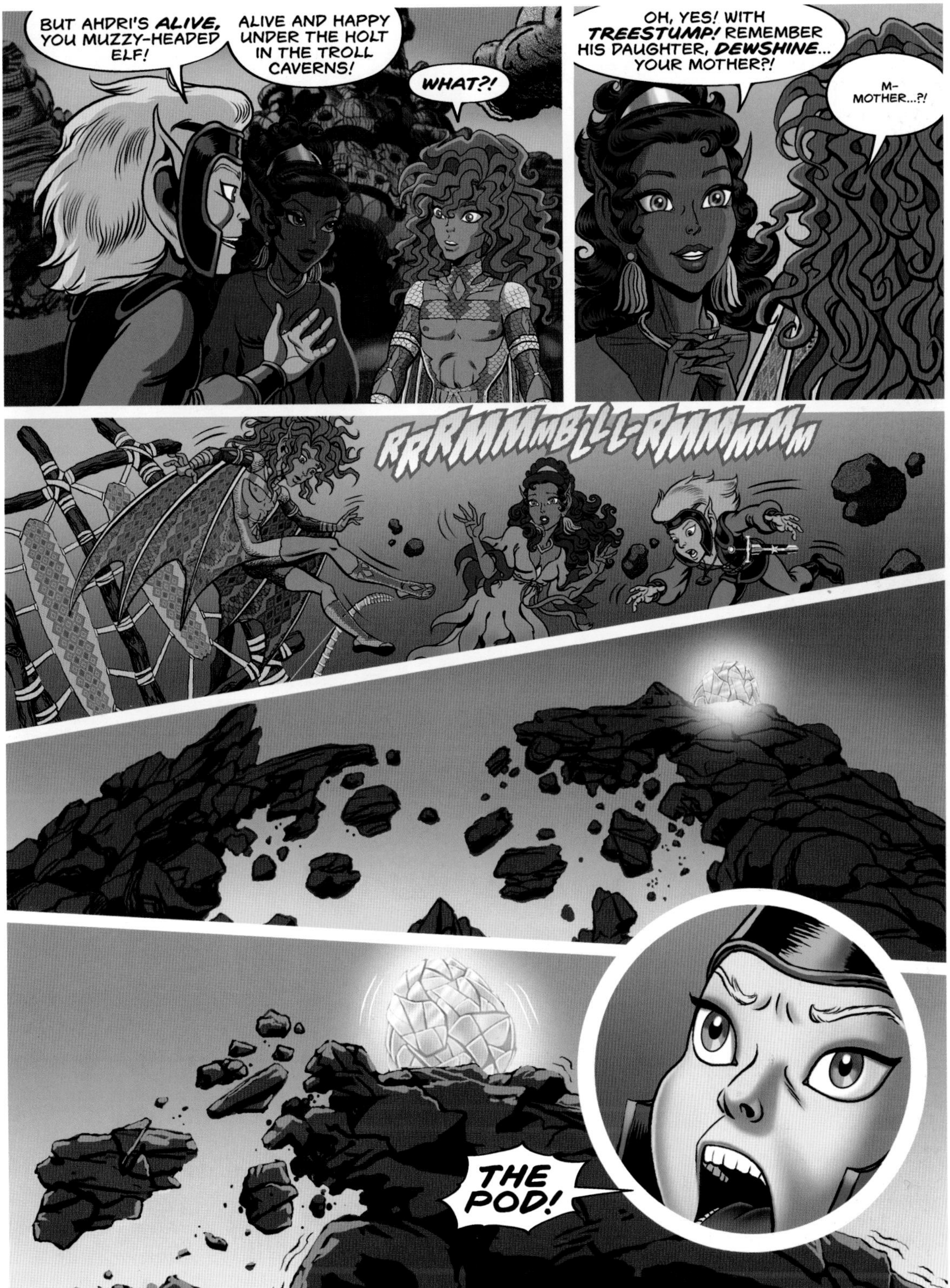
BUT AHDRI'S ALIVE, YOU MUZZY-HEADED ELF!
ALIVE AND HAPPY UNDER THE HOLT IN THE TROLL CAVERNS!
WHAT?!
OH, YES! WITH TREESTUMP! REMEMBER HIS DAUGHTER, DEWSHINE... YOUR MOTHER?!
M-MOTHER...?!
RRRMMMMBLLL-RMMMMMM
THE POD!

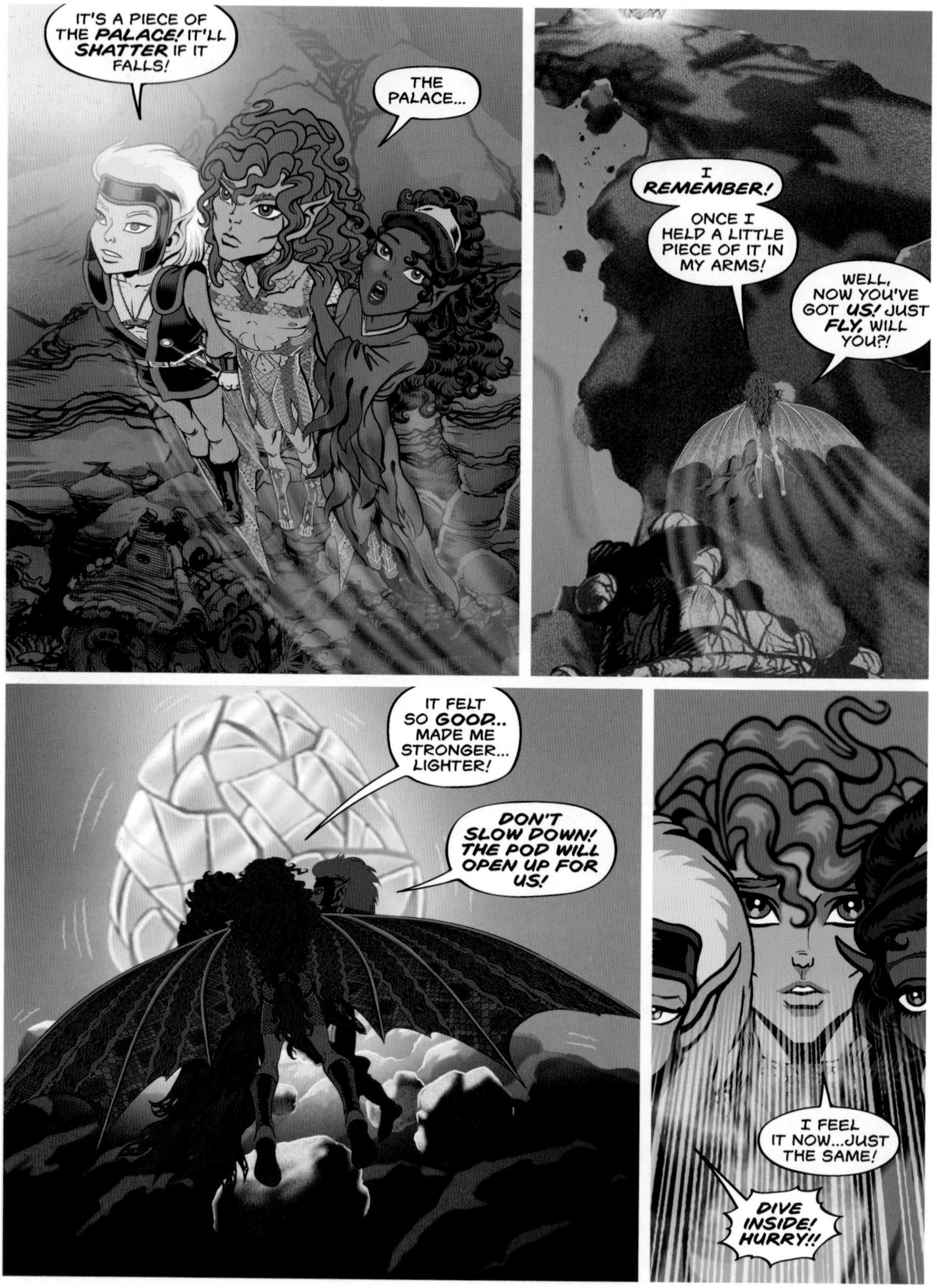
IT'S A PIECE OF THE PALACE! IT'LL SHATTER IF IT FALLS!
THE PALACE...
I REMEMBER!
ONCE I HELD A LITTLE PIECE OF IT IN MY ARMS!
WELL, NOW YOU'VE GOT US! JUST FLY, WILL YOU?!
IT FELT SO GOOD... MADE ME STRONGER... LIGHTER!
DON'T SLOW DOWN! THE POD WILL OPEN UP FOR US!
I FEEL IT NOW...JUST THE SAME!
DIVE INSIDE! HURRY!!

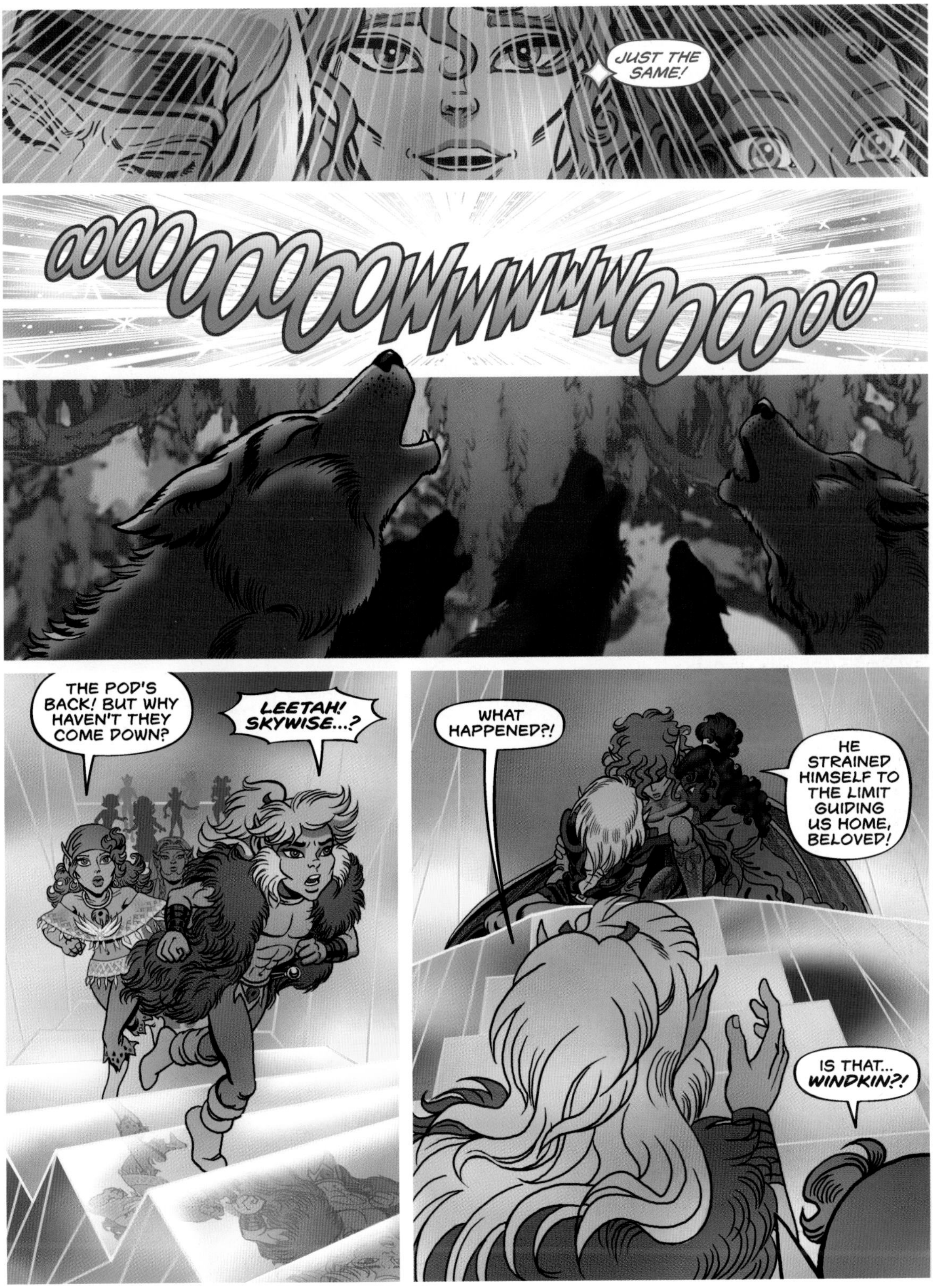
JUST THE SAME!
OOOOOOOOWWWWWWOOOOOO
THE POD'S BACK! BUT WHY HAVEN'T THEY COME DOWN?
LEETAH! SKYWISE...?
WHAT HAPPENED?!
HE STRAINED HIMSELF TO THE LIMIT GUIDING US HOME, BELOVED!
IS THAT... WINDKIN?!

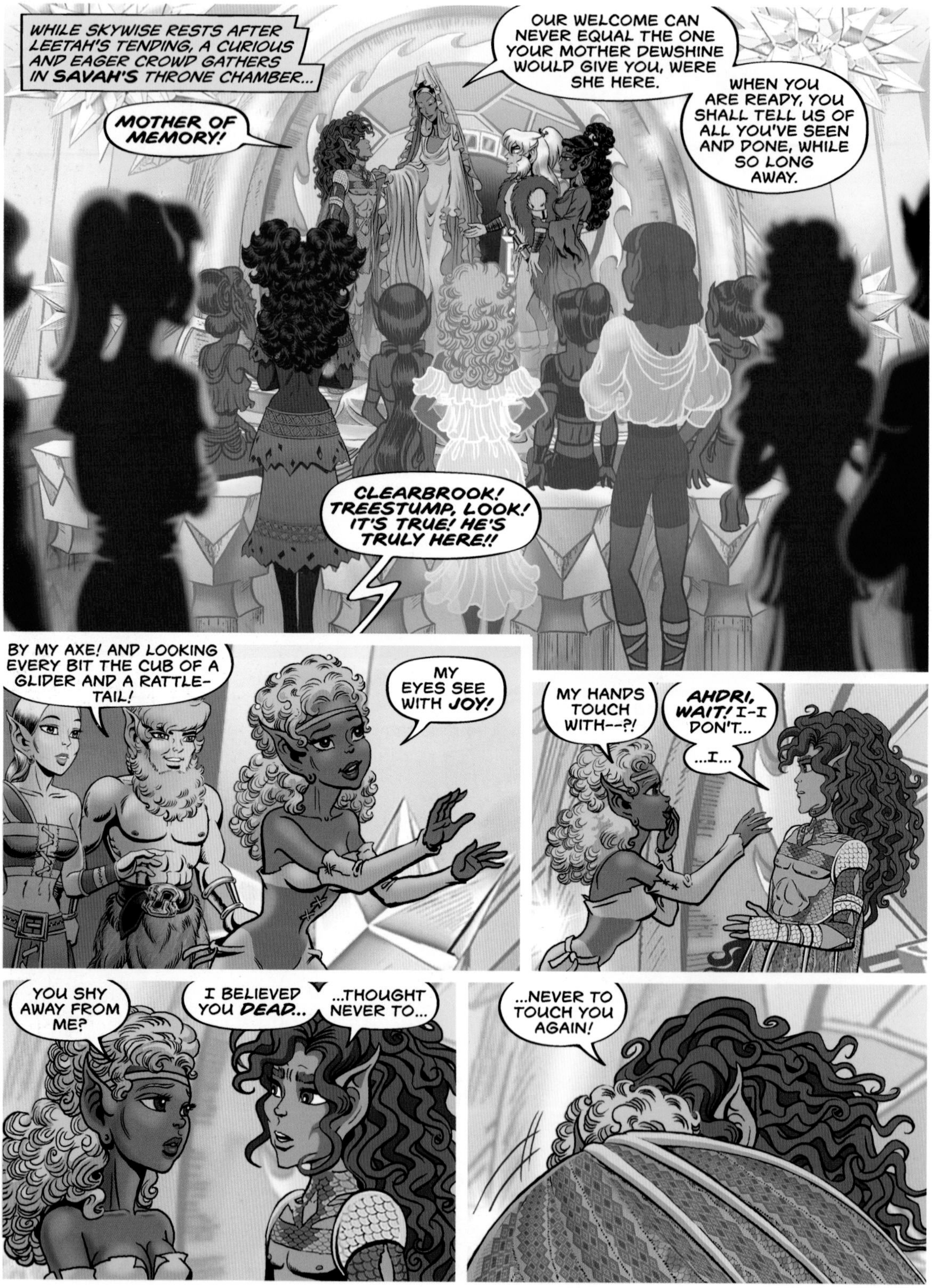
WHILE SKYWISE RESTS AFTER LEETAH'S TENDING, A CURIOUS AND EAGER CROWD GATHERS IN SAVAH'S THRONE CHAMBER...
OUR WELCOME CAN NEVER EQUAL THE ONE YOUR MOTHER DEWSHINE WOULD GIVE YOU, WERE SHE HERE.
WHEN YOU ARE READY, YOU SHALL TELL US OF ALL YOU'VE SEEN AND DONE, WHILE SO LONG AWAY.
MOTHER OF MEMORY!
CLEARBROOK! TREESTUMP, LOOK! IT'S TRUE! HE'S TRULY HERE!!
BY MY AXE! AND LOOKING EVERY BIT THE CUB OF A GLIDER AND A RATTLE-TAIL!
MY EYES SEE WITH JOY!
MY HANDS TOUCH WITH--?!
AHDRI, WAIT! I-I DON'T...
...I...
YOU SHY AWAY FROM ME?
I BELIEVED YOU DEAD...
...THOUGHT NEVER TO...
...NEVER TO TOUCH YOU AGAIN!

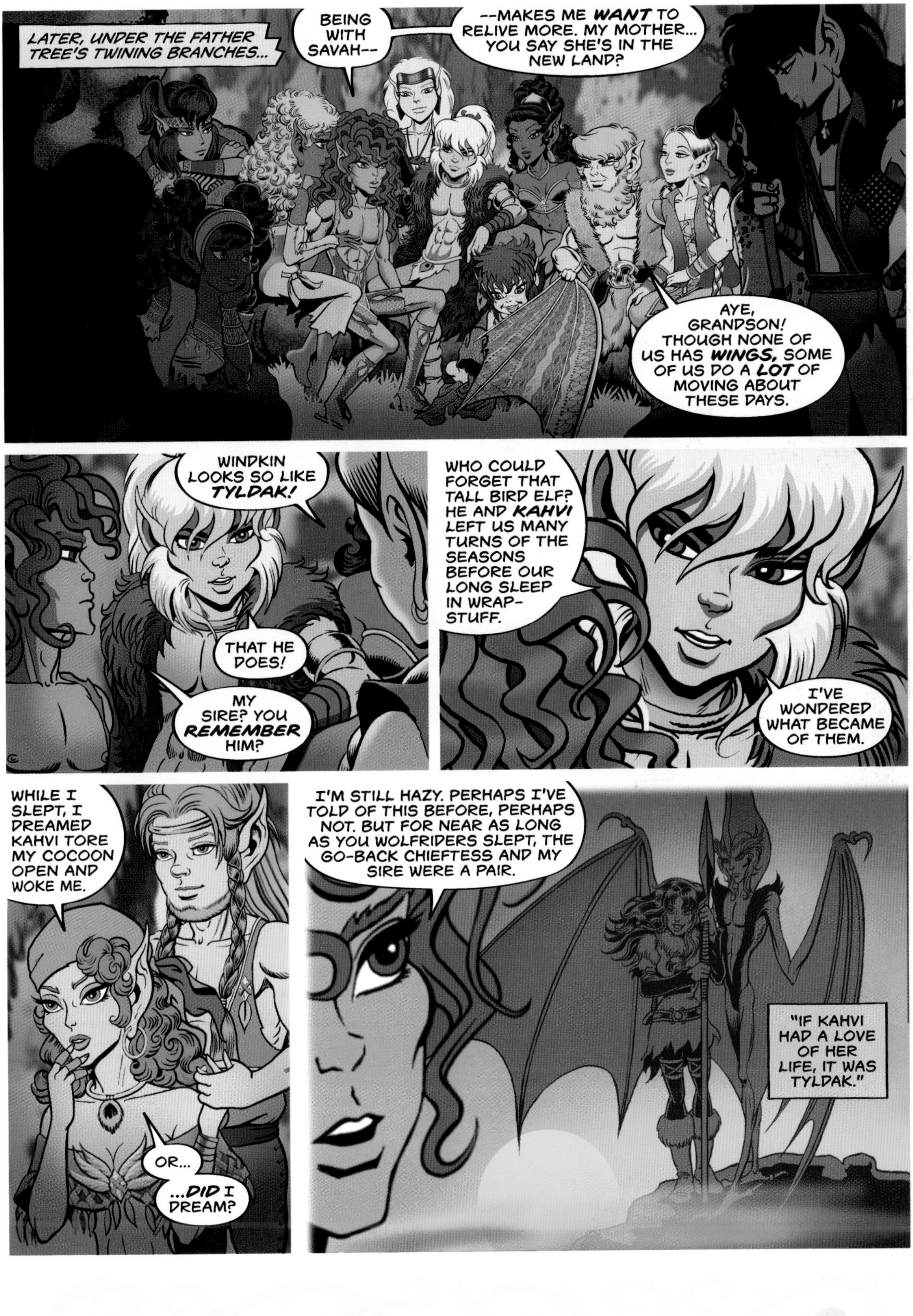
LATER, UNDER THE FATHER TREE'S TWINING BRANCHES...
BEING WITH SAVAH--
--MAKES ME WANT TO RELIVE MORE. MY MOTHER... YOU SAY SHE'S IN THE NEW LAND?
AYE, GRANDSON! THOUGH NONE OF US HAS WINGS, SOME OF US DO A LOT OF MOVING ABOUT THESE DAYS.
WINDKIN LOOKS SO LIKE TYLDAK!
THAT HE DOES!
MY SIRE? YOU REMEMBER HIM?
WHO COULD FORGET THAT TALL BIRD ELF? HE AND KAHVI LEFT US MANY TURNS OF THE SEASONS BEFORE OUR LONG SLEEP IN WRAP-STUFF.
I'VE WONDERED WHAT BECAME OF THEM.
WHILE I SLEPT, I DREAMED KAHVI TORE MY COCOON OPEN AND WOKE ME.
OR...
...DID I DREAM?
I'M STILL HAZY. PERHAPS I'VE TOLD OF THIS BEFORE, PERHAPS NOT. BUT FOR NEAR AS LONG AS YOU WOLFRIDERS SLEPT, THE GO-BACK CHIEFTESS AND MY SIRE WERE A PAIR.
"IF KAHVI HAD A LOVE OF HER LIFE, IT WAS TYLDAK."

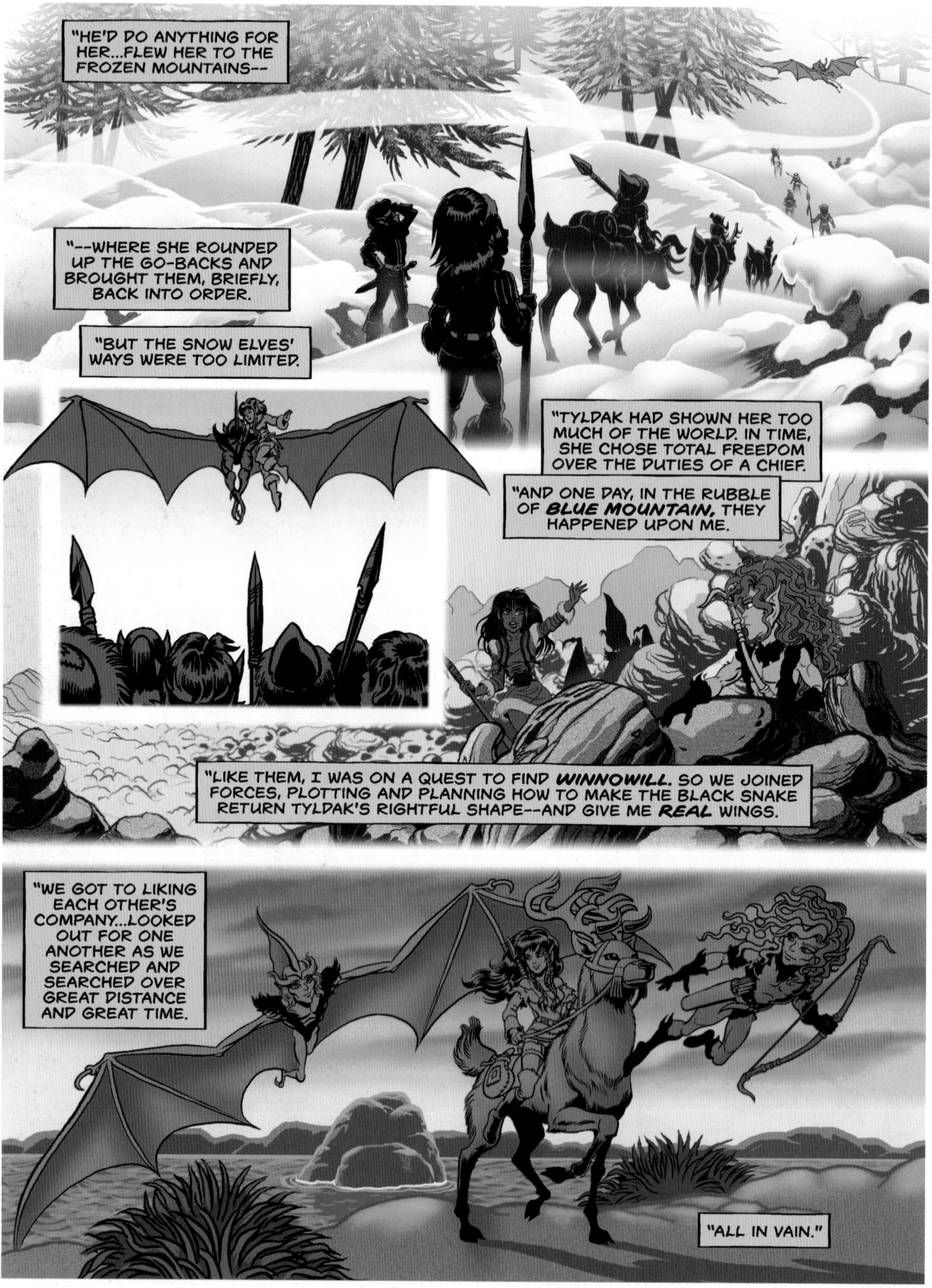
"HE'D DO ANYTHING FOR HER...FLEW HER TO THE FROZEN MOUNTAINS--
"--WHERE SHE ROUNDED UP THE GO-BACKS AND BROUGHT THEM, BRIEFLY, BACK INTO ORDER.
"BUT THE SNOW ELVES' WAYS WERE TOO LIMITED.
"TYLDAK HAD SHOWN HER TOO MUCH OF THE WORLD. IN TIME, SHE CHOSE TOTAL FREEDOM OVER THE DUTIES OF A CHIEF.
"AND ONE DAY, IN THE RUBBLE OF BLUE MOUNTAIN, THEY HAPPENED UPON ME.
"LIKE THEM, I WAS ON A QUEST TO FIND WINNOWILL. SO WE JOINED FORCES, PLOTTING AND PLANNING HOW TO MAKE THE BLACK SNAKE RETURN TYLDAK'S RIGHTFUL SHAPE--AND GIVE ME REAL WINGS.
"WE GOT TO LIKING EACH OTHER'S COMPANY...LOOKED OUT FOR ONE ANOTHER AS WE SEARCHED AND SEARCHED OVER GREAT DISTANCE AND GREAT TIME.
"ALL IN VAIN."

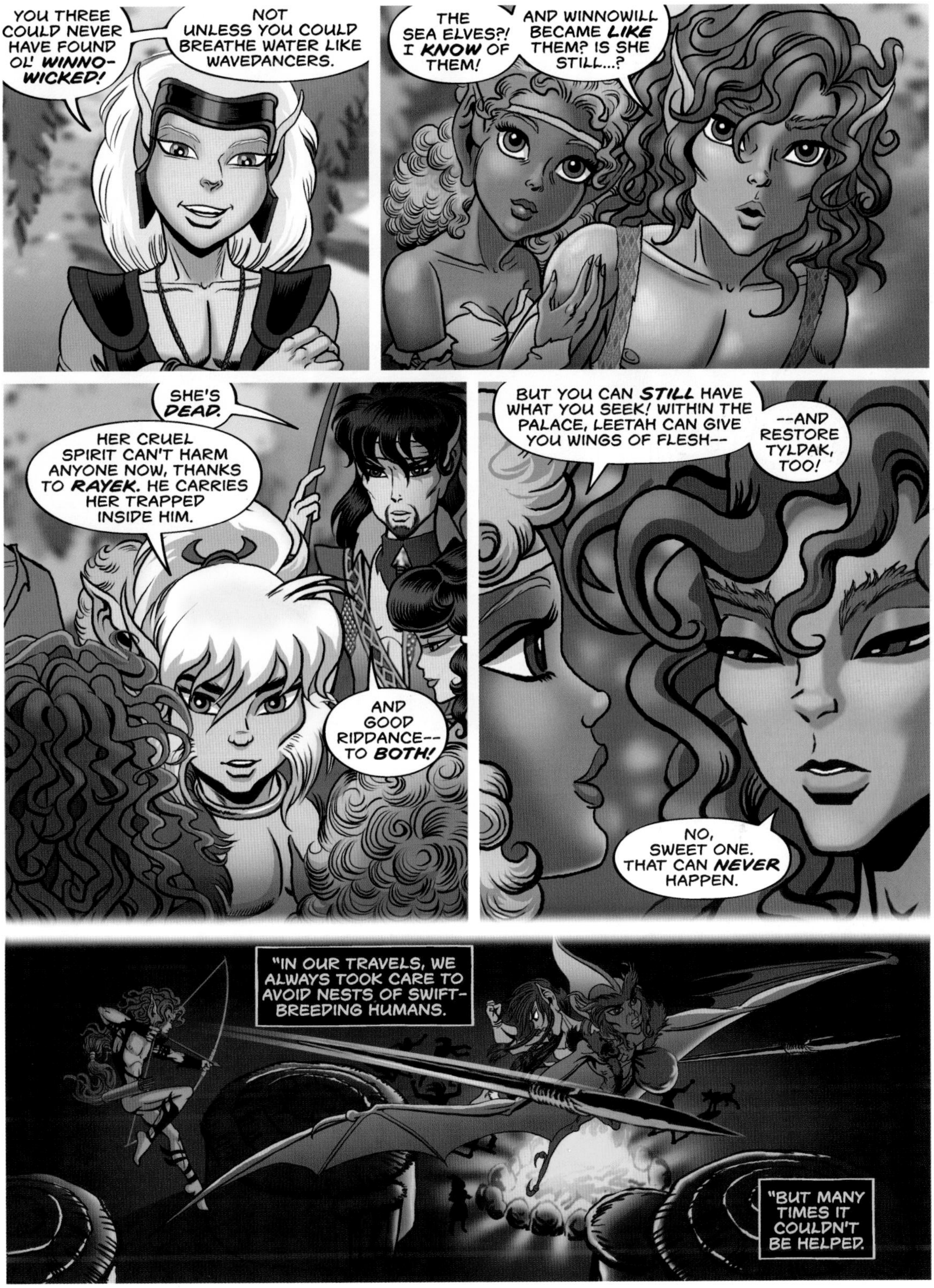

YOU THREE COULD NEVER HAVE FOUND OL' WINNO-WICKED!
NOT UNLESS YOU COULD BREATHE WATER LIKE WAVEDANCERS.
THE SEA ELVES?! I KNOW OF THEM!
AND WINNOWILL BECAME LIKE THEM? IS SHE STILL...?
SHE'S DEAD.
HER CRUEL SPIRIT CAN'T HARM ANYONE NOW, THANKS TO RAYEK. HE CARRIES HER TRAPPED INSIDE HIM.
AND GOOD RIDDANCE--TO BOTH!
BUT YOU CAN STILL HAVE WHAT YOU SEEK! WITHIN THE PALACE, LEETAH CAN GIVE YOU WINGS OF FLESH--
--AND RESTORE TYLDAK, TOO!
NO, SWEET ONE. THAT CAN NEVER HAPPEN.
"IN OUR TRAVELS, WE ALWAYS TOOK CARE TO AVOID NESTS OF SWIFT-BREEDING HUMANS.
"BUT MANY TIMES IT COULDN'T BE HELPED.

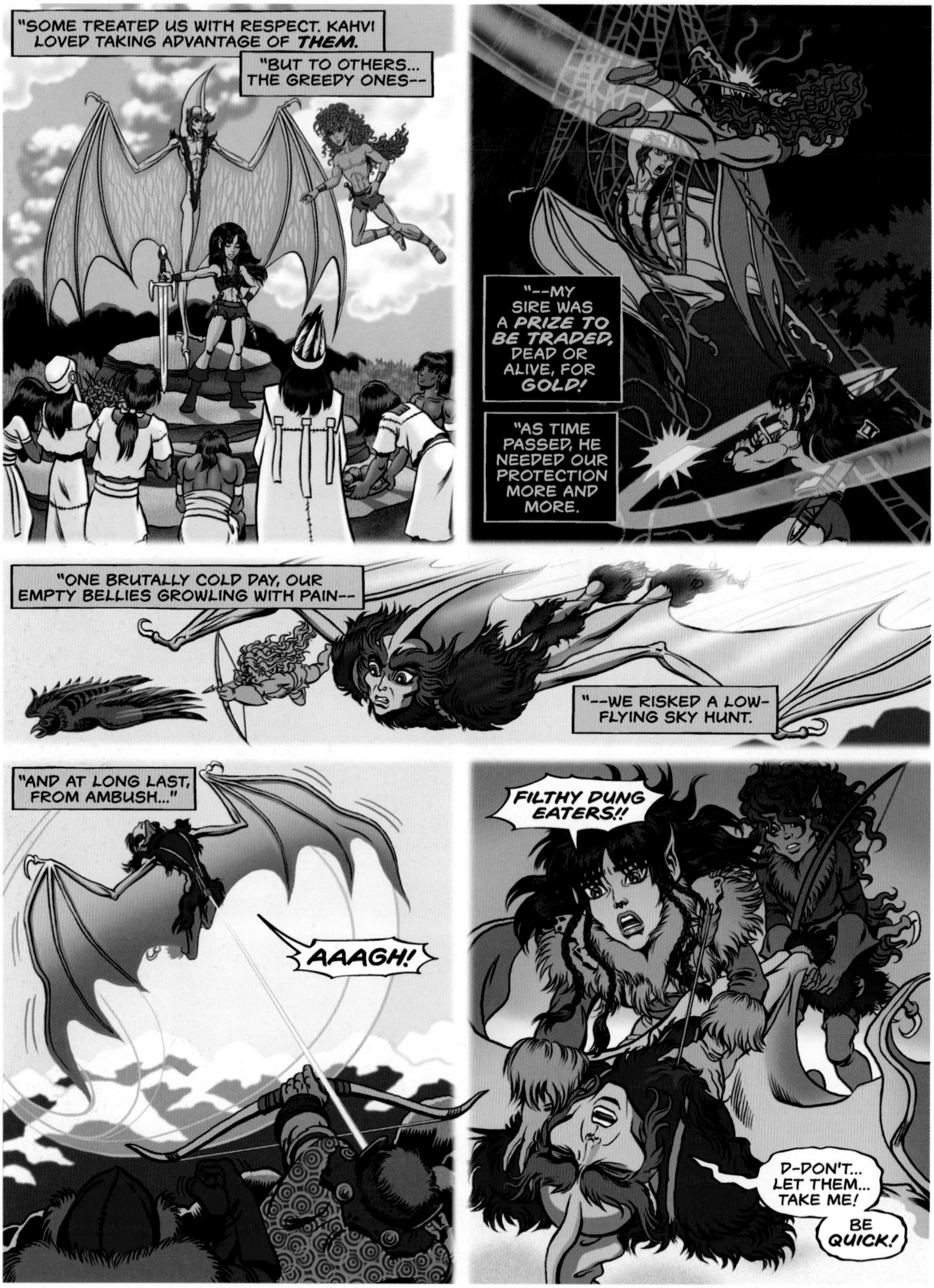

"SOME TREATED US WITH RESPECT. KAHVI LOVED TAKING ADVANTAGE OF *THEM.*
"BUT TO OTHERS... THE GREEDY ONES--
"--MY SIRE WAS A *PRIZE TO BE TRADED,* DEAD OR ALIVE, FOR *GOLD!*
"AS TIME PASSED, HE NEEDED OUR PROTECTION MORE AND MORE.
"ONE BRUTALLY COLD DAY, OUR EMPTY BELLIES GROWLING WITH PAIN--
"--WE RISKED A LOW-FLYING SKY HUNT.
"AND AT LONG LAST, FROM AMBUSH..."
AAAGH!
FILTHY DUNG EATERS!!
D-DON'T... LET THEM... TAKE ME!
BE QUICK!

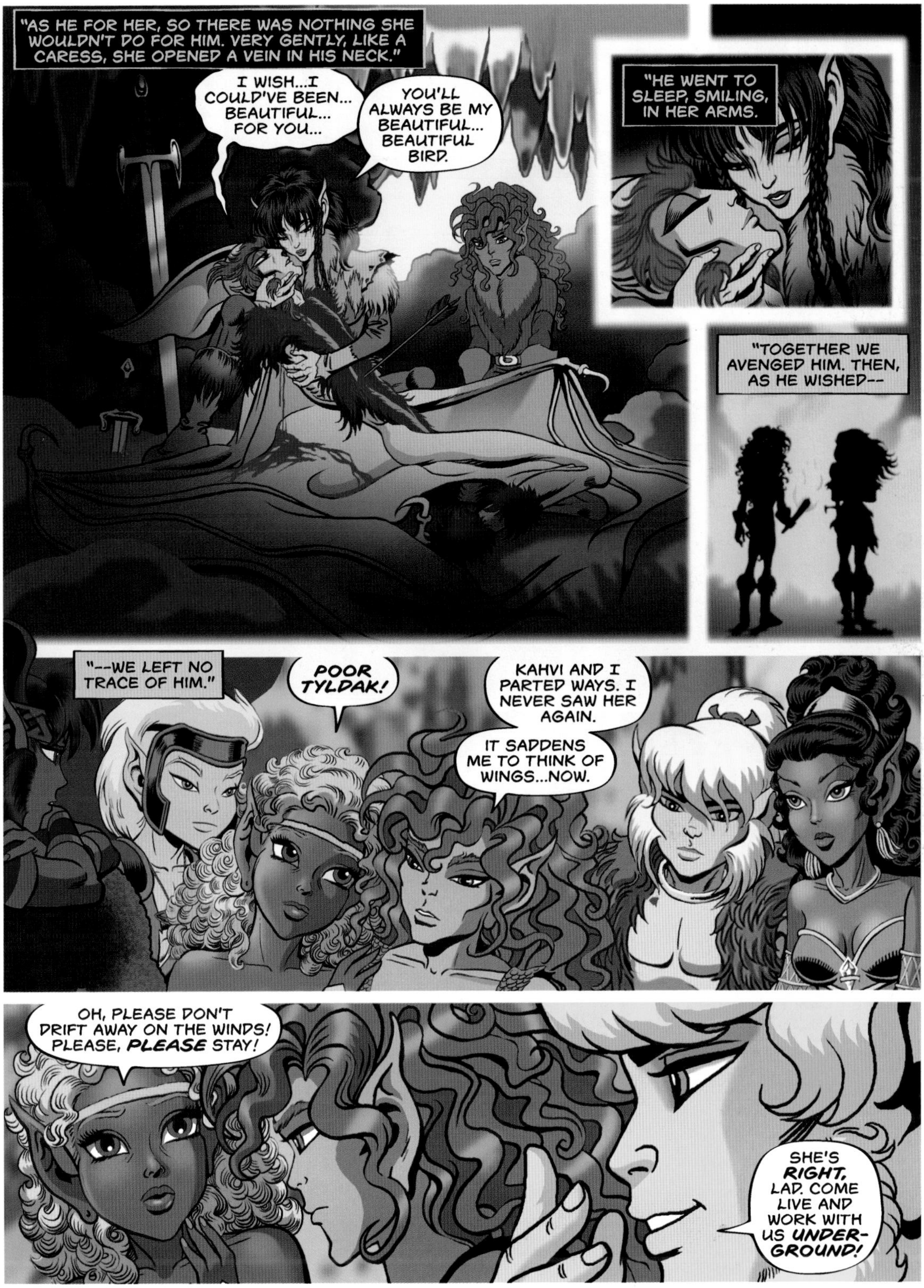
"AS HE FOR HER, SO THERE WAS NOTHING SHE WOULDN'T DO FOR HIM. VERY GENTLY, LIKE A CARESS, SHE OPENED A VEIN IN HIS NECK."
I WISH...I COULD'VE BEEN... BEAUTIFUL... FOR YOU...
YOU'LL ALWAYS BE MY BEAUTIFUL... BEAUTIFUL BIRD.
"HE WENT TO SLEEP, SMILING, IN HER ARMS.
"TOGETHER WE AVENGED HIM. THEN, AS HE WISHED--
"--WE LEFT NO TRACE OF HIM."
POOR TYLDAK!
KAHVI AND I PARTED WAYS. I NEVER SAW HER AGAIN.
IT SADDENS ME TO THINK OF WINGS...NOW.
OH, PLEASE DON'T DRIFT AWAY ON THE WINDS! PLEASE, PLEASE STAY!
SHE'S RIGHT, LAD. COME LIVE AND WORK WITH US UNDER-GROUND!

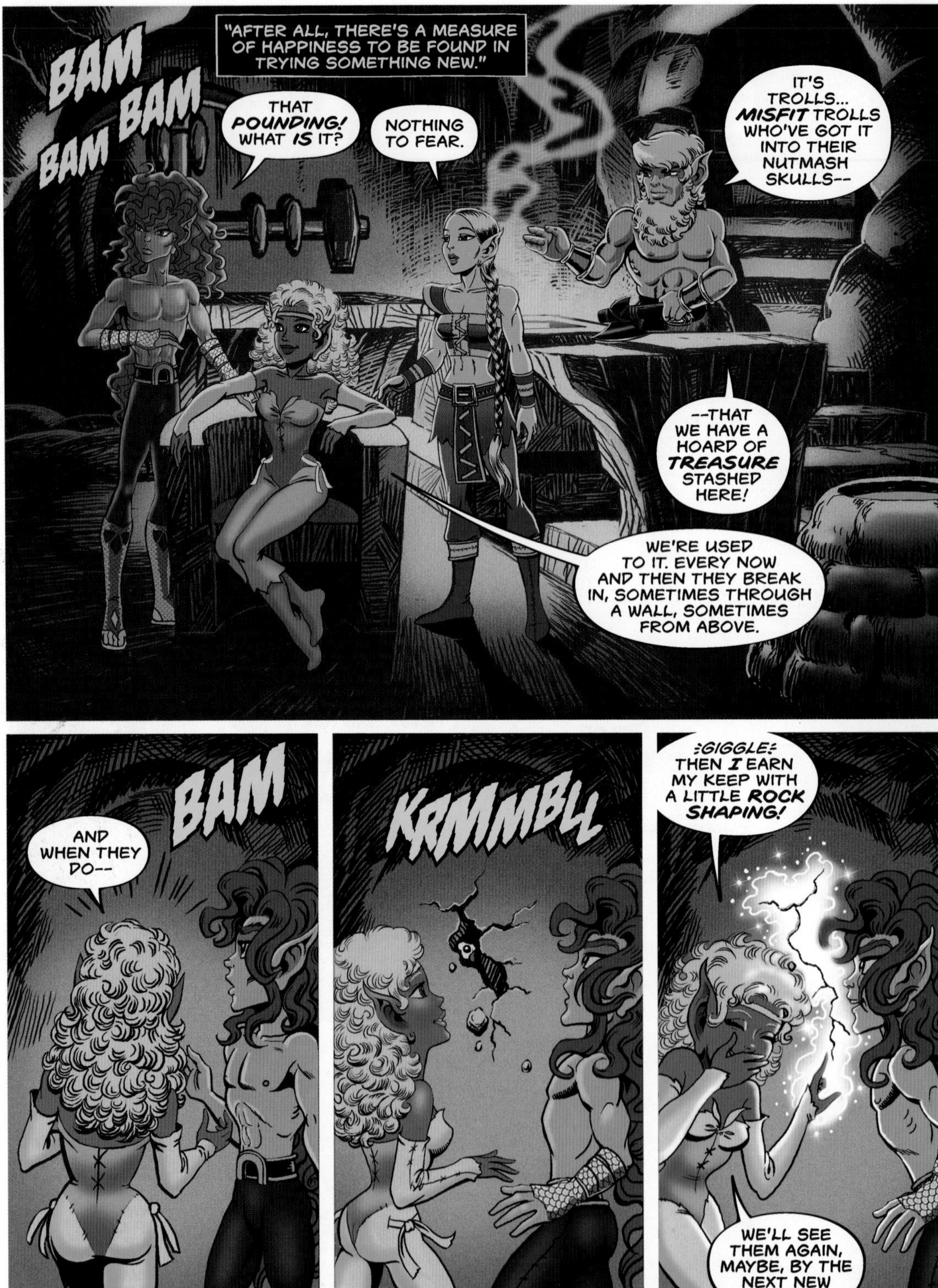
"AFTER ALL, THERE'S A MEASURE OF HAPPINESS TO BE FOUND IN TRYING SOMETHING NEW."
BAM BAM BAM
THAT POUNDING! WHAT IS IT?
NOTHING TO FEAR.
IT'S TROLLS... MISFIT TROLLS WHO'VE GOT IT INTO THEIR NUTMASH SKULLS--
--THAT WE HAVE A HOARD OF TREASURE STASHED HERE!
WE'RE USED TO IT. EVERY NOW AND THEN THEY BREAK IN, SOMETIMES THROUGH A WALL, SOMETIMES FROM ABOVE.
AND WHEN THEY DO--
BAM
KRMMBLL
GIGGLE
THEN I EARN MY KEEP WITH A LITTLE ROCK SHAPING!
WE'LL SEE THEM AGAIN, MAYBE, BY THE NEXT NEW GREEN.

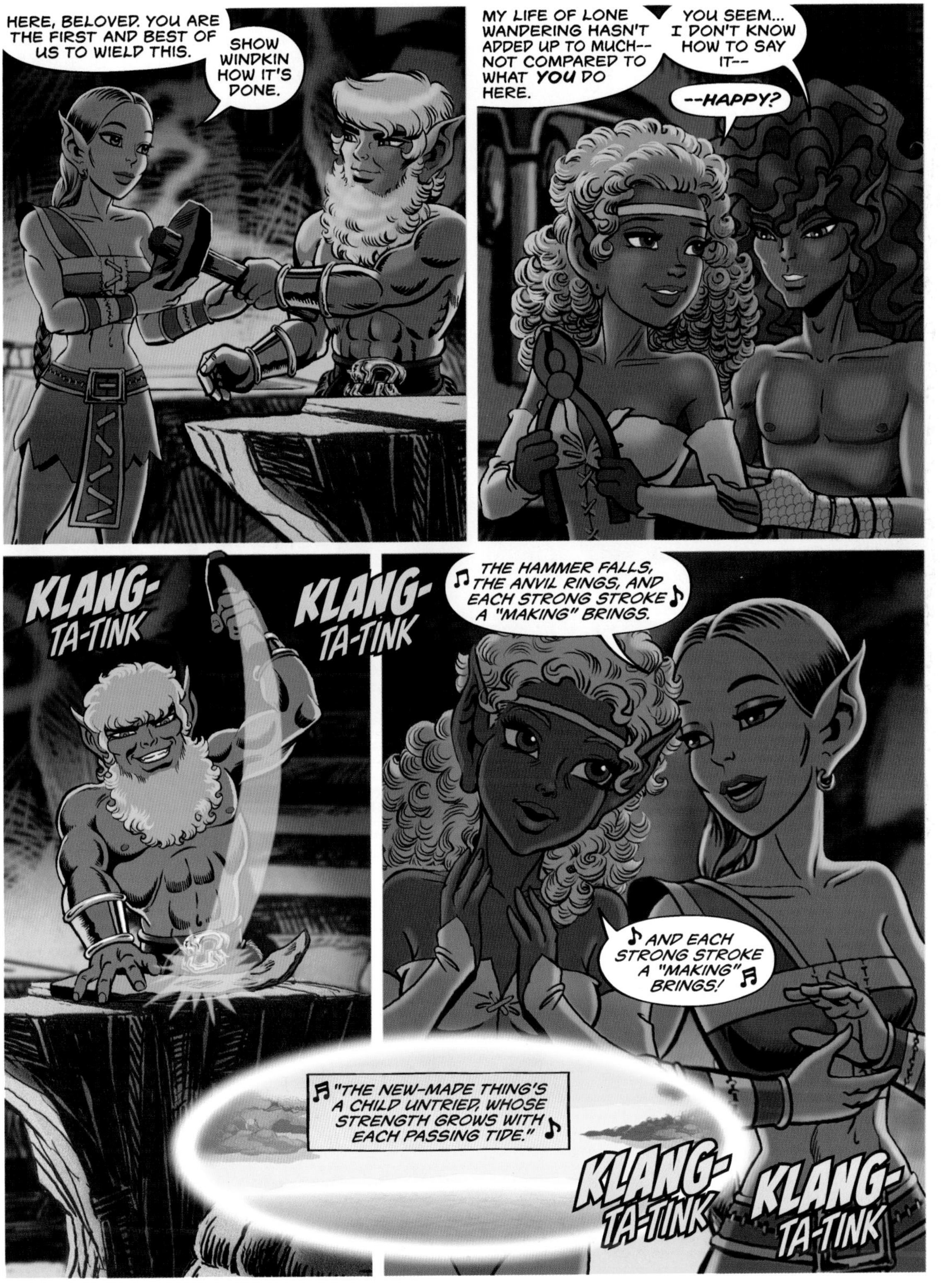

HERE, BELOVED. YOU ARE THE FIRST AND BEST OF US TO WIELD THIS.
SHOW WINDKIN HOW IT'S DONE.
MY LIFE OF LONE WANDERING HASN'T ADDED UP TO MUCH-- NOT COMPARED TO WHAT YOU DO HERE.
YOU SEEM... I DON'T KNOW HOW TO SAY IT--
--HAPPY?
KLANG-TA-TINK
KLANG-TA-TINK
♫ THE HAMMER FALLS, THE ANVIL RINGS, AND EACH STRONG STROKE A "MAKING" BRINGS. ♪
♪ AND EACH STRONG STROKE A "MAKING" BRINGS! ♫
♫ "THE NEW-MADE THING'S A CHILD UNTRIED, WHOSE STRENGTH GROWS WITH EACH PASSING TIDE." ♪
KLANG-TA-TINK
KLANG-TA-TINK

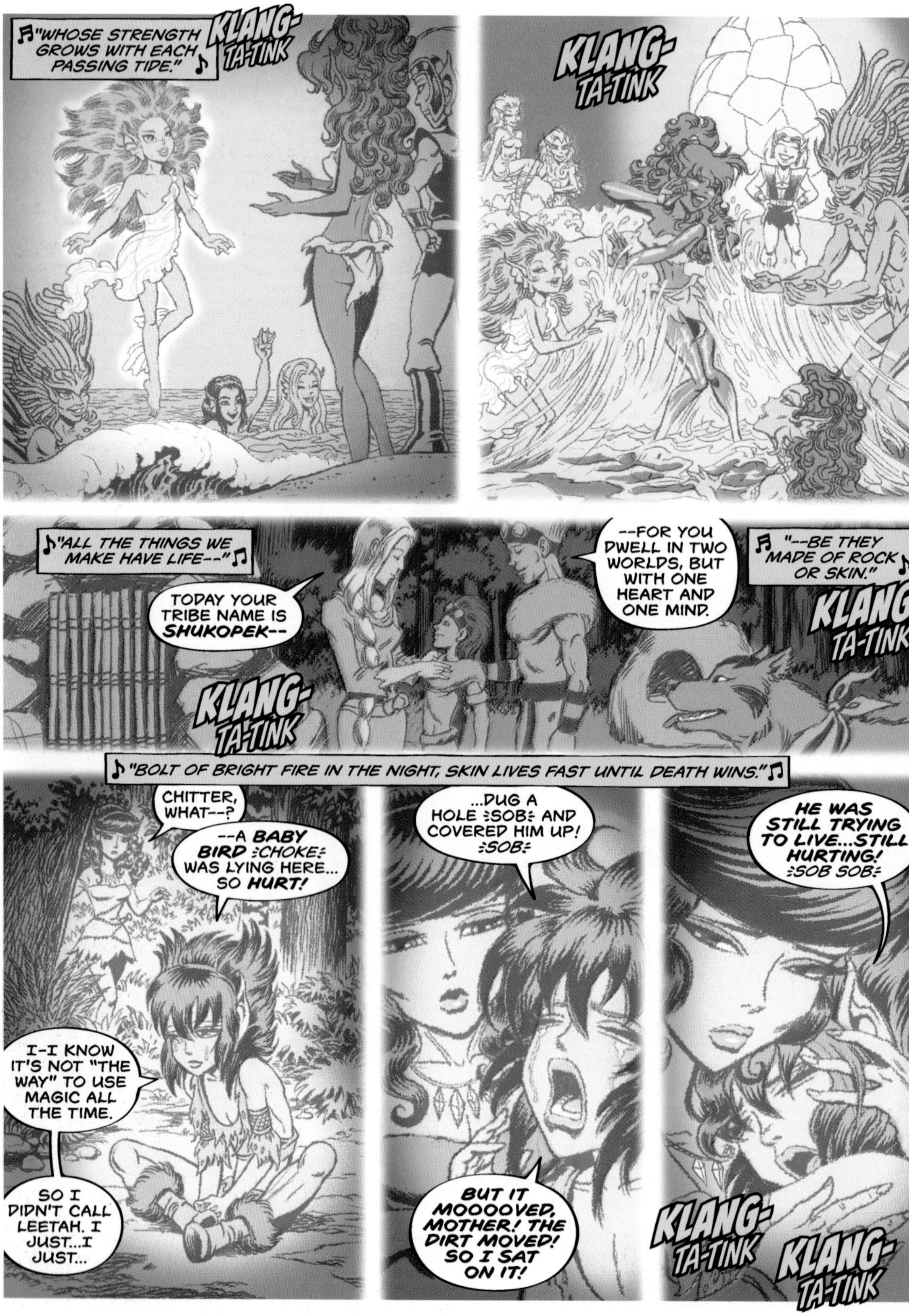
♫"WHOSE STRENGTH GROWS WITH EACH PASSING TIDE."♪
KLANG-TA-TINK
KLANG-TA-TINK
♪"ALL THE THINGS WE MAKE HAVE LIFE--"♫
TODAY YOUR TRIBE NAME IS SHUKOPEK--
--FOR YOU DWELL IN TWO WORLDS, BUT WITH ONE HEART AND ONE MIND.
♫"--BE THEY MADE OF ROCK OR SKIN."♪
KLANG-TA-TINK
KLANG-TA-TINK
♪"BOLT OF BRIGHT FIRE IN THE NIGHT, SKIN LIVES FAST UNTIL DEATH WINS."♫
CHITTER, WHAT--?
--A BABY BIRD :CHOKE: WAS LYING HERE... SO HURT!
I-I KNOW IT'S NOT "THE WAY" TO USE MAGIC ALL THE TIME.
SO I DIDN'T CALL LEETAH. I JUST...I JUST...
...DUG A HOLE :SOB: AND COVERED HIM UP! :SOB:
BUT IT MOOOOVED, MOTHER! THE DIRT MOVED! SO I SAT ON IT!
HE WAS STILL TRYING TO LIVE...STILL HURTING! :SOB SOB:
KLANG-TA-TINK
KLANG-TA-TINK

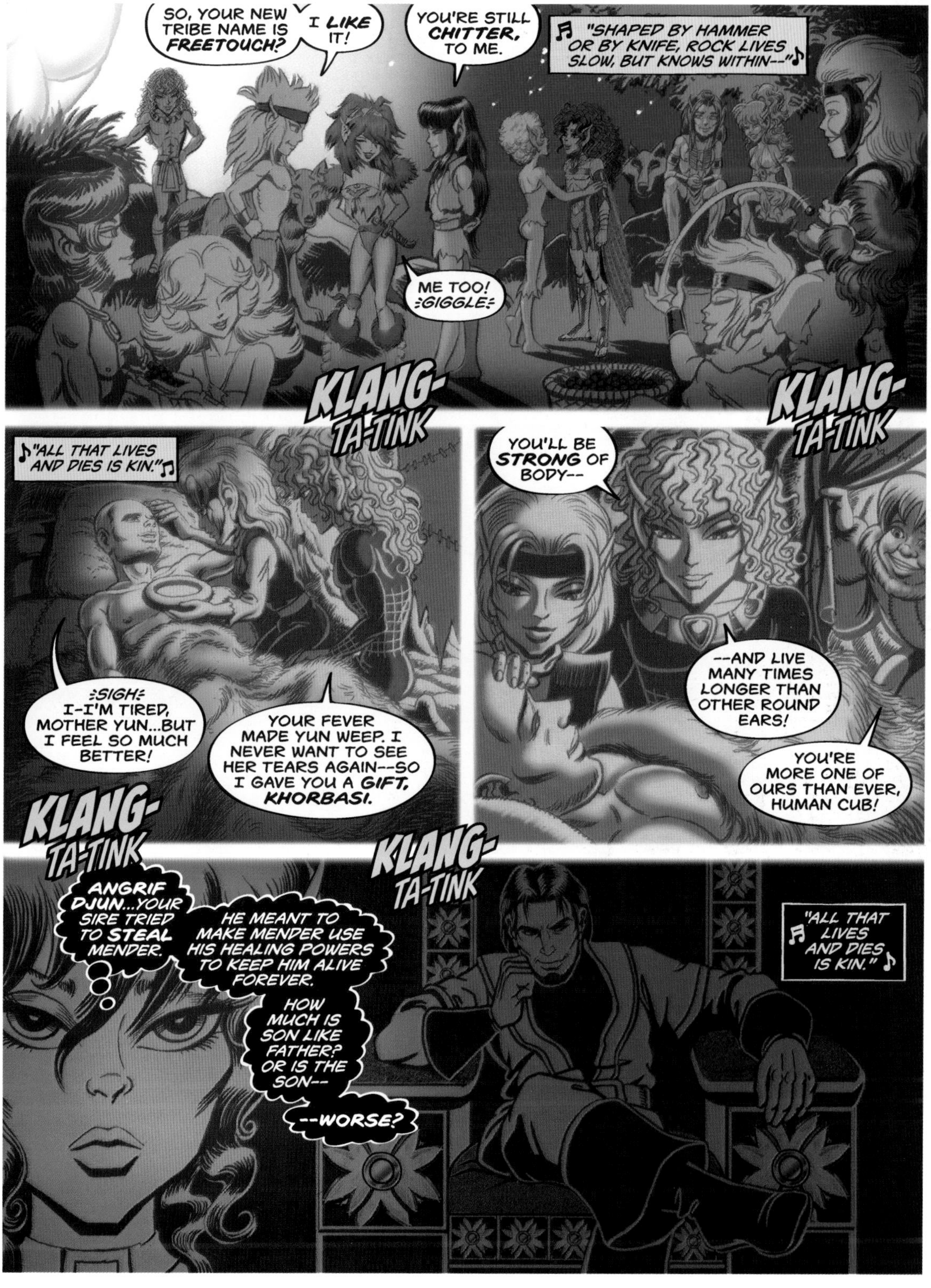

SO, YOUR NEW TRIBE NAME IS FREETOUCH?
I LIKE IT!
YOU'RE STILL CHITTER, TO ME.
♫ "SHAPED BY HAMMER OR BY KNIFE, ROCK LIVES SLOW, BUT KNOWS WITHIN--" ♪
ME TOO! :GIGGLE:
KLANG-TA-TINK
KLANG-TA-TINK
♪ "ALL THAT LIVES AND DIES IS KIN." ♫
:SIGH: I-I'M TIRED, MOTHER YUN...BUT I FEEL SO MUCH BETTER!
YOUR FEVER MADE YUN WEEP. I NEVER WANT TO SEE HER TEARS AGAIN--SO I GAVE YOU A GIFT, KHORBASI.
YOU'LL BE STRONG OF BODY--
--AND LIVE MANY TIMES LONGER THAN OTHER ROUND EARS!
YOU'RE MORE ONE OF OURS THAN EVER, HUMAN CUB!
KLANG-TA-TINK
KLANG-TA-TINK
ANGRIF DJUN...YOUR SIRE TRIED TO STEAL MENDER.
HE MEANT TO MAKE MENDER USE HIS HEALING POWERS TO KEEP HIM ALIVE FOREVER.
HOW MUCH IS SON LIKE FATHER? OR IS THE SON--
--WORSE?
♫ "ALL THAT LIVES AND DIES IS KIN." ♪

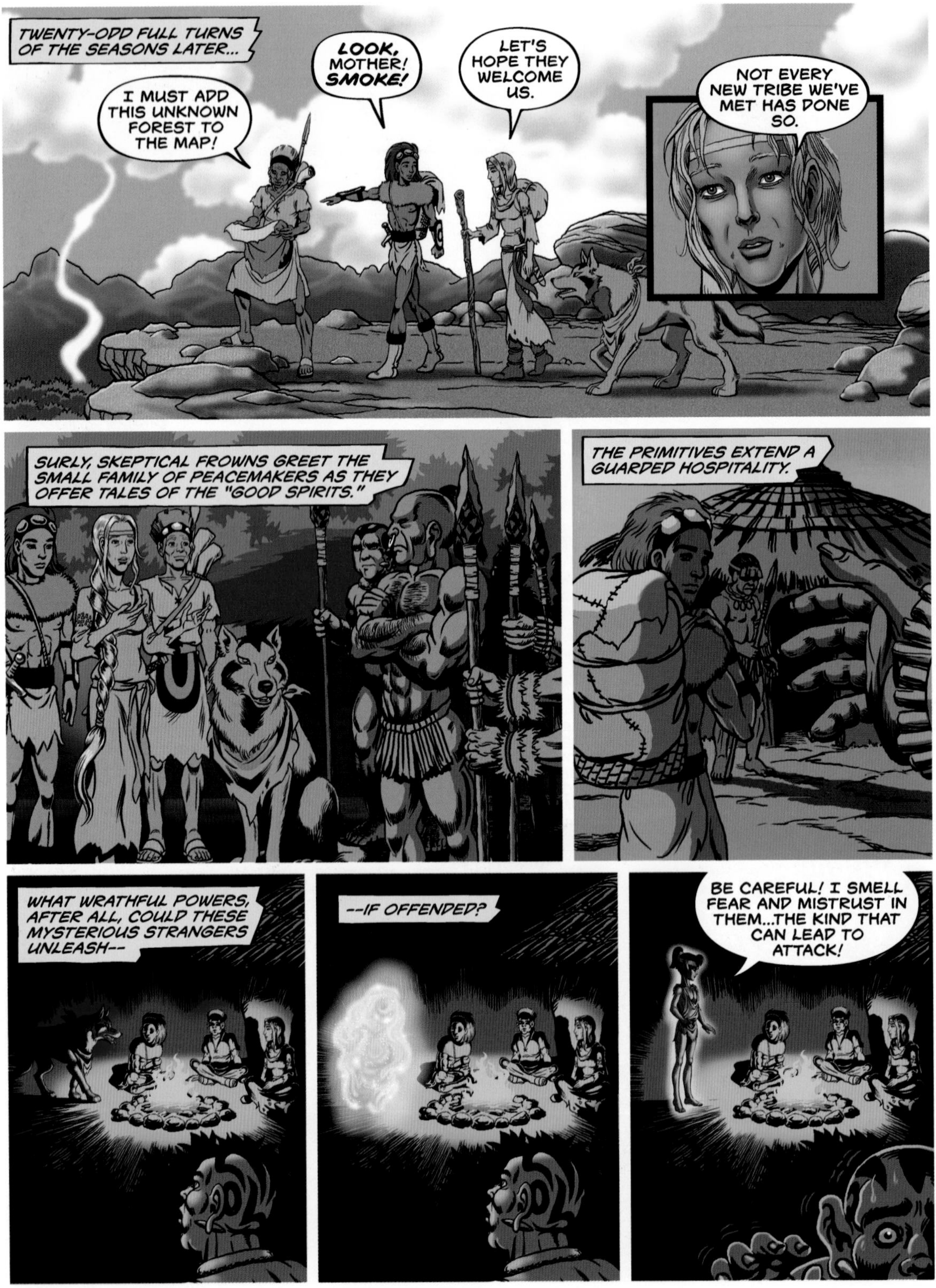
TWENTY-ODD FULL TURNS OF THE SEASONS LATER...
I MUST ADD THIS UNKNOWN FOREST TO THE MAP!
LOOK, MOTHER! SMOKE!
LET'S HOPE THEY WELCOME US.
NOT EVERY NEW TRIBE WE'VE MET HAS DONE SO.
SURLY, SKEPTICAL FROWNS GREET THE SMALL FAMILY OF PEACEMAKERS AS THEY OFFER TALES OF THE "GOOD SPIRITS."
THE PRIMITIVES EXTEND A GUARDED HOSPITALITY.
WHAT WRATHFUL POWERS, AFTER ALL, COULD THESE MYSTERIOUS STRANGERS UNLEASH--
--IF OFFENDED?
BE CAREFUL! I SMELL FEAR AND MISTRUST IN THEM...THE KIND THAT CAN LEAD TO ATTACK!

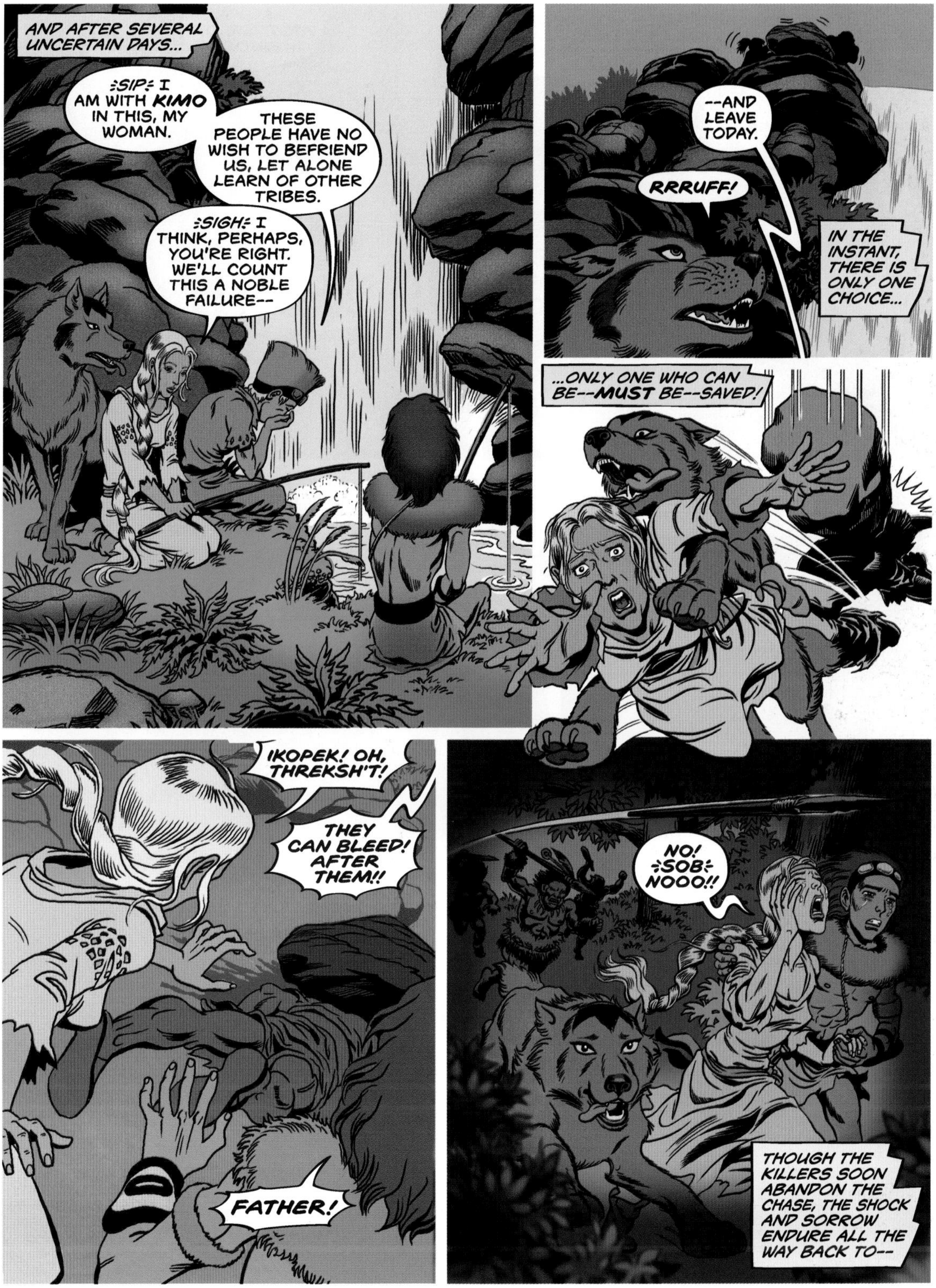
AND AFTER SEVERAL UNCERTAIN DAYS...
SIP I AM WITH KIMO IN THIS, MY WOMAN.
THESE PEOPLE HAVE NO WISH TO BEFRIEND US, LET ALONE LEARN OF OTHER TRIBES.
SIGH I THINK, PERHAPS, YOU'RE RIGHT. WE'LL COUNT THIS A NOBLE FAILURE--
--AND LEAVE TODAY.
RRRUFF!
IN THE INSTANT, THERE IS ONLY ONE CHOICE...
...ONLY ONE WHO CAN BE--MUST BE--SAVED!
IKOPEK! OH, THREKSH'T!
THEY CAN BLEED! AFTER THEM!!
FATHER!
NO! SOB NOOO!!
THOUGH THE KILLERS SOON ABANDON THE CHASE, THE SHOCK AND SORROW ENDURE ALL THE WAY BACK TO--

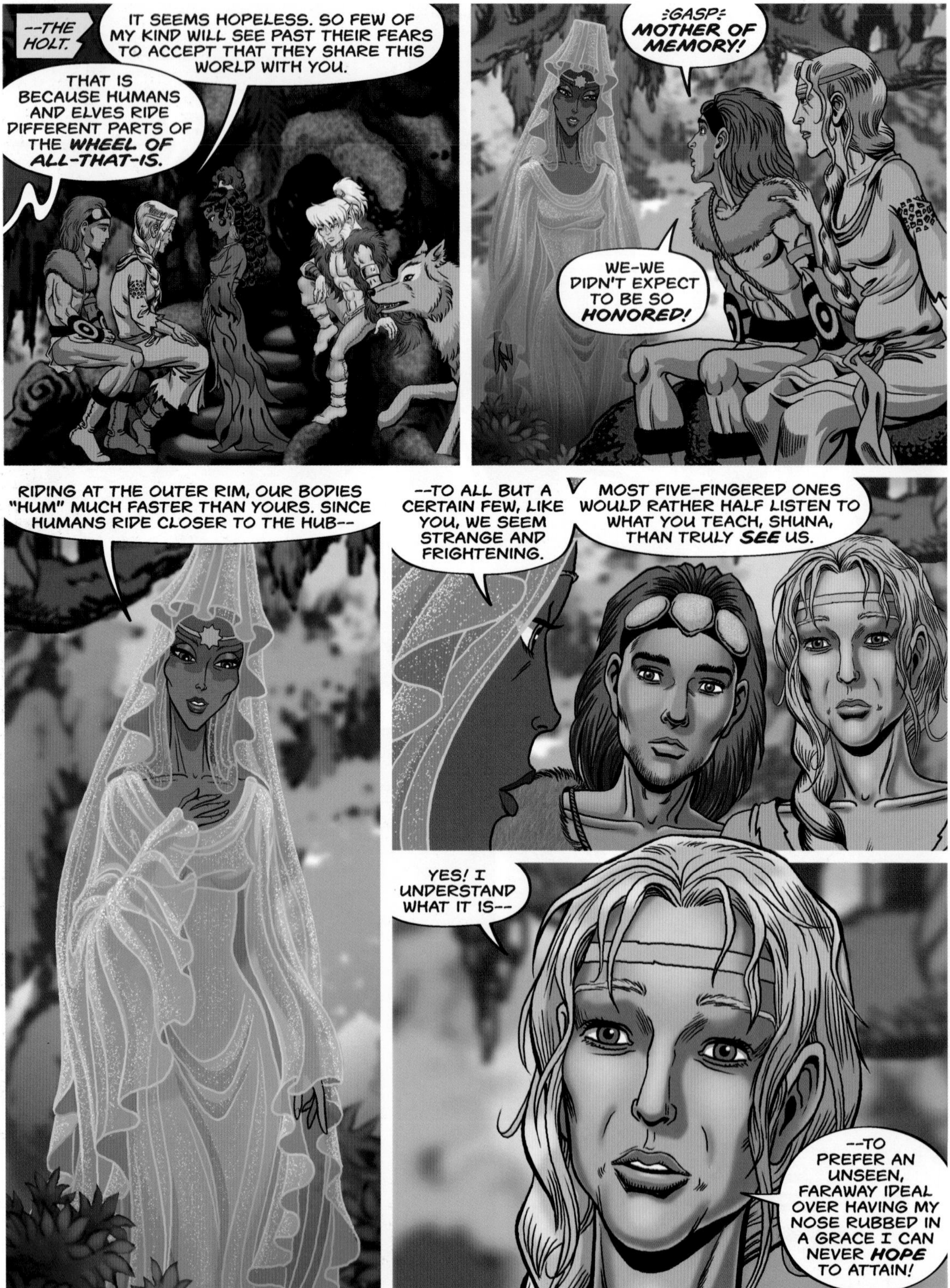

--THE HOLT.
IT SEEMS HOPELESS. SO FEW OF MY KIND WILL SEE PAST THEIR FEARS TO ACCEPT THAT THEY SHARE THIS WORLD WITH YOU.
THAT IS BECAUSE HUMANS AND ELVES RIDE DIFFERENT PARTS OF THE **WHEEL OF ALL-THAT-IS.**
GASP
MOTHER OF MEMORY!
WE-WE DIDN'T EXPECT TO BE SO **HONORED!**
RIDING AT THE OUTER RIM, OUR BODIES "HUM" MUCH FASTER THAN YOURS. SINCE HUMANS RIDE CLOSER TO THE HUB--
--TO ALL BUT A CERTAIN FEW, LIKE YOU, WE SEEM STRANGE AND FRIGHTENING.
MOST FIVE-FINGERED ONES WOULD RATHER HALF LISTEN TO WHAT YOU TEACH, SHUNA, THAN TRULY **SEE** US.
YES! I UNDERSTAND WHAT IT IS--
--TO PREFER AN UNSEEN, FARAWAY IDEAL OVER HAVING MY NOSE RUBBED IN A GRACE I CAN NEVER **HOPE** TO ATTAIN!

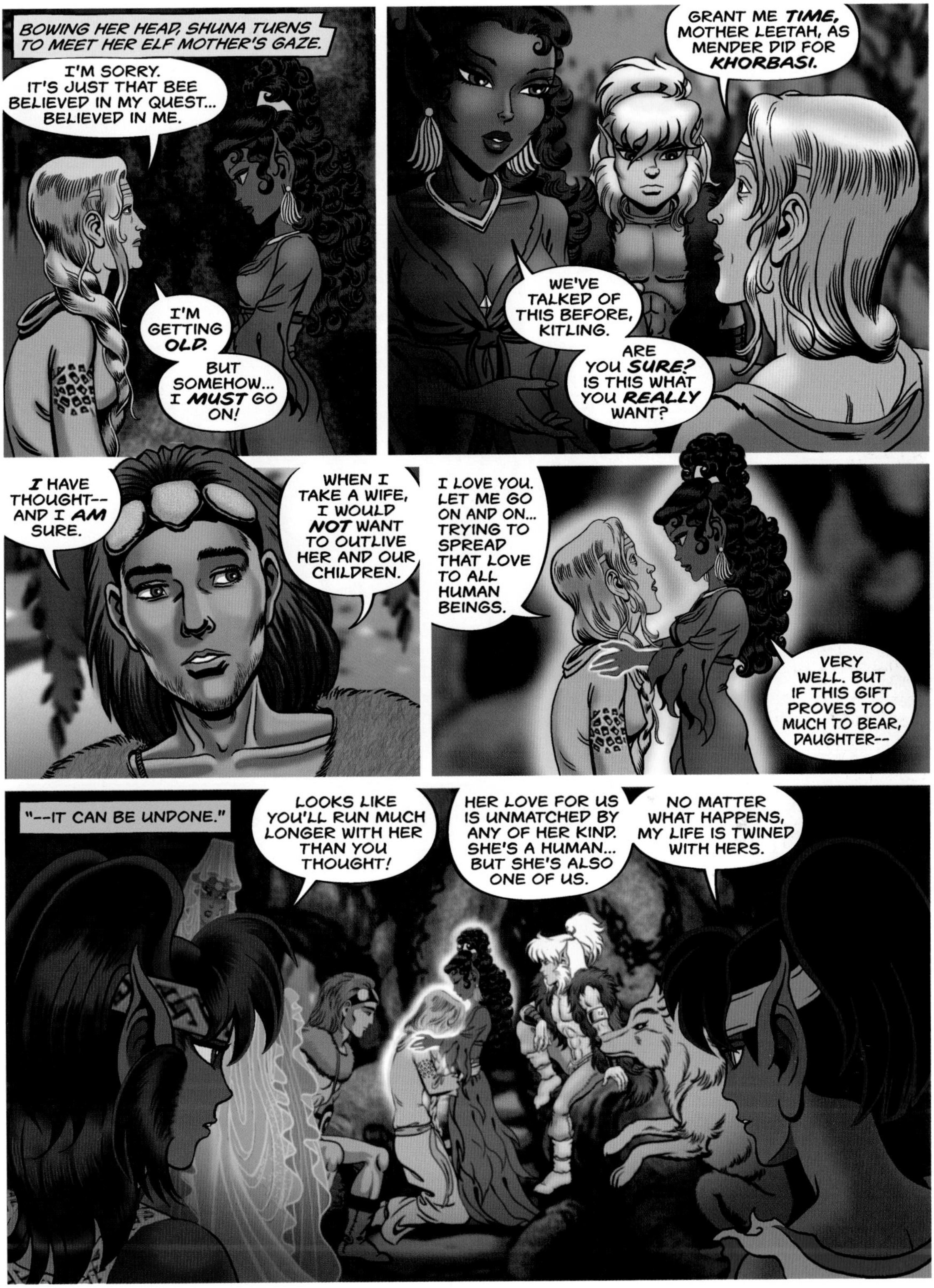
BOWING HER HEAD, SHUNA TURNS TO MEET HER ELF MOTHER'S GAZE.
I'M SORRY. IT'S JUST THAT BEE BELIEVED IN MY QUEST... BELIEVED IN ME.
I'M GETTING OLD.
BUT SOMEHOW... I MUST GO ON!
GRANT ME TIME, MOTHER LEETAH, AS MENDER DID FOR KHORBASI.
WE'VE TALKED OF THIS BEFORE, KITLING.
ARE YOU SURE? IS THIS WHAT YOU REALLY WANT?
I HAVE THOUGHT-- AND I AM SURE.
WHEN I TAKE A WIFE, I WOULD NOT WANT TO OUTLIVE HER AND OUR CHILDREN.
I LOVE YOU. LET ME GO ON AND ON... TRYING TO SPREAD THAT LOVE TO ALL HUMAN BEINGS.
VERY WELL. BUT IF THIS GIFT PROVES TOO MUCH TO BEAR, DAUGHTER--
"--IT CAN BE UNDONE."
LOOKS LIKE YOU'LL RUN MUCH LONGER WITH HER THAN YOU THOUGHT!
HER LOVE FOR US IS UNMATCHED BY ANY OF HER KIND. SHE'S A HUMAN... BUT SHE'S ALSO ONE OF US.
NO MATTER WHAT HAPPENS, MY LIFE IS TWINED WITH HERS.

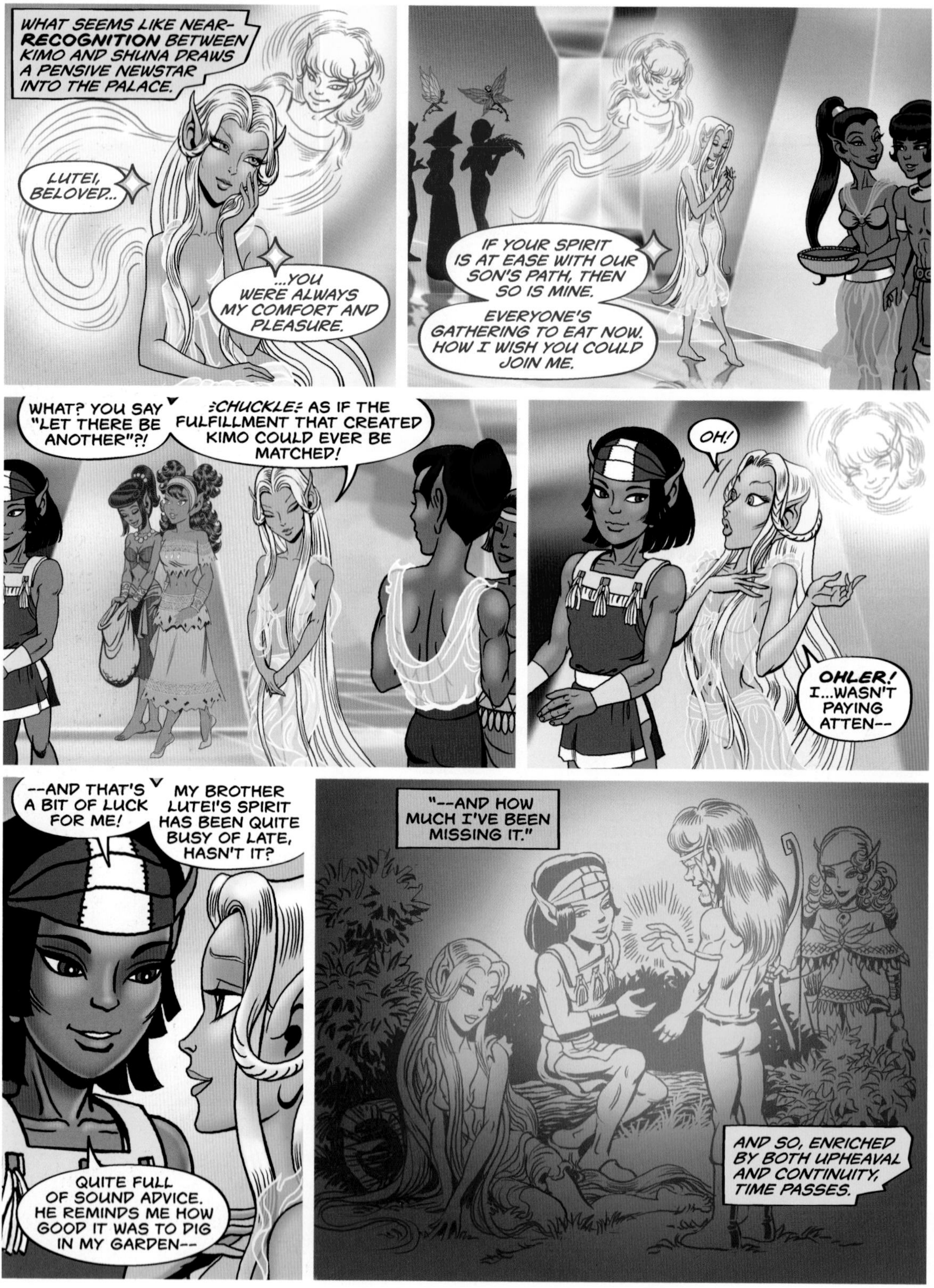
WHAT SEEMS LIKE NEAR-RECOGNITION BETWEEN KIMO AND SHUNA DRAWS A PENSIVE NEWSTAR INTO THE PALACE.
LUTEI, BELOVED...
...YOU WERE ALWAYS MY COMFORT AND PLEASURE.
IF YOUR SPIRIT IS AT EASE WITH OUR SON'S PATH, THEN SO IS MINE.
EVERYONE'S GATHERING TO EAT NOW. HOW I WISH YOU COULD JOIN ME.
WHAT? YOU SAY "LET THERE BE ANOTHER"?!
=CHUCKLE= AS IF THE FULFILLMENT THAT CREATED KIMO COULD EVER BE MATCHED!
OH!
OHLER! I...WASN'T PAYING ATTEN--
--AND THAT'S A BIT OF LUCK FOR ME!
MY BROTHER LUTEI'S SPIRIT HAS BEEN QUITE BUSY OF LATE, HASN'T IT?
QUITE FULL OF SOUND ADVICE. HE REMINDS ME HOW GOOD IT WAS TO DIG IN MY GARDEN--
"--AND HOW MUCH I'VE BEEN MISSING IT."
AND SO, ENRICHED BY BOTH UPHEAVAL AND CONTINUITY, TIME PASSES.

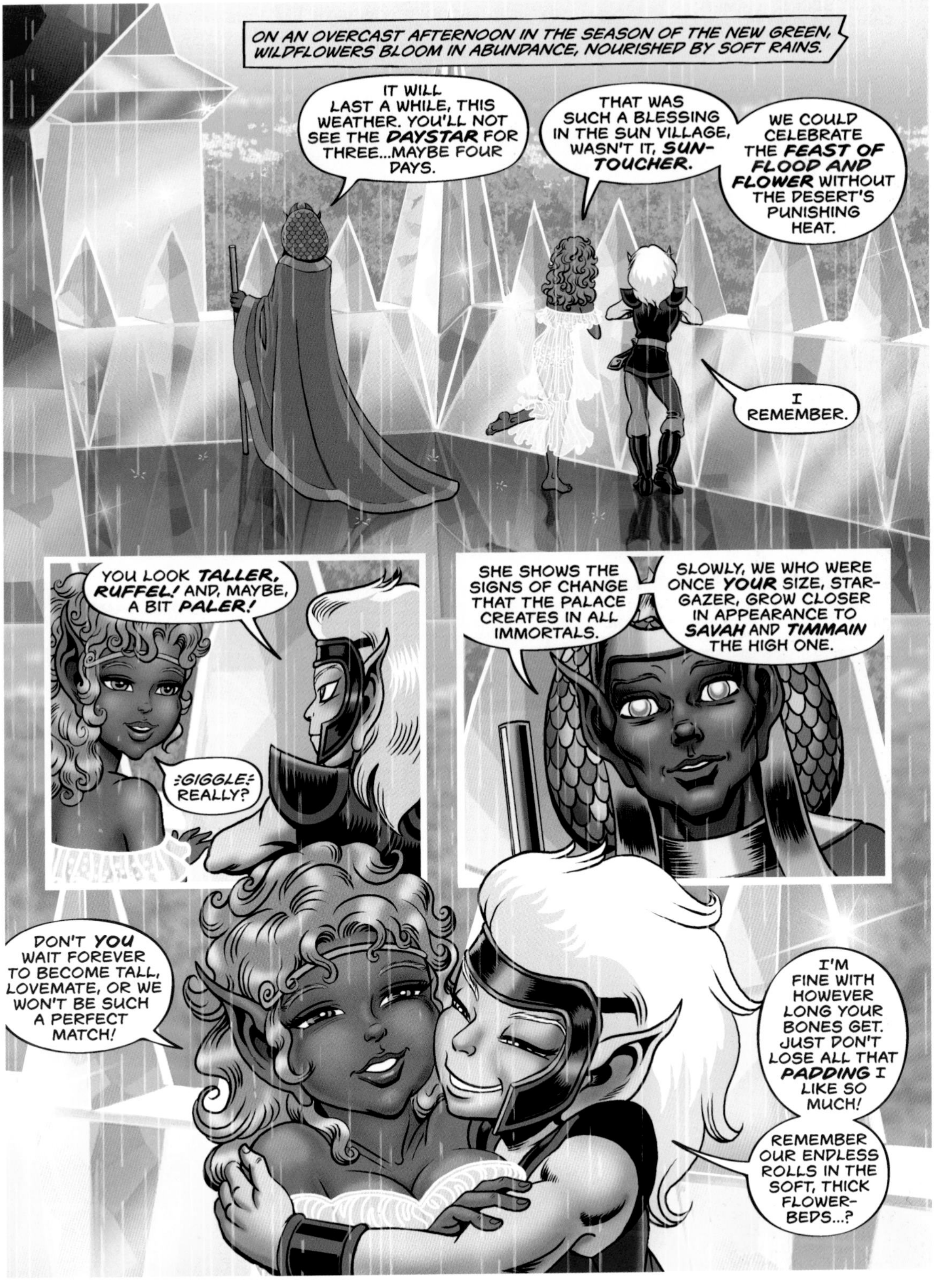
ON AN OVERCAST AFTERNOON IN THE SEASON OF THE NEW GREEN, WILDFLOWERS BLOOM IN ABUNDANCE, NOURISHED BY SOFT RAINS.
IT WILL LAST A WHILE, THIS WEATHER. YOU'LL NOT SEE THE DAYSTAR FOR THREE...MAYBE FOUR DAYS.
THAT WAS SUCH A BLESSING IN THE SUN VILLAGE, WASN'T IT, SUN-TOUCHER.
WE COULD CELEBRATE THE FEAST OF FLOOD AND FLOWER WITHOUT THE DESERT'S PUNISHING HEAT.
I REMEMBER.
YOU LOOK TALLER, RUFFEL! AND, MAYBE, A BIT PALER!
:GIGGLE: REALLY?
SHE SHOWS THE SIGNS OF CHANGE THAT THE PALACE CREATES IN ALL IMMORTALS.
SLOWLY, WE WHO WERE ONCE YOUR SIZE, STAR-GAZER, GROW CLOSER IN APPEARANCE TO SAVAH AND TIMMAIN THE HIGH ONE.
DON'T YOU WAIT FOREVER TO BECOME TALL, LOVEMATE, OR WE WON'T BE SUCH A PERFECT MATCH!
I'M FINE WITH HOWEVER LONG YOUR BONES GET. JUST DON'T LOSE ALL THAT PADDING I LIKE SO MUCH!
REMEMBER OUR ENDLESS ROLLS IN THE SOFT, THICK FLOWER-BEDS...?

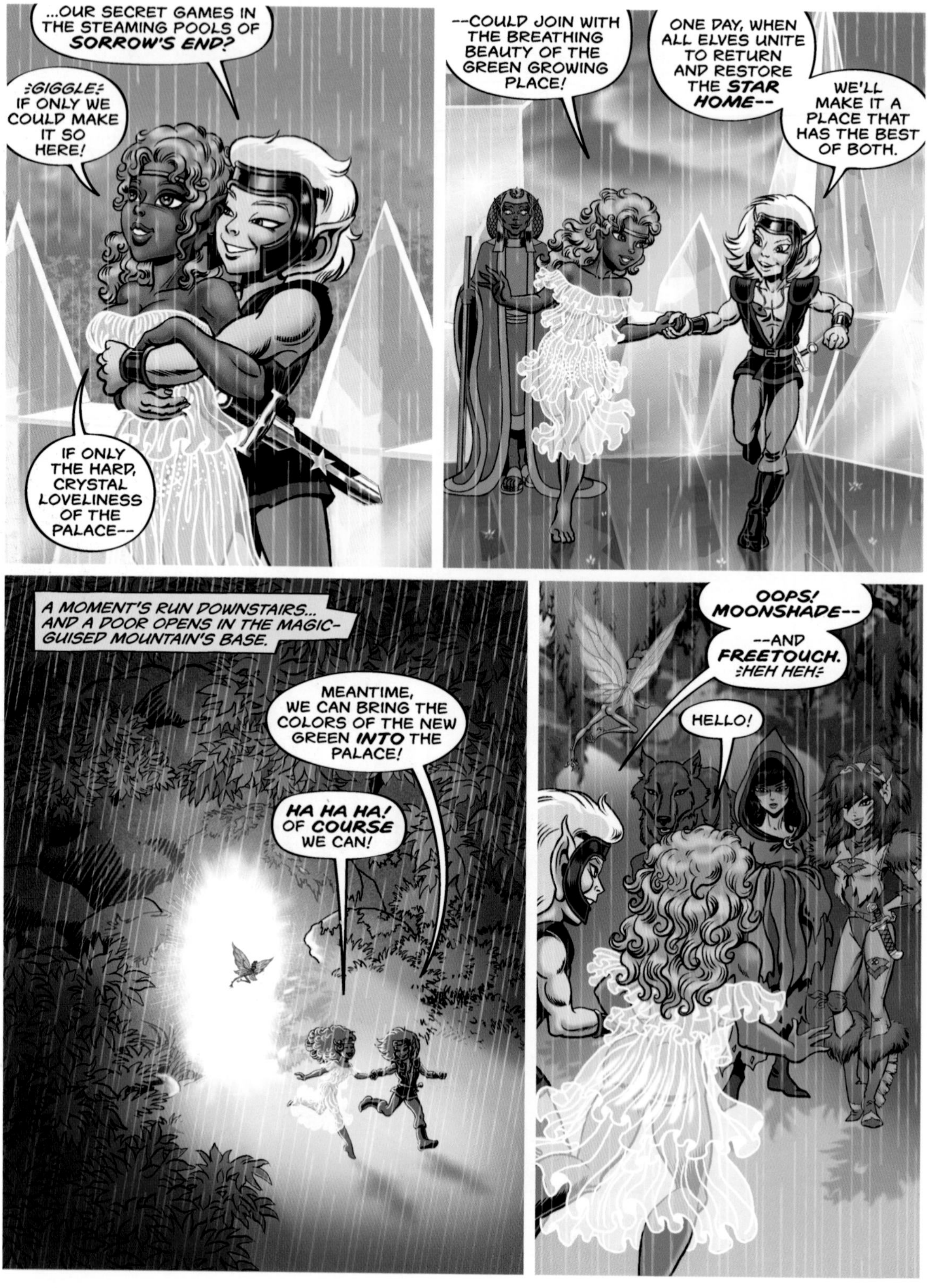
...OUR SECRET GAMES IN THE STEAMING POOLS OF SORROW'S END?
:GIGGLE: IF ONLY WE COULD MAKE IT SO HERE!
IF ONLY THE HARD, CRYSTAL LOVELINESS OF THE PALACE--
--COULD JOIN WITH THE BREATHING BEAUTY OF THE GREEN GROWING PLACE!
ONE DAY, WHEN ALL ELVES UNITE TO RETURN AND RESTORE THE STAR HOME--
WE'LL MAKE IT A PLACE THAT HAS THE BEST OF BOTH.
A MOMENT'S RUN DOWNSTAIRS... AND A DOOR OPENS IN THE MAGIC-GUISED MOUNTAIN'S BASE.
MEANTIME, WE CAN BRING THE COLORS OF THE NEW GREEN INTO THE PALACE!
HA HA HA! OF COURSE WE CAN!
OOPS! MOONSHADE--
--AND FREETOUCH. :HEH HEH:
HELLO!

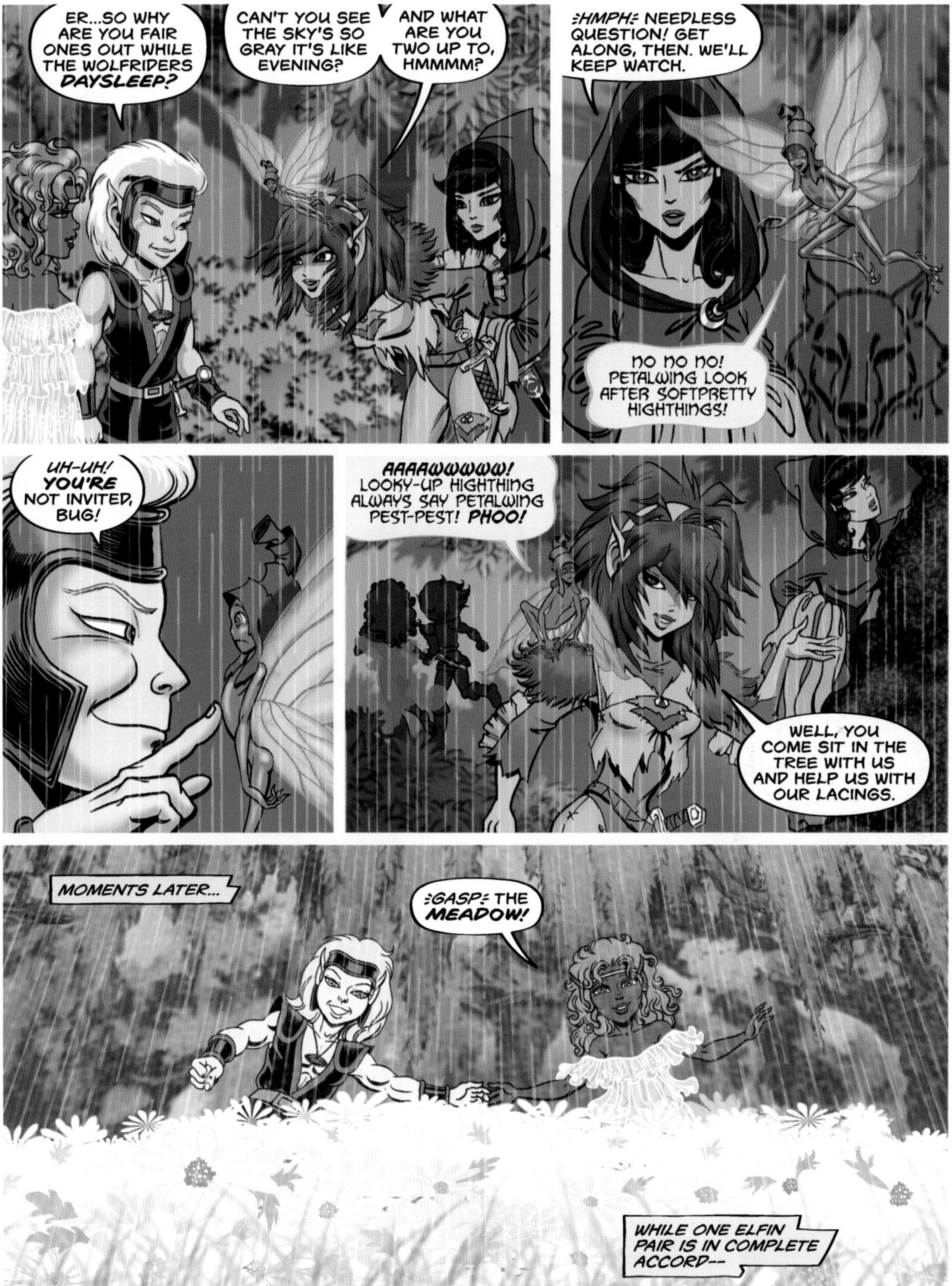
ER...SO WHY ARE YOU FAIR ONES OUT WHILE THE WOLFRIDERS DAYSLEEP?
CAN'T YOU SEE THE SKY'S SO GRAY IT'S LIKE EVENING?
AND WHAT ARE YOU TWO UP TO, HMMMM?
=HMPH= NEEDLESS QUESTION! GET ALONG, THEN. WE'LL KEEP WATCH.
NO NO NO! PETALWING LOOK AFTER SOFTPRETTY HIGHTHINGS!
UH-UH! YOU'RE NOT INVITED, BUG!
AAAAWWWWW! LOOKY-UP HIGHTHING ALWAYS SAY PETALWING PEST-PEST! PHOO!
WELL, YOU COME SIT IN THE TREE WITH US AND HELP US WITH OUR LACINGS.
MOMENTS LATER...
=GASP= THE MEADOW!
WHILE ONE ELFIN PAIR IS IN COMPLETE ACCORD--

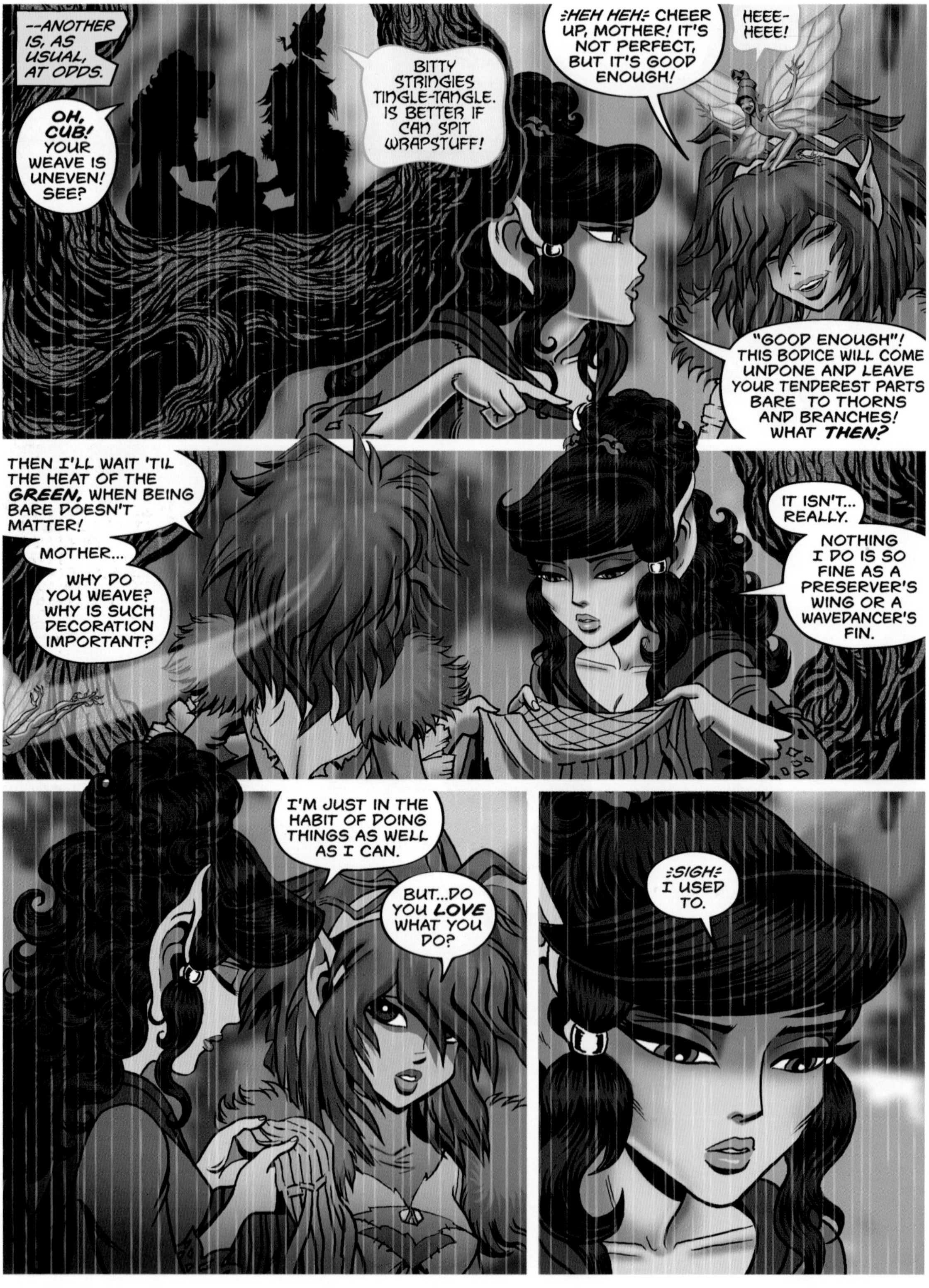
--ANOTHER IS, AS USUAL, AT ODDS.
OH, CUB! YOUR WEAVE IS UNEVEN! SEE?
BITTY STRINGIES TINGLE-TANGLE. IS BETTER IF CAN SPIT WRAPSTUFF!
:HEH HEH: CHEER UP, MOTHER! IT'S NOT PERFECT, BUT IT'S GOOD ENOUGH!
HEEE-HEEE!
"GOOD ENOUGH"! THIS BODICE WILL COME UNDONE AND LEAVE YOUR TENDEREST PARTS BARE TO THORNS AND BRANCHES! WHAT THEN?
THEN I'LL WAIT 'TIL THE HEAT OF THE GREEN, WHEN BEING BARE DOESN'T MATTER!
MOTHER...
WHY DO YOU WEAVE? WHY IS SUCH DECORATION IMPORTANT?
IT ISN'T... REALLY.
NOTHING I DO IS SO FINE AS A PRESERVER'S WING OR A WAVEDANCER'S FIN.
I'M JUST IN THE HABIT OF DOING THINGS AS WELL AS I CAN.
BUT...DO YOU LOVE WHAT YOU DO?
:SIGH: I USED TO.

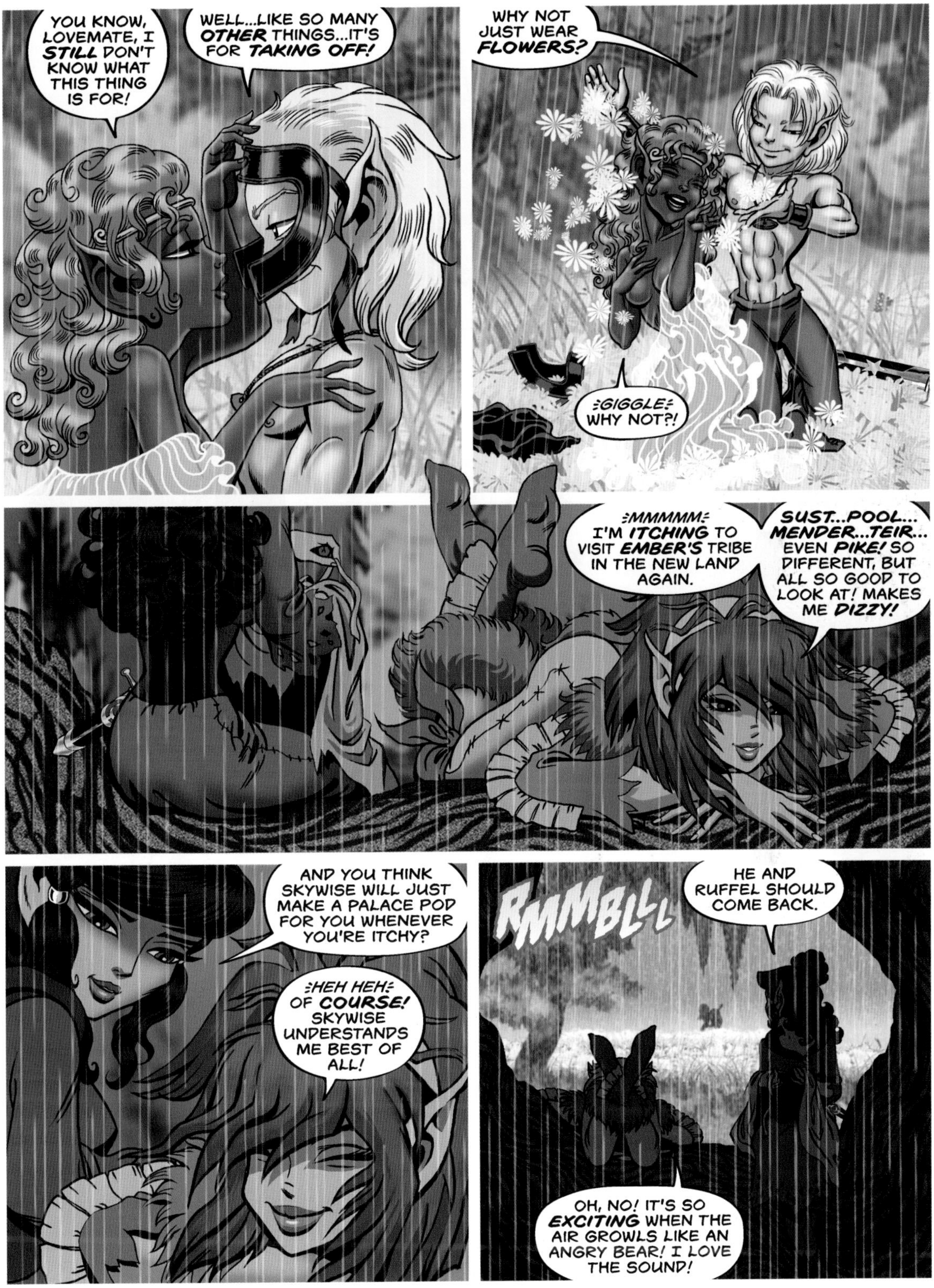
YOU KNOW, LOVEMATE, I **STILL** DON'T KNOW WHAT THIS THING IS FOR!
WELL...LIKE SO MANY **OTHER** THINGS...IT'S FOR **TAKING OFF!**
WHY NOT JUST WEAR **FLOWERS?**
GIGGLE WHY NOT?!
MMMMM I'M **ITCHING** TO VISIT **EMBER'S** TRIBE IN THE NEW LAND AGAIN.
SUST...POOL... MENDER...TEIR... EVEN **PIKE!** SO DIFFERENT, BUT ALL SO GOOD TO LOOK AT! MAKES ME **DIZZY!**
AND YOU THINK SKYWISE WILL JUST MAKE A PALACE POD FOR YOU WHENEVER YOU'RE ITCHY?
HEH HEH OF **COURSE!** SKYWISE UNDERSTANDS ME BEST OF ALL!
RMMBLLL
HE AND RUFFEL SHOULD COME BACK.
OH, NO! IT'S SO **EXCITING** WHEN THE AIR GROWLS LIKE AN ANGRY BEAR! I LOVE THE SOUND!

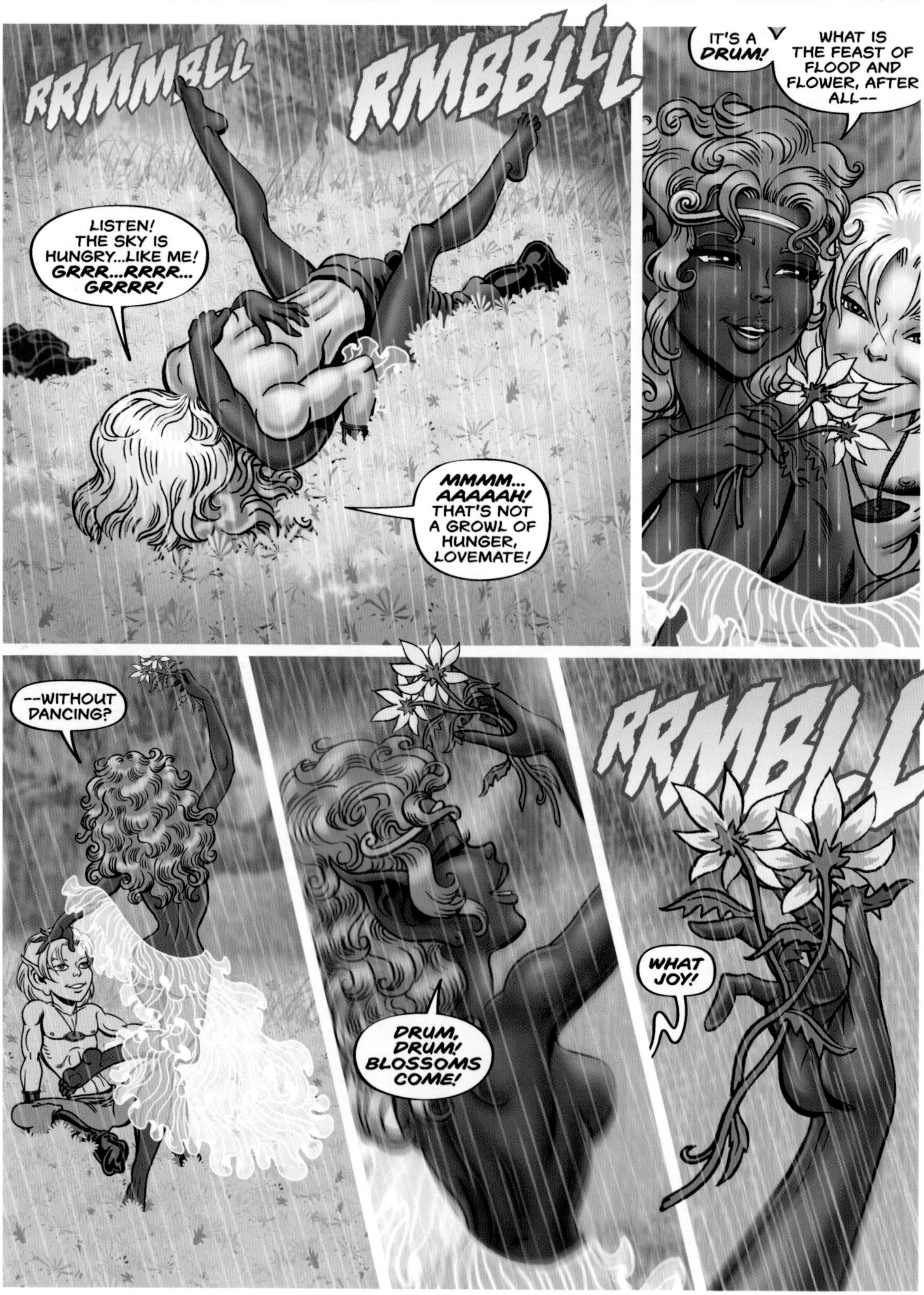
RRMMBLL
RMBBLLL
LISTEN! THE SKY IS HUNGRY...LIKE ME! GRRR...RRRR... GRRRR!
MMMM... AAAAAH! THAT'S NOT A GROWL OF HUNGER, LOVEMATE!
IT'S A DRUM!
WHAT IS THE FEAST OF FLOOD AND FLOWER, AFTER ALL--
--WITHOUT DANCING?
DRUM, DRUM! BLOSSOMS COME!
RRMBLLL
WHAT JOY!

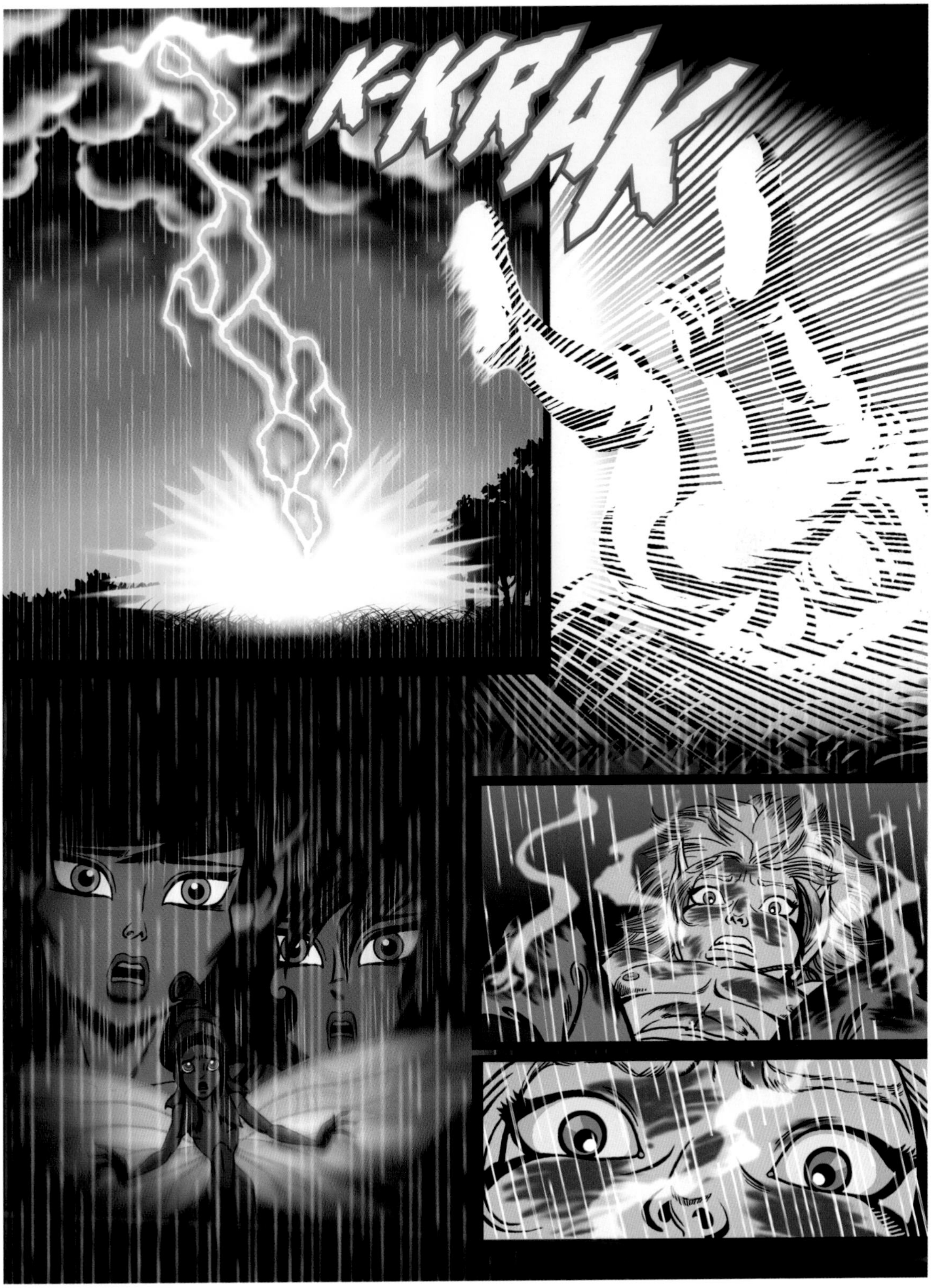
K-KRAK!

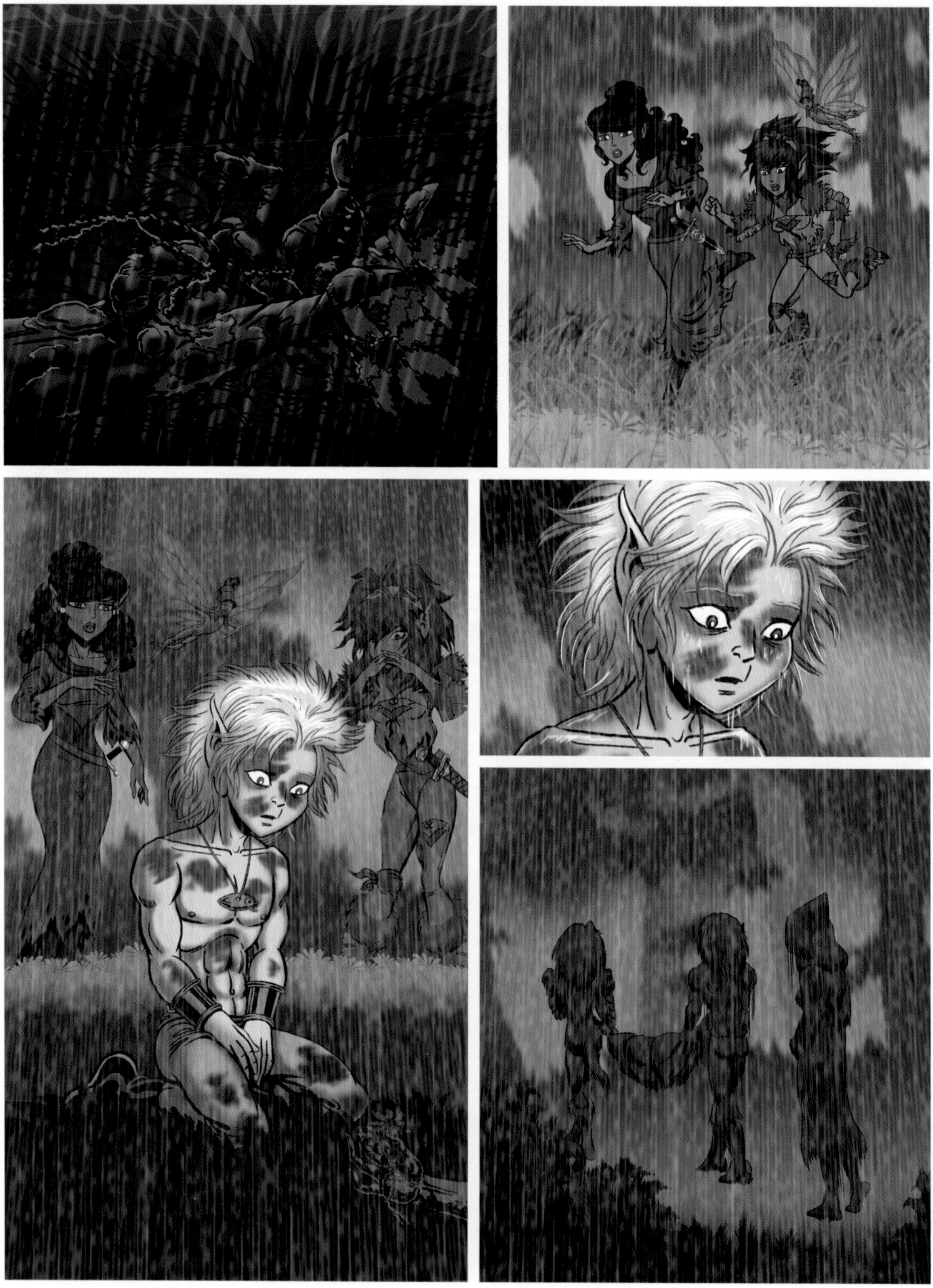

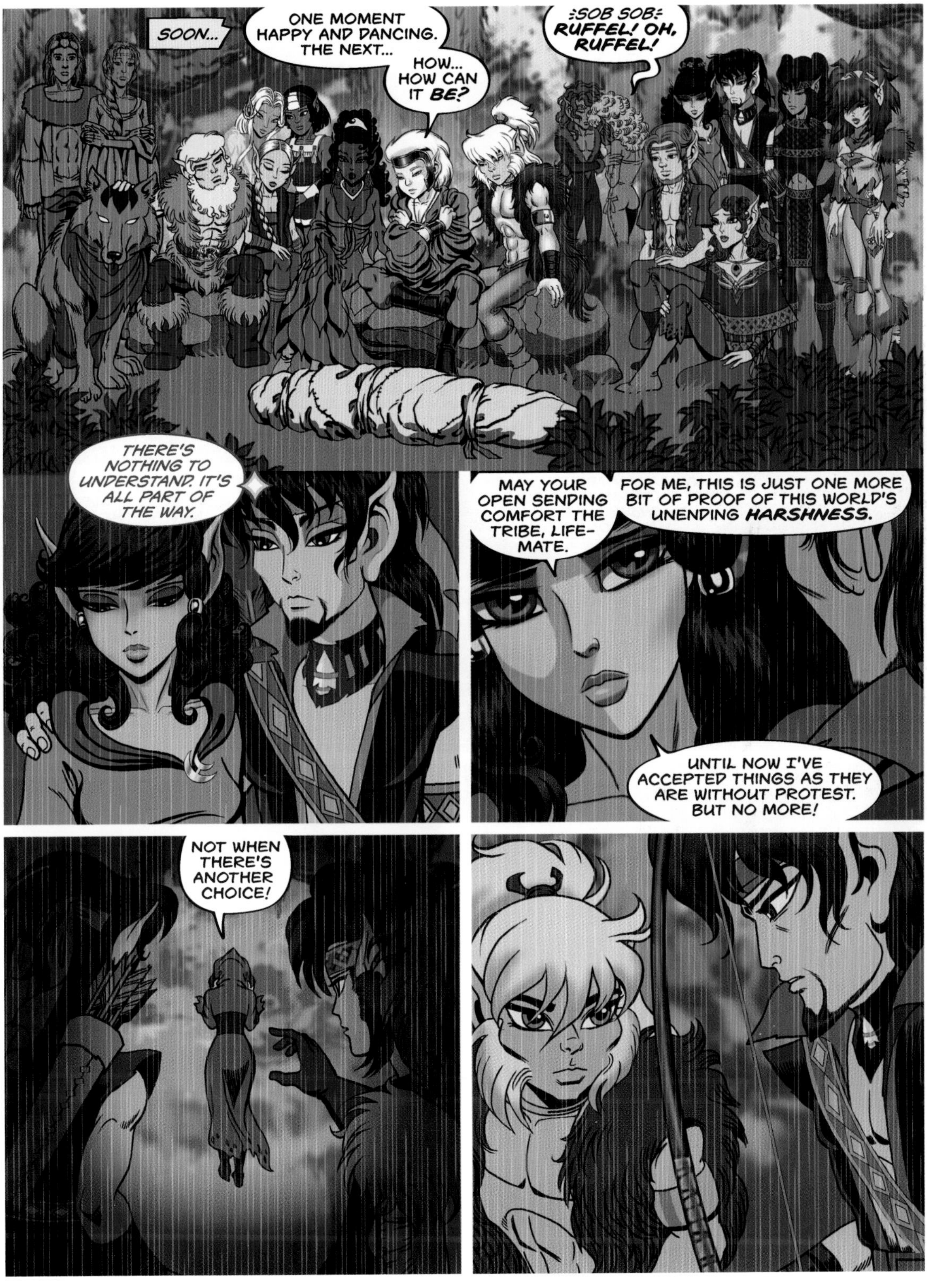
SOON...
ONE MOMENT HAPPY AND DANCING. THE NEXT...
HOW... HOW CAN IT BE?
:SOB SOB: RUFFEL! OH, RUFFEL!
THERE'S NOTHING TO UNDERSTAND. IT'S ALL PART OF THE WAY.
MAY YOUR OPEN SENDING COMFORT THE TRIBE, LIFE-MATE.
FOR ME, THIS IS JUST ONE MORE BIT OF PROOF OF THIS WORLD'S UNENDING HARSHNESS.
UNTIL NOW I'VE ACCEPTED THINGS AS THEY ARE WITHOUT PROTEST. BUT NO MORE!
NOT WHEN THERE'S ANOTHER CHOICE!

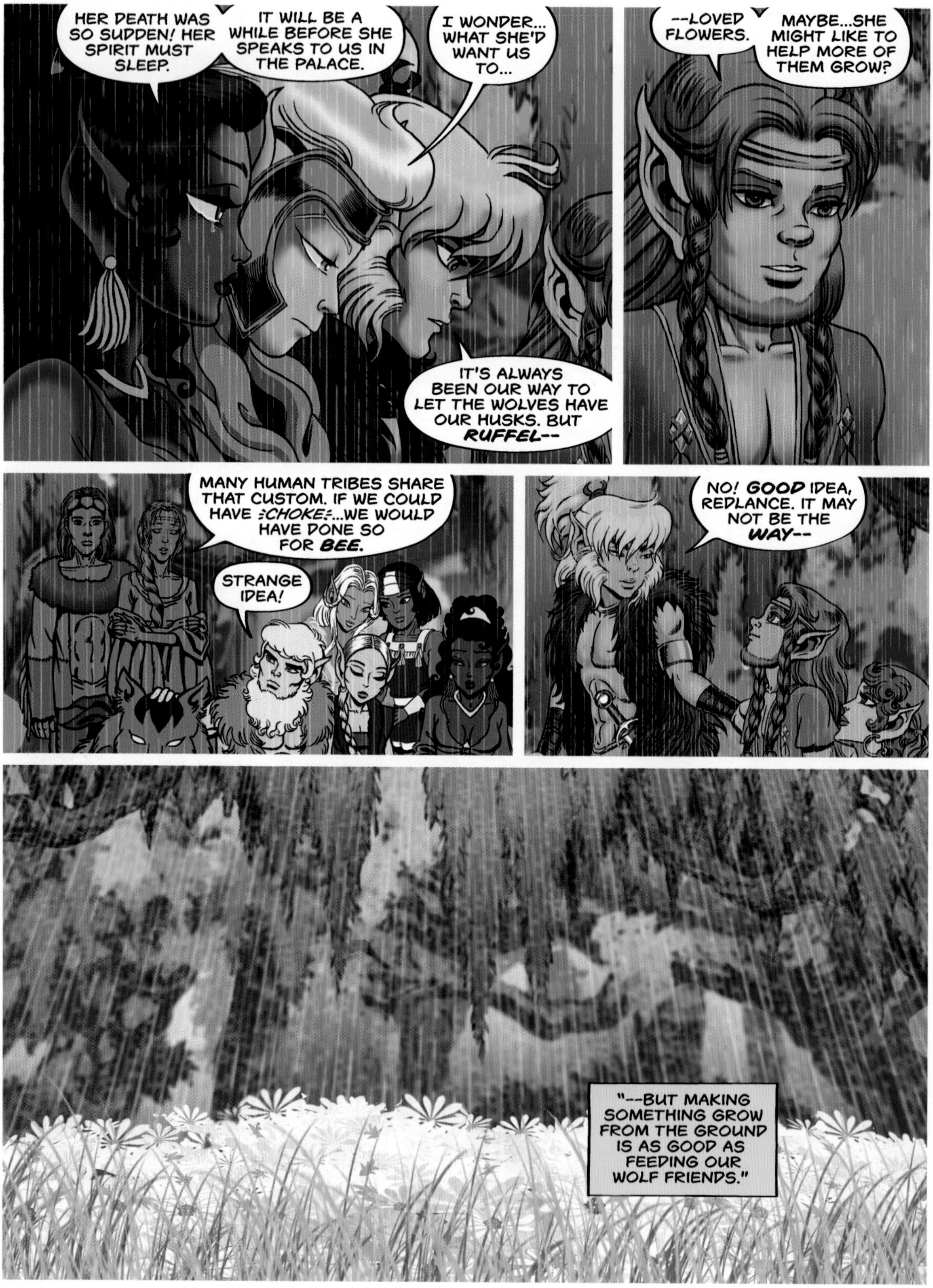
HER DEATH WAS SO SUDDEN! HER SPIRIT MUST SLEEP.
IT WILL BE A WHILE BEFORE SHE SPEAKS TO US IN THE PALACE.
I WONDER... WHAT SHE'D WANT US TO...
IT'S ALWAYS BEEN OUR WAY TO LET THE WOLVES HAVE OUR HUSKS. BUT RUFFEL--
--LOVED FLOWERS.
MAYBE...SHE MIGHT LIKE TO HELP MORE OF THEM GROW?
MANY HUMAN TRIBES SHARE THAT CUSTOM. IF WE COULD HAVE =CHOKE=...WE WOULD HAVE DONE SO FOR BEE.
STRANGE IDEA!
NO! GOOD IDEA, REDLANCE. IT MAY NOT BE THE WAY--
"--BUT MAKING SOMETHING GROW FROM THE GROUND IS AS GOOD AS FEEDING OUR WOLF FRIENDS."

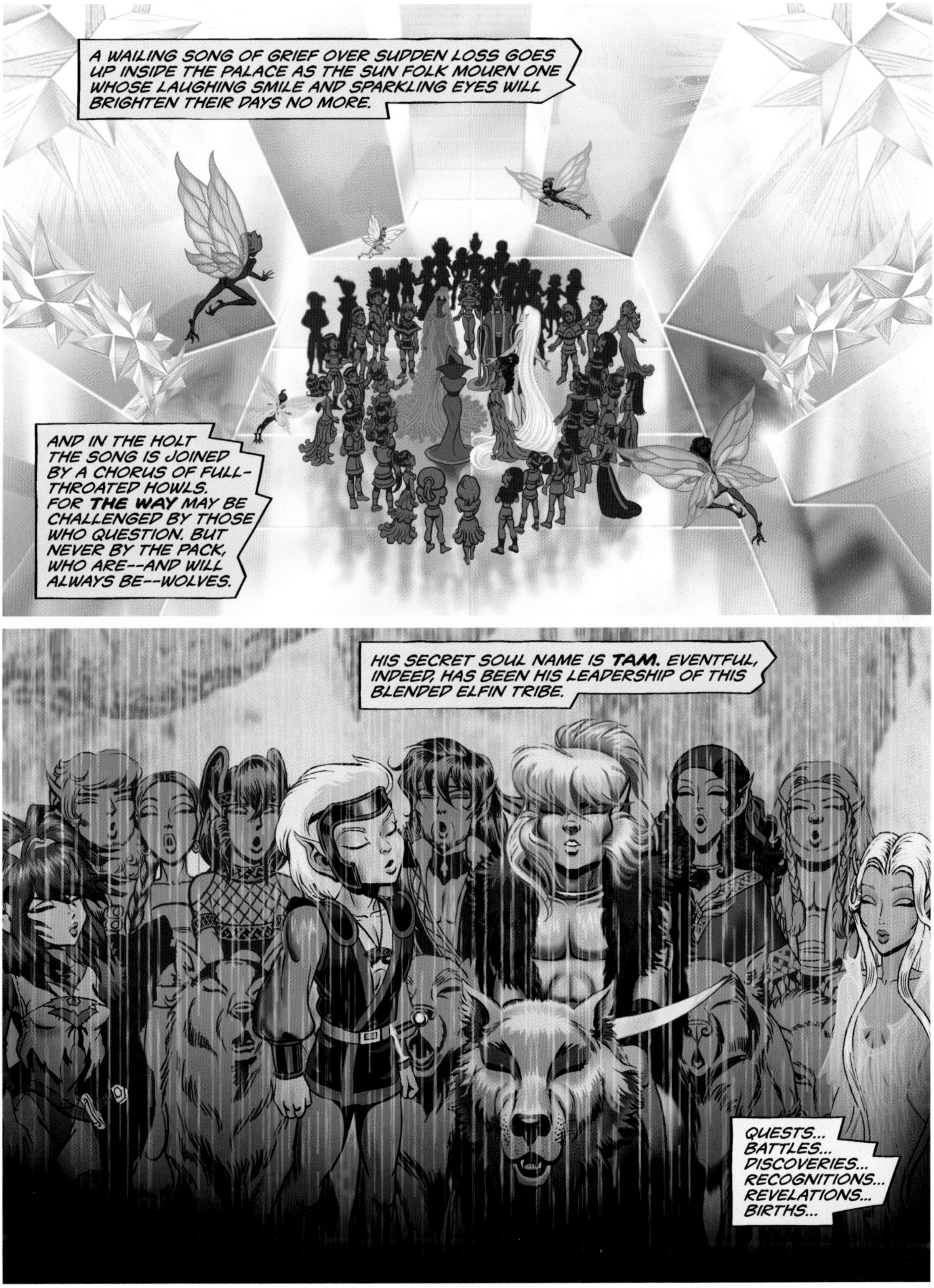
A WAILING SONG OF GRIEF OVER SUDDEN LOSS GOES UP INSIDE THE PALACE AS THE SUN FOLK MOURN ONE WHOSE LAUGHING SMILE AND SPARKLING EYES WILL BRIGHTEN THEIR DAYS NO MORE.
AND IN THE HOLT THE SONG IS JOINED BY A CHORUS OF FULL-THROATED HOWLS. FOR **THE WAY** MAY BE CHALLENGED BY THOSE WHO QUESTION. BUT NEVER BY THE PACK, WHO ARE--AND WILL ALWAYS BE--WOLVES.
HIS SECRET SOUL NAME IS **TAM.** EVENTFUL, INDEED, HAS BEEN HIS LEADERSHIP OF THIS BLENDED ELFIN TRIBE.
QUESTS... BATTLES... DISCOVERIES... RECOGNITIONS... REVELATIONS... BIRTHS...

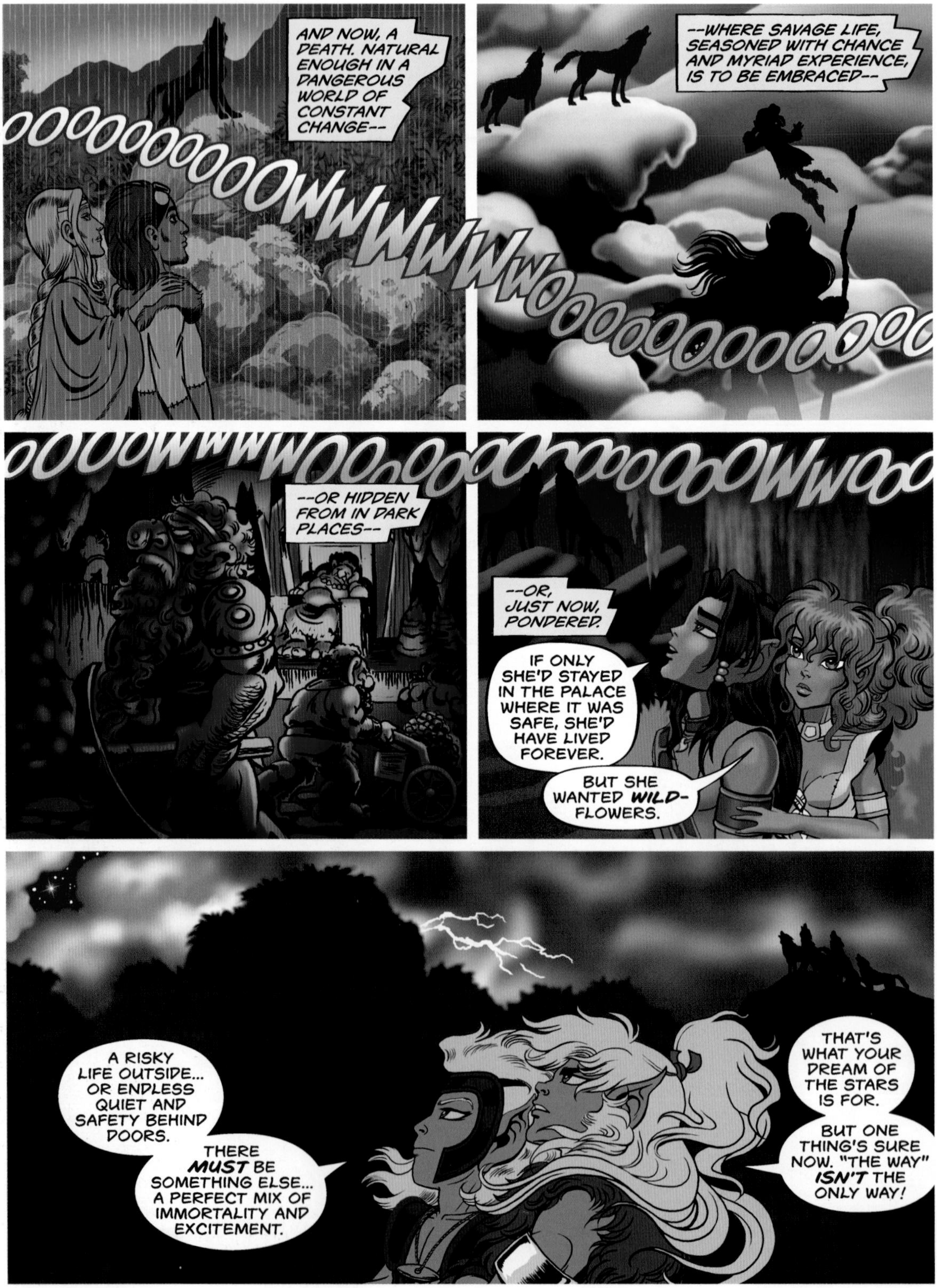
AND NOW, A DEATH. NATURAL ENOUGH IN A DANGEROUS WORLD OF CONSTANT CHANGE--
OOOOOOOOOOOOWWWWWWWWOOOOOOOOOOOOO
--WHERE SAVAGE LIFE, SEASONED WITH CHANCE AND MYRIAD EXPERIENCE, IS TO BE EMBRACED--
OOOOOWWWWWWOOOOOOOOOOOOOOOOOWWOOO
--OR HIDDEN FROM IN DARK PLACES--
--OR, JUST NOW, PONDERED.
IF ONLY SHE'D STAYED IN THE PALACE WHERE IT WAS SAFE, SHE'D HAVE LIVED FOREVER.
BUT SHE WANTED WILD-FLOWERS.
A RISKY LIFE OUTSIDE... OR ENDLESS QUIET AND SAFETY BEHIND DOORS.
THERE MUST BE SOMETHING ELSE... A PERFECT MIX OF IMMORTALITY AND EXCITEMENT.
THAT'S WHAT YOUR DREAM OF THE STARS IS FOR.
BUT ONE THING'S SURE NOW. "THE WAY" ISN'T THE ONLY WAY!

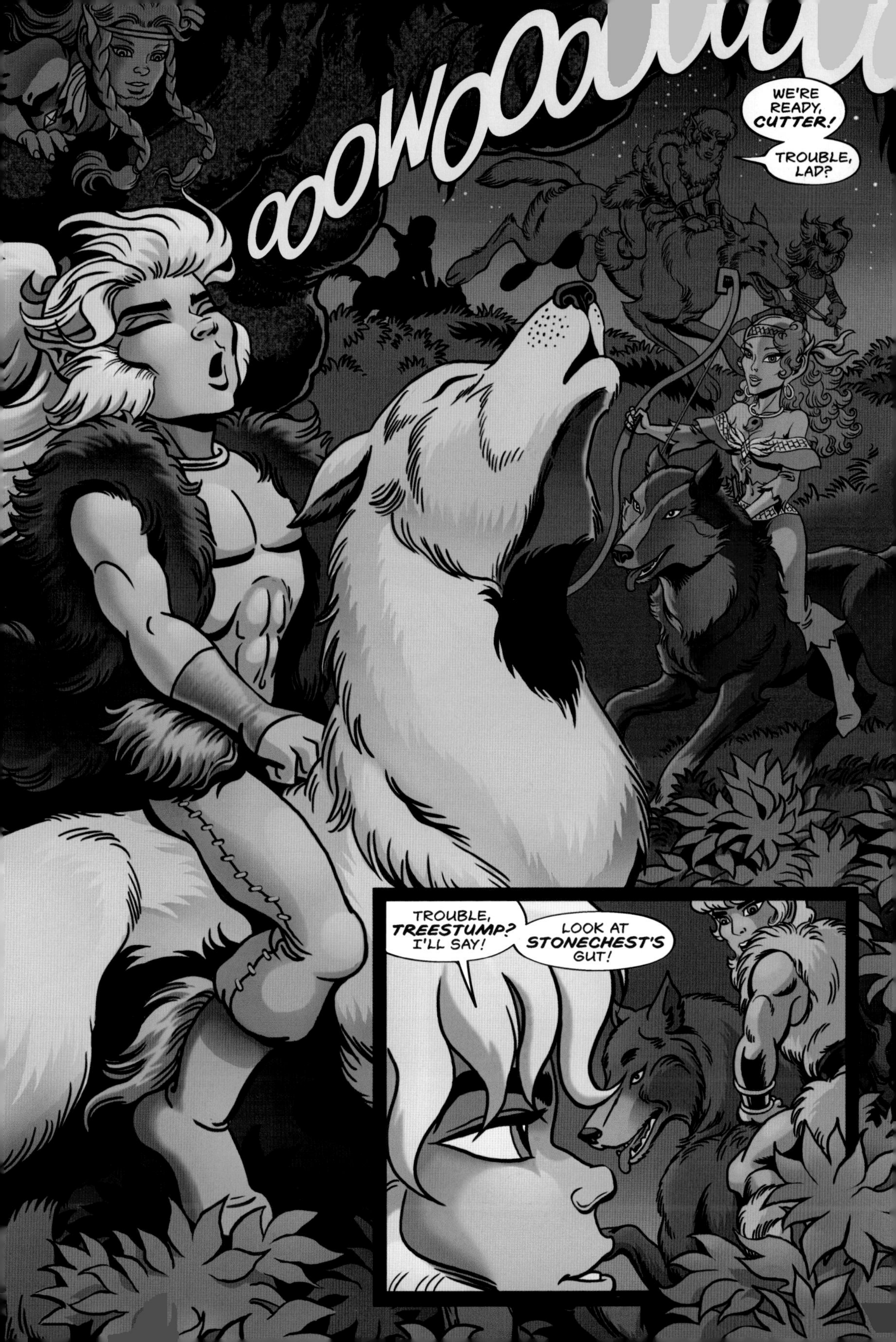
aaoWOOaaaaa
WE'RE READY, CUTTER!
TROUBLE, LAD?
TROUBLE, TREESTUMP? I'LL SAY!
LOOK AT STONECHEST'S GUT!

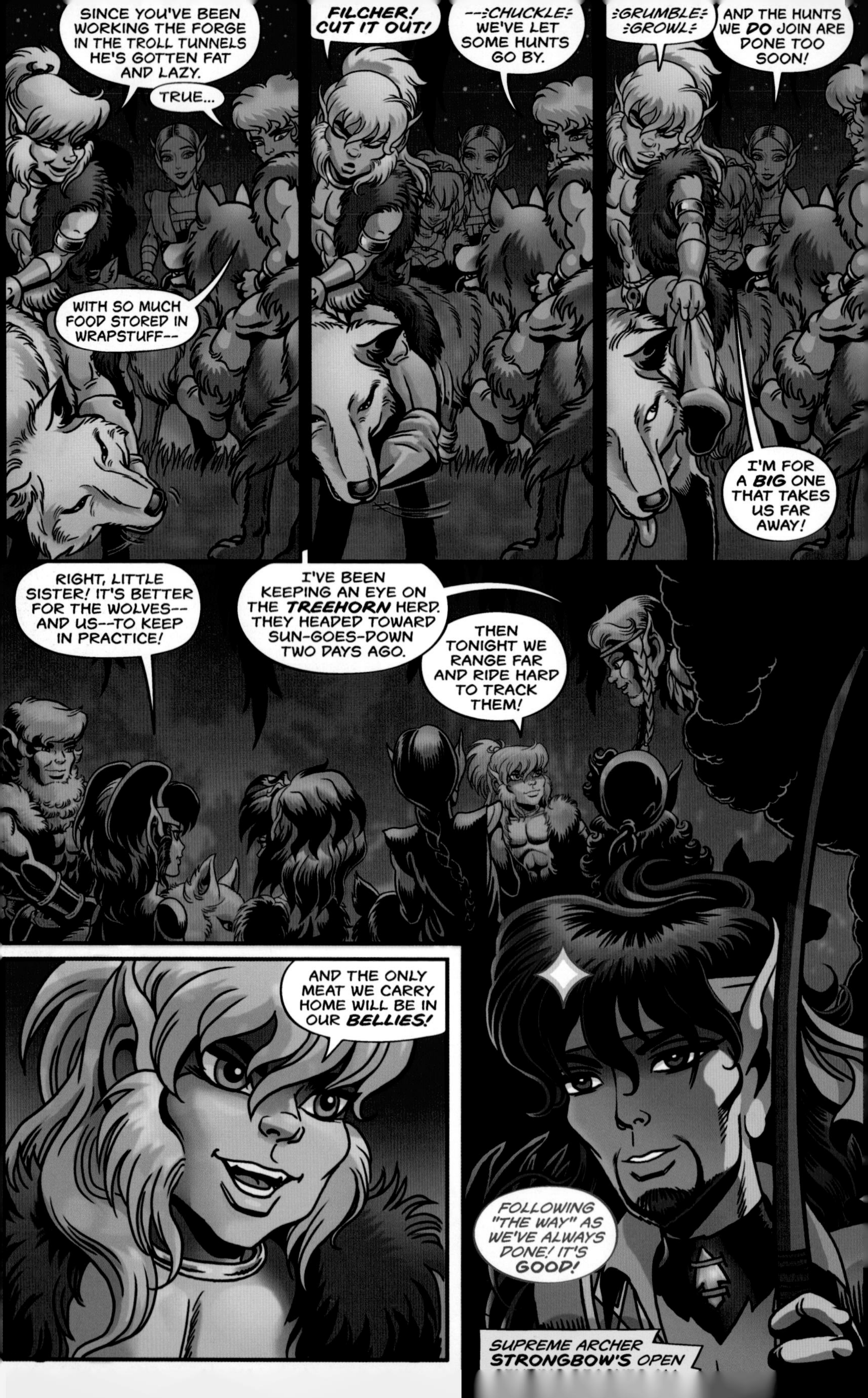
SINCE YOU'VE BEEN WORKING THE FORGE IN THE TROLL TUNNELS HE'S GOTTEN FAT AND LAZY.
TRUE...
WITH SO MUCH FOOD STORED IN WRAPSTUFF--
FILCHER! CUT IT OUT!
--:CHUCKLE: WE'VE LET SOME HUNTS GO BY.
:GRUMBLE: :GROWL:
AND THE HUNTS WE DO JOIN ARE DONE TOO SOON!
I'M FOR A BIG ONE THAT TAKES US FAR AWAY!
RIGHT, LITTLE SISTER! IT'S BETTER FOR THE WOLVES--AND US--TO KEEP IN PRACTICE!
I'VE BEEN KEEPING AN EYE ON THE TREEHORN HERD. THEY HEADED TOWARD SUN-GOES-DOWN TWO DAYS AGO.
THEN TONIGHT WE RANGE FAR AND RIDE HARD TO TRACK THEM!
AND THE ONLY MEAT WE CARRY HOME WILL BE IN OUR BELLIES!
FOLLOWING "THE WAY" AS WE'VE ALWAYS DONE! IT'S GOOD!
SUPREME ARCHER STRONGBOW'S OPEN

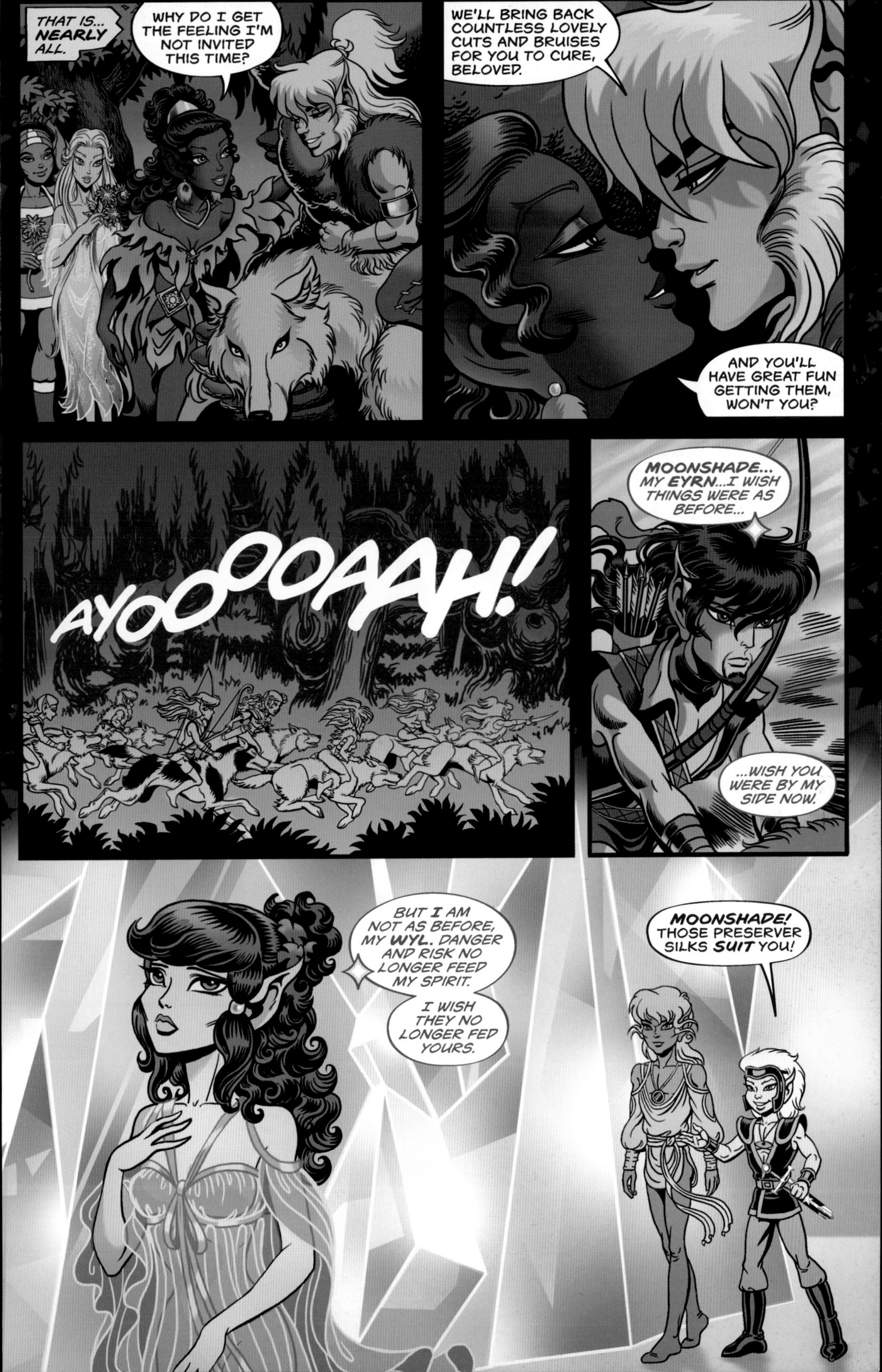
THAT IS... NEARLY ALL.
WHY DO I GET THE FEELING I'M NOT INVITED THIS TIME?
WE'LL BRING BACK COUNTLESS LOVELY CUTS AND BRUISES FOR YOU TO CURE, BELOVED.
AND YOU'LL HAVE GREAT FUN GETTING THEM, WON'T YOU?
AYOOOOAAH!
MOONSHADE... MY EYRN...I WISH THINGS WERE AS BEFORE...
...WISH YOU WERE BY MY SIDE NOW.
BUT I AM NOT AS BEFORE, MY WYL. DANGER AND RISK NO LONGER FEED MY SPIRIT.
I WISH THEY NO LONGER FED YOURS.
MOONSHADE! THOSE PRESERVER SILKS SUIT YOU!

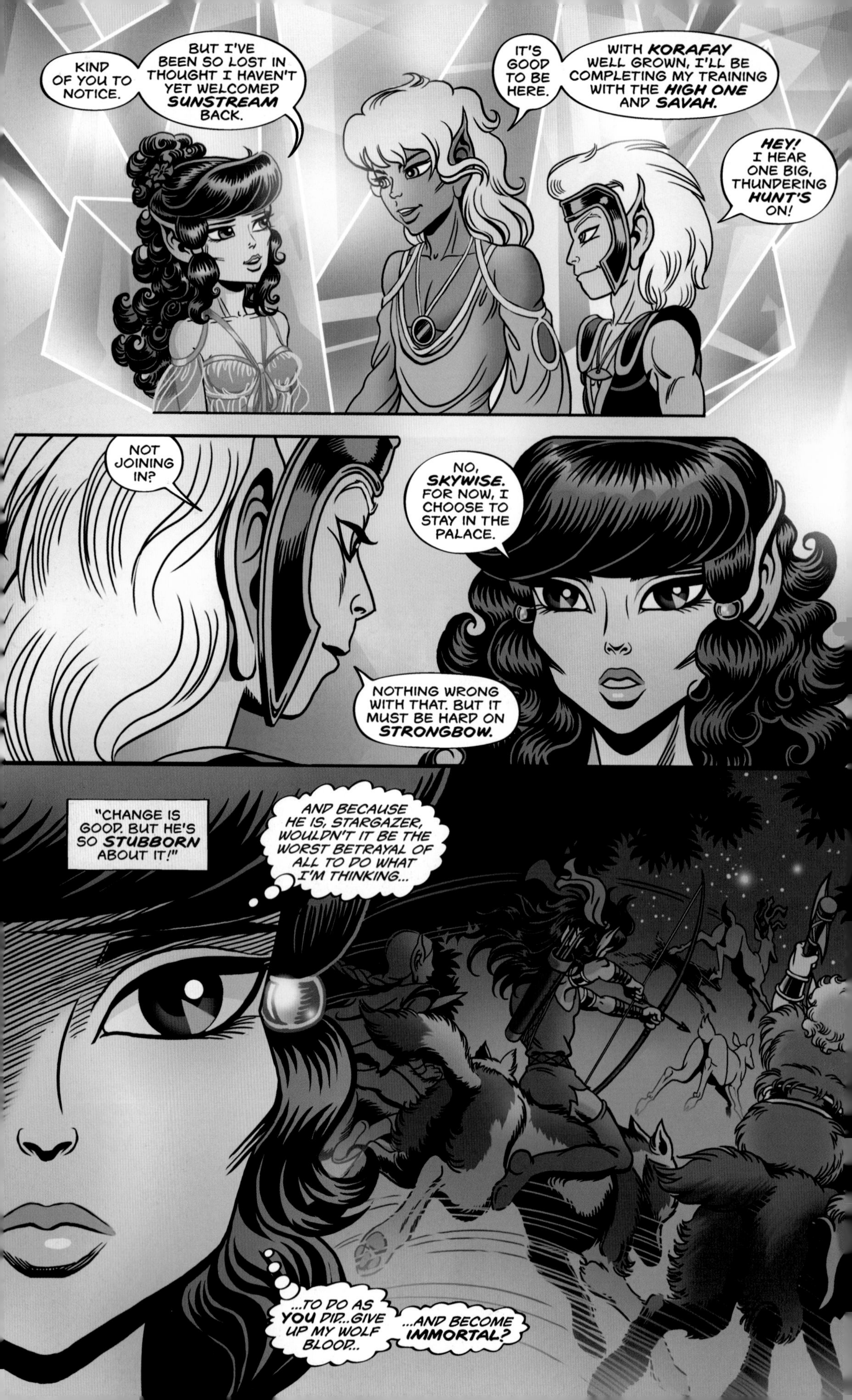
KIND OF YOU TO NOTICE.
BUT I'VE BEEN SO LOST IN THOUGHT I HAVEN'T YET WELCOMED SUNSTREAM BACK.
IT'S GOOD TO BE HERE.
WITH KORAFAY WELL GROWN, I'LL BE COMPLETING MY TRAINING WITH THE HIGH ONE AND SAVAH.
HEY! I HEAR ONE BIG, THUNDERING HUNT'S ON!
NOT JOINING IN?
NO, SKYWISE. FOR NOW, I CHOOSE TO STAY IN THE PALACE.
NOTHING WRONG WITH THAT. BUT IT MUST BE HARD ON STRONGBOW.
"CHANGE IS GOOD. BUT HE'S SO STUBBORN ABOUT IT!"
AND BECAUSE HE IS, STARGAZER, WOULDN'T IT BE THE WORST BETRAYAL OF ALL TO DO WHAT I'M THINKING...
...TO DO AS YOU DID...GIVE UP MY WOLF BLOOD...
...AND BECOME IMMORTAL?

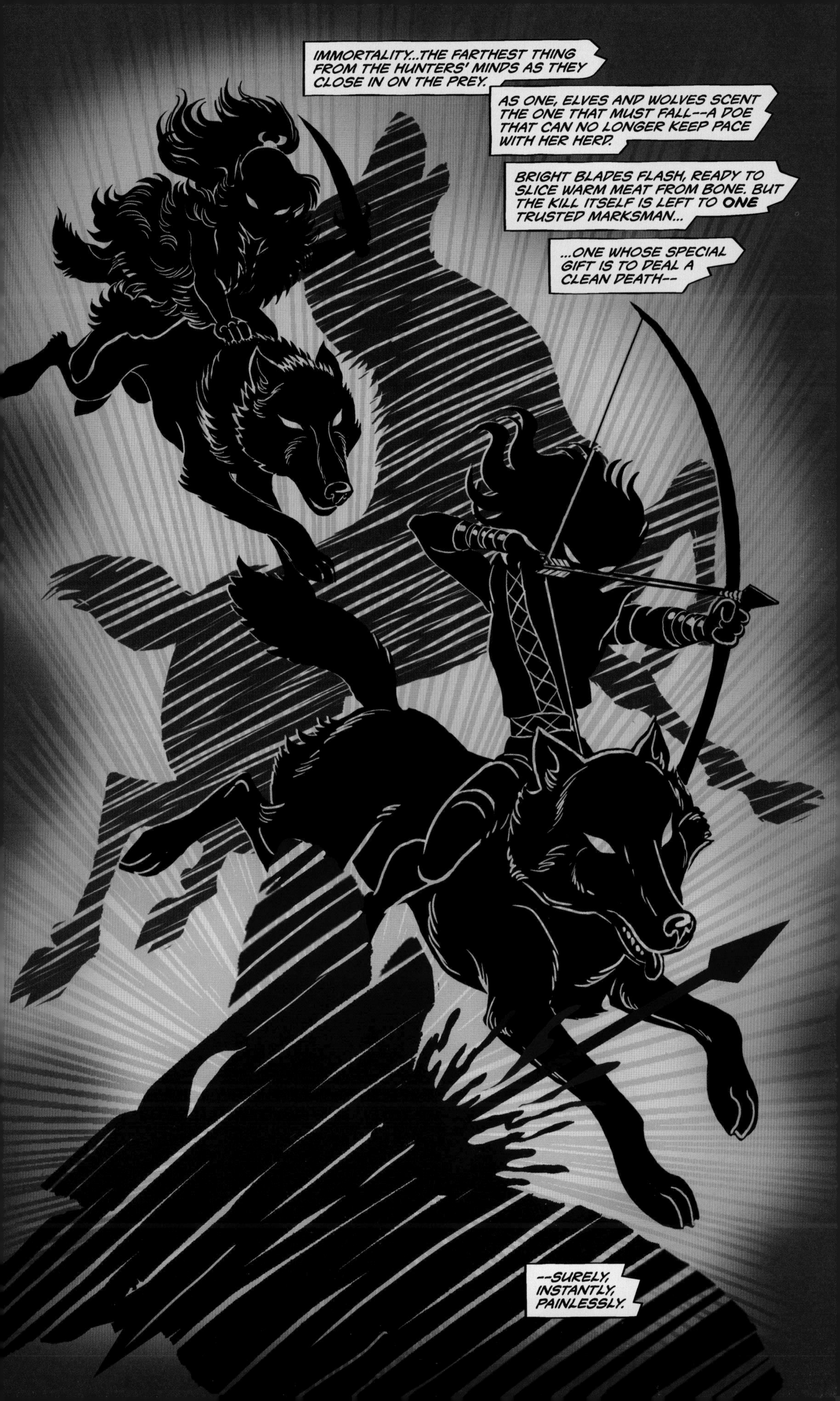
IMMORTALITY...THE FARTHEST THING FROM THE HUNTERS' MINDS AS THEY CLOSE IN ON THE PREY.
AS ONE, ELVES AND WOLVES SCENT THE ONE THAT MUST FALL--A DOE THAT CAN NO LONGER KEEP PACE WITH HER HERD.
BRIGHT BLADES FLASH, READY TO SLICE WARM MEAT FROM BONE. BUT THE KILL ITSELF IS LEFT TO ONE TRUSTED MARKSMAN...
...ONE WHOSE SPECIAL GIFT IS TO DEAL A CLEAN DEATH--
--SURELY, INSTANTLY, PAINLESSLY.

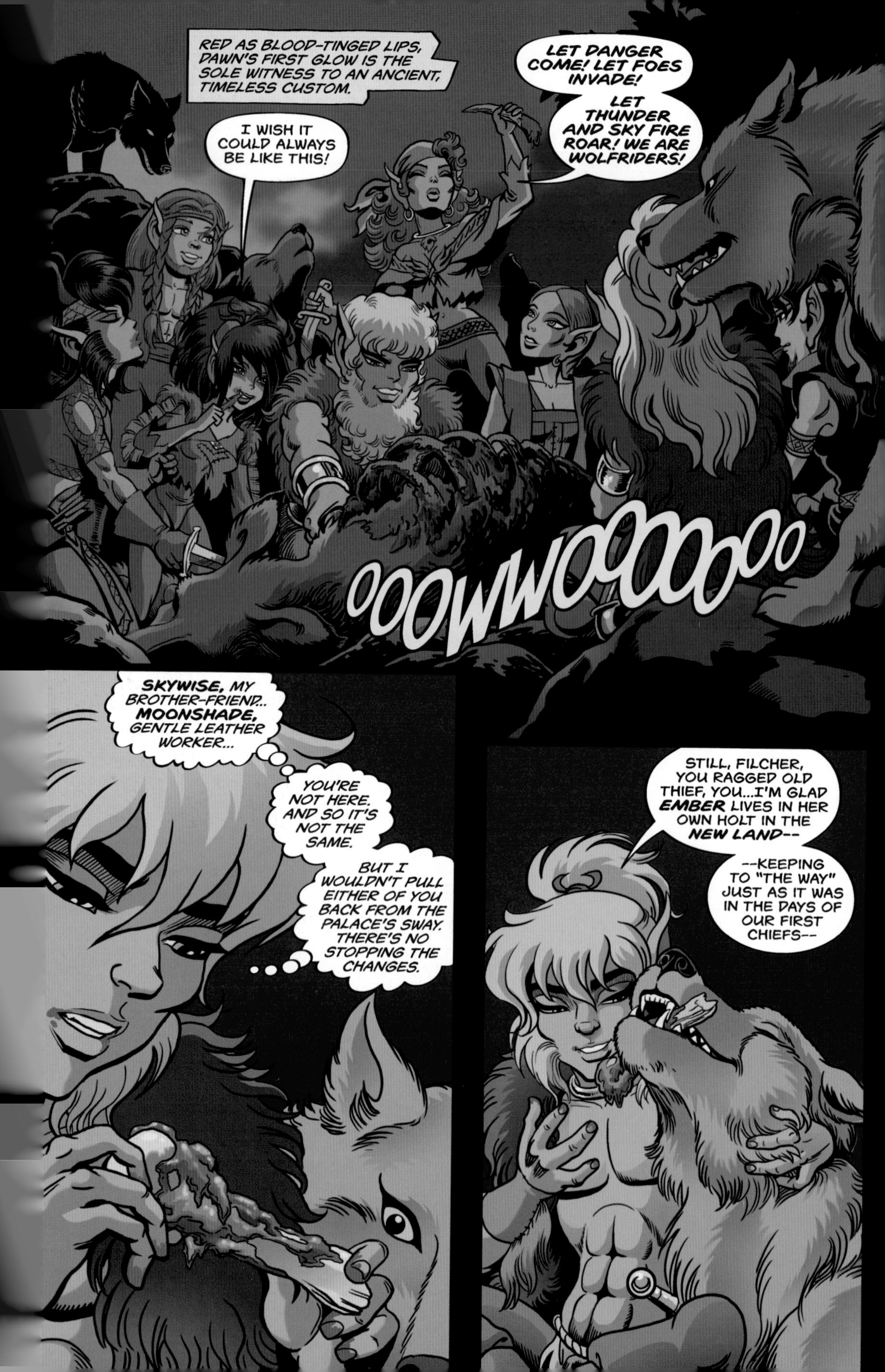
RED AS BLOOD-TINGED LIPS, DAWN'S FIRST GLOW IS THE SOLE WITNESS TO AN ANCIENT, TIMELESS CUSTOM.
I WISH IT COULD ALWAYS BE LIKE THIS!
LET DANGER COME! LET FOES INVADE!
LET THUNDER AND SKY FIRE ROAR! WE ARE WOLFRIDERS!
OOOWWOOOOOOO
SKYWISE, MY BROTHER-FRIEND.. MOONSHADE, GENTLE LEATHER WORKER...
YOU'RE NOT HERE. AND SO IT'S NOT THE SAME.
BUT I WOULDN'T PULL EITHER OF YOU BACK FROM THE PALACE'S SWAY. THERE'S NO STOPPING THE CHANGES.
STILL, FILCHER, YOU RAGGED OLD THIEF, YOU...I'M GLAD EMBER LIVES IN HER OWN HOLT IN THE NEW LAND--
--KEEPING TO "THE WAY" JUST AS IT WAS IN THE DAYS OF OUR FIRST CHIEFS--

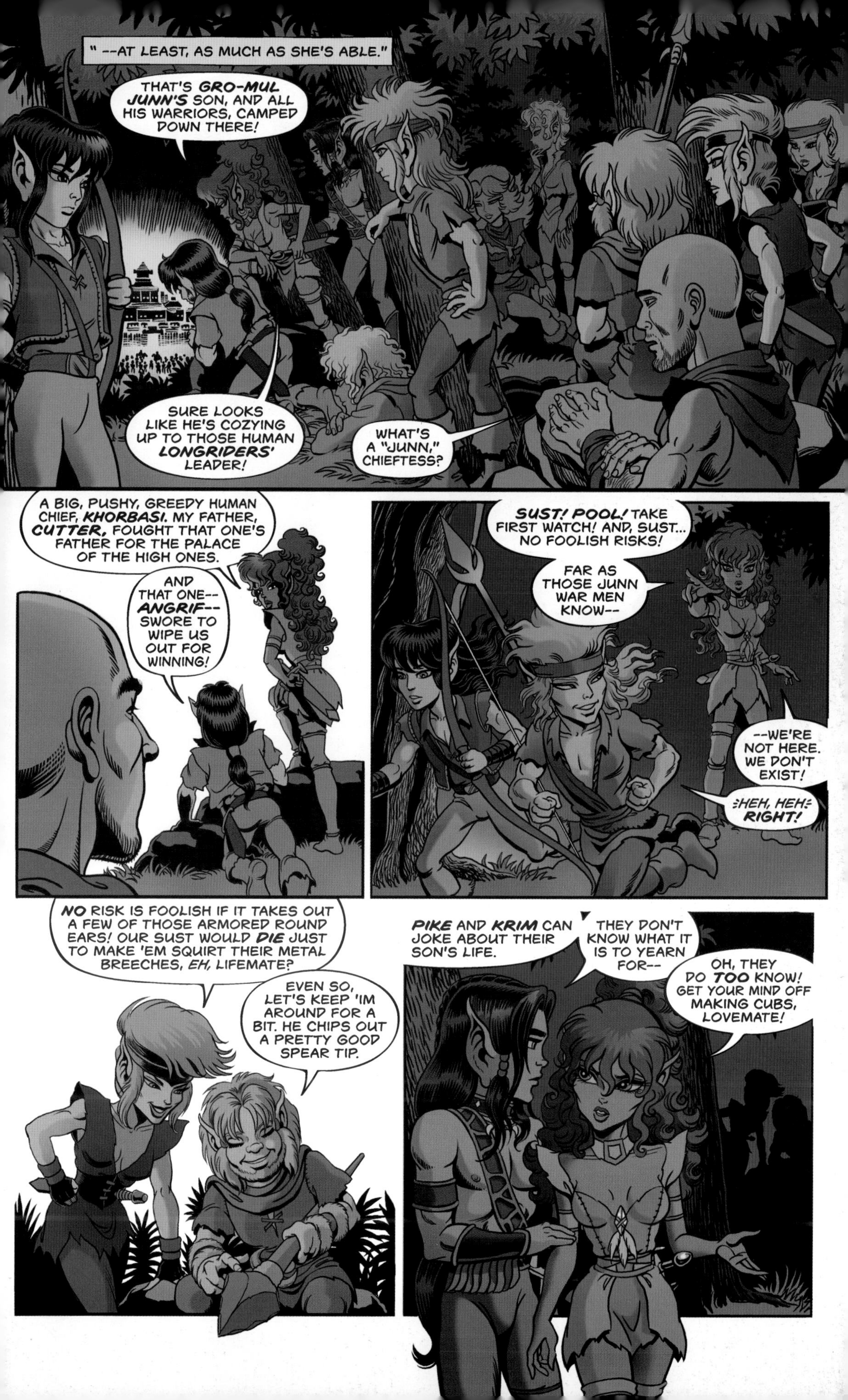
" --AT LEAST, AS MUCH AS SHE'S ABLE."
THAT'S GRO-MUL JUNN'S SON, AND ALL HIS WARRIORS, CAMPED DOWN THERE!
SURE LOOKS LIKE HE'S COZYING UP TO THOSE HUMAN LONGRIDERS' LEADER!
WHAT'S A "JUNN," CHIEFTESS?
A BIG, PUSHY, GREEDY HUMAN CHIEF, KHORBASI. MY FATHER, CUTTER, FOUGHT THAT ONE'S FATHER FOR THE PALACE OF THE HIGH ONES.
AND THAT ONE-- ANGRIF-- SWORE TO WIPE US OUT FOR WINNING!
SUST! POOL! TAKE FIRST WATCH! AND, SUST... NO FOOLISH RISKS!
FAR AS THOSE JUNN WAR MEN KNOW--
--WE'RE NOT HERE. WE DON'T EXIST!
HEH, HEH RIGHT!
NO RISK IS FOOLISH IF IT TAKES OUT A FEW OF THOSE ARMORED ROUND EARS! OUR SUST WOULD DIE JUST TO MAKE 'EM SQUIRT THEIR METAL BREECHES, EH, LIFEMATE?
EVEN SO, LET'S KEEP 'IM AROUND FOR A BIT. HE CHIPS OUT A PRETTY GOOD SPEAR TIP.
PIKE AND KRIM CAN JOKE ABOUT THEIR SON'S LIFE.
THEY DON'T KNOW WHAT IT IS TO YEARN FOR--
OH, THEY DO TOO KNOW! GET YOUR MIND OFF MAKING CUBS, LOVEMATE!

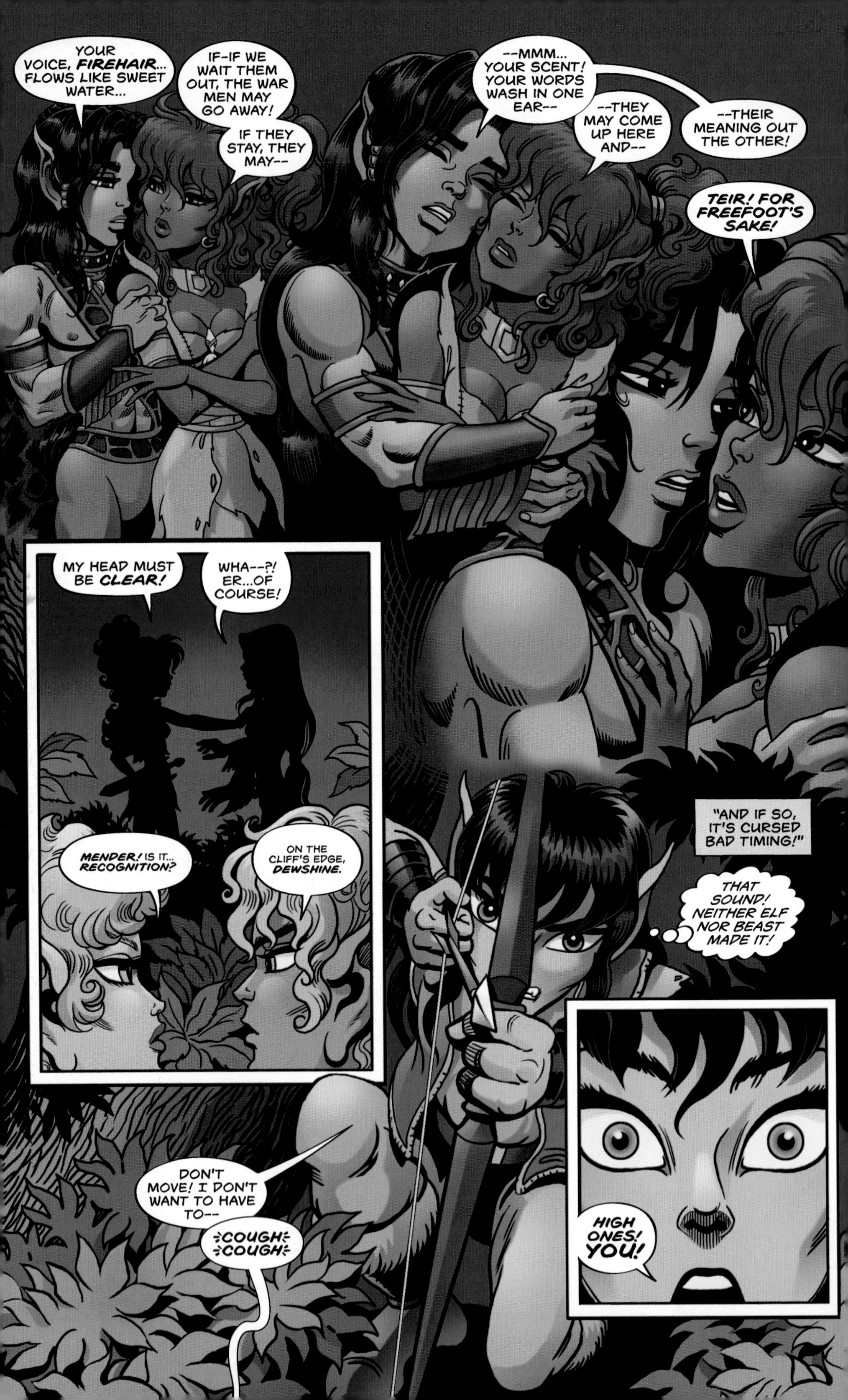

YOUR VOICE, FIREHAIR... FLOWS LIKE SWEET WATER...
IF-IF WE WAIT THEM OUT, THE WAR MEN MAY GO AWAY!
IF THEY STAY, THEY MAY--
--MMM... YOUR SCENT! YOUR WORDS WASH IN ONE EAR--
--THEY MAY COME UP HERE AND--
--THEIR MEANING OUT THE OTHER!
TEIR! FOR FREEFOOT'S SAKE!
MY HEAD MUST BE CLEAR!
WHA--?! ER...OF COURSE!
MENDER! IS IT... RECOGNITION?
ON THE CLIFF'S EDGE, DEWSHINE.
"AND IF SO, IT'S CURSED BAD TIMING!"
THAT SOUND! NEITHER ELF NOR BEAST MADE IT!
DON'T MOVE! I DON'T WANT TO HAVE TO--
COUGH COUGH
HIGH ONES! YOU!

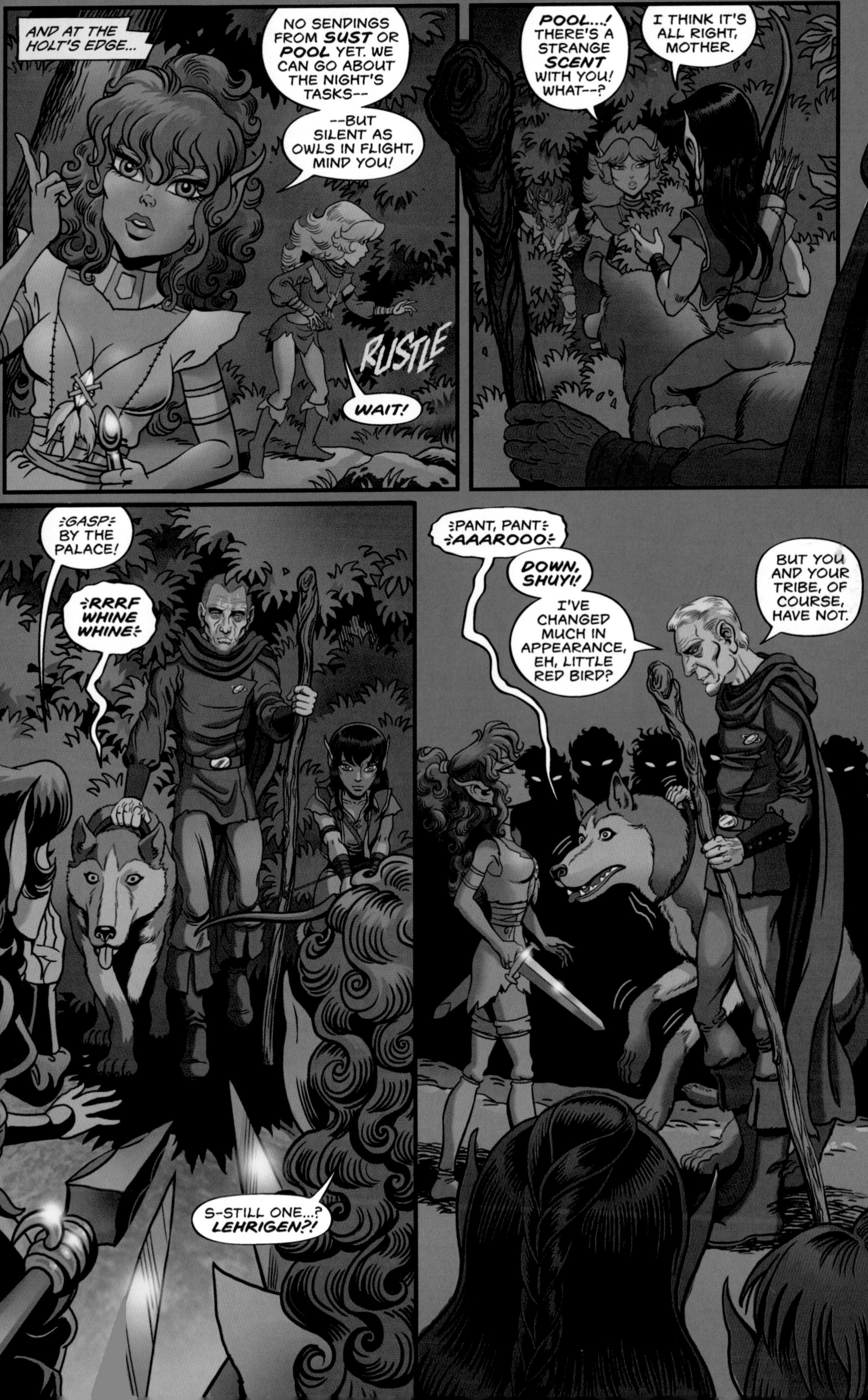
AND AT THE HOLT'S EDGE...
NO SENDINGS FROM SUST OR POOL YET. WE CAN GO ABOUT THE NIGHT'S TASKS--
--BUT SILENT AS OWLS IN FLIGHT, MIND YOU!
RUSTLE
WAIT!
POOL...! THERE'S A STRANGE SCENT WITH YOU! WHAT--?
I THINK IT'S ALL RIGHT, MOTHER.
GASP BY THE PALACE!
RRRF WHINE WHINE
S-STILL ONE...? LEHRIGEN?!
PANT, PANT AAAROOO
DOWN, SHUYI!
I'VE CHANGED MUCH IN APPEARANCE, EH, LITTLE RED BIRD?
BUT YOU AND YOUR TRIBE, OF COURSE, HAVE NOT.

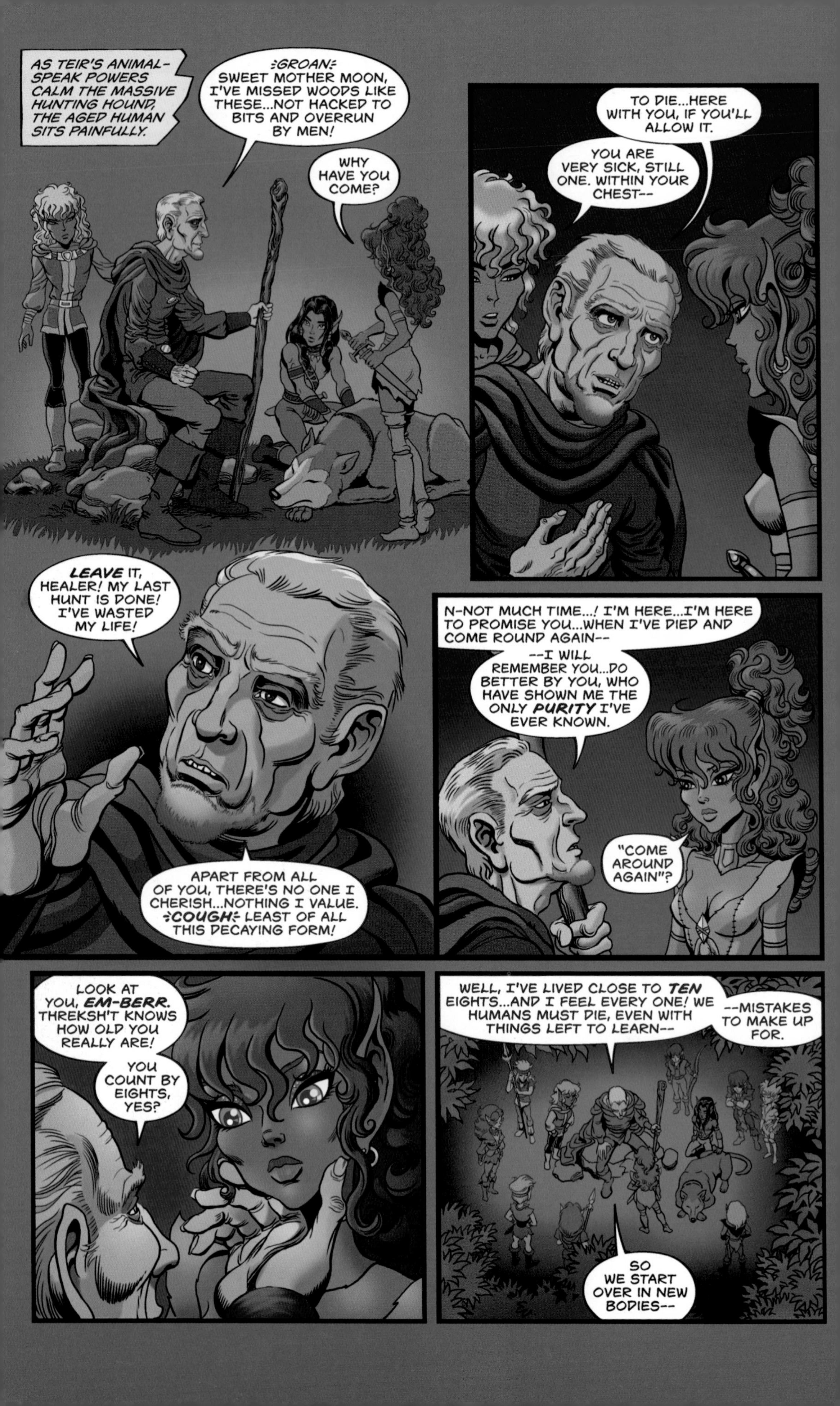
AS TEIR'S ANIMAL-SPEAK POWERS CALM THE MASSIVE HUNTING HOUND, THE AGED HUMAN SITS PAINFULLY.
GROAN SWEET MOTHER MOON, I'VE MISSED WOODS LIKE THESE...NOT HACKED TO BITS AND OVERRUN BY MEN!
WHY HAVE YOU COME?
TO DIE...HERE WITH YOU, IF YOU'LL ALLOW IT.
YOU ARE VERY SICK, STILL ONE. WITHIN YOUR CHEST--
LEAVE IT, HEALER! MY LAST HUNT IS DONE! I'VE WASTED MY LIFE!
APART FROM ALL OF YOU, THERE'S NO ONE I CHERISH...NOTHING I VALUE. COUGH LEAST OF ALL THIS DECAYING FORM!
N-NOT MUCH TIME...! I'M HERE...I'M HERE TO PROMISE YOU...WHEN I'VE DIED AND COME ROUND AGAIN--
--I WILL REMEMBER YOU...DO BETTER BY YOU, WHO HAVE SHOWN ME THE ONLY PURITY I'VE EVER KNOWN.
"COME AROUND AGAIN"?
LOOK AT YOU, EM-BERR. THREKSH'T KNOWS HOW OLD YOU REALLY ARE!
YOU COUNT BY EIGHTS, YES?
WELL, I'VE LIVED CLOSE TO TEN EIGHTS...AND I FEEL EVERY ONE! WE HUMANS MUST DIE, EVEN WITH THINGS LEFT TO LEARN--
--MISTAKES TO MAKE UP FOR.
SO WE START OVER IN NEW BODIES--

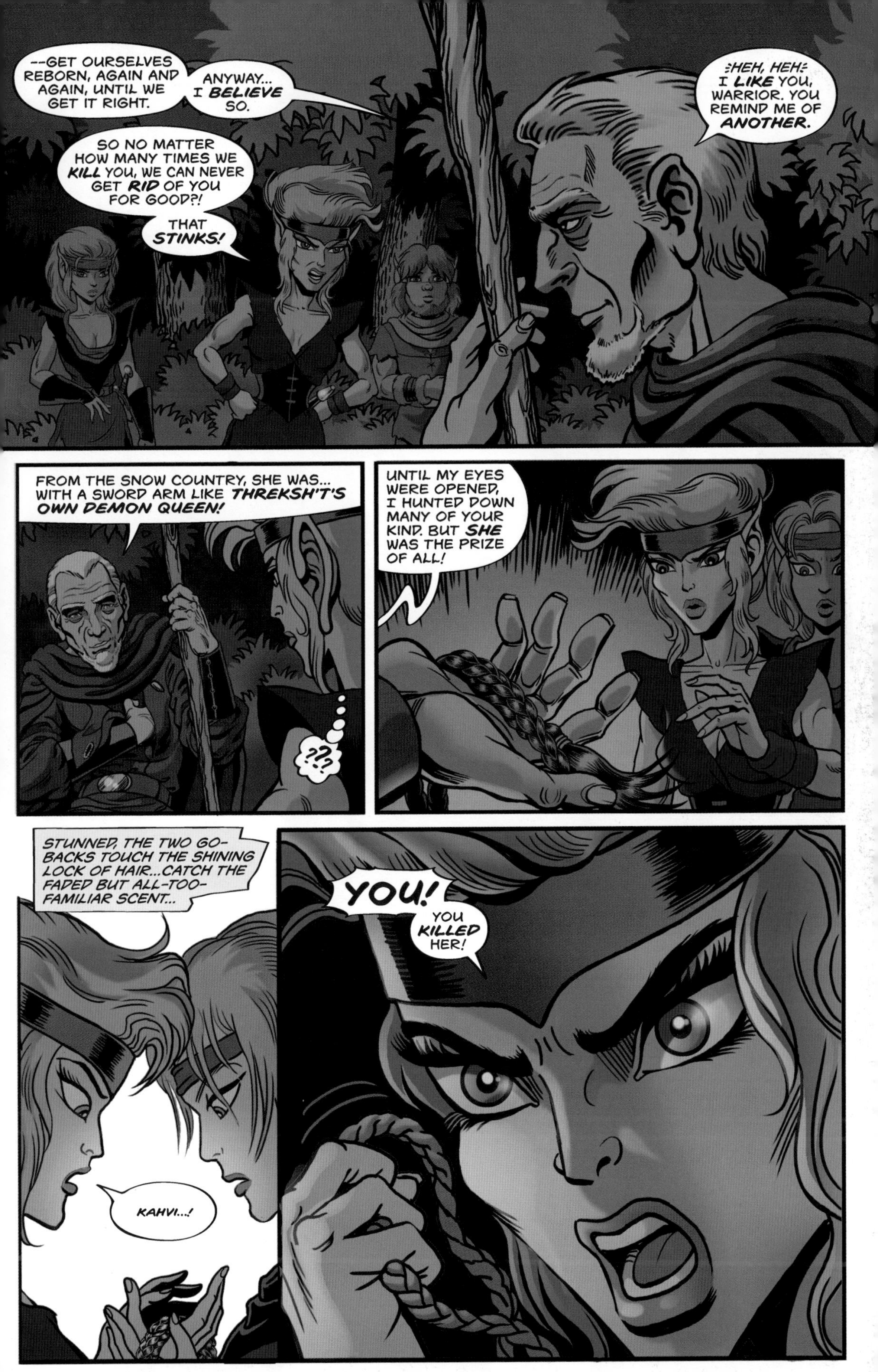
--GET OURSELVES REBORN, AGAIN AND AGAIN, UNTIL WE GET IT RIGHT.
ANYWAY... I BELIEVE SO.
SO NO MATTER HOW MANY TIMES WE KILL YOU, WE CAN NEVER GET RID OF YOU FOR GOOD?!
THAT STINKS!
HEH, HEH I LIKE YOU, WARRIOR. YOU REMIND ME OF ANOTHER.
FROM THE SNOW COUNTRY, SHE WAS... WITH A SWORD ARM LIKE THREKSH'T'S OWN DEMON QUEEN!
???
UNTIL MY EYES WERE OPENED, I HUNTED DOWN MANY OF YOUR KIND. BUT SHE WAS THE PRIZE OF ALL!
STUNNED, THE TWO GO-BACKS TOUCH THE SHINING LOCK OF HAIR...CATCH THE FADED BUT ALL-TOO-FAMILIAR SCENT...
KAHVI...!
YOU!
YOU KILLED HER!

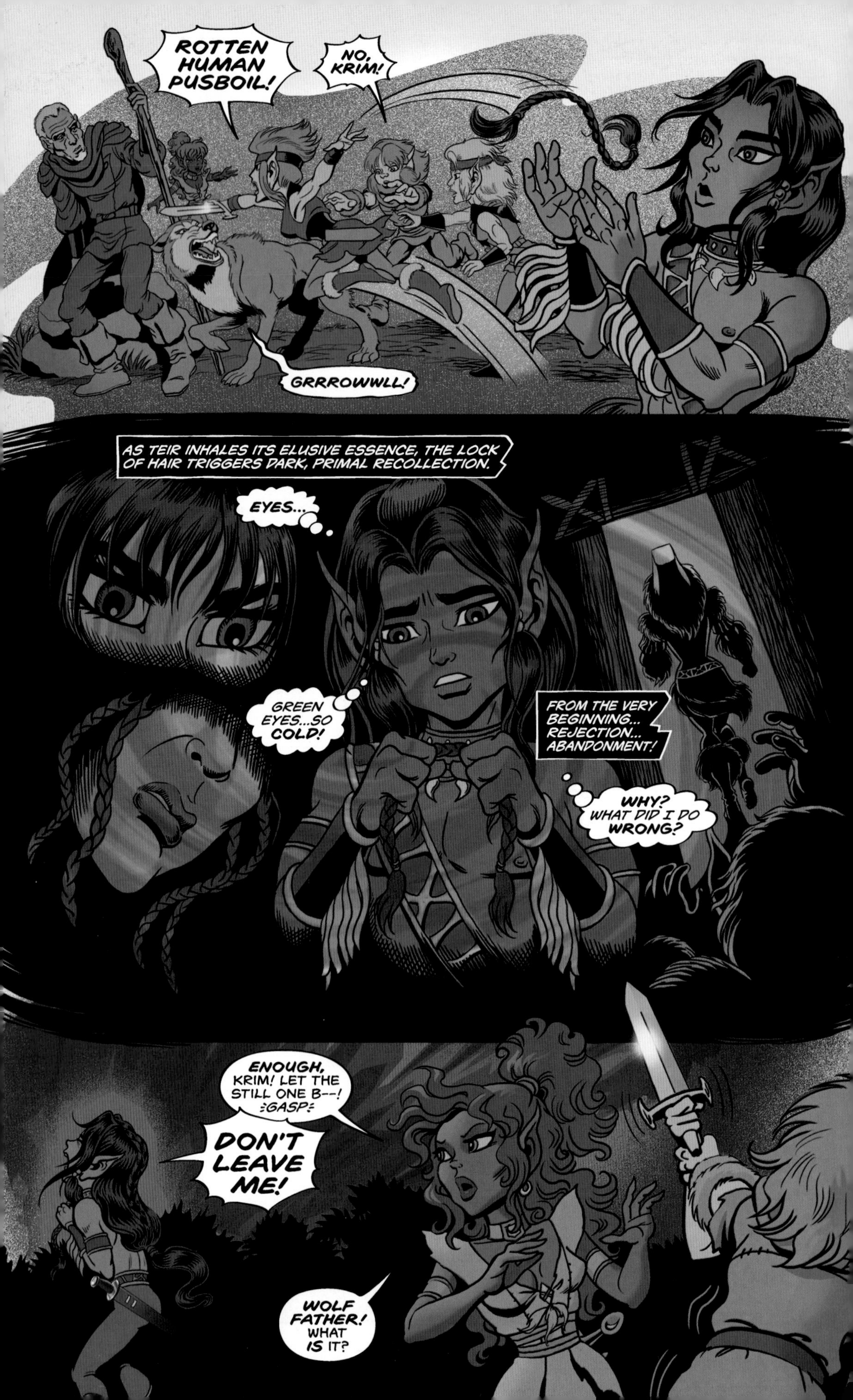
ROTTEN HUMAN PUSBOIL!
NO, KRIM!
GRRROWWLL!
AS TEIR INHALES ITS ELUSIVE ESSENCE, THE LOCK OF HAIR TRIGGERS DARK, PRIMAL RECOLLECTION.
EYES...
GREEN EYES...SO COLD!
FROM THE VERY BEGINNING... REJECTION... ABANDONMENT!
WHY? WHAT DID I DO WRONG?
ENOUGH, KRIM! LET THE STILL ONE B--! GASP
DON'T LEAVE ME!
WOLF FATHER! WHAT IS IT?

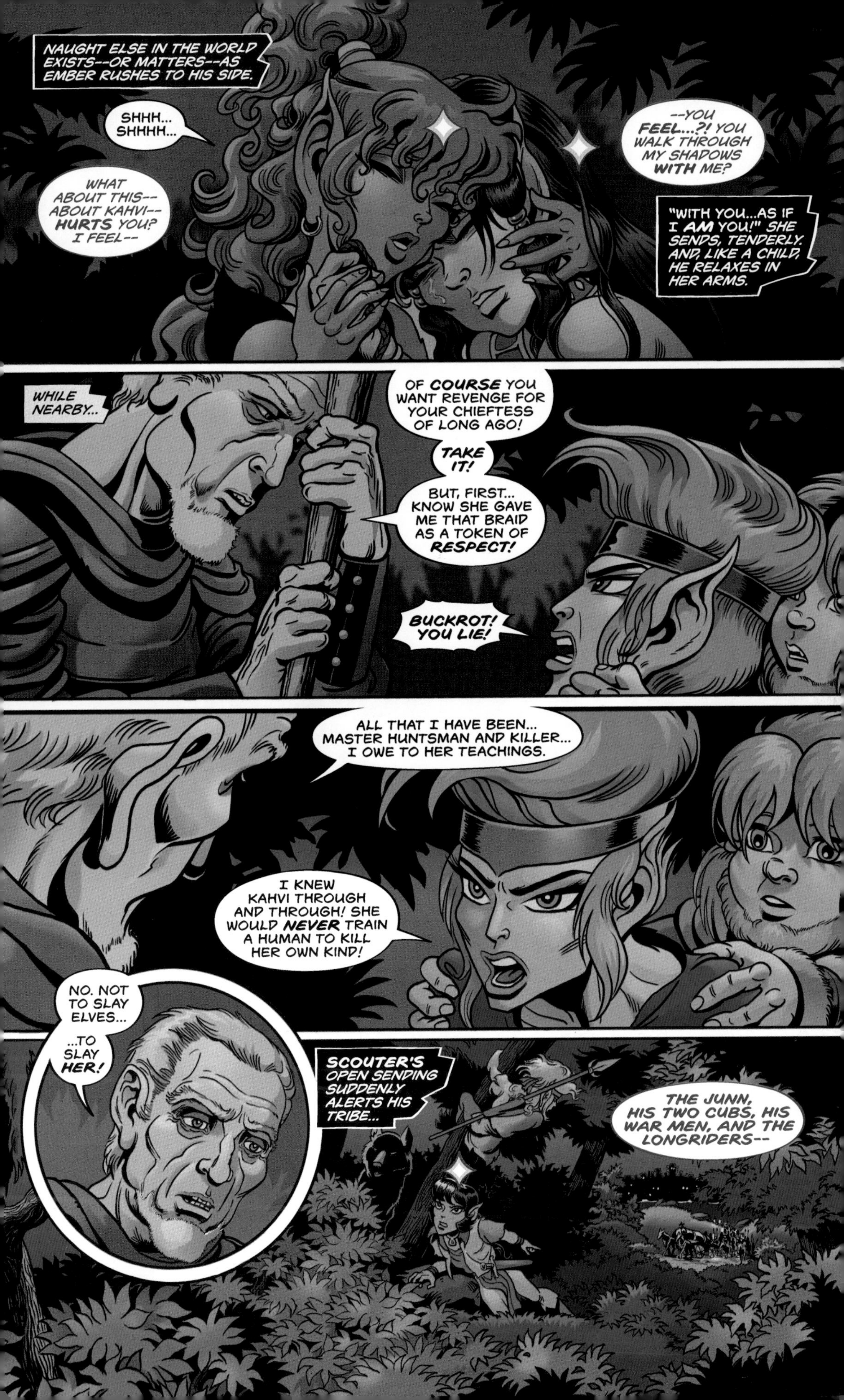
NAUGHT ELSE IN THE WORLD EXISTS--OR MATTERS--AS EMBER RUSHES TO HIS SIDE.
SHHH... SHHHH...
WHAT ABOUT THIS-- ABOUT KAHVI-- HURTS YOU? I FEEL--
--YOU FEEL...?! YOU WALK THROUGH MY SHADOWS WITH ME?
"WITH YOU...AS IF I AM YOU!" SHE SENDS, TENDERLY. AND, LIKE A CHILD, HE RELAXES IN HER ARMS.
WHILE NEARBY...
OF COURSE YOU WANT REVENGE FOR YOUR CHIEFTESS OF LONG AGO!
TAKE IT!
BUT, FIRST... KNOW SHE GAVE ME THAT BRAID AS A TOKEN OF RESPECT!
BUCKROT! YOU LIE!
ALL THAT I HAVE BEEN... MASTER HUNTSMAN AND KILLER... I OWE TO HER TEACHINGS.
I KNEW KAHVI THROUGH AND THROUGH! SHE WOULD NEVER TRAIN A HUMAN TO KILL HER OWN KIND!
NO. NOT TO SLAY ELVES...
...TO SLAY HER!
SCOUTER'S OPEN SENDING SUDDENLY ALERTS HIS TRIBE...
THE JUNN, HIS TWO CUBS, HIS WAR MEN, AND THE LONGRIDERS--

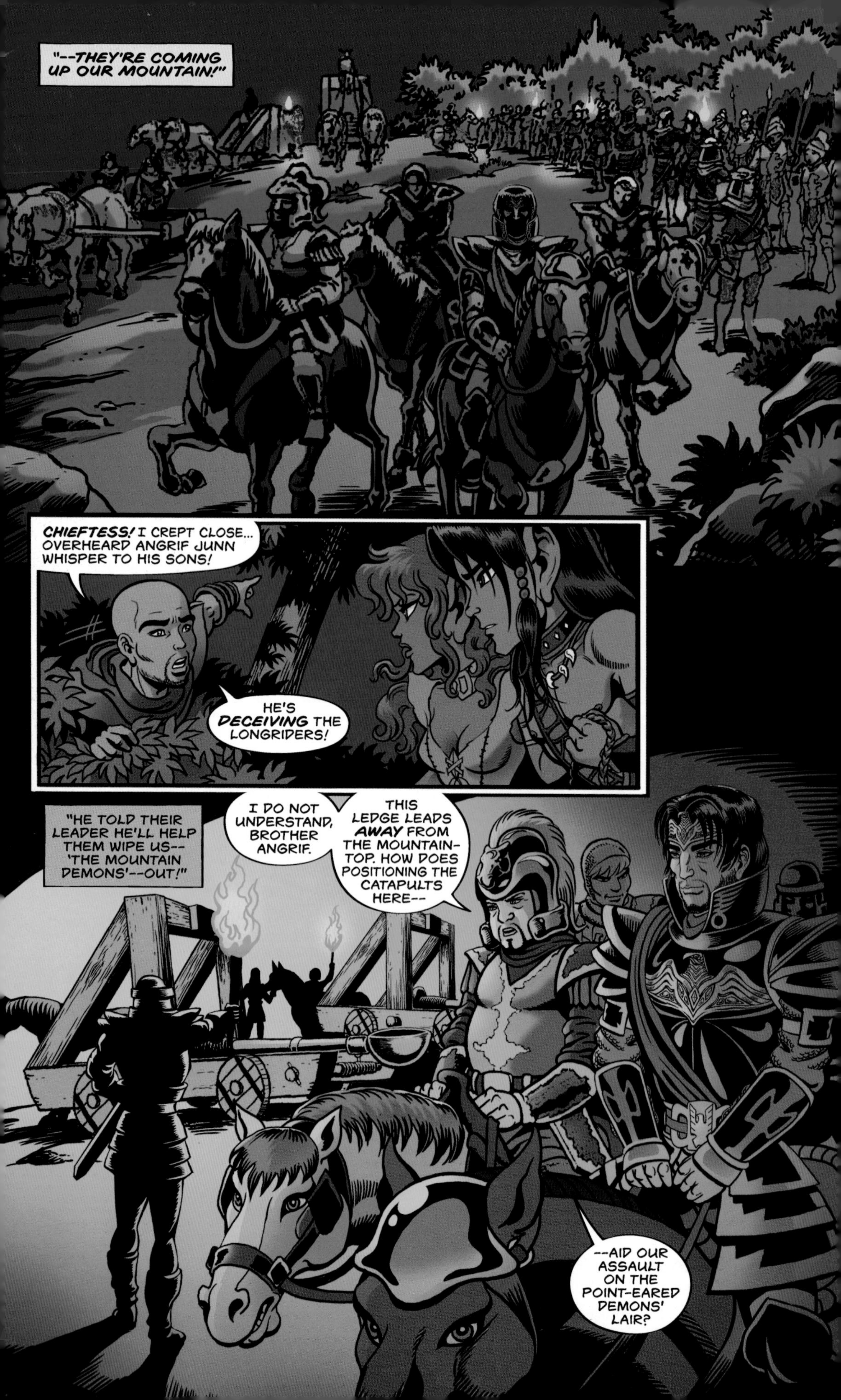
"--THEY'RE COMING UP OUR MOUNTAIN!"
CHIEFTESS! I CREPT CLOSE... OVERHEARD ANGRIF JUNN WHISPER TO HIS SONS!
HE'S DECEIVING THE LONGRIDERS!
"HE TOLD THEIR LEADER HE'LL HELP THEM WIPE US-- 'THE MOUNTAIN DEMONS'--OUT!"
I DO NOT UNDERSTAND, BROTHER ANGRIF.
THIS LEDGE LEADS AWAY FROM THE MOUNTAIN-TOP. HOW DOES POSITIONING THE CATAPULTS HERE--
--AID OUR ASSAULT ON THE POINT-EARED DEMONS' LAIR?

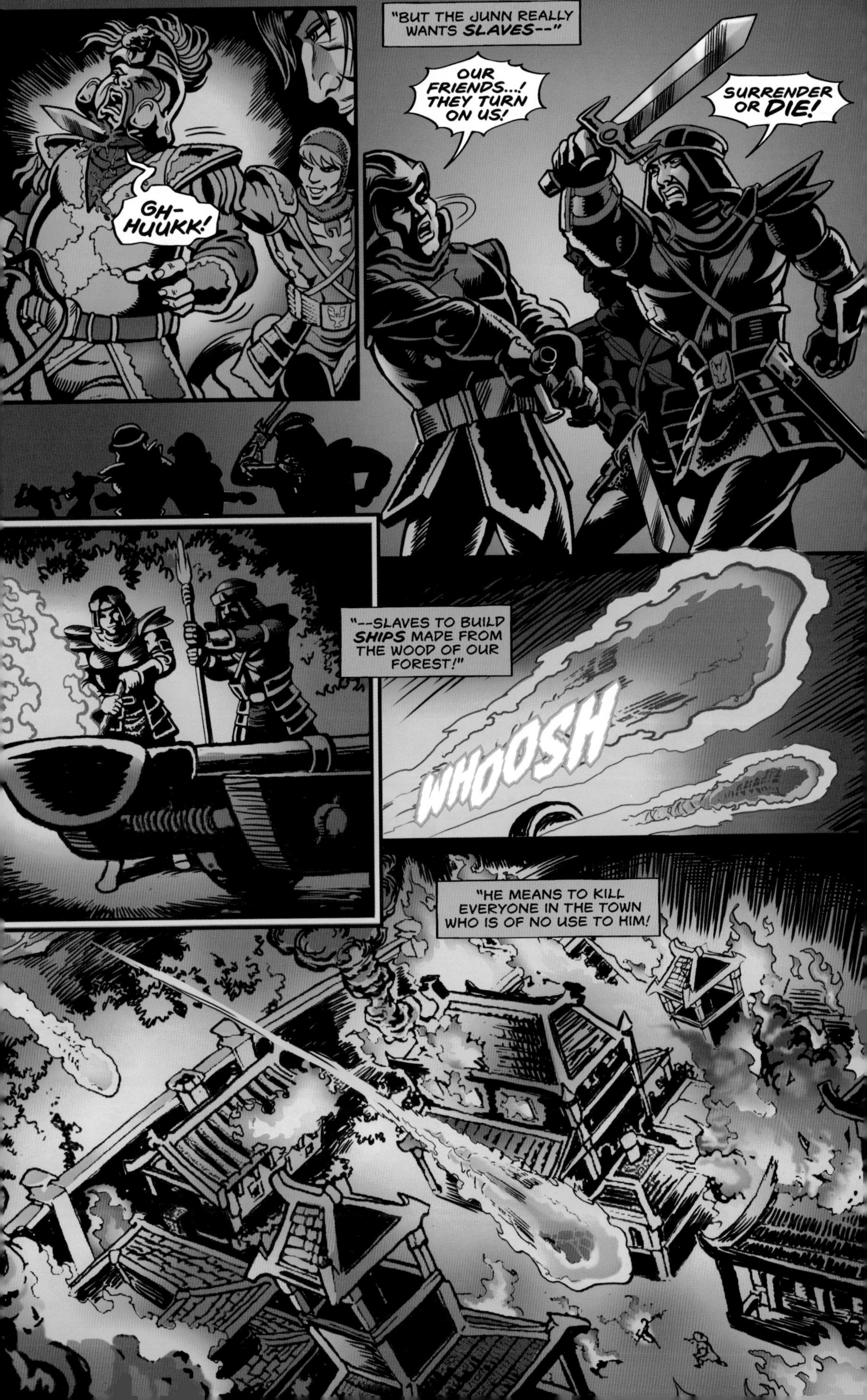
"BUT THE JUNN REALLY WANTS SLAVES--"
GH-HUUKK!
OUR FRIENDS...! THEY TURN ON US!
SURRENDER OR DIE!
"--SLAVES TO BUILD SHIPS MADE FROM THE WOOD OF OUR FOREST!"
WHOOSH
"HE MEANS TO KILL EVERYONE IN THE TOWN WHO IS OF NO USE TO HIM!

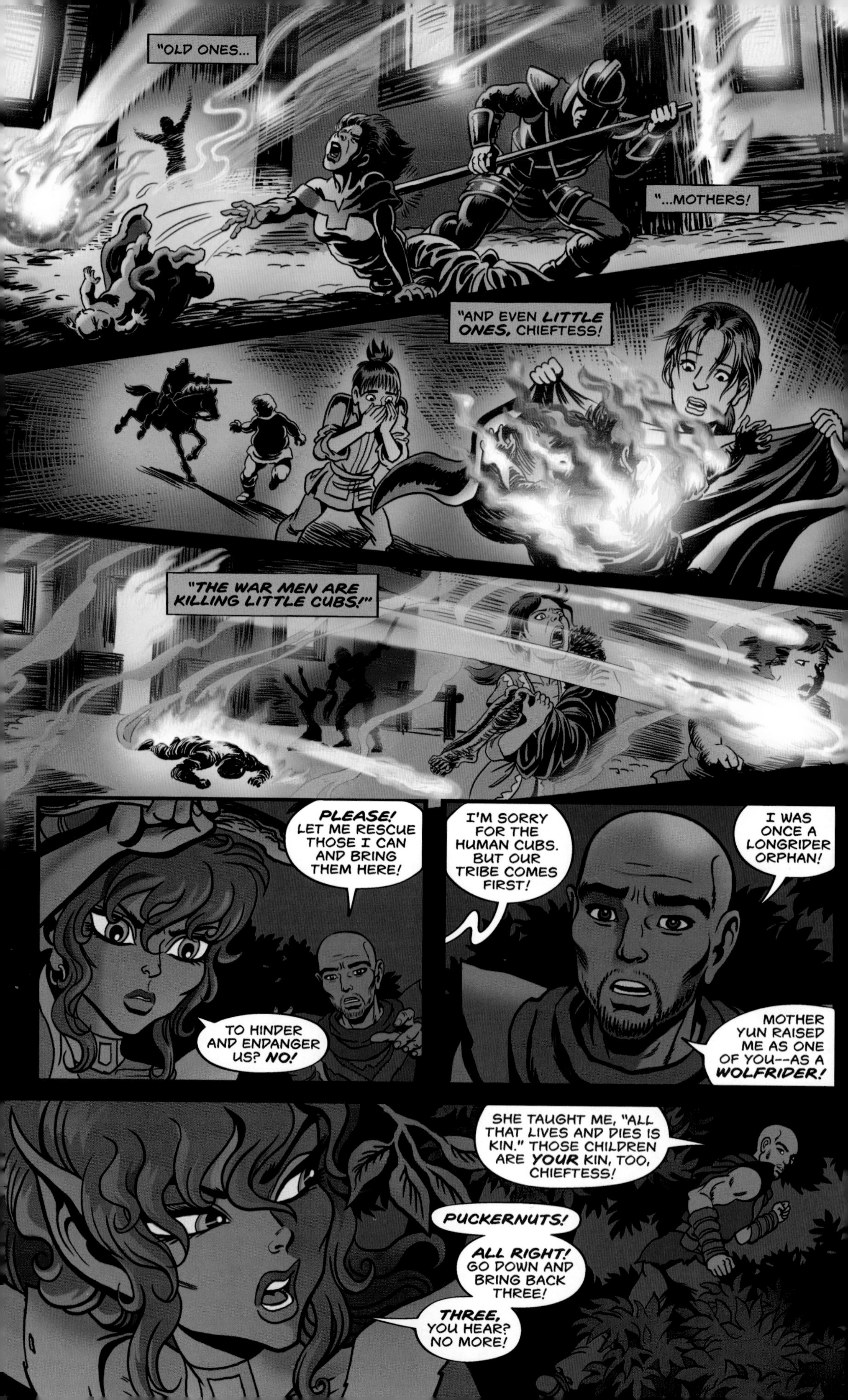

"OLD ONES...
"...MOTHERS!
"AND EVEN LITTLE ONES, CHIEFTESS!
"THE WAR MEN ARE KILLING LITTLE CUBS!"
PLEASE! LET ME RESCUE THOSE I CAN AND BRING THEM HERE!
TO HINDER AND ENDANGER US? NO!
I'M SORRY FOR THE HUMAN CUBS. BUT OUR TRIBE COMES FIRST!
I WAS ONCE A LONGRIDER ORPHAN!
MOTHER YUN RAISED ME AS ONE OF YOU--AS A WOLFRIDER!
SHE TAUGHT ME, "ALL THAT LIVES AND DIES IS KIN." THOSE CHILDREN ARE YOUR KIN, TOO, CHIEFTESS!
PUCKERNUTS!
ALL RIGHT! GO DOWN AND BRING BACK THREE!
THREE, YOU HEAR? NO MORE!

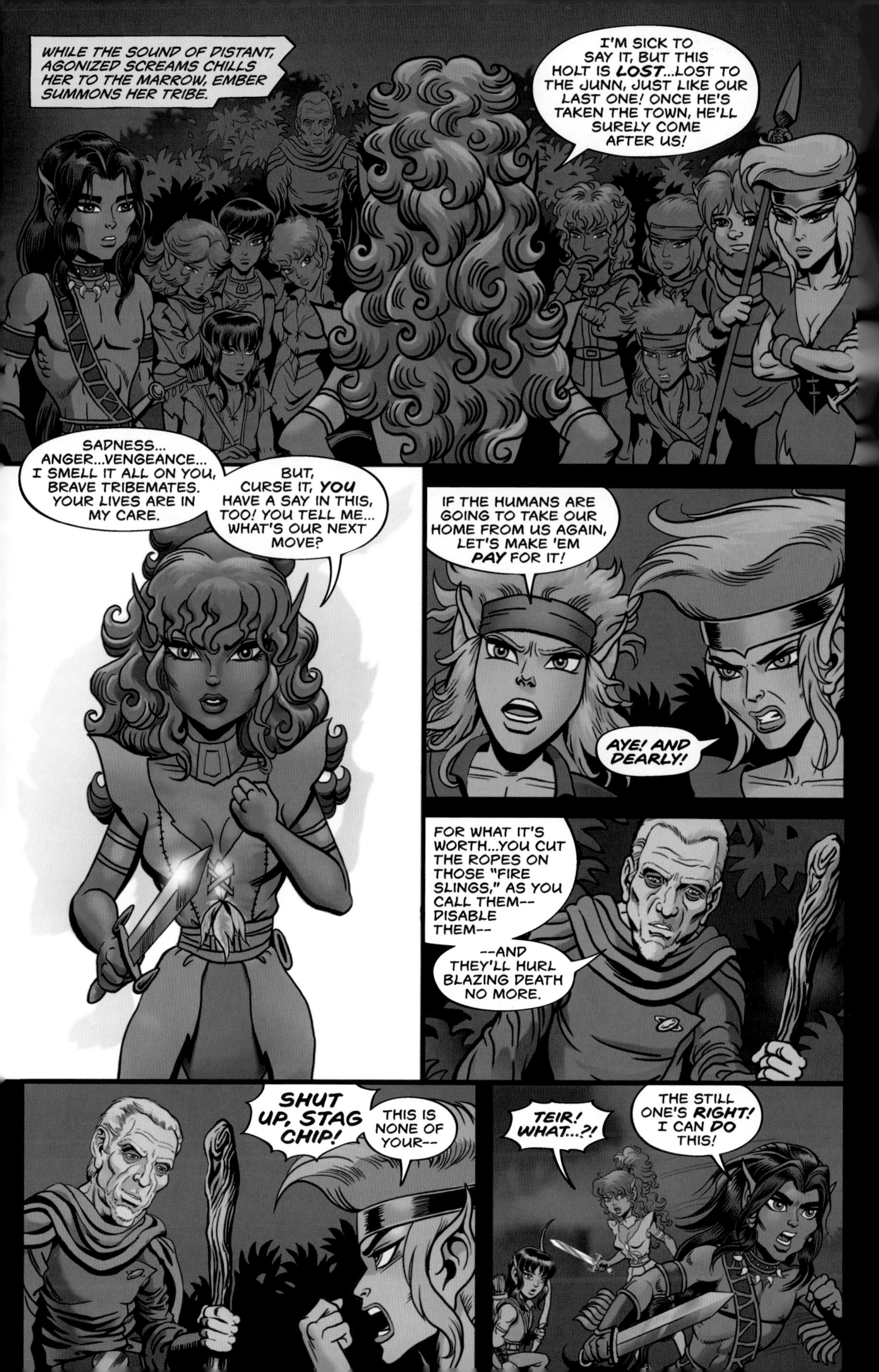
WHILE THE SOUND OF DISTANT, AGONIZED SCREAMS CHILLS HER TO THE MARROW, EMBER SUMMONS HER TRIBE.
I'M SICK TO SAY IT, BUT THIS HOLT IS LOST...LOST TO THE JUNN, JUST LIKE OUR LAST ONE! ONCE HE'S TAKEN THE TOWN, HE'LL SURELY COME AFTER US!
SADNESS... ANGER...VENGEANCE... I SMELL IT ALL ON YOU, BRAVE TRIBEMATES. YOUR LIVES ARE IN MY CARE.
BUT, CURSE IT, YOU HAVE A SAY IN THIS, TOO! YOU TELL ME... WHAT'S OUR NEXT MOVE?
IF THE HUMANS ARE GOING TO TAKE OUR HOME FROM US AGAIN, LET'S MAKE 'EM PAY FOR IT!
AYE! AND DEARLY!
FOR WHAT IT'S WORTH...YOU CUT THE ROPES ON THOSE "FIRE SLINGS," AS YOU CALL THEM-- DISABLE THEM--
--AND THEY'LL HURL BLAZING DEATH NO MORE.
SHUT UP, STAG CHIP!
THIS IS NONE OF YOUR--
TEIR! WHAT...?!
THE STILL ONE'S RIGHT! I CAN DO THIS!

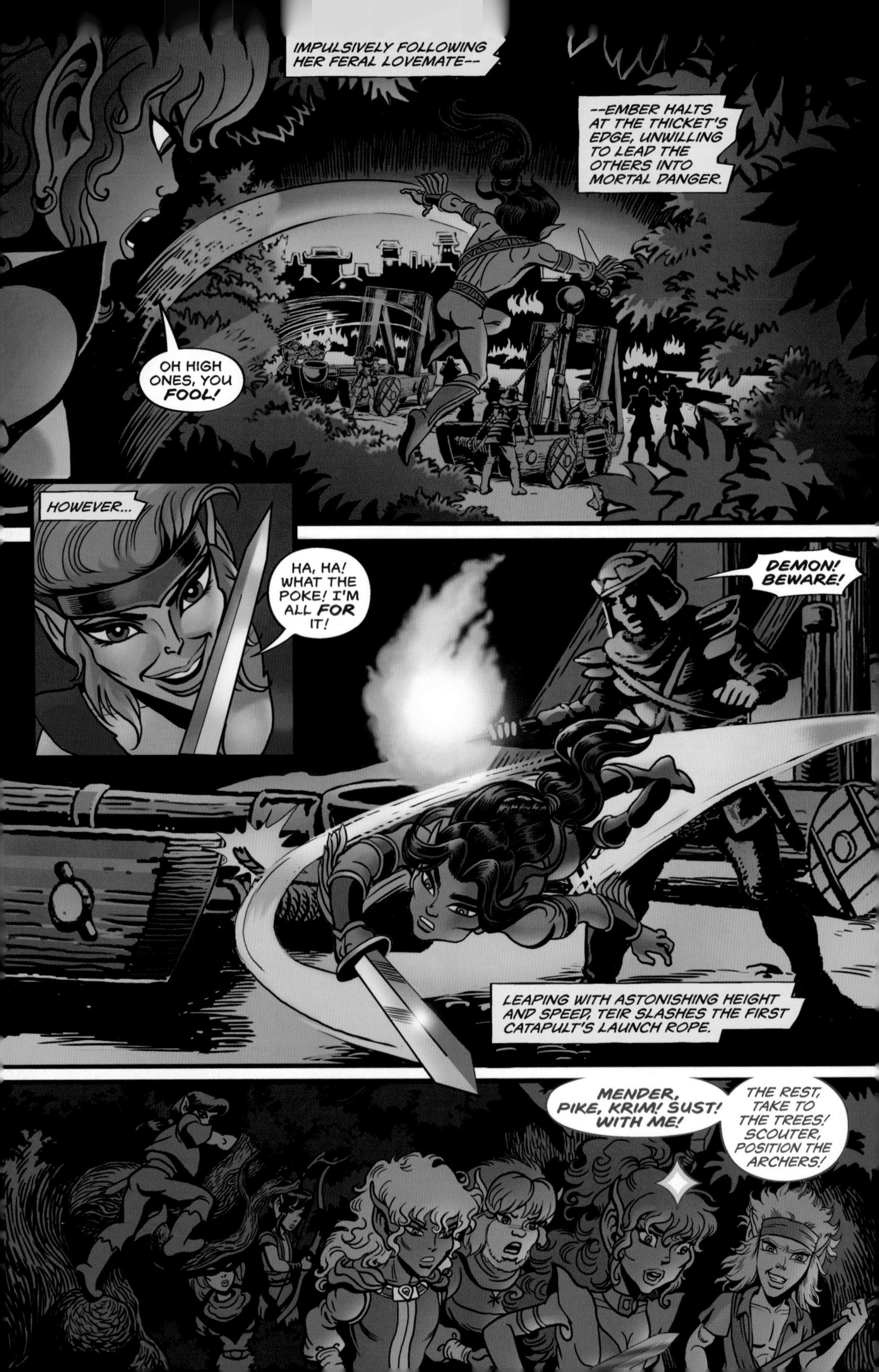

IMPULSIVELY FOLLOWING HER FERAL LOVEMATE--
--EMBER HALTS AT THE THICKET'S EDGE, UNWILLING TO LEAD THE OTHERS INTO MORTAL DANGER.
OH HIGH ONES, YOU FOOL!
HOWEVER...
HA, HA! WHAT THE POKE! I'M ALL FOR IT!
DEMON! BEWARE!
LEAPING WITH ASTONISHING HEIGHT AND SPEED, TEIR SLASHES THE FIRST CATAPULT'S LAUNCH ROPE.
MENDER, PIKE, KRIM! SUST! WITH ME!
THE REST, TAKE TO THE TREES! SCOUTER, POSITION THE ARCHERS!

A HEARTBEAT LATER, THEIR SECOND WAR MACHINE MADE USELESS, THE STARTLED DJUNSMEN GALVANIZE.

SLAY IT!

MONSTER! YOU'RE MINE!

SLASH

AAAGH!

LIKE DUNG HE'S YOURS!

UNNOTICED AND UNINVITED, ANOTHER JOINS THE FRAY...

HEEEYAH!

BEHIND YOU!

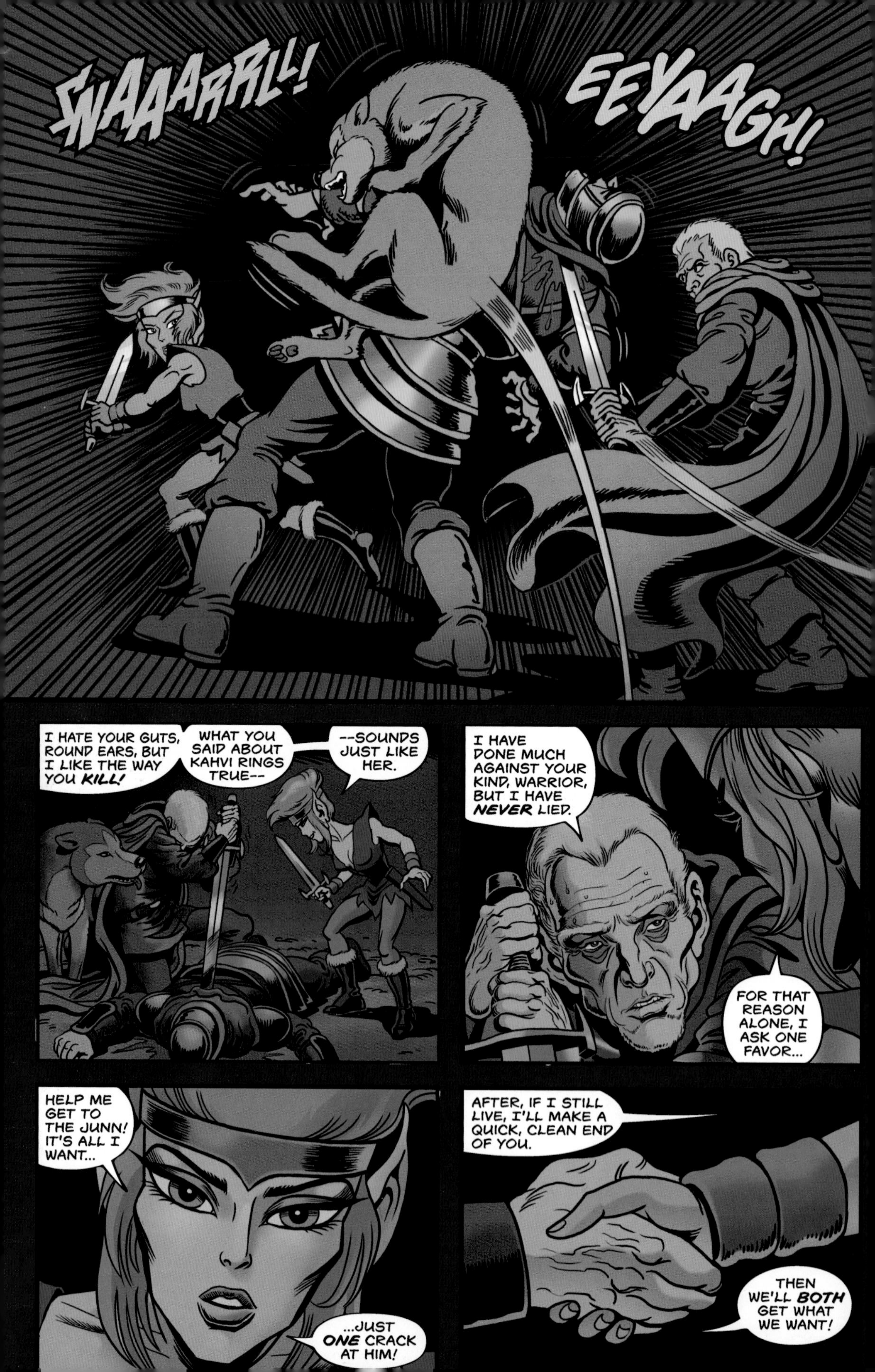
SWAAARRLL!
EEYAAGH!
I HATE YOUR GUTS, ROUND EARS, BUT I LIKE THE WAY YOU KILL!
WHAT YOU SAID ABOUT KAHVI RINGS TRUE--
--SOUNDS JUST LIKE HER.
I HAVE DONE MUCH AGAINST YOUR KIND, WARRIOR, BUT I HAVE NEVER LIED.
FOR THAT REASON ALONE, I ASK ONE FAVOR...
HELP ME GET TO THE JUNN! IT'S ALL I WANT...
...JUST ONE CRACK AT HIM!
AFTER, IF I STILL LIVE, I'LL MAKE A QUICK, CLEAN END OF YOU.
THEN WE'LL BOTH GET WHAT WE WANT!

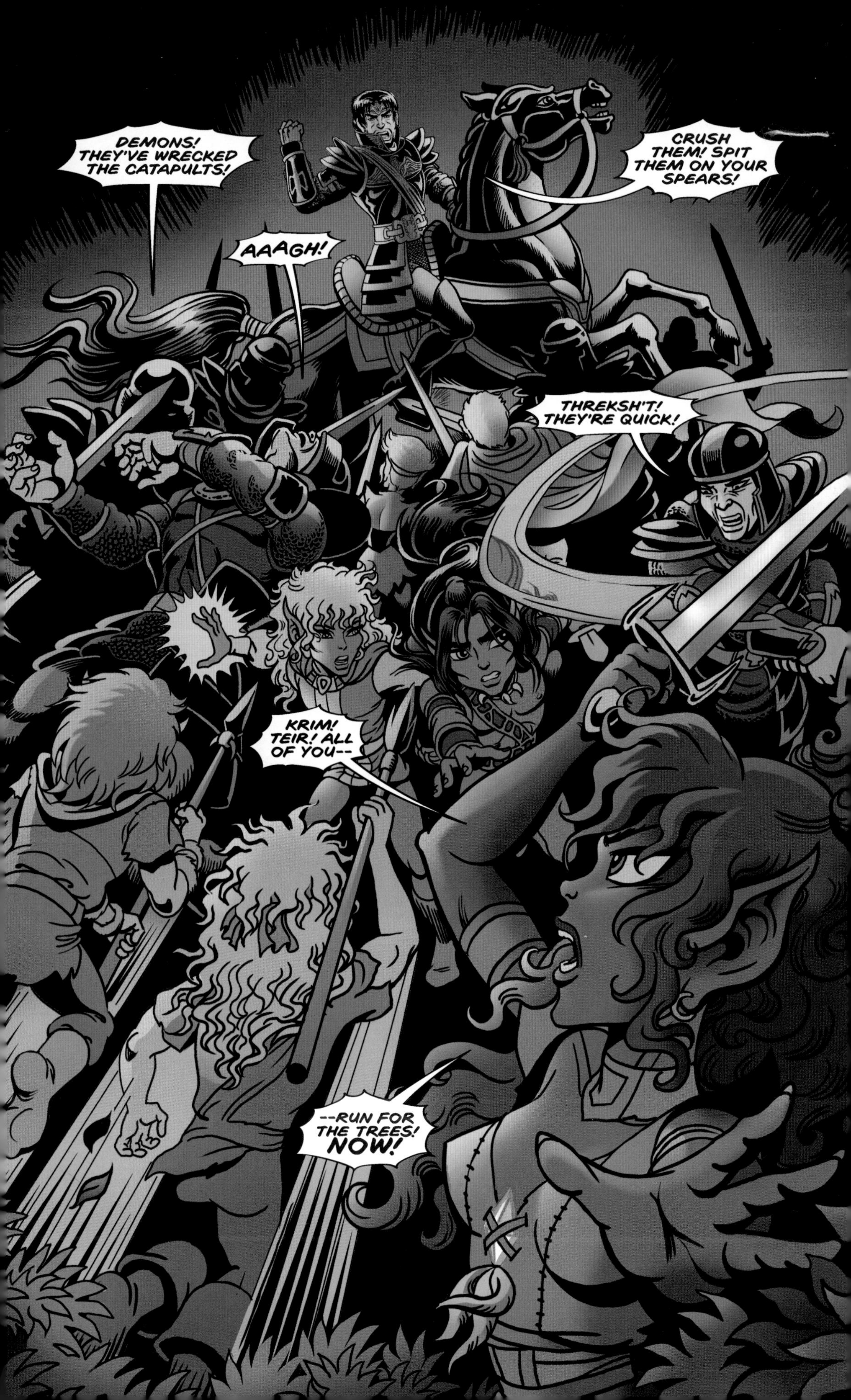
DEMONS! THEY'VE WRECKED THE CATAPULTS!
CRUSH THEM! SPIT THEM ON YOUR SPEARS!
AAAGH!
THREKSH'T! THEY'RE QUICK!
KRIM! TEIR! ALL OF YOU--
--RUN FOR THE TREES! NOW!

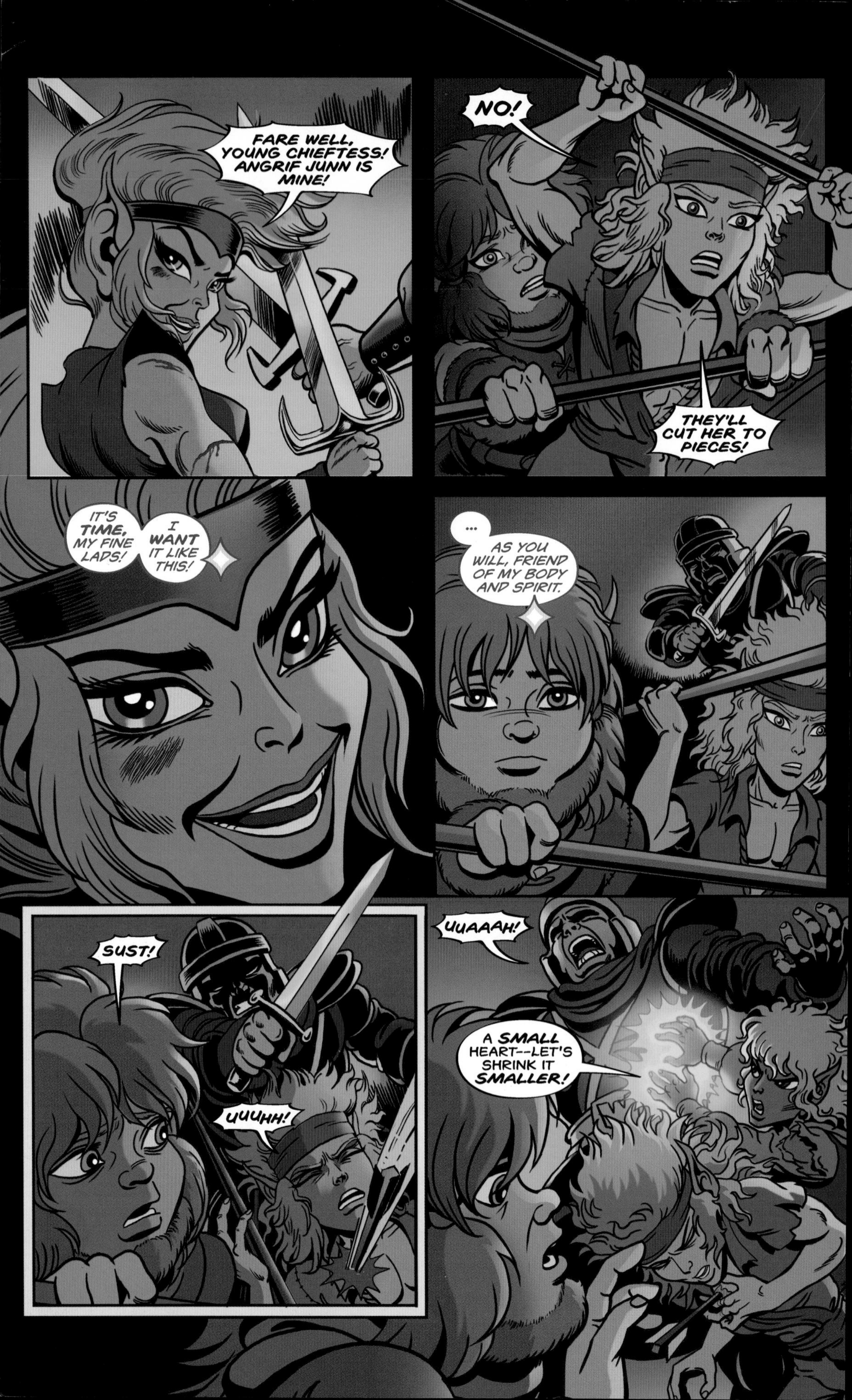
FARE WELL, YOUNG CHIEFTESS! ANGRIF JUNN IS MINE!
NO!
THEY'LL CUT HER TO PIECES!
IT'S TIME, MY FINE LADS!
I WANT IT LIKE THIS!
...
AS YOU WILL, FRIEND OF MY BODY AND SPIRIT.
SUST!
UUUHH!
UUAAAH!
A SMALL HEART--LET'S SHRINK IT SMALLER!

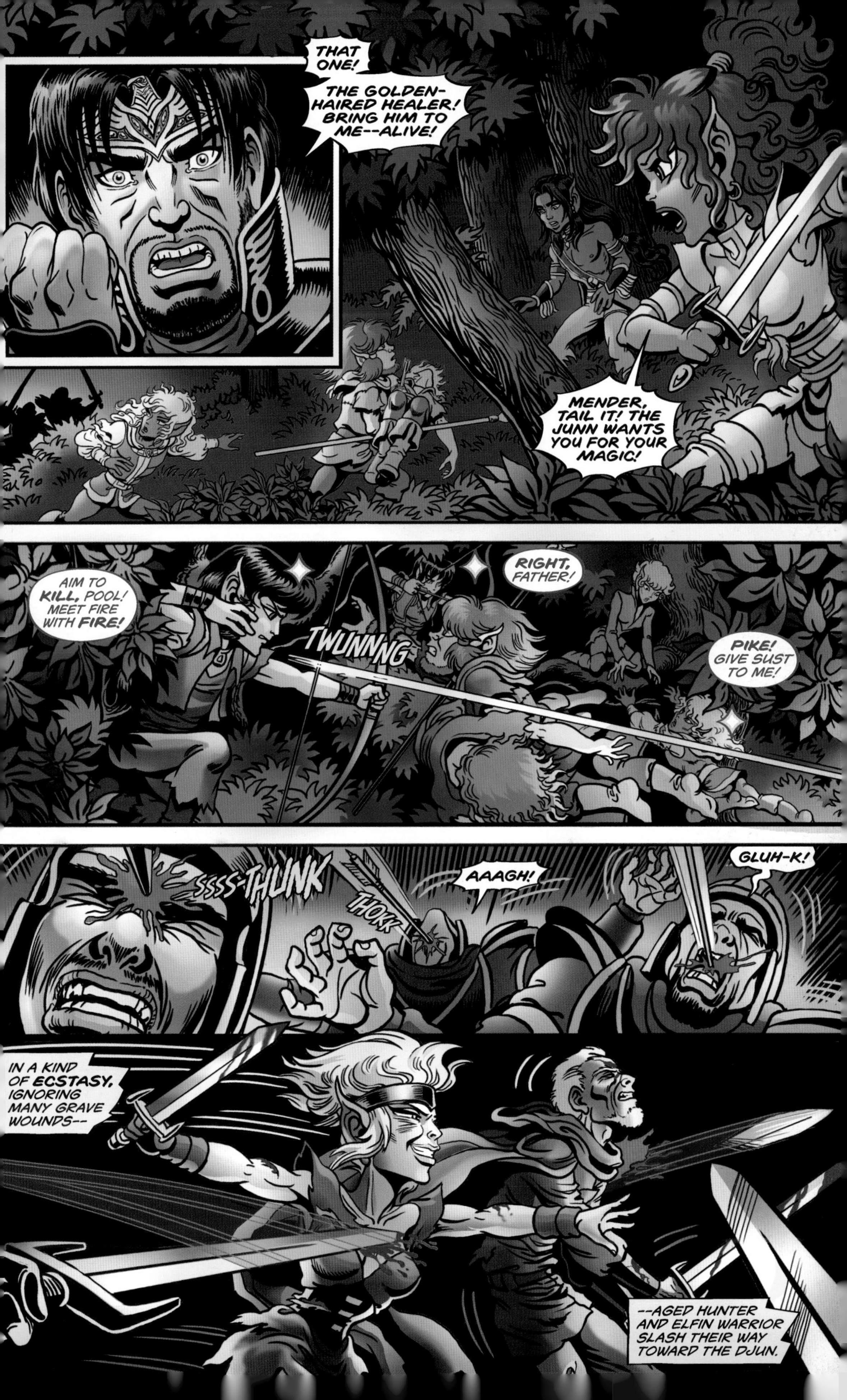
THAT ONE!
THE GOLDEN-HAIRED HEALER! BRING HIM TO ME--ALIVE!
MENDER, TAIL IT! THE JUNN WANTS YOU FOR YOUR MAGIC!
AIM TO KILL, POOL! MEET FIRE WITH FIRE!
TWUNNNG
RIGHT, FATHER!
PIKE! GIVE SUST TO ME!
SSSS-THUNK
THOKK
AAAGH!
GLUH-K!
IN A KIND OF ECSTASY, IGNORING MANY GRAVE WOUNDS--
--AGED HUNTER AND ELFIN WARRIOR SLASH THEIR WAY TOWARD THE DJUN.

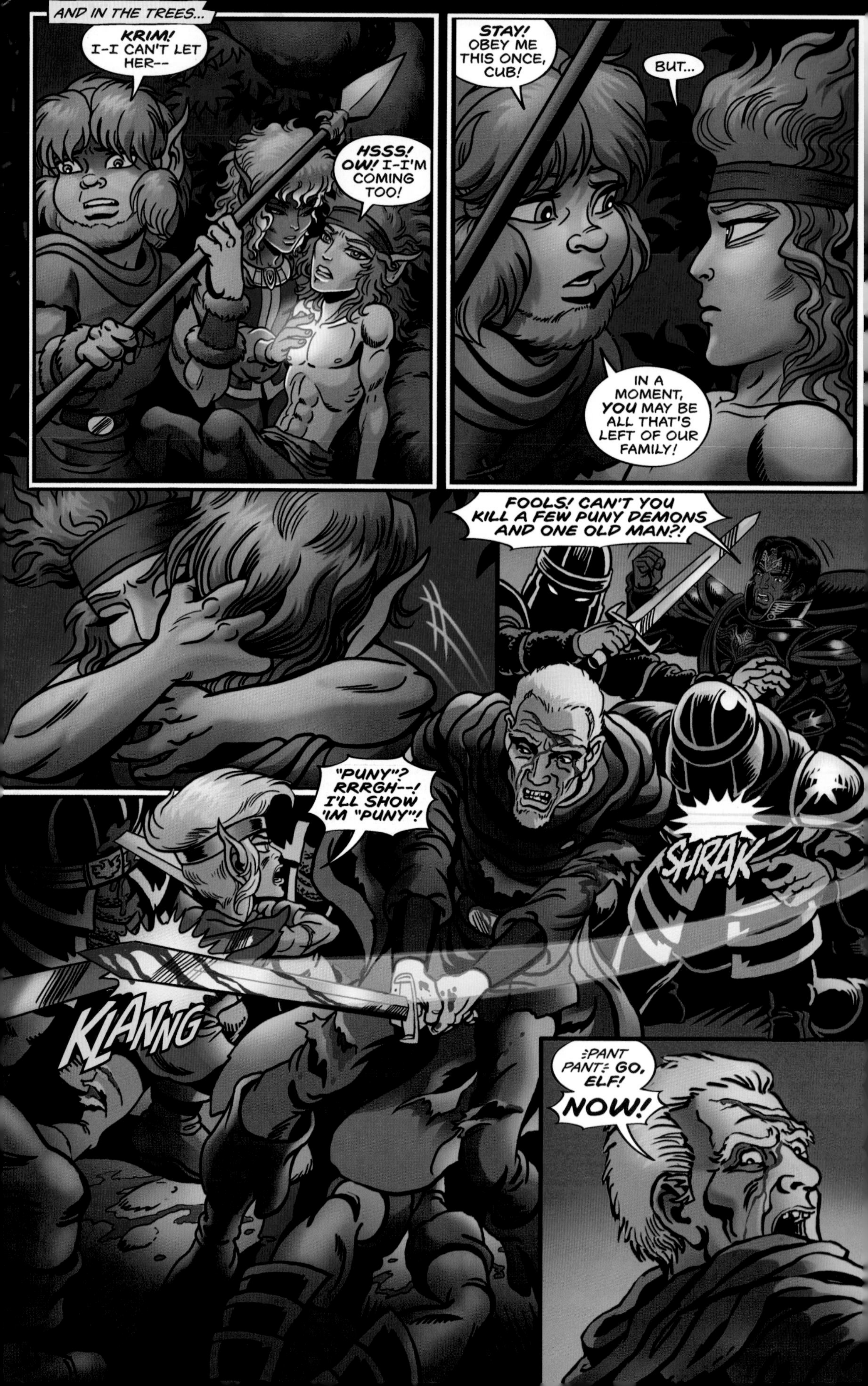
AND IN THE TREES...
KRIM! I-I CAN'T LET HER--
HSSS! OW! I-I'M COMING TOO!
STAY! OBEY ME THIS ONCE, CUB!
BUT...
IN A MOMENT, YOU MAY BE ALL THAT'S LEFT OF OUR FAMILY!
FOOLS! CAN'T YOU KILL A FEW PUNY DEMONS AND ONE OLD MAN?!
"PUNY"? RRRGH--! I'LL SHOW 'IM "PUNY"!
SHRAK
KLANNG
PANT PANT GO, ELF!
NOW!

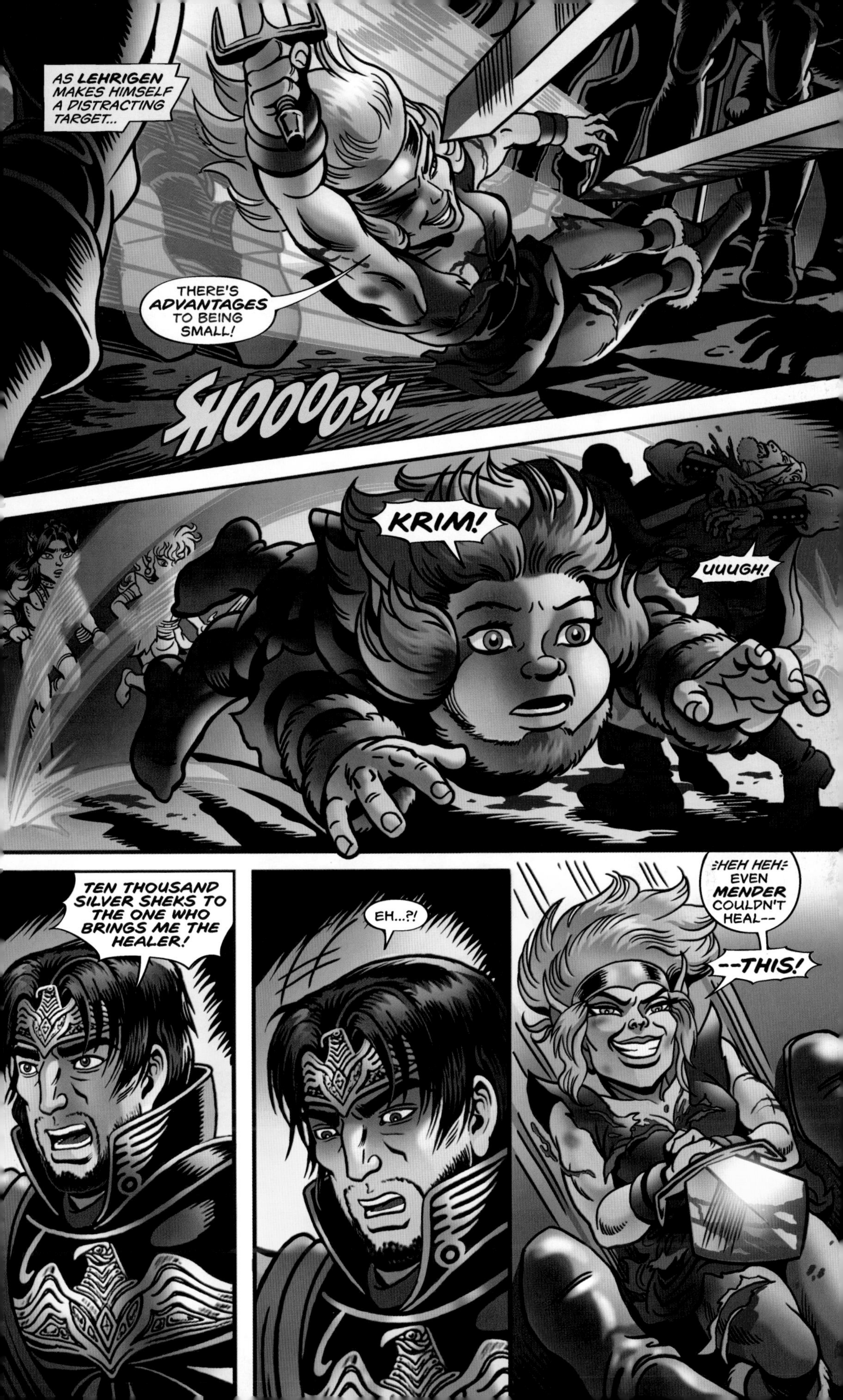
AS LEHRIGEN MAKES HIMSELF A DISTRACTING TARGET...
THERE'S ADVANTAGES TO BEING SMALL!
SHOOOOSH
KRIM!
UUUGH!
TEN THOUSAND SILVER SHEKS TO THE ONE WHO BRINGS ME THE HEALER!
EH...?!
HEH HEH EVEN MENDER COULDN'T HEAL--
--THIS!

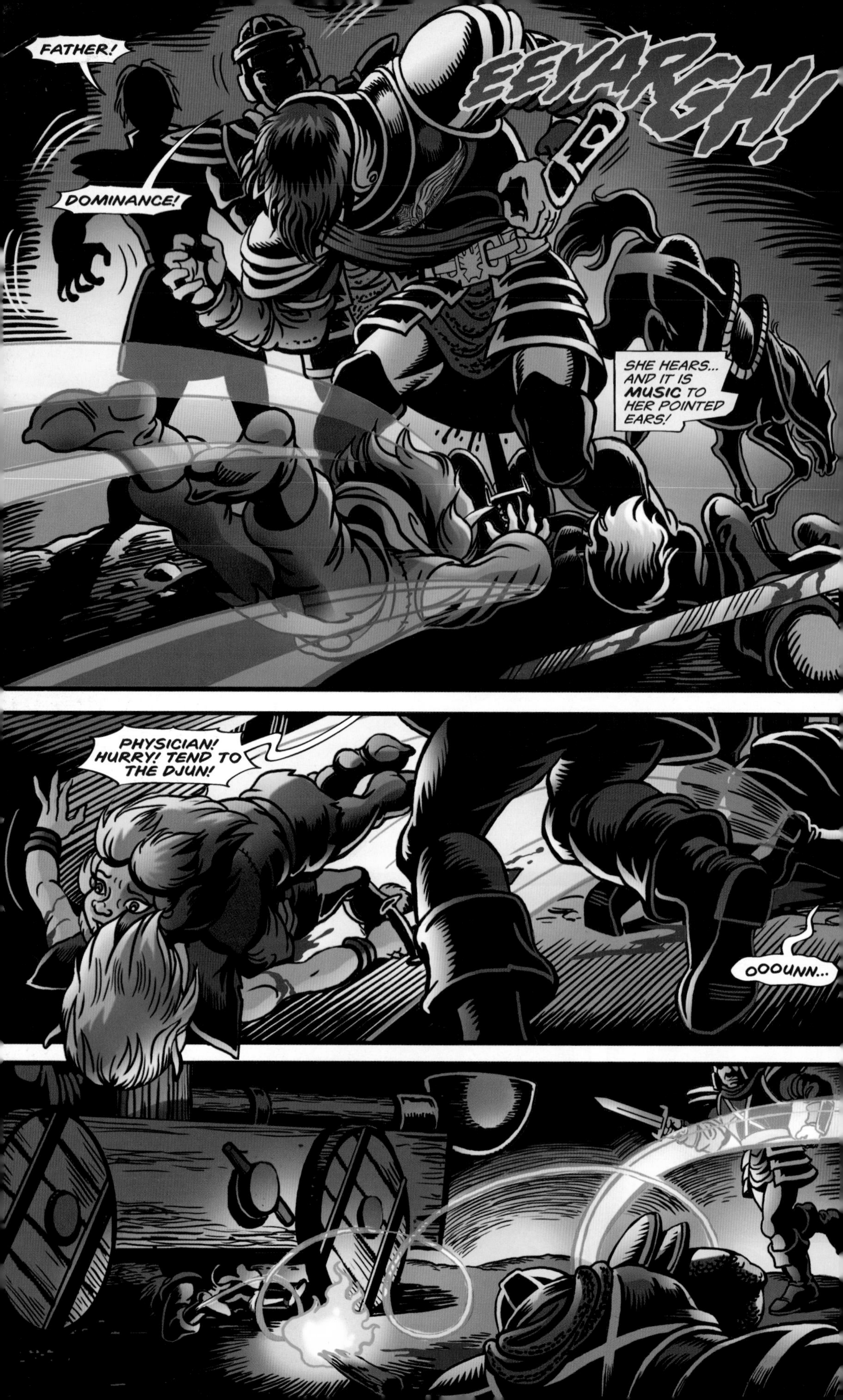

FATHER!
EEYARGH!
DOMINANCE!
SHE HEARS... AND IT IS MUSIC TO HER POINTED EARS!
PHYSICIAN! HURRY! TEND TO THE DJUN!
OOOUNN...

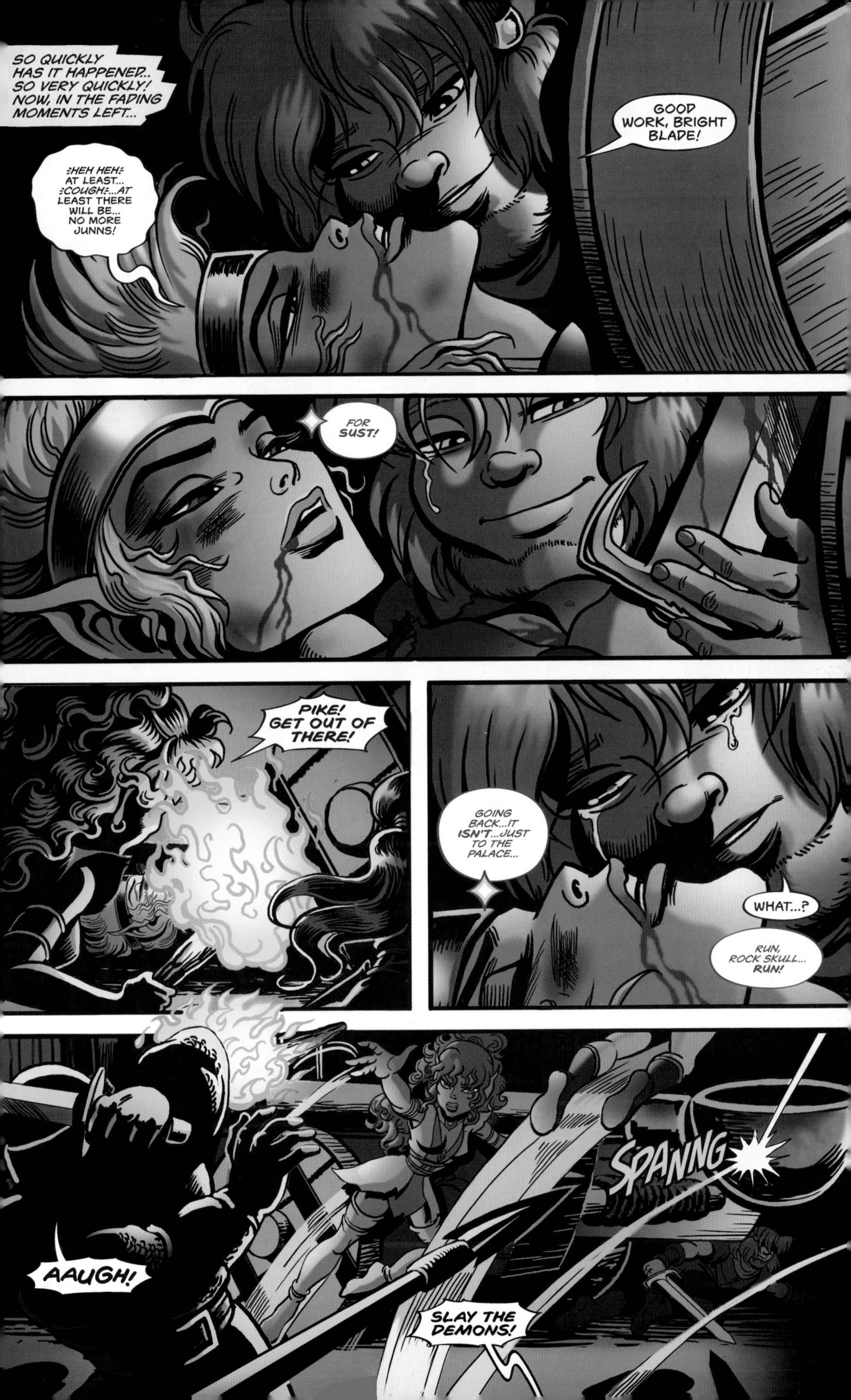
SO QUICKLY HAS IT HAPPENED.. SO VERY QUICKLY! NOW, IN THE FADING MOMENTS LEFT...
GOOD WORK, BRIGHT BLADE!
=HEH HEH= AT LEAST... =COUGH=...AT LEAST THERE WILL BE... NO MORE JUNNS!
FOR SUST!
PIKE! GET OUT OF THERE!
GOING BACK...IT ISN'T...JUST TO THE PALACE...
WHAT...?
RUN, ROCK SKULL... RUN!
SPANNG
AAUGH!
SLAY THE DEMONS!

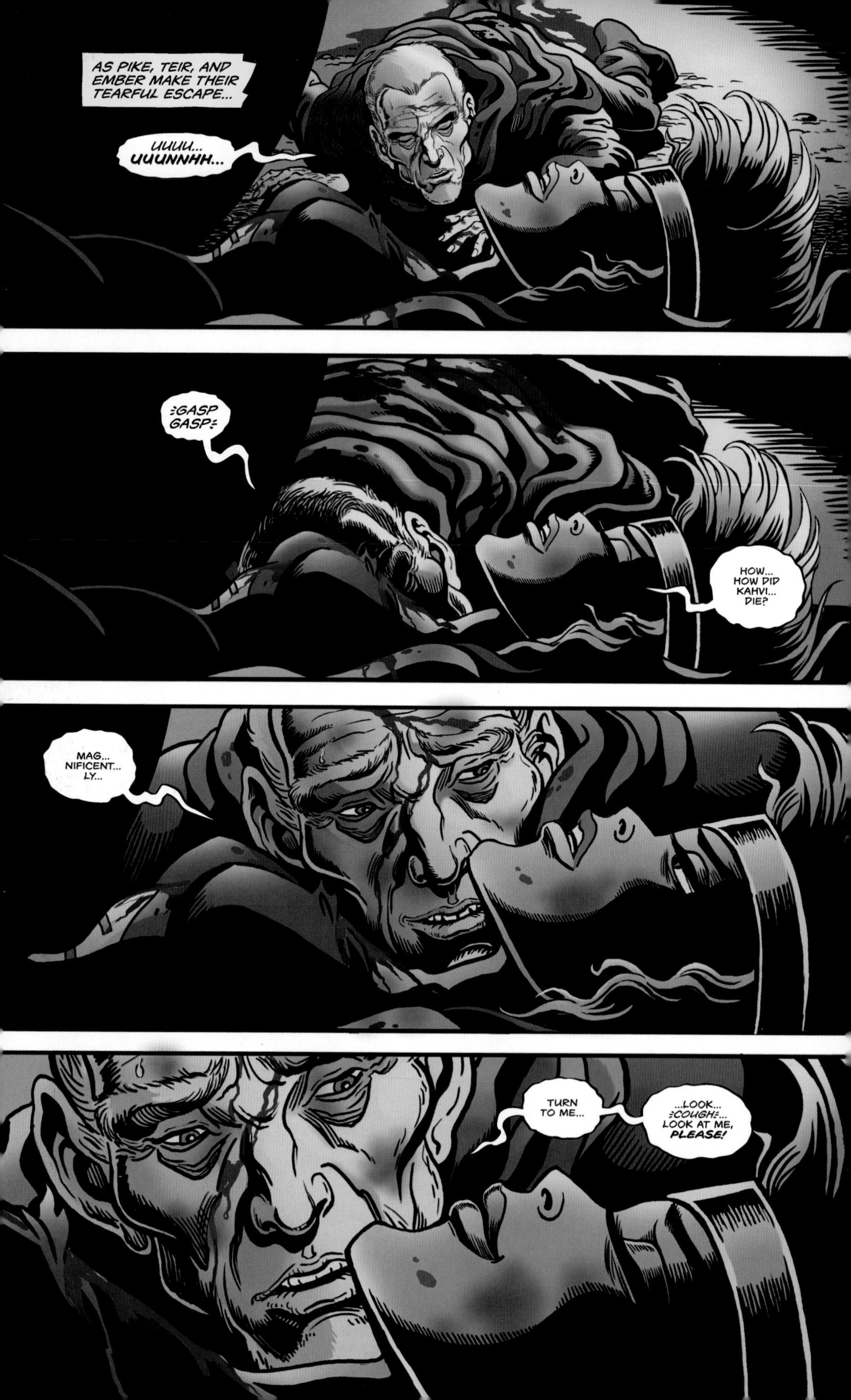
AS PIKE, TEIR, AND EMBER MAKE THEIR TEARFUL ESCAPE...
UUUU... UUUNNHH...
GASP GASP
HOW... HOW DID KAHVI... DIE?
MAG... NIFICENT... LY...
TURN TO ME...
...LOOK... COUGH... LOOK AT ME, PLEASE!

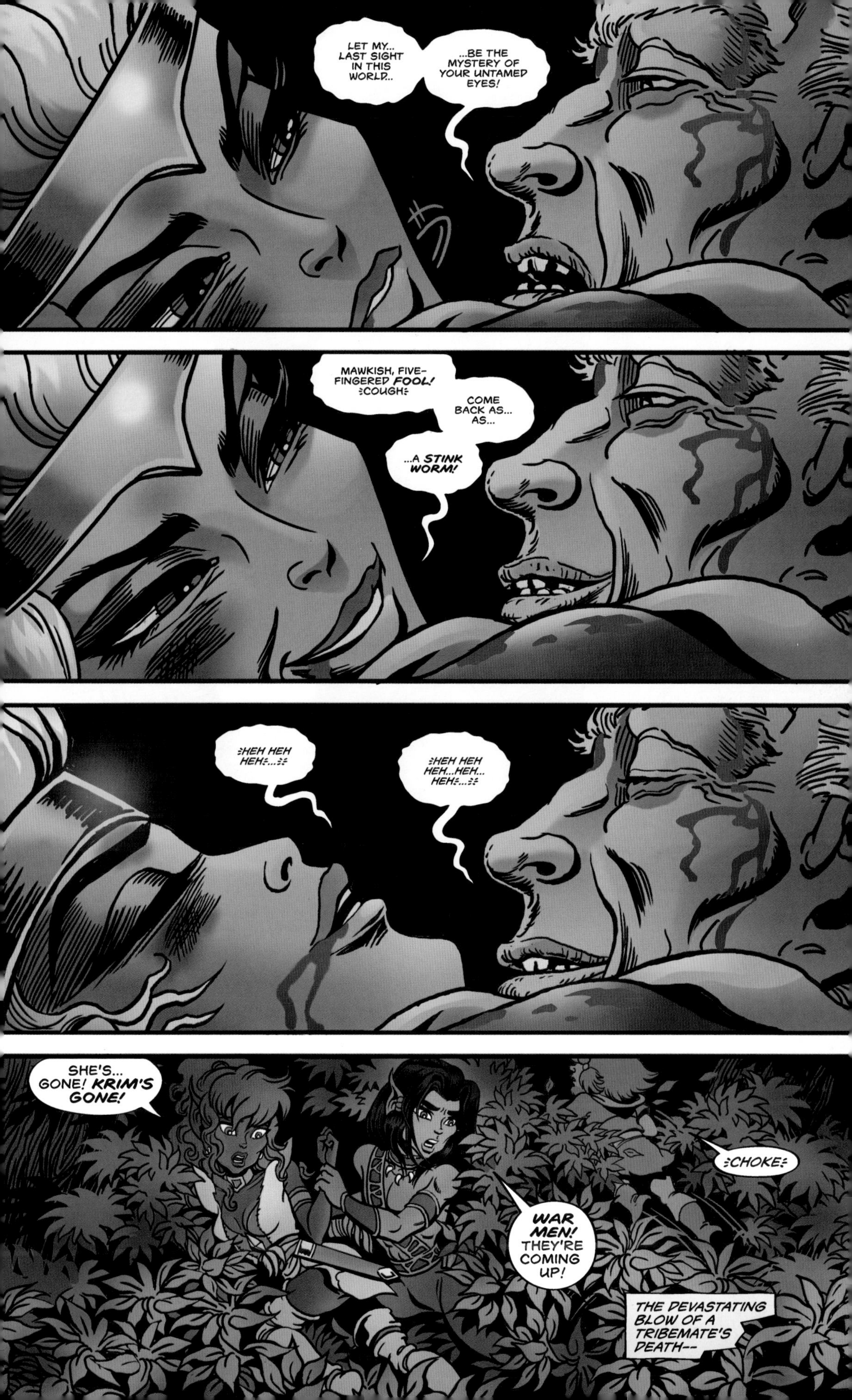
LET MY... LAST SIGHT IN THIS WORLD...
...BE THE MYSTERY OF YOUR UNTAMED EYES!
MAWKISH, FIVE-FINGERED FOOL! COUGH
COME BACK AS... AS...
...A STINK WORM!
HEH HEH HEH...
HEH HEH HEH...HEH... HEH...
SHE'S... GONE! KRIM'S GONE!
CHOKE
WAR MEN! THEY'RE COMING UP!
THE DEVASTATING BLOW OF A TRIBEMATE'S DEATH--

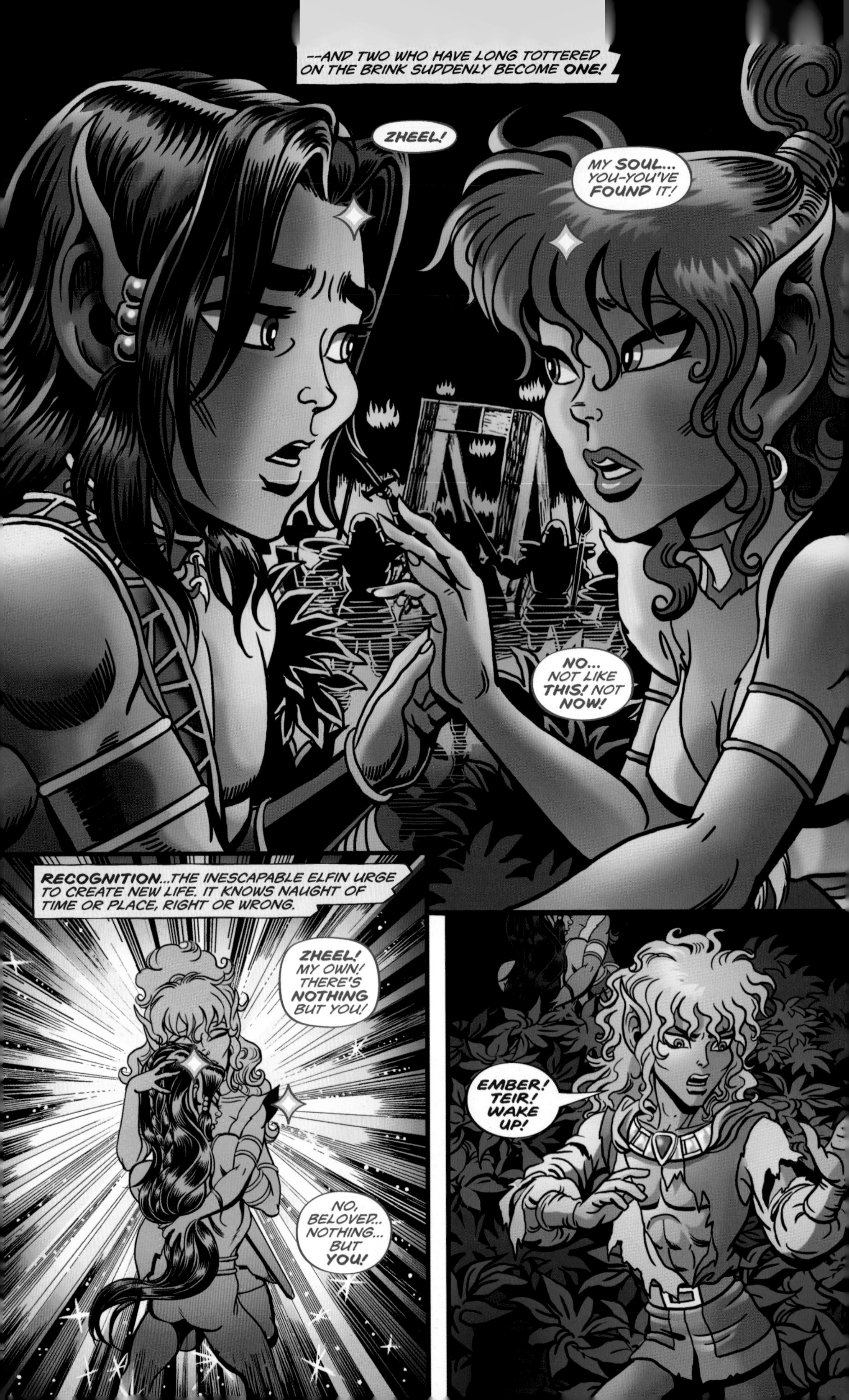
--AND TWO WHO HAVE LONG TOTTERED ON THE BRINK SUDDENLY BECOME ONE!
ZHEEL!
MY SOUL... YOU-YOU'VE FOUND IT!
NO... NOT LIKE THIS! NOT NOW!
RECOGNITION...THE INESCAPABLE ELFIN URGE TO CREATE NEW LIFE. IT KNOWS NAUGHT OF TIME OR PLACE, RIGHT OR WRONG.
ZHEEL! MY OWN! THERE'S NOTHING BUT YOU!
NO, BELOVED... NOTHING... BUT YOU!
EMBER! TEIR! WAKE UP!

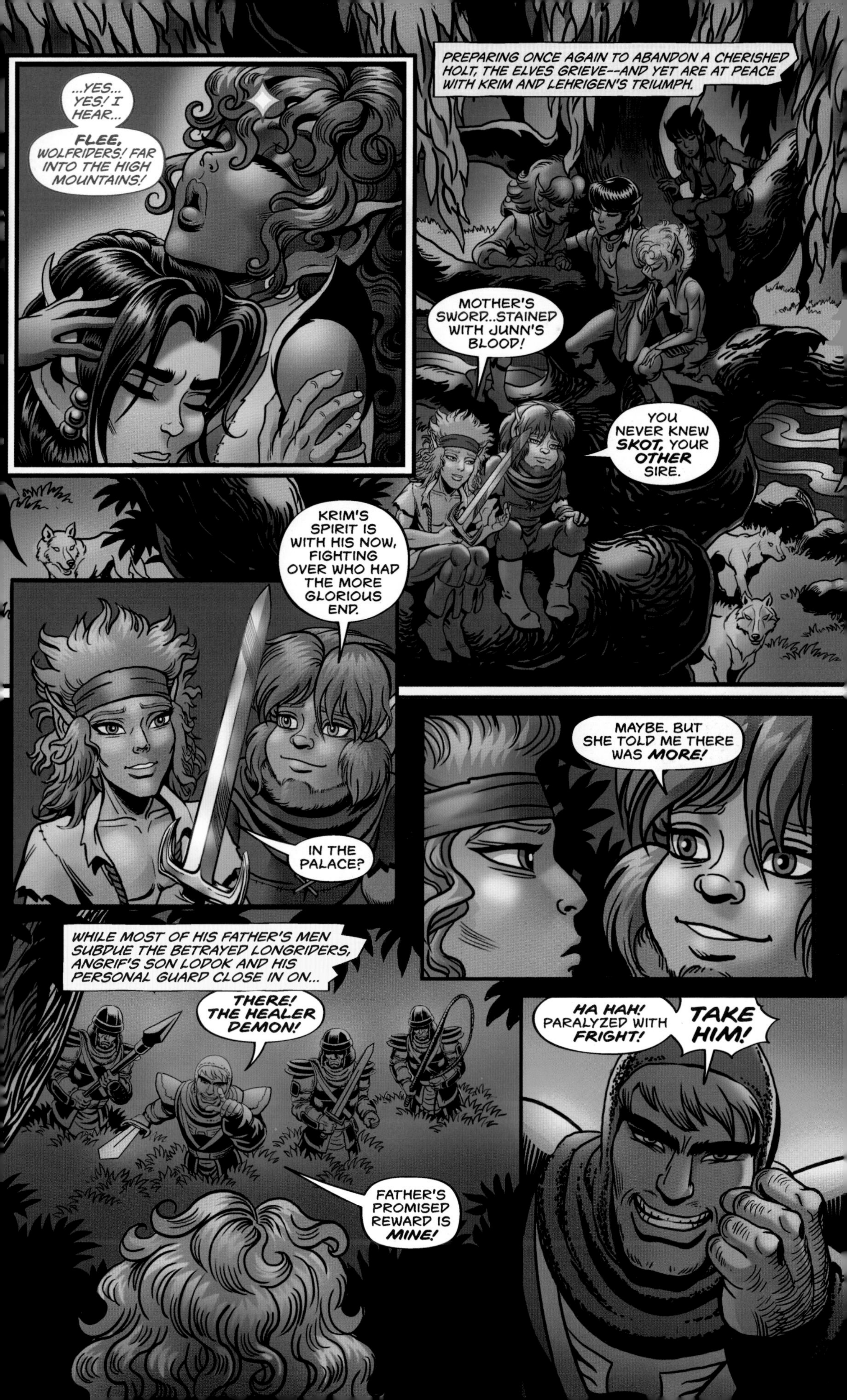

...YES... YES! I HEAR...
FLEE, WOLFRIDERS! FAR INTO THE HIGH MOUNTAINS!
PREPARING ONCE AGAIN TO ABANDON A CHERISHED HOLT, THE ELVES GRIEVE--AND YET ARE AT PEACE WITH KRIM AND LEHRIGEN'S TRIUMPH.
MOTHER'S SWORD...STAINED WITH JUNN'S BLOOD!
YOU NEVER KNEW SKOT, YOUR OTHER SIRE.
KRIM'S SPIRIT IS WITH HIS NOW, FIGHTING OVER WHO HAD THE MORE GLORIOUS END.
IN THE PALACE?
MAYBE. BUT SHE TOLD ME THERE WAS MORE!
WHILE MOST OF HIS FATHER'S MEN SUBDUE THE BETRAYED LONGRIDERS, ANGRIF'S SON LODOK AND HIS PERSONAL GUARD CLOSE IN ON...
THERE! THE HEALER DEMON!
FATHER'S PROMISED REWARD IS MINE!
HA HAH! PARALYZED WITH FRIGHT!
TAKE HIM!

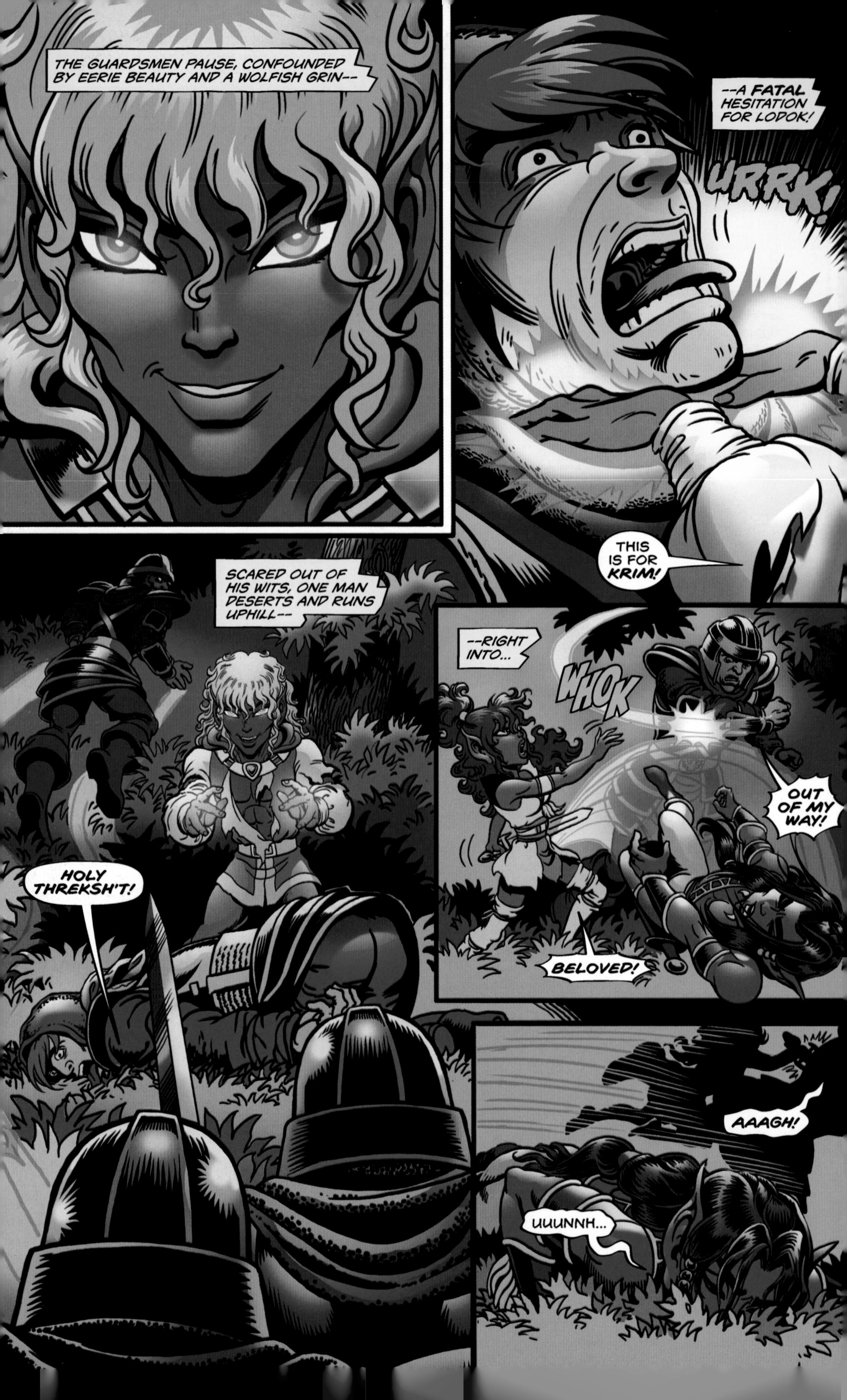
THE GUARDSMEN PAUSE, CONFOUNDED BY EERIE BEAUTY AND A WOLFISH GRIN--
--A FATAL HESITATION FOR LODOK!
URRK!
THIS IS FOR KRIM!
SCARED OUT OF HIS WITS, ONE MAN DESERTS AND RUNS UPHILL--
HOLY THREKSH'T!
--RIGHT INTO...
WHOK
OUT OF MY WAY!
BELOVED!
AAAGH!
UUUNNH...

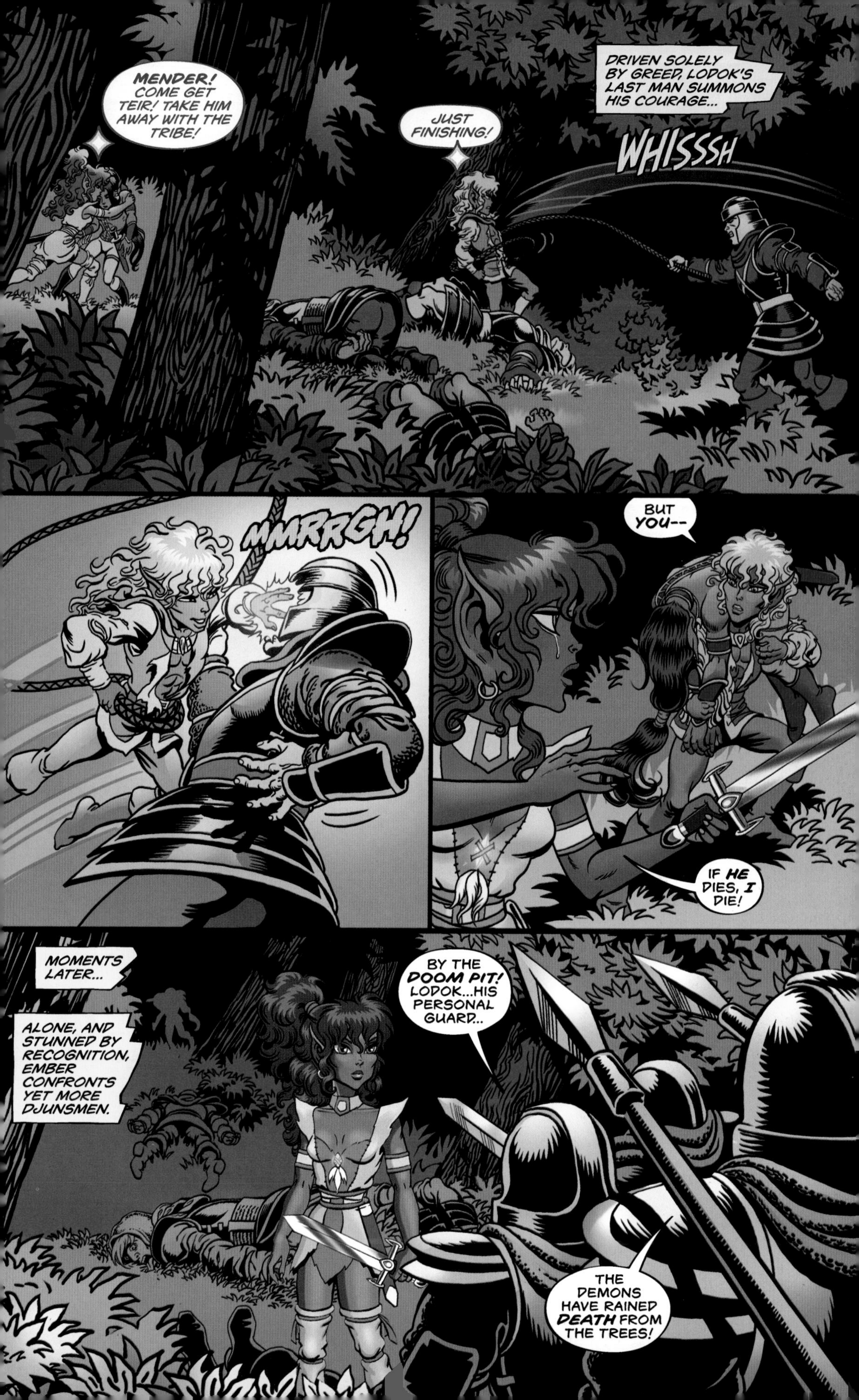
MENDER! COME GET TEIR! TAKE HIM AWAY WITH THE TRIBE!
JUST FINISHING!
DRIVEN SOLELY BY GREED, LODOK'S LAST MAN SUMMONS HIS COURAGE...
WHISSSH
MMRRGH!
BUT YOU--
IF HE DIES, I DIE!
MOMENTS LATER...
ALONE, AND STUNNED BY RECOGNITION, EMBER CONFRONTS YET MORE DJUNSMEN.
BY THE DOOM PIT! LODOK...HIS PERSONAL GUARD...
THE DEMONS HAVE RAINED DEATH FROM THE TREES!

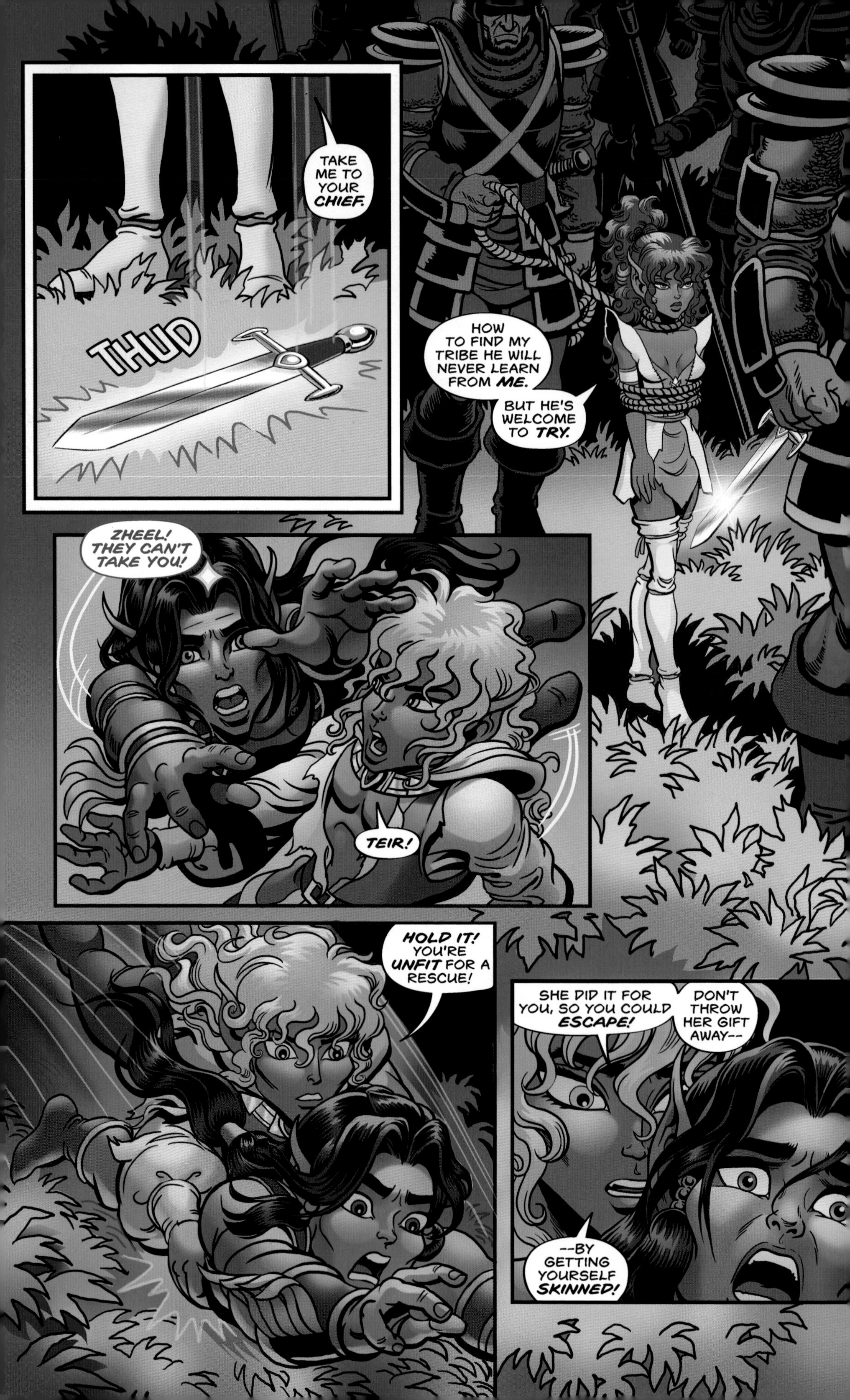
TAKE ME TO YOUR CHIEF.
THUD
HOW TO FIND MY TRIBE HE WILL NEVER LEARN FROM ME.
BUT HE'S WELCOME TO TRY.
ZHEEL! THEY CAN'T TAKE YOU!
TEIR!
HOLD IT! YOU'RE UNFIT FOR A RESCUE!
SHE DID IT FOR YOU, SO YOU COULD ESCAPE!
DON'T THROW HER GIFT AWAY--
--BY GETTING YOURSELF SKINNED!

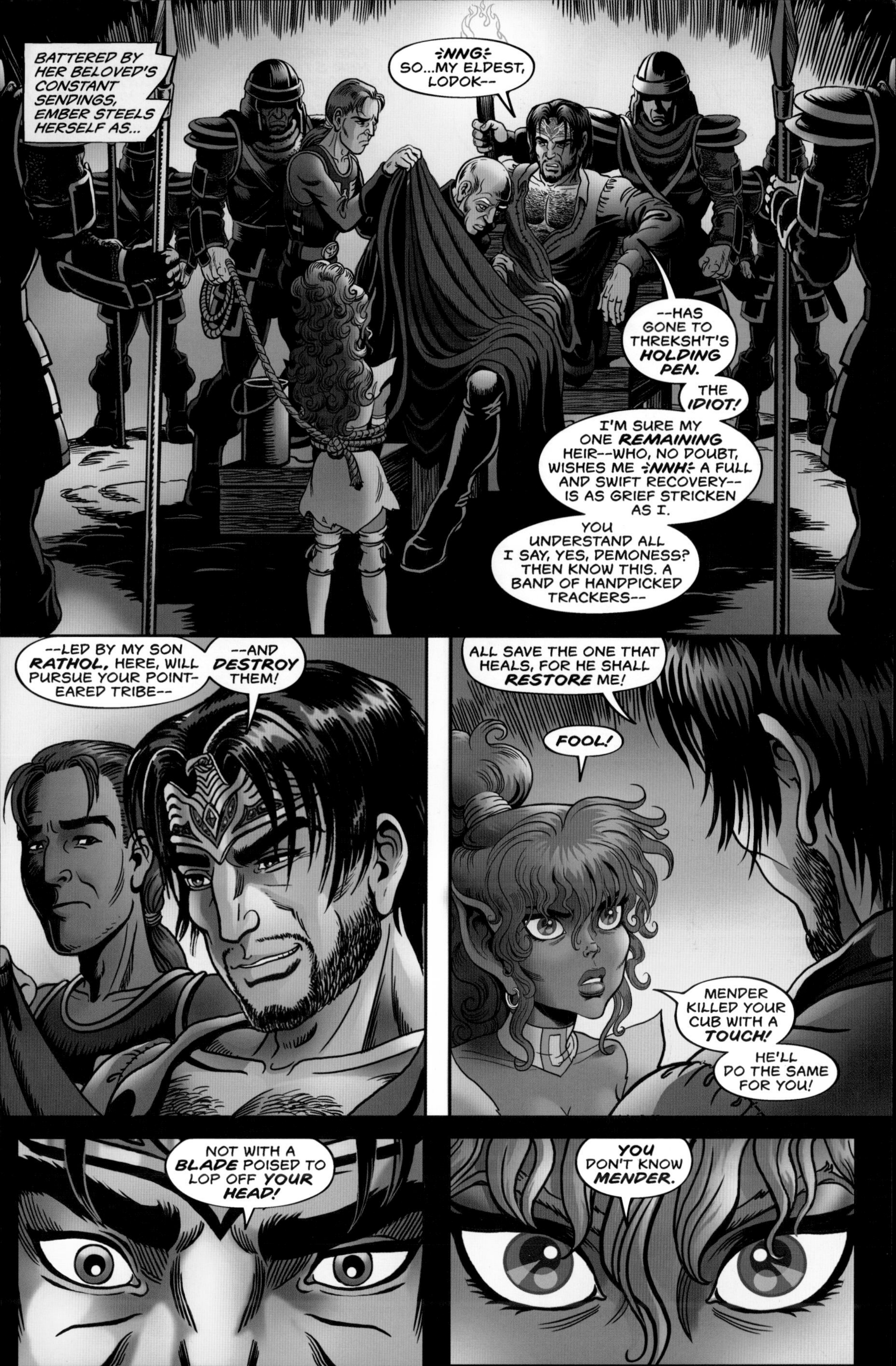
BATTERED BY HER BELOVED'S CONSTANT SENDINGS, EMBER STEELS HERSELF AS...
NNG SO...MY ELDEST, LODOK--
--HAS GONE TO THREKSH'T'S HOLDING PEN.
THE IDIOT!
I'M SURE MY ONE REMAINING HEIR--WHO, NO DOUBT, WISHES ME NNH A FULL AND SWIFT RECOVERY--IS AS GRIEF STRICKEN AS I.
YOU UNDERSTAND ALL I SAY, YES, DEMONESS? THEN KNOW THIS. A BAND OF HANDPICKED TRACKERS--
--LED BY MY SON RATHOL, HERE, WILL PURSUE YOUR POINT-EARED TRIBE--
--AND DESTROY THEM!
ALL SAVE THE ONE THAT HEALS, FOR HE SHALL RESTORE ME!
FOOL!
MENDER KILLED YOUR CUB WITH A TOUCH!
HE'LL DO THE SAME FOR YOU!
NOT WITH A BLADE POISED TO LOP OFF YOUR HEAD!
YOU DON'T KNOW MENDER.

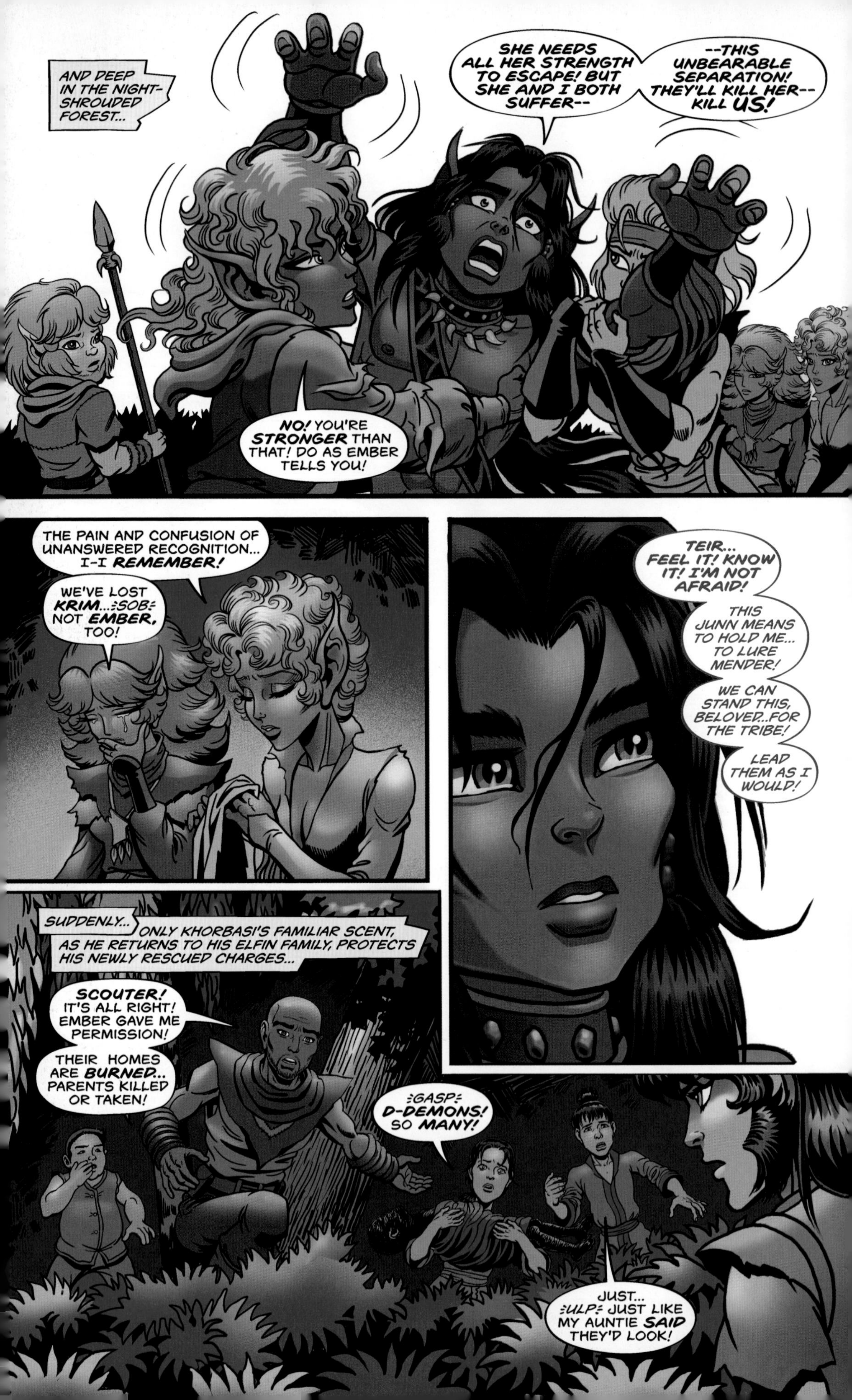
AND DEEP IN THE NIGHT-SHROUDED FOREST...
SHE NEEDS ALL HER STRENGTH TO ESCAPE! BUT SHE AND I BOTH SUFFER--
--THIS UNBEARABLE SEPARATION! THEY'LL KILL HER-- KILL US!
NO! YOU'RE STRONGER THAN THAT! DO AS EMBER TELLS YOU!
THE PAIN AND CONFUSION OF UNANSWERED RECOGNITION... I-I REMEMBER!
WE'VE LOST KRIM... SOB NOT EMBER, TOO!
TEIR... FEEL IT! KNOW IT! I'M NOT AFRAID!
THIS JUNN MEANS TO HOLD ME... TO LURE MENDER!
WE CAN STAND THIS, BELOVED...FOR THE TRIBE!
LEAD THEM AS I WOULD!
SUDDENLY...
ONLY KHORBASI'S FAMILIAR SCENT, AS HE RETURNS TO HIS ELFIN FAMILY, PROTECTS HIS NEWLY RESCUED CHARGES...
SCOUTER! IT'S ALL RIGHT! EMBER GAVE ME PERMISSION!
THEIR HOMES ARE BURNED... PARENTS KILLED OR TAKEN!
GASP D-DEMONS! SO MANY!
JUST... ULP JUST LIKE MY AUNTIE SAID THEY'D LOOK!

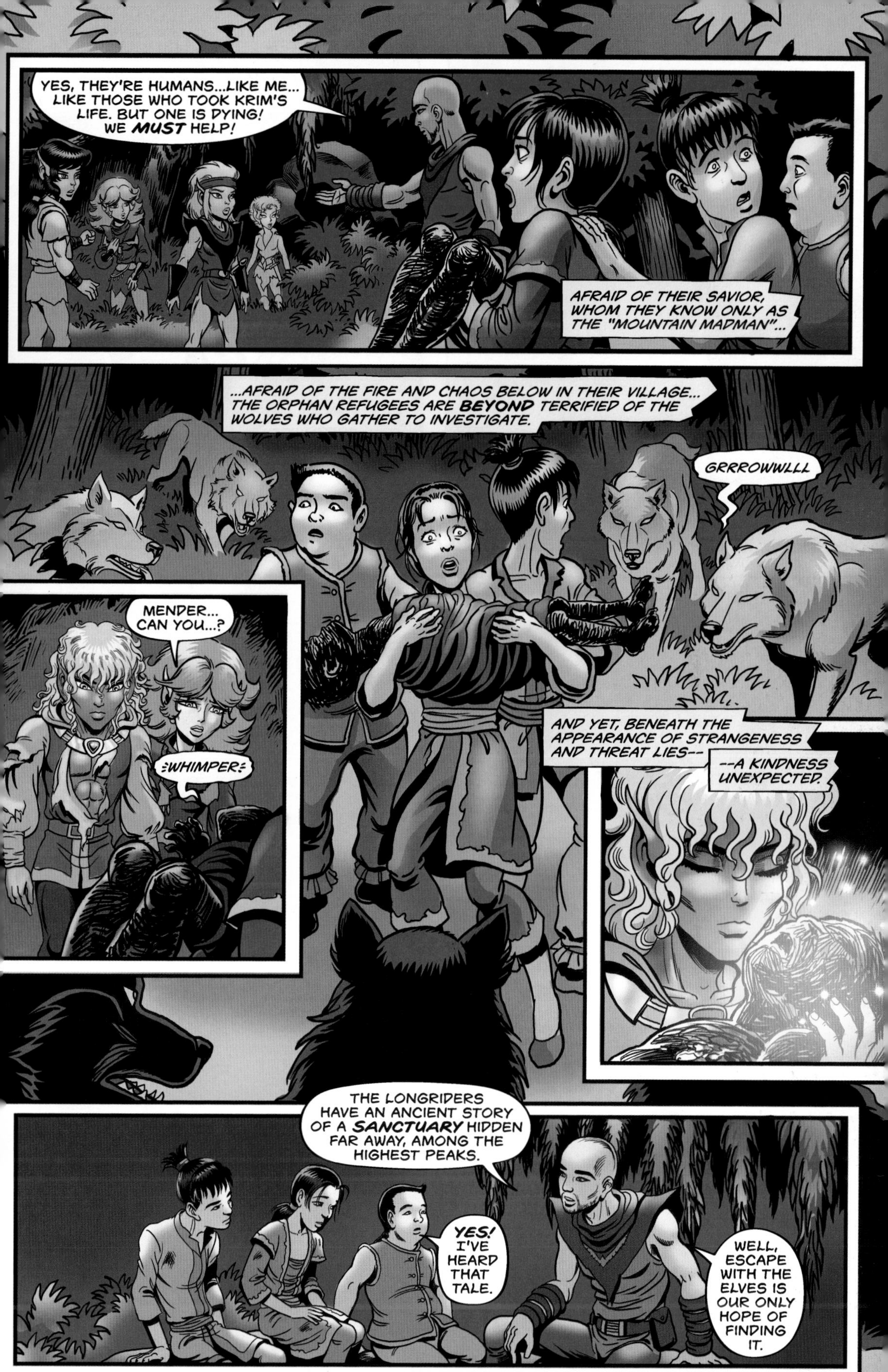
YES, THEY'RE HUMANS...LIKE ME... LIKE THOSE WHO TOOK KRIM'S LIFE. BUT ONE IS DYING! WE MUST HELP!
AFRAID OF THEIR SAVIOR, WHOM THEY KNOW ONLY AS THE "MOUNTAIN MADMAN"...
...AFRAID OF THE FIRE AND CHAOS BELOW IN THEIR VILLAGE... THE ORPHAN REFUGEES ARE BEYOND TERRIFIED OF THE WOLVES WHO GATHER TO INVESTIGATE.
GRRROWWLLL
MENDER... CAN YOU...?
:WHIMPER:
AND YET, BENEATH THE APPEARANCE OF STRANGENESS AND THREAT LIES--
--A KINDNESS UNEXPECTED.
THE LONGRIDERS HAVE AN ANCIENT STORY OF A SANCTUARY HIDDEN FAR AWAY, AMONG THE HIGHEST PEAKS.
YES! I'VE HEARD THAT TALE.
WELL, ESCAPE WITH THE ELVES IS OUR ONLY HOPE OF FINDING IT.

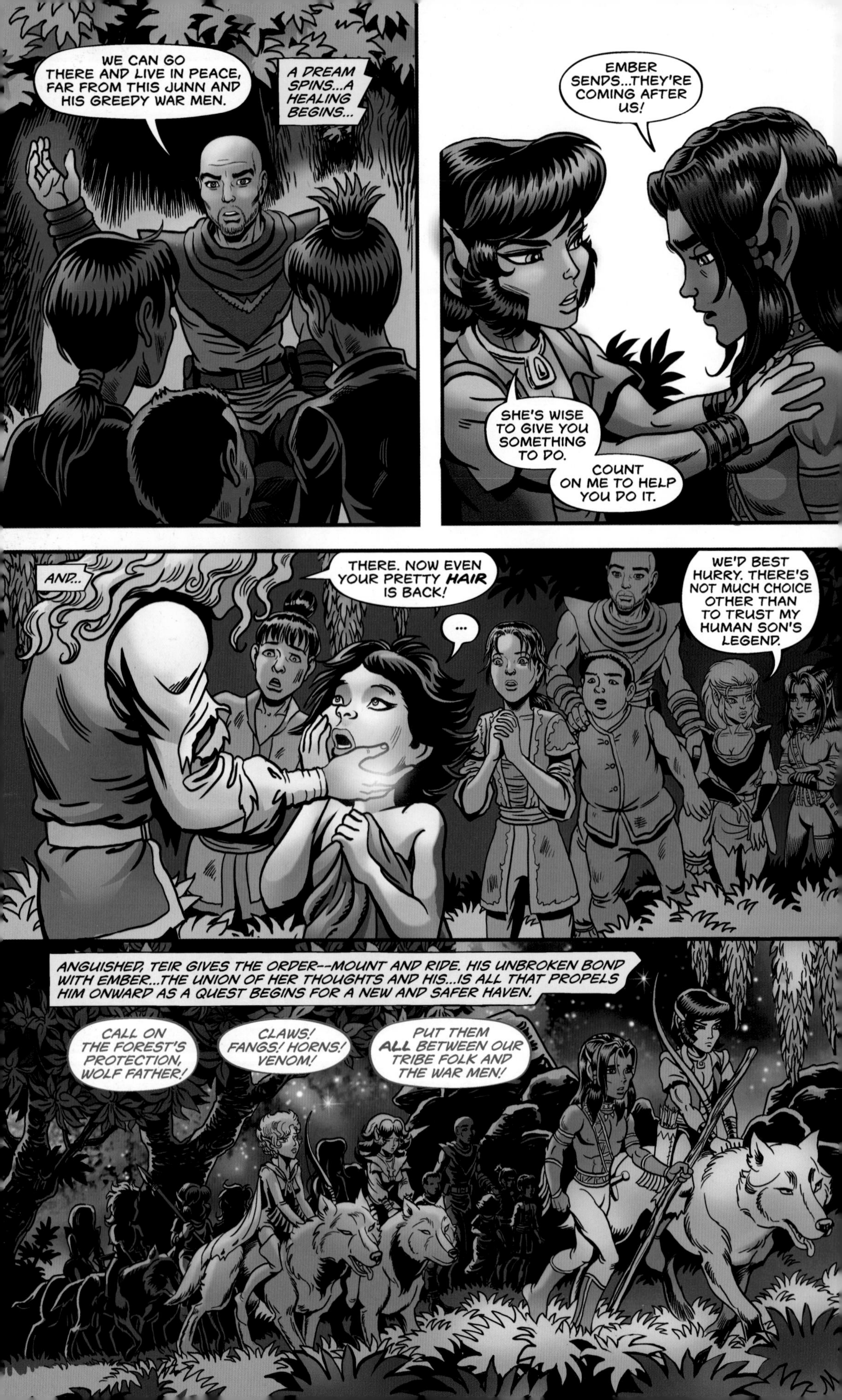
WE CAN GO THERE AND LIVE IN PEACE, FAR FROM THIS JUNN AND HIS GREEDY WAR MEN.
A DREAM SPINS...A HEALING BEGINS...
EMBER SENDS...THEY'RE COMING AFTER US!
SHE'S WISE TO GIVE YOU SOMETHING TO DO.
COUNT ON ME TO HELP YOU DO IT.
AND...
THERE. NOW EVEN YOUR PRETTY HAIR IS BACK!
...
WE'D BEST HURRY. THERE'S NOT MUCH CHOICE OTHER THAN TO TRUST MY HUMAN SON'S LEGEND.
ANGUISHED, TEIR GIVES THE ORDER--MOUNT AND RIDE. HIS UNBROKEN BOND WITH EMBER...THE UNION OF HER THOUGHTS AND HIS...IS ALL THAT PROPELS HIM ONWARD AS A QUEST BEGINS FOR A NEW AND SAFER HAVEN.
CALL ON THE FOREST'S PROTECTION, WOLF FATHER!
CLAWS! FANGS! HORNS! VENOM!
PUT THEM ALL BETWEEN OUR TRIBE FOLK AND THE WAR MEN!

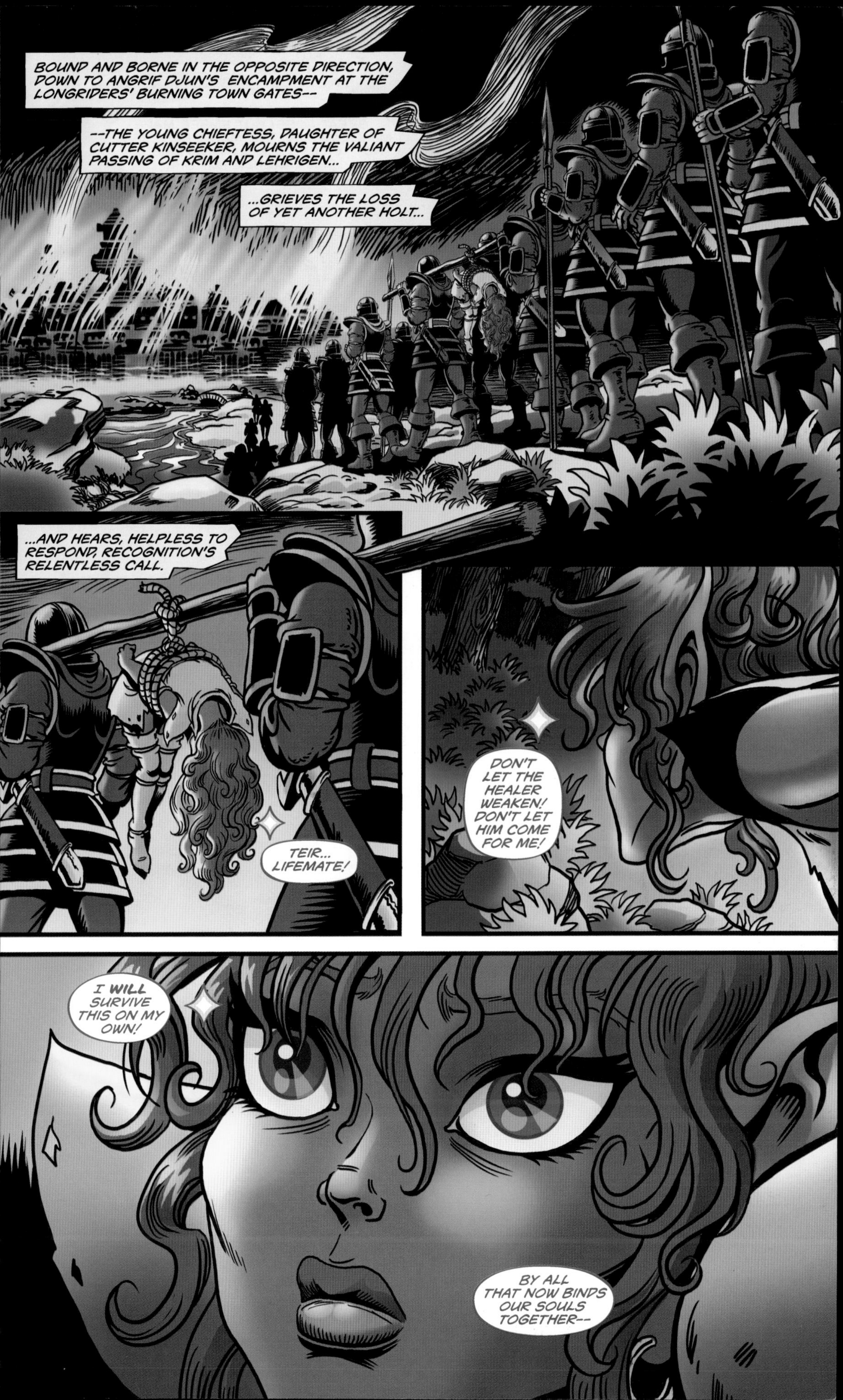
BOUND AND BORNE IN THE OPPOSITE DIRECTION, DOWN TO ANGRIF DJUN'S ENCAMPMENT AT THE LONGRIDERS' BURNING TOWN GATES--
--THE YOUNG CHIEFTESS, DAUGHTER OF CUTTER KINSEEKER, MOURNS THE VALIANT PASSING OF KRIM AND LEHRIGEN...
...GRIEVES THE LOSS OF YET ANOTHER HOLT...
...AND HEARS, HELPLESS TO RESPOND, RECOGNITION'S RELENTLESS CALL.
TEIR... LIFEMATE!
DON'T LET THE HEALER WEAKEN! DON'T LET HIM COME FOR ME!
I WILL SURVIVE THIS ON MY OWN!
BY ALL THAT NOW BINDS OUR SOULS TOGETHER--

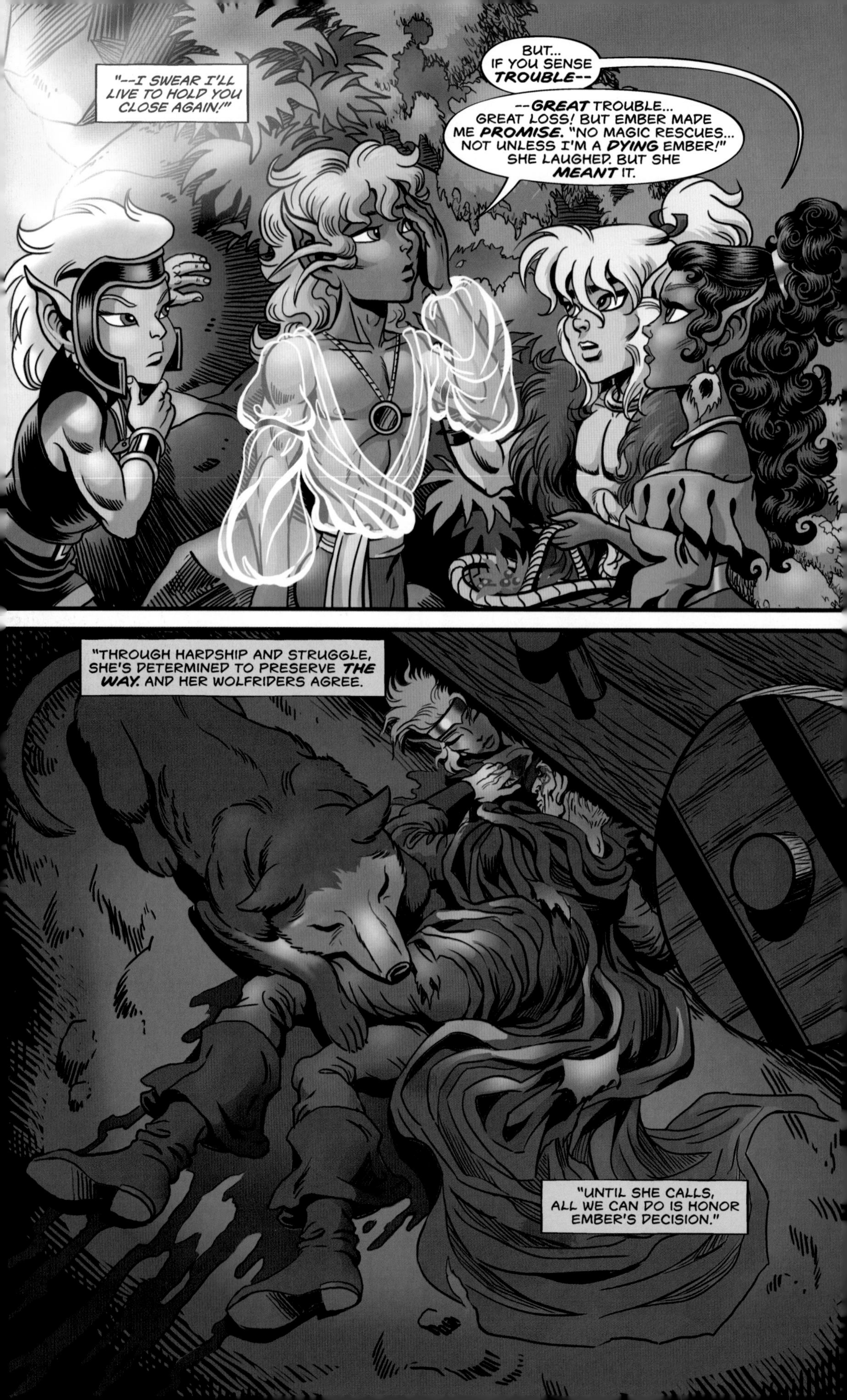
"--I SWEAR I'LL LIVE TO HOLD YOU CLOSE AGAIN!"
BUT... IF YOU SENSE TROUBLE--
--GREAT TROUBLE... GREAT LOSS! BUT EMBER MADE ME PROMISE. "NO MAGIC RESCUES... NOT UNLESS I'M A DYING EMBER!" SHE LAUGHED. BUT SHE MEANT IT.
"THROUGH HARDSHIP AND STRUGGLE, SHE'S DETERMINED TO PRESERVE THE WAY. AND HER WOLFRIDERS AGREE.
"UNTIL SHE CALLS, ALL WE CAN DO IS HONOR EMBER'S DECISION."

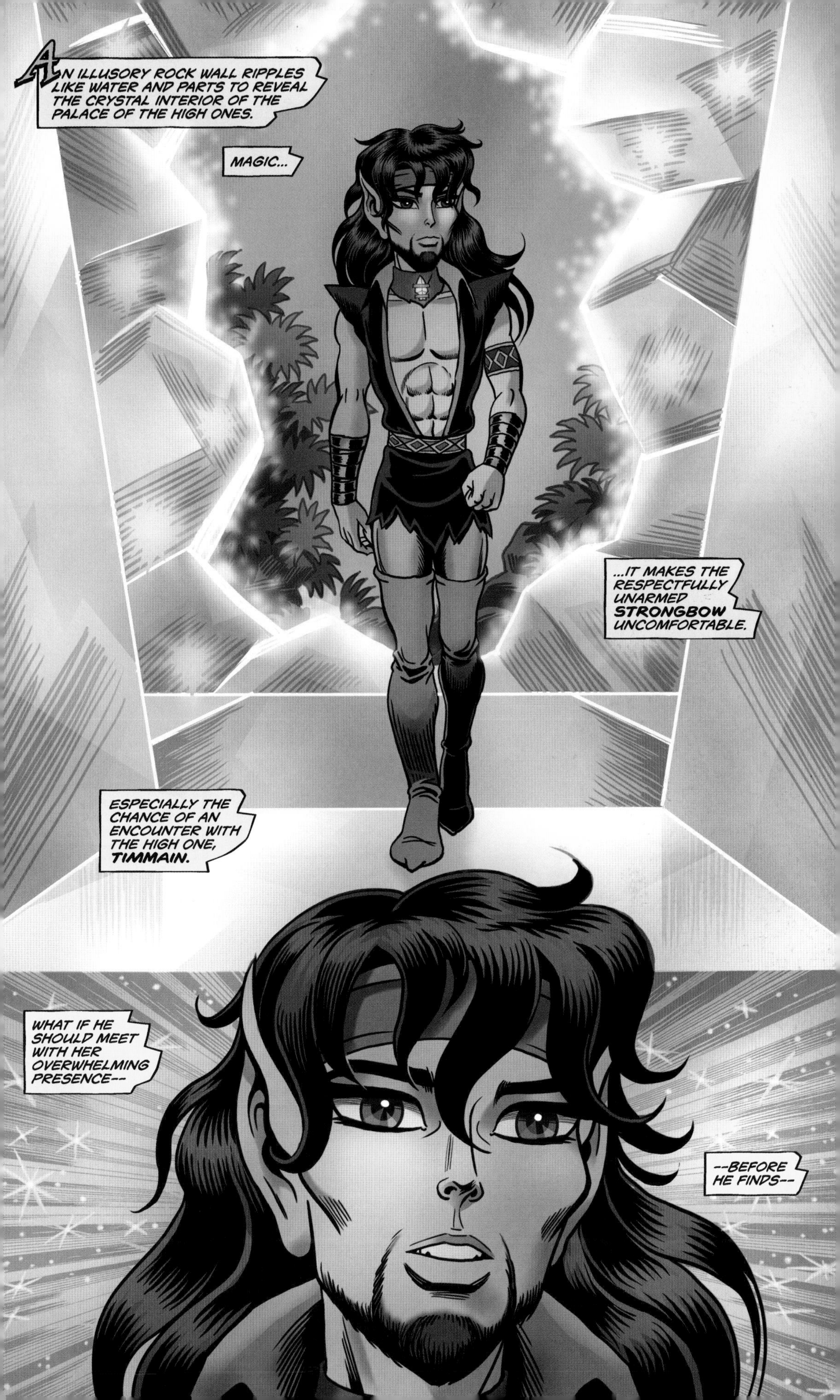
AN ILLUSORY ROCK WALL RIPPLES LIKE WATER AND PARTS TO REVEAL THE CRYSTAL INTERIOR OF THE PALACE OF THE HIGH ONES.
MAGIC...
...IT MAKES THE RESPECTFULLY UNARMED STRONGBOW UNCOMFORTABLE.
ESPECIALLY THE CHANCE OF AN ENCOUNTER WITH THE HIGH ONE, TIMMAIN.
WHAT IF HE SHOULD MEET WITH HER OVERWHELMING PRESENCE--
--BEFORE HE FINDS--

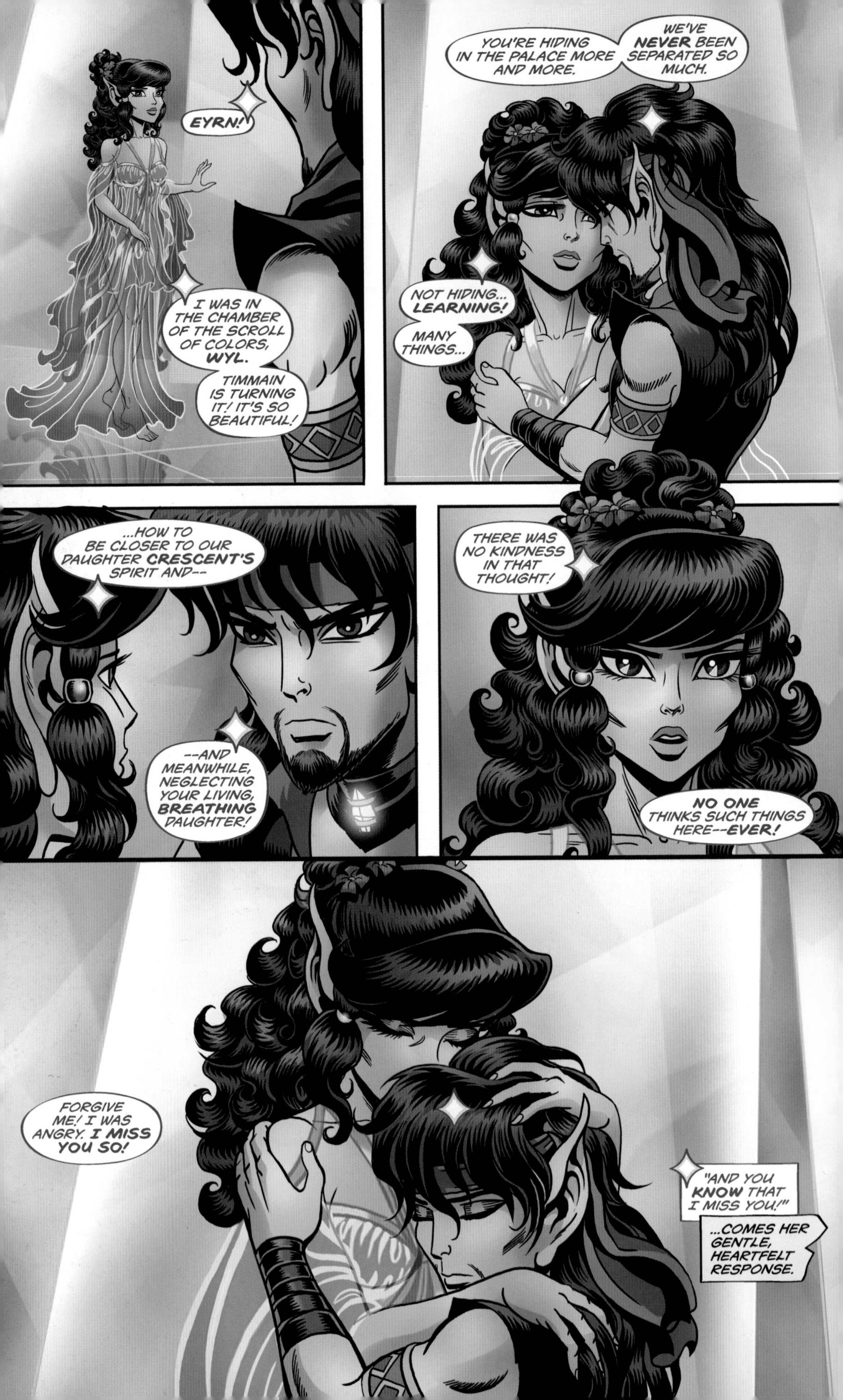
EYRN!
I WAS IN THE CHAMBER OF THE SCROLL OF COLORS, WYL.
TIMMAIN IS TURNING IT! IT'S SO BEAUTIFUL!
YOU'RE HIDING IN THE PALACE MORE AND MORE.
WE'VE NEVER BEEN SEPARATED SO MUCH.
NOT HIDING... LEARNING!
MANY THINGS...
...HOW TO BE CLOSER TO OUR DAUGHTER CRESCENT'S SPIRIT AND--
--AND MEANWHILE, NEGLECTING YOUR LIVING, BREATHING DAUGHTER!
THERE WAS NO KINDNESS IN THAT THOUGHT!
NO ONE THINKS SUCH THINGS HERE--EVER!
FORGIVE ME! I WAS ANGRY. I MISS YOU SO!
"AND YOU KNOW THAT I MISS YOU!"
...COMES HER GENTLE, HEARTFELT RESPONSE.

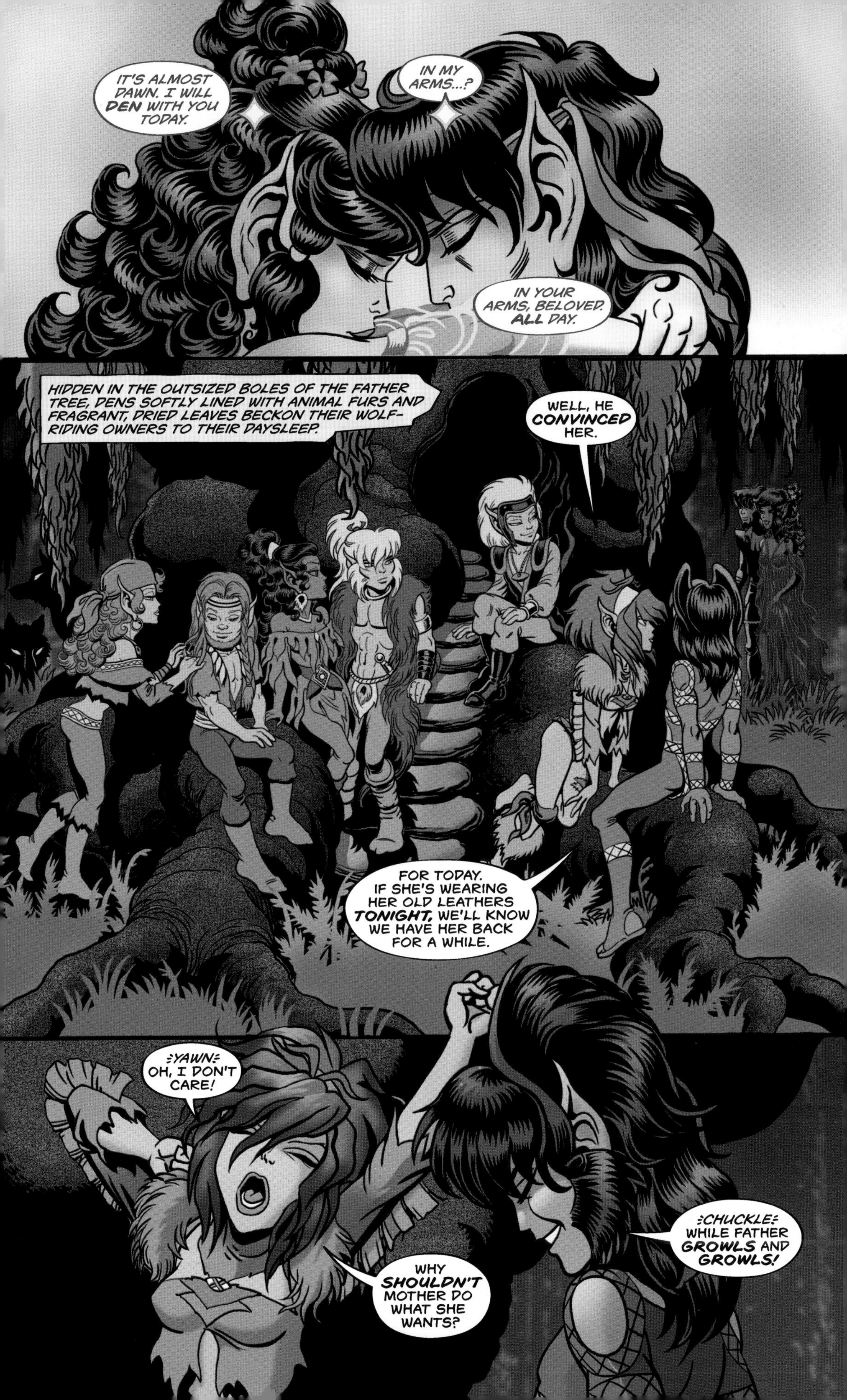
IT'S ALMOST DAWN. I WILL DEN WITH YOU TODAY.
IN MY ARMS...?
IN YOUR ARMS, BELOVED. ALL DAY.
HIDDEN IN THE OUTSIZED BOLES OF THE FATHER TREE, DENS SOFTLY LINED WITH ANIMAL FURS AND FRAGRANT, DRIED LEAVES BECKON THEIR WOLF-RIDING OWNERS TO THEIR DAYSLEEP.
WELL, HE CONVINCED HER.
FOR TODAY. IF SHE'S WEARING HER OLD LEATHERS TONIGHT, WE'LL KNOW WE HAVE HER BACK FOR A WHILE.
YAWN OH, I DON'T CARE!
WHY SHOULDN'T MOTHER DO WHAT SHE WANTS?
CHUCKLE WHILE FATHER GROWLS AND GROWLS!

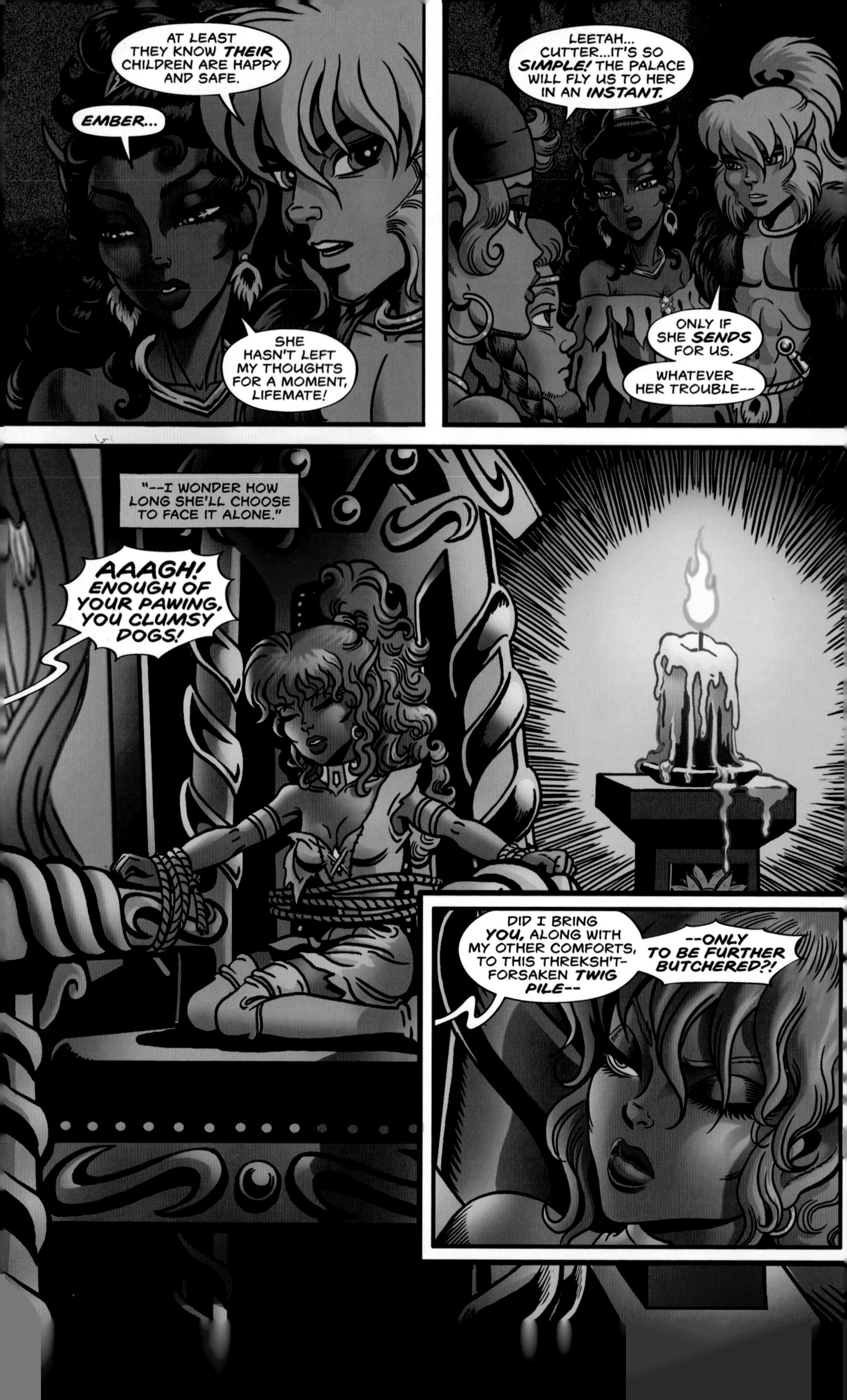
AT LEAST THEY KNOW THEIR CHILDREN ARE HAPPY AND SAFE.
EMBER...
SHE HASN'T LEFT MY THOUGHTS FOR A MOMENT, LIFEMATE!
LEETAH... CUTTER...IT'S SO SIMPLE! THE PALACE WILL FLY US TO HER IN AN INSTANT.
ONLY IF SHE SENDS FOR US.
WHATEVER HER TROUBLE--
"--I WONDER HOW LONG SHE'LL CHOOSE TO FACE IT ALONE."
AAAGH! ENOUGH OF YOUR PAWING, YOU CLUMSY DOGS!
DID I BRING YOU, ALONG WITH MY OTHER COMFORTS, TO THIS THREKSH'T-FORSAKEN TWIG PILE--
--ONLY TO BE FURTHER BUTCHERED?!

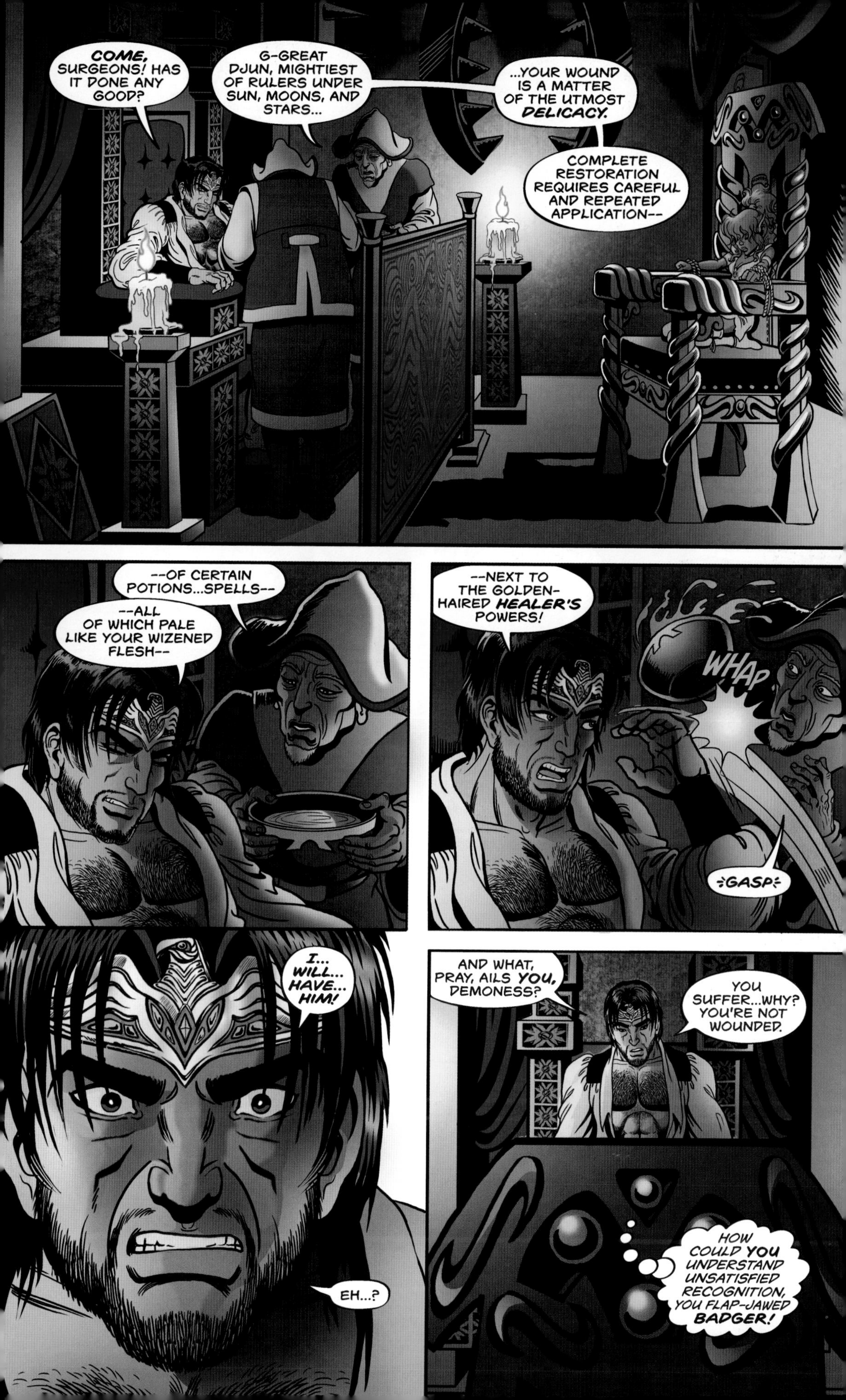
COME, SURGEONS! HAS IT DONE ANY GOOD?
G-GREAT DJUN, MIGHTIEST OF RULERS UNDER SUN, MOONS, AND STARS...
...YOUR WOUND IS A MATTER OF THE UTMOST DELICACY.
COMPLETE RESTORATION REQUIRES CAREFUL AND REPEATED APPLICATION--
--OF CERTAIN POTIONS...SPELLS--
--ALL OF WHICH PALE LIKE YOUR WIZENED FLESH--
--NEXT TO THE GOLDEN-HAIRED HEALER'S POWERS!
WHAP
GASP
I... WILL... HAVE... HIM!
EH...?
AND WHAT, PRAY, AILS YOU, DEMONESS?
YOU SUFFER...WHY? YOU'RE NOT WOUNDED.
HOW COULD YOU UNDERSTAND UNSATISFIED RECOGNITION, YOU FLAP-JAWED BADGER!

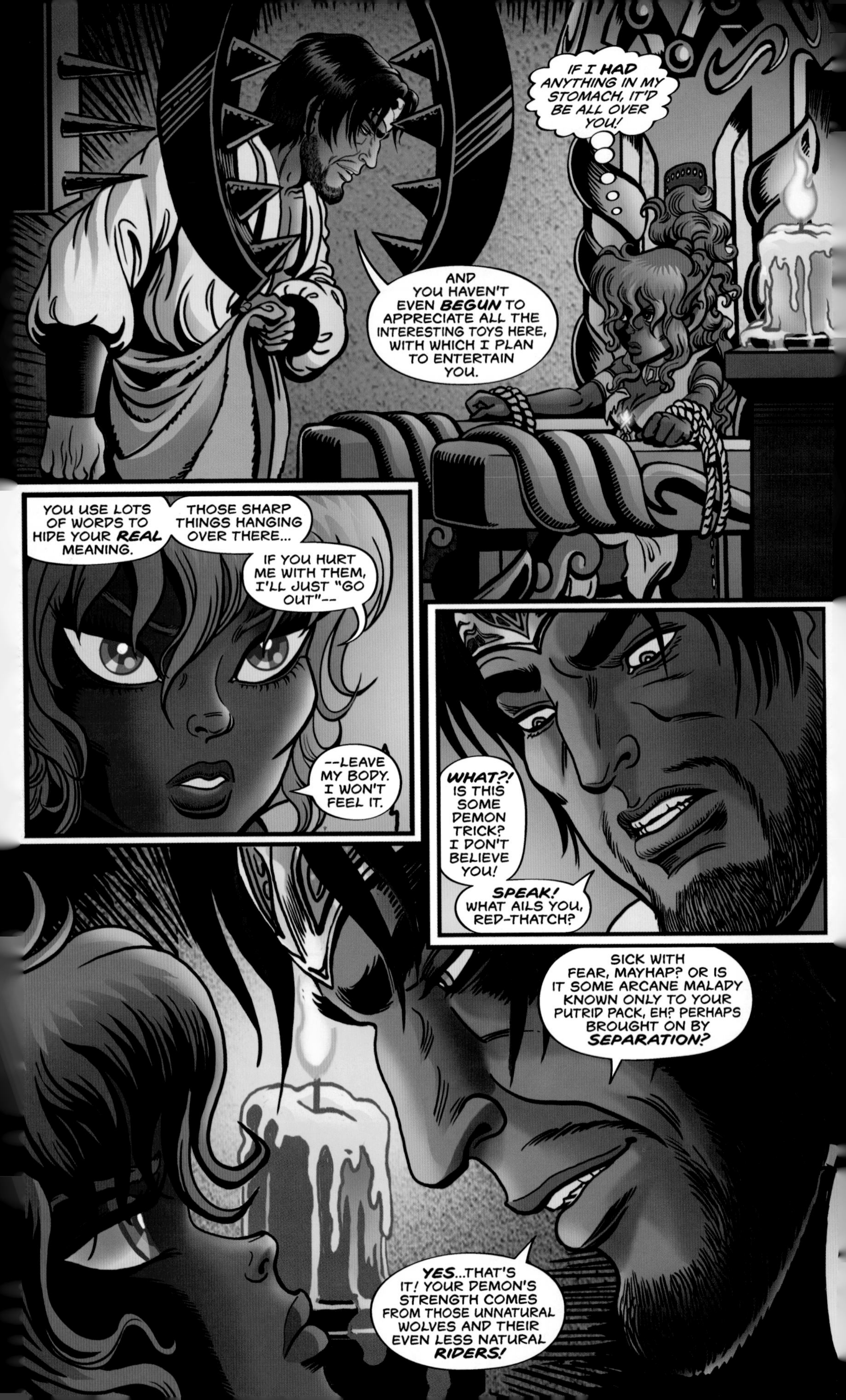

IF I HAD ANYTHING IN MY STOMACH, IT'D BE ALL OVER YOU!
AND YOU HAVEN'T EVEN BEGUN TO APPRECIATE ALL THE INTERESTING TOYS HERE, WITH WHICH I PLAN TO ENTERTAIN YOU.
YOU USE LOTS OF WORDS TO HIDE YOUR REAL MEANING.
THOSE SHARP THINGS HANGING OVER THERE...
IF YOU HURT ME WITH THEM, I'LL JUST "GO OUT"--
--LEAVE MY BODY. I WON'T FEEL IT.
WHAT?! IS THIS SOME DEMON TRICK? I DON'T BELIEVE YOU!
SPEAK! WHAT AILS YOU, RED-THATCH?
SICK WITH FEAR, MAYHAP? OR IS IT SOME ARCANE MALADY KNOWN ONLY TO YOUR PUTRID PACK, EH? PERHAPS BROUGHT ON BY SEPARATION?
YES...THAT'S IT! YOUR DEMON'S STRENGTH COMES FROM THOSE UNNATURAL WOLVES AND THEIR EVEN LESS NATURAL RIDERS!

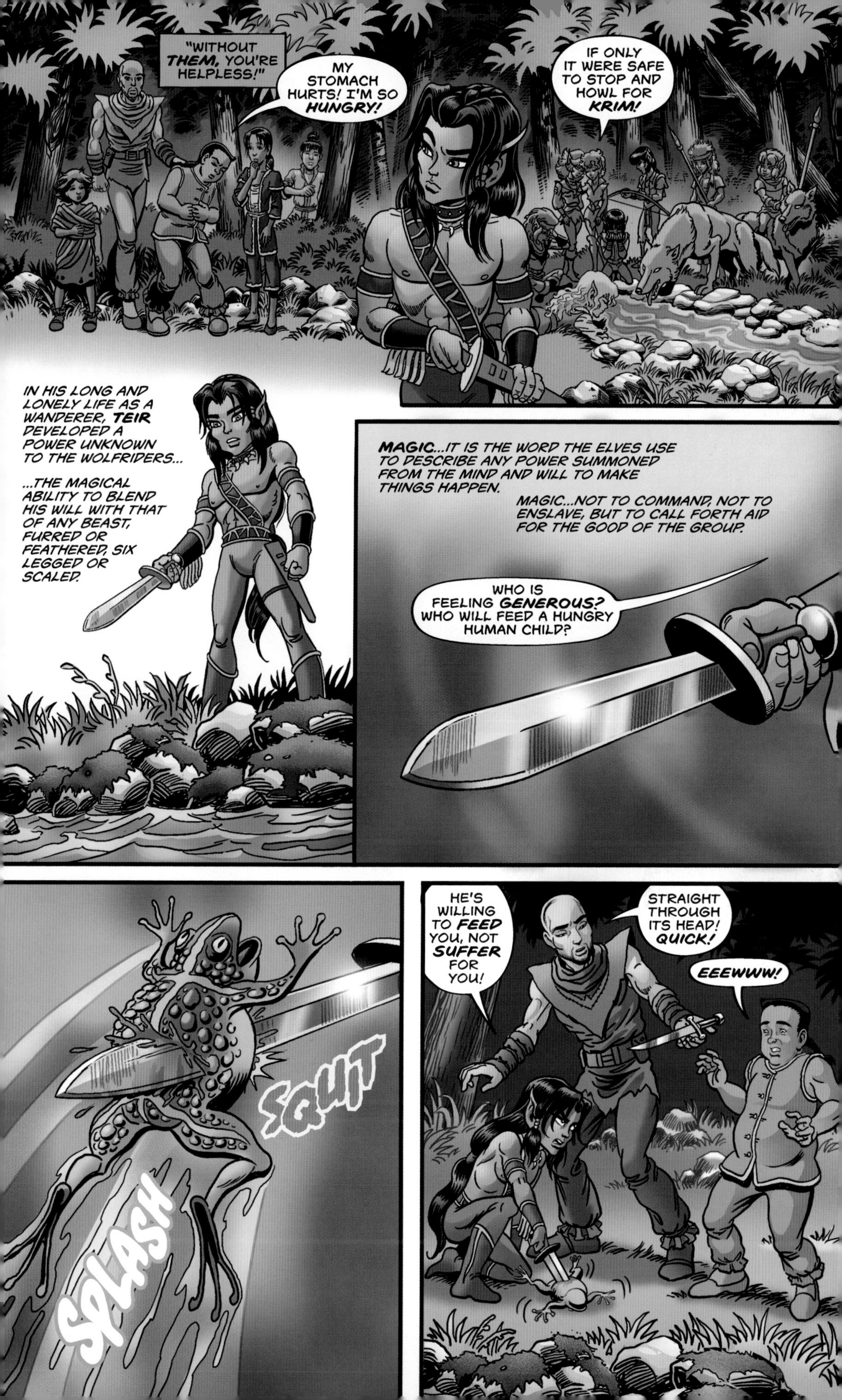
"WITHOUT THEM, YOU'RE HELPLESS!"
MY STOMACH HURTS! I'M SO HUNGRY!
IF ONLY IT WERE SAFE TO STOP AND HOWL FOR KRIM!
IN HIS LONG AND LONELY LIFE AS A WANDERER, TEIR DEVELOPED A POWER UNKNOWN TO THE WOLFRIDERS...
...THE MAGICAL ABILITY TO BLEND HIS WILL WITH THAT OF ANY BEAST, FURRED OR FEATHERED, SIX LEGGED OR SCALED.
MAGIC...IT IS THE WORD THE ELVES USE TO DESCRIBE ANY POWER SUMMONED FROM THE MIND AND WILL TO MAKE THINGS HAPPEN.
MAGIC...NOT TO COMMAND, NOT TO ENSLAVE, BUT TO CALL FORTH AID FOR THE GOOD OF THE GROUP.
WHO IS FEELING GENEROUS? WHO WILL FEED A HUNGRY HUMAN CHILD?
SQUIT
SPLASH
HE'S WILLING TO FEED YOU, NOT SUFFER FOR YOU!
STRAIGHT THROUGH ITS HEAD! QUICK!
EEEWWW!

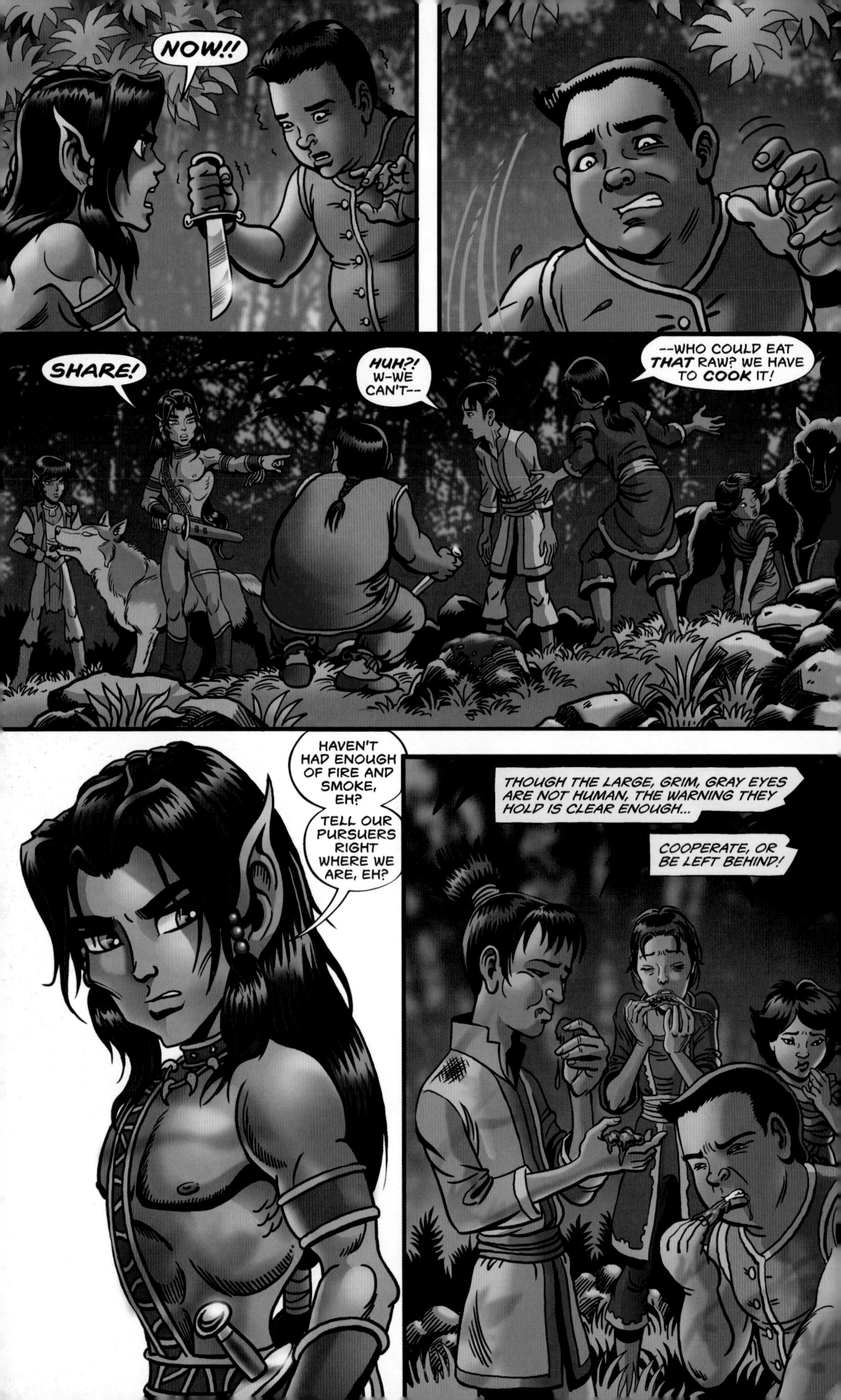
NOW!!
SHARE!
HUH?! W-WE CAN'T--
--WHO COULD EAT THAT RAW? WE HAVE TO COOK IT!
HAVEN'T HAD ENOUGH OF FIRE AND SMOKE, EH?
TELL OUR PURSUERS RIGHT WHERE WE ARE, EH?
THOUGH THE LARGE, GRIM, GRAY EYES ARE NOT HUMAN, THE WARNING THEY HOLD IS CLEAR ENOUGH...
COOPERATE, OR BE LEFT BEHIND!

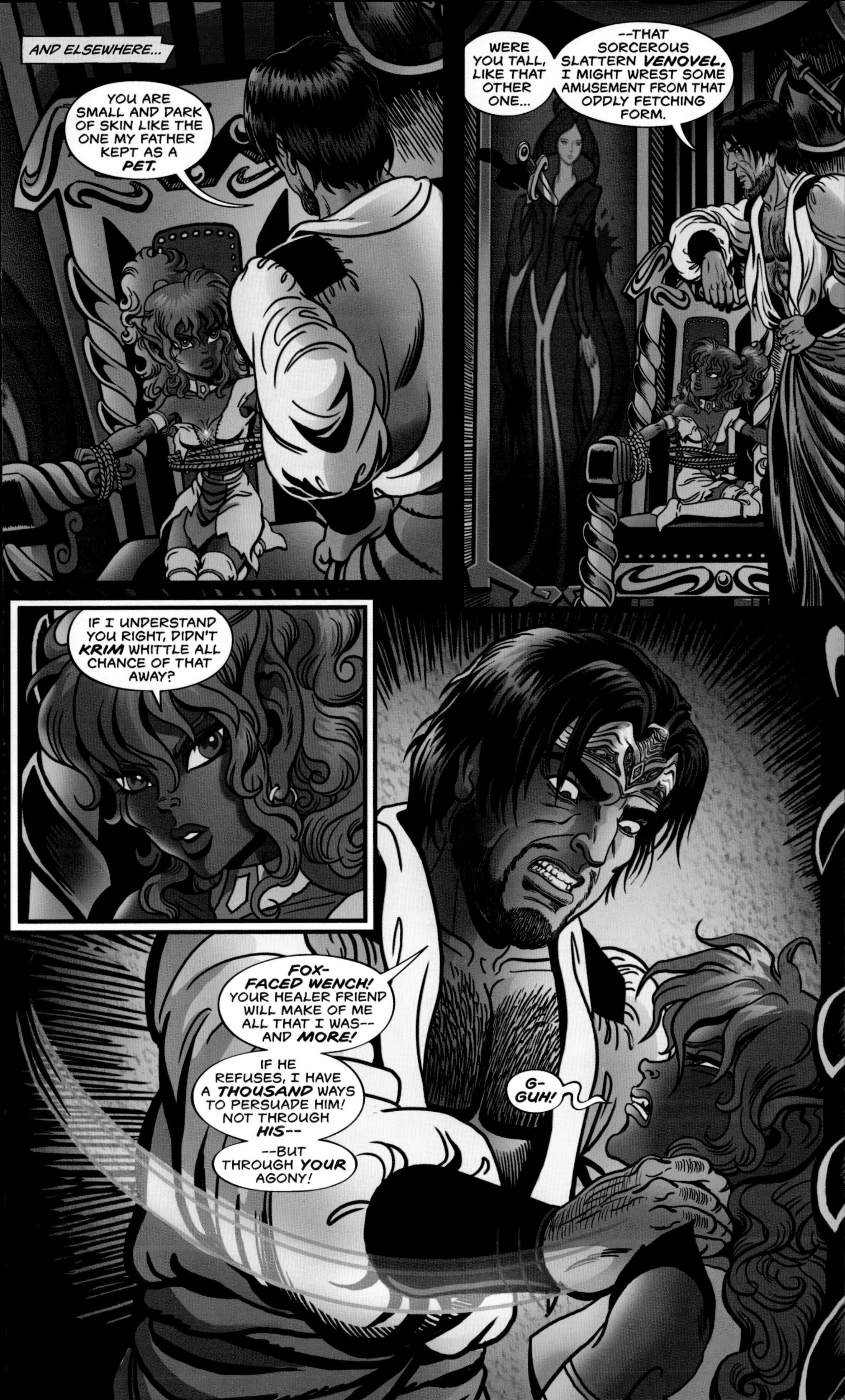
AND ELSEWHERE...
YOU ARE SMALL AND DARK OF SKIN LIKE THE ONE MY FATHER KEPT AS A PET.
WERE YOU TALL, LIKE THAT OTHER ONE...
--THAT SORCEROUS SLATTERN VENOVEL, I MIGHT WREST SOME AMUSEMENT FROM THAT ODDLY FETCHING FORM.
IF I UNDERSTAND YOU RIGHT, DIDN'T KRIM WHITTLE ALL CHANCE OF THAT AWAY?
FOX-FACED WENCH! YOUR HEALER FRIEND WILL MAKE OF ME ALL THAT I WAS-- AND MORE!
IF HE REFUSES, I HAVE A THOUSAND WAYS TO PERSUADE HIM! NOT THROUGH HIS--
--BUT THROUGH YOUR AGONY!
G-GUH!

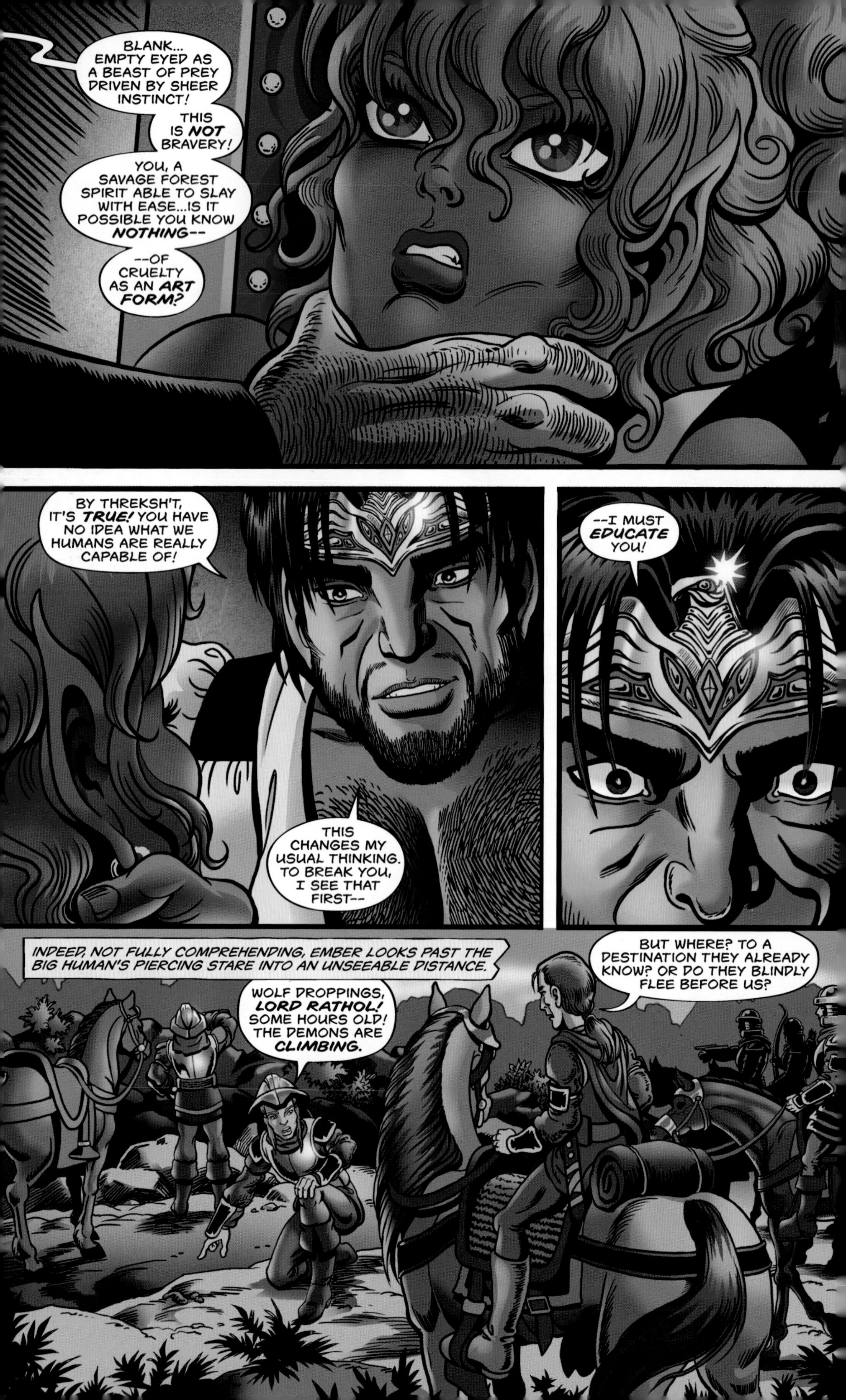

BLANK... EMPTY EYED AS A BEAST OF PREY DRIVEN BY SHEER INSTINCT!
THIS IS NOT BRAVERY!
YOU, A SAVAGE FOREST SPIRIT ABLE TO SLAY WITH EASE...IS IT POSSIBLE YOU KNOW NOTHING--
--OF CRUELTY AS AN ART FORM?
BY THREKSH'T, IT'S TRUE! YOU HAVE NO IDEA WHAT WE HUMANS ARE REALLY CAPABLE OF!
THIS CHANGES MY USUAL THINKING. TO BREAK YOU, I SEE THAT FIRST--
--I MUST EDUCATE YOU!
INDEED, NOT FULLY COMPREHENDING, EMBER LOOKS PAST THE BIG HUMAN'S PIERCING STARE INTO AN UNSEEABLE DISTANCE.
WOLF DROPPINGS, LORD RATHOL! SOME HOURS OLD! THE DEMONS ARE CLIMBING.
BUT WHERE? TO A DESTINATION THEY ALREADY KNOW? OR DO THEY BLINDLY FLEE BEFORE US?

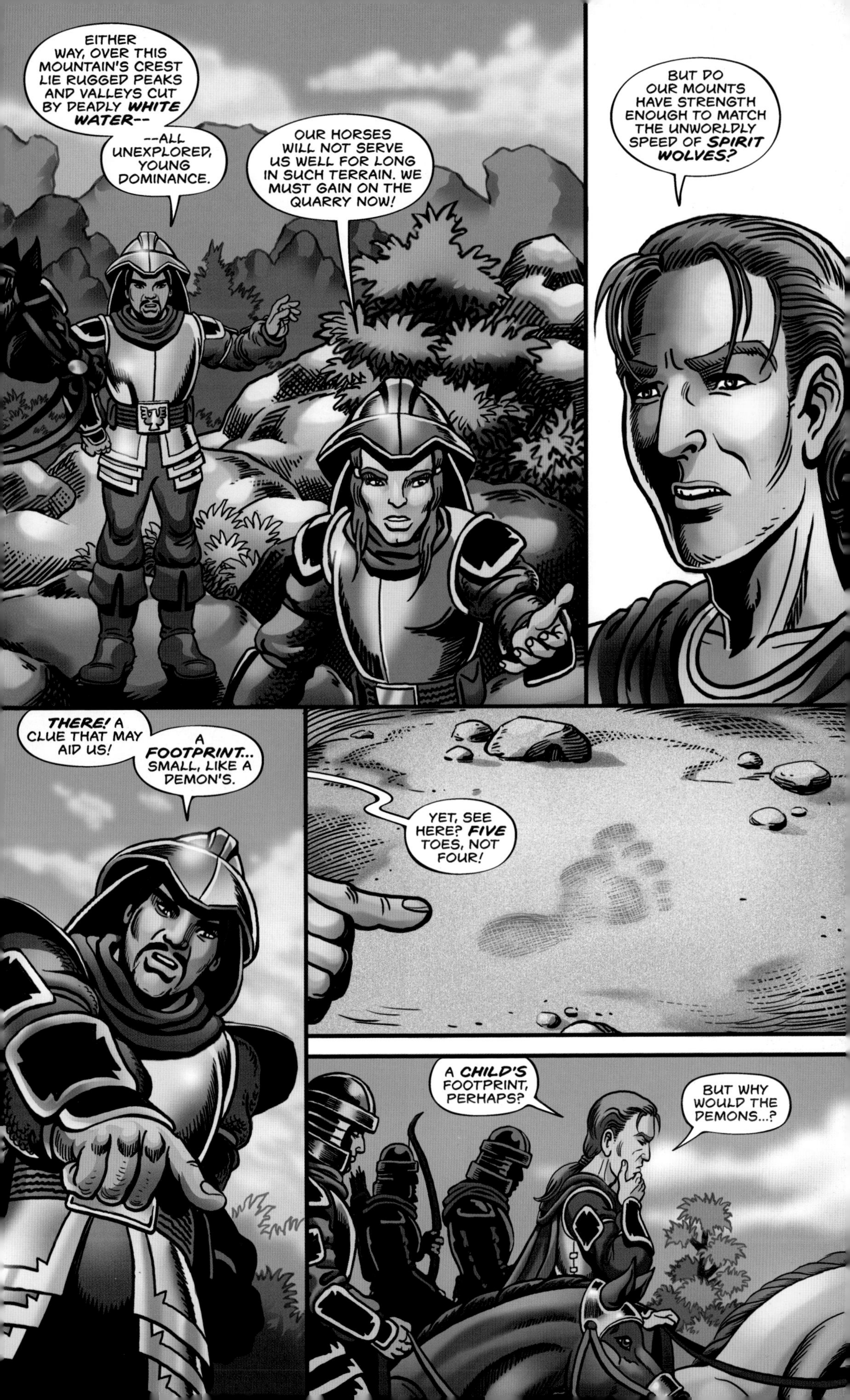
EITHER WAY, OVER THIS MOUNTAIN'S CREST LIE RUGGED PEAKS AND VALLEYS CUT BY DEADLY **WHITE WATER--**
--ALL UNEXPLORED, YOUNG DOMINANCE.
OUR HORSES WILL NOT SERVE US WELL FOR LONG IN SUCH TERRAIN. WE MUST GAIN ON THE QUARRY NOW!
BUT DO OUR MOUNTS HAVE STRENGTH ENOUGH TO MATCH THE UNWORLDLY SPEED OF **SPIRIT WOLVES?**
THERE! A CLUE THAT MAY AID US!
A **FOOTPRINT...** SMALL, LIKE A DEMON'S.
YET, SEE HERE? **FIVE** TOES, NOT FOUR!
A **CHILD'S** FOOTPRINT, PERHAPS?
BUT WHY WOULD THE DEMONS...?

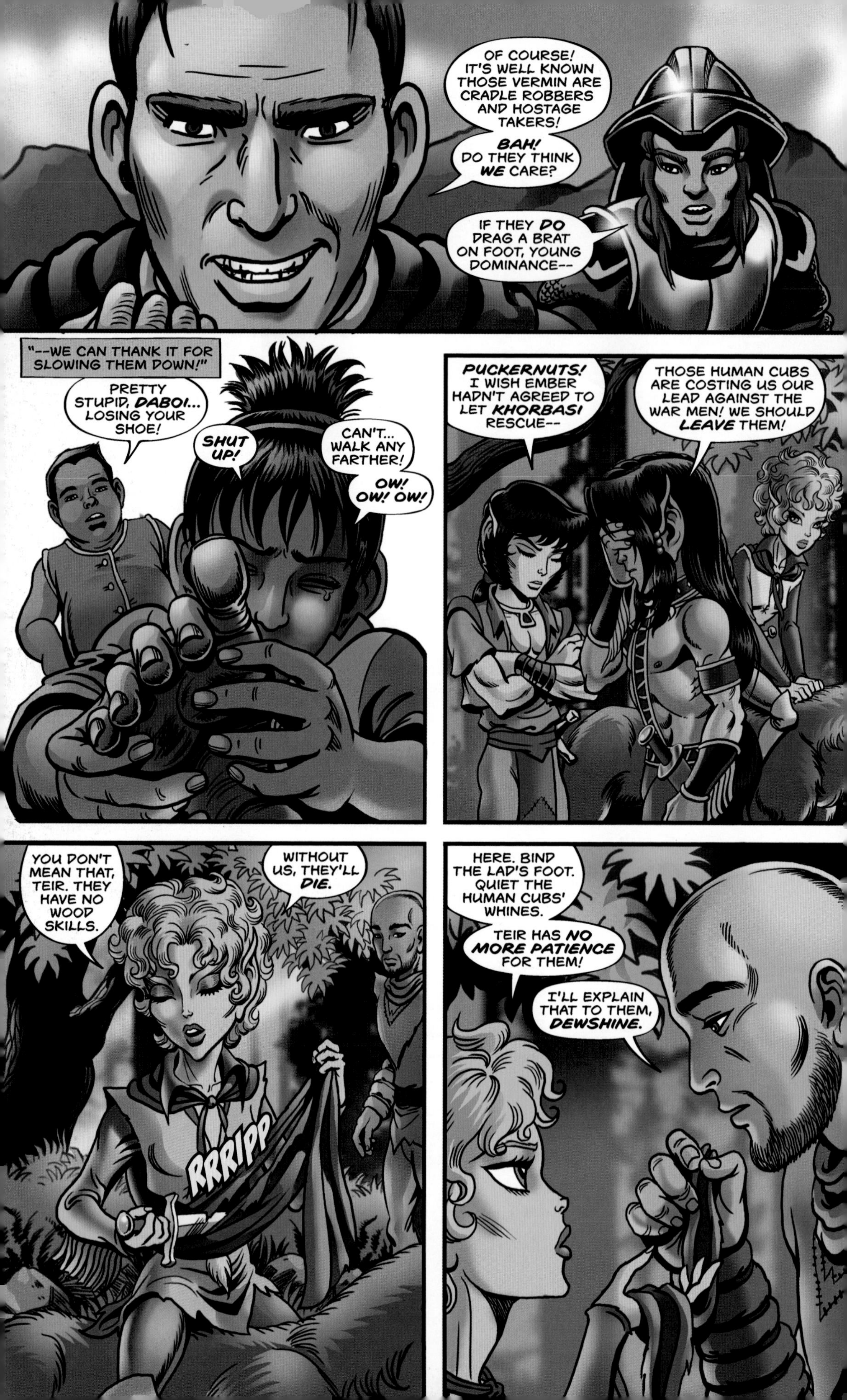
OF COURSE! IT'S WELL KNOWN THOSE VERMIN ARE CRADLE ROBBERS AND HOSTAGE TAKERS!
BAH! DO THEY THINK WE CARE?
IF THEY DO DRAG A BRAT ON FOOT, YOUNG DOMINANCE--
"--WE CAN THANK IT FOR SLOWING THEM DOWN!"
PRETTY STUPID, DABOI... LOSING YOUR SHOE!
SHUT UP!
CAN'T... WALK ANY FARTHER!
OW! OW! OW!
PUCKERNUTS! I WISH EMBER HADN'T AGREED TO LET KHORBASI RESCUE--
THOSE HUMAN CUBS ARE COSTING US OUR LEAD AGAINST THE WAR MEN! WE SHOULD LEAVE THEM!
YOU DON'T MEAN THAT, TEIR. THEY HAVE NO WOOD SKILLS.
WITHOUT US, THEY'LL DIE.
RRRIPP
HERE. BIND THE LAD'S FOOT. QUIET THE HUMAN CUBS' WHINES.
TEIR HAS NO MORE PATIENCE FOR THEM!
I'LL EXPLAIN THAT TO THEM, DEWSHINE.

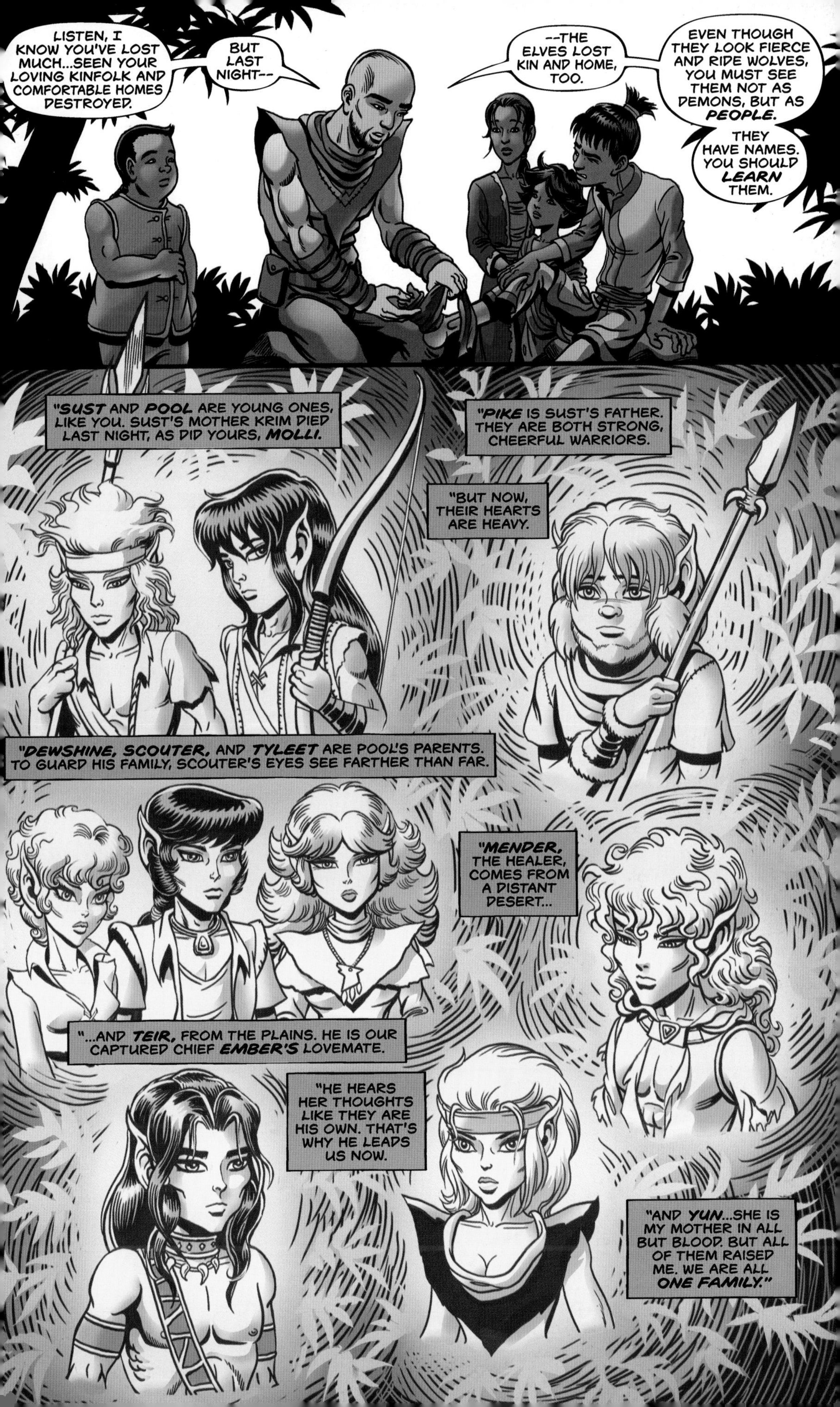
LISTEN, I KNOW YOU'VE LOST MUCH...SEEN YOUR LOVING KINFOLK AND COMFORTABLE HOMES DESTROYED.
BUT LAST NIGHT--
--THE ELVES LOST KIN AND HOME, TOO.
EVEN THOUGH THEY LOOK FIERCE AND RIDE WOLVES, YOU MUST SEE THEM NOT AS DEMONS, BUT AS PEOPLE.
THEY HAVE NAMES. YOU SHOULD LEARN THEM.
"SUST AND POOL ARE YOUNG ONES, LIKE YOU. SUST'S MOTHER KRIM DIED LAST NIGHT, AS DID YOURS, MOLLI.
"PIKE IS SUST'S FATHER. THEY ARE BOTH STRONG, CHEERFUL WARRIORS.
"BUT NOW, THEIR HEARTS ARE HEAVY.
"DEWSHINE, SCOUTER, AND TYLEET ARE POOL'S PARENTS. TO GUARD HIS FAMILY, SCOUTER'S EYES SEE FARTHER THAN FAR.
"MENDER, THE HEALER, COMES FROM A DISTANT DESERT...
"...AND TEIR, FROM THE PLAINS. HE IS OUR CAPTURED CHIEF EMBER'S LOVEMATE.
"HE HEARS HER THOUGHTS LIKE THEY ARE HIS OWN. THAT'S WHY HE LEADS US NOW.
"AND YUN...SHE IS MY MOTHER IN ALL BUT BLOOD. BUT ALL OF THEM RAISED ME. WE ARE ALL ONE FAMILY."

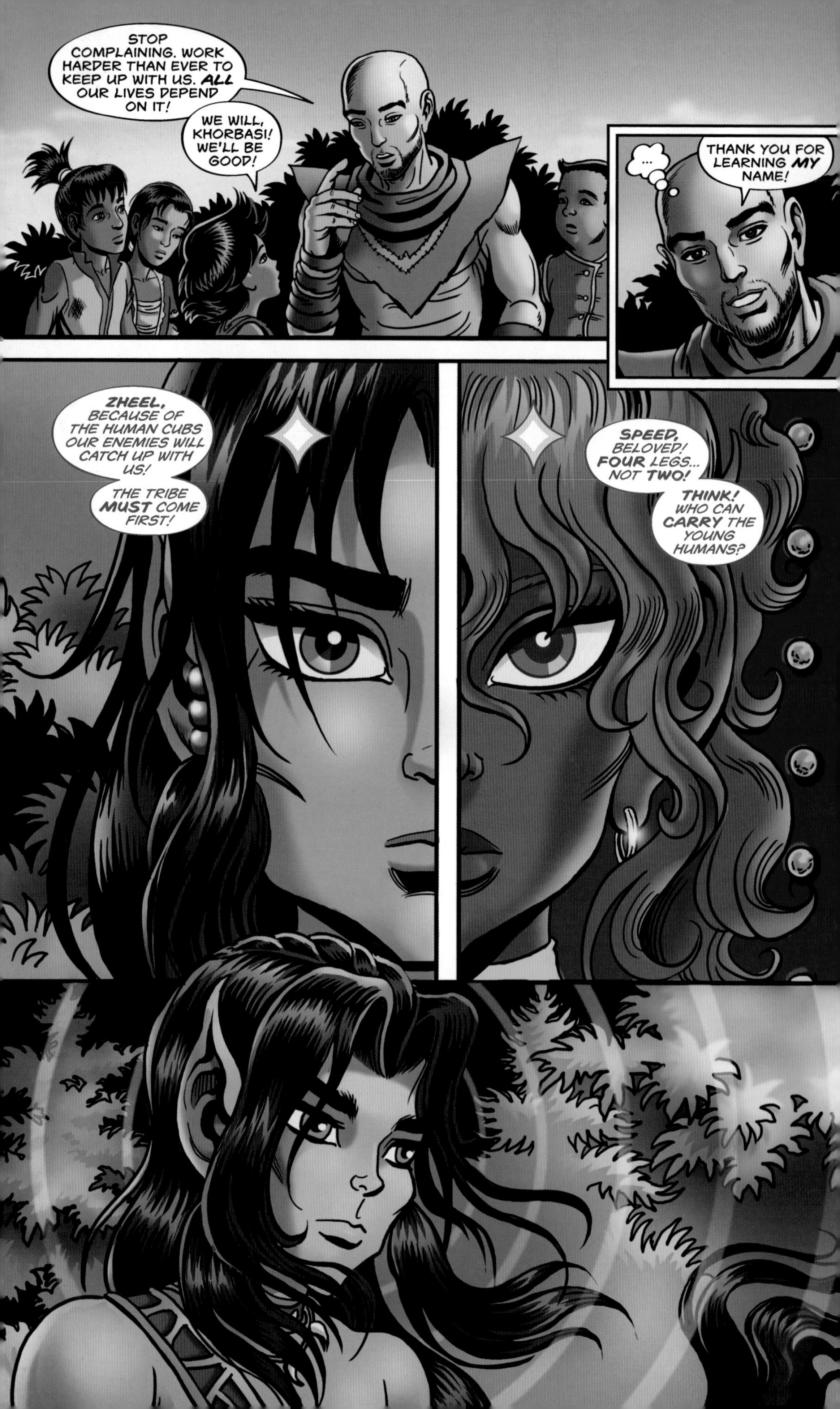
STOP COMPLAINING. WORK HARDER THAN EVER TO KEEP UP WITH US. ALL OUR LIVES DEPEND ON IT!
WE WILL, KHORBASI! WE'LL BE GOOD!
...
THANK YOU FOR LEARNING MY NAME!
ZHEEL, BECAUSE OF THE HUMAN CUBS OUR ENEMIES WILL CATCH UP WITH US!
THE TRIBE MUST COME FIRST!
SPEED, BELOVED! FOUR LEGS... NOT TWO!
THINK! WHO CAN CARRY THE YOUNG HUMANS?

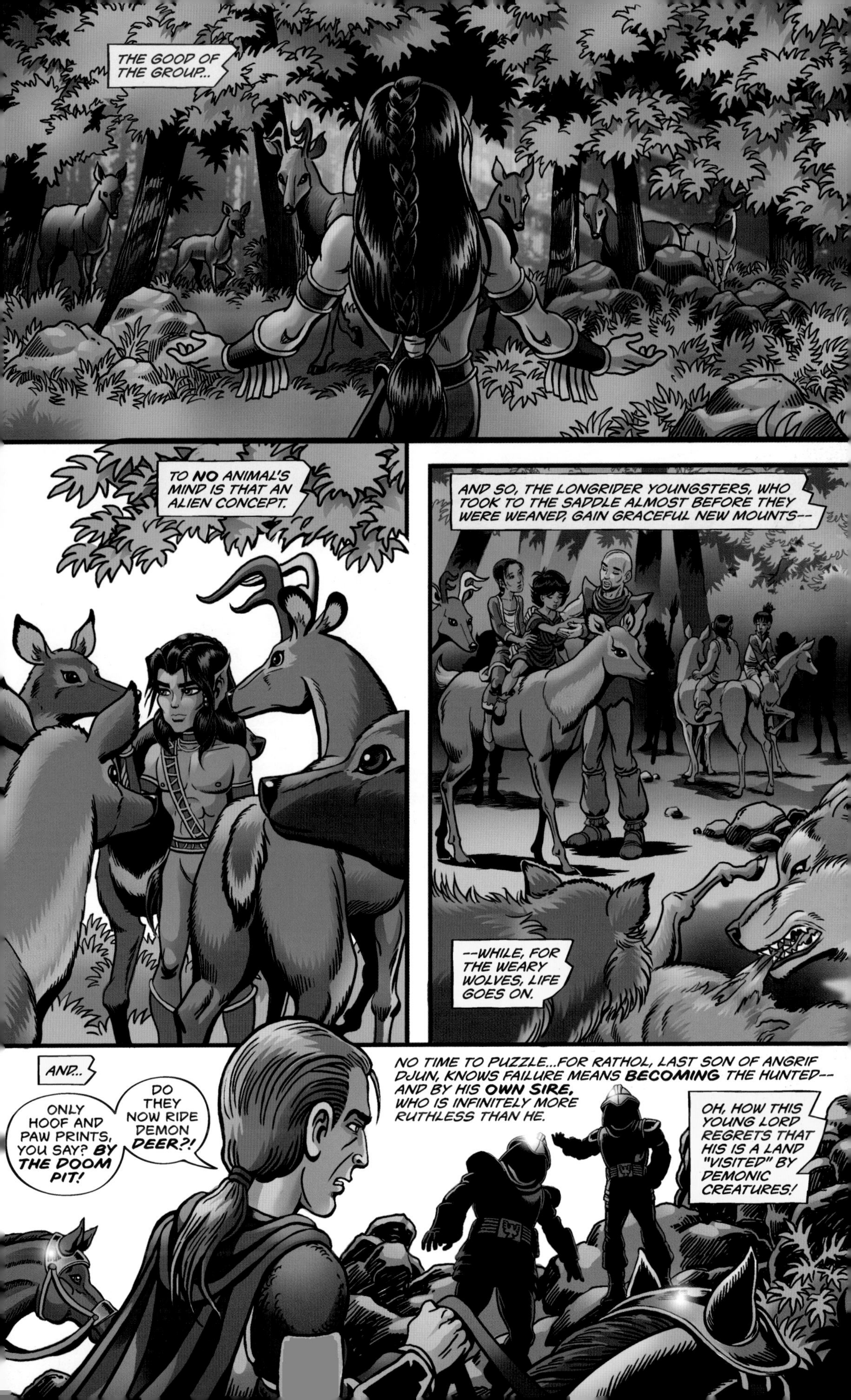
THE GOOD OF THE GROUP...
TO NO ANIMAL'S MIND IS THAT AN ALIEN CONCEPT.
AND SO, THE LONGRIDER YOUNGSTERS, WHO TOOK TO THE SADDLE ALMOST BEFORE THEY WERE WEANED, GAIN GRACEFUL NEW MOUNTS--
--WHILE, FOR THE WEARY WOLVES, LIFE GOES ON.
AND...
ONLY HOOF AND PAW PRINTS, YOU SAY? BY THE DOOM PIT!
DO THEY NOW RIDE DEMON DEER?!
NO TIME TO PUZZLE...FOR RATHOL, LAST SON OF ANGRIF DJUN, KNOWS FAILURE MEANS BECOMING THE HUNTED--AND BY HIS OWN SIRE, WHO IS INFINITELY MORE RUTHLESS THAN HE.
OH, HOW THIS YOUNG LORD REGRETS THAT HIS IS A LAND "VISITED" BY DEMONIC CREATURES!

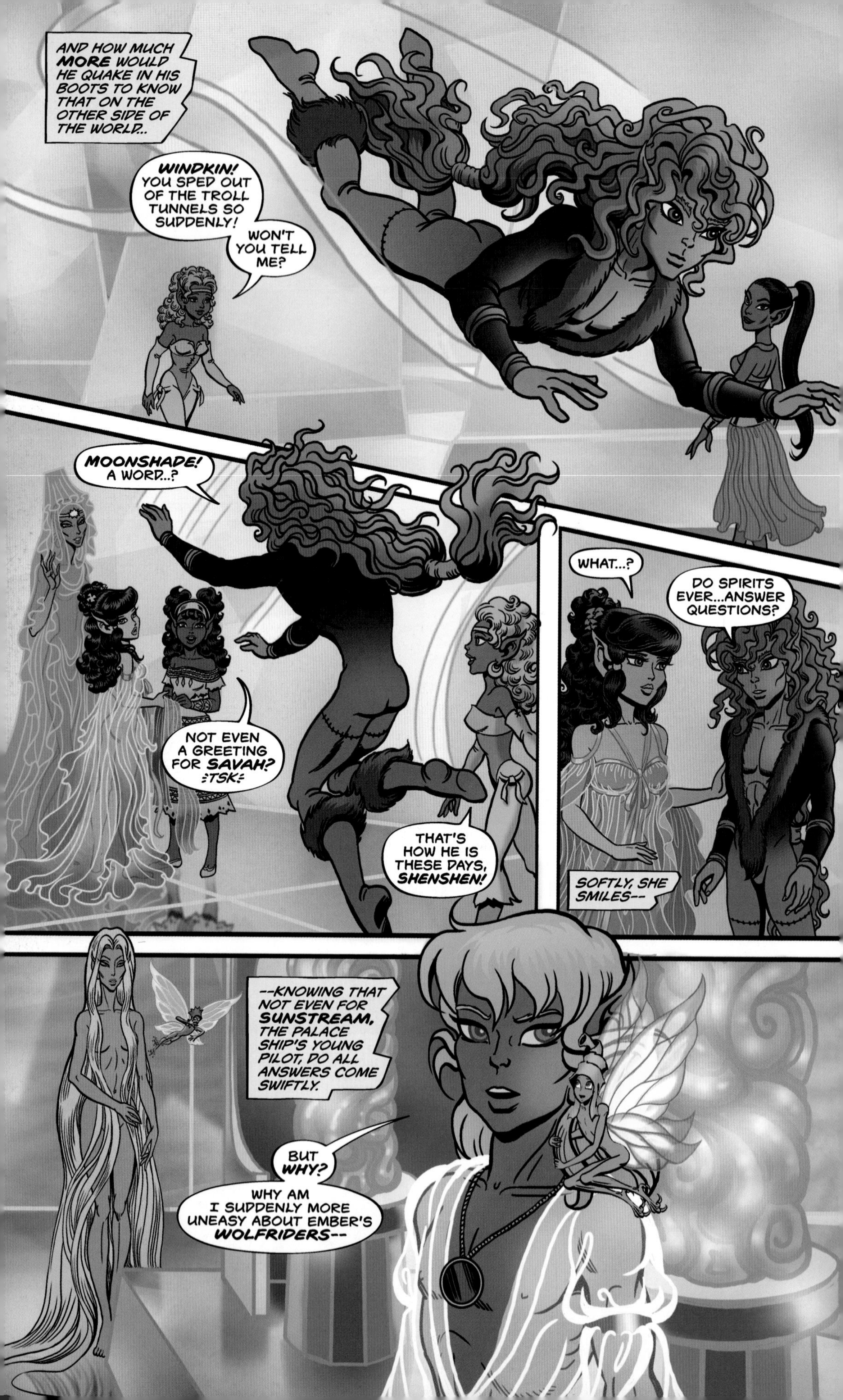
AND HOW MUCH MORE WOULD HE QUAKE IN HIS BOOTS TO KNOW THAT ON THE OTHER SIDE OF THE WORLD..
WINDKIN! YOU SPED OUT OF THE TROLL TUNNELS SO SUDDENLY!
WON'T YOU TELL ME?
MOONSHADE! A WORD...?
NOT EVEN A GREETING FOR SAVAH? TSK
THAT'S HOW HE IS THESE DAYS, SHENSHEN!
WHAT...?
DO SPIRITS EVER...ANSWER QUESTIONS?
SOFTLY, SHE SMILES--
--KNOWING THAT NOT EVEN FOR SUNSTREAM, THE PALACE SHIP'S YOUNG PILOT, DO ALL ANSWERS COME SWIFTLY.
BUT WHY?
WHY AM I SUDDENLY MORE UNEASY ABOUT EMBER'S WOLFRIDERS--

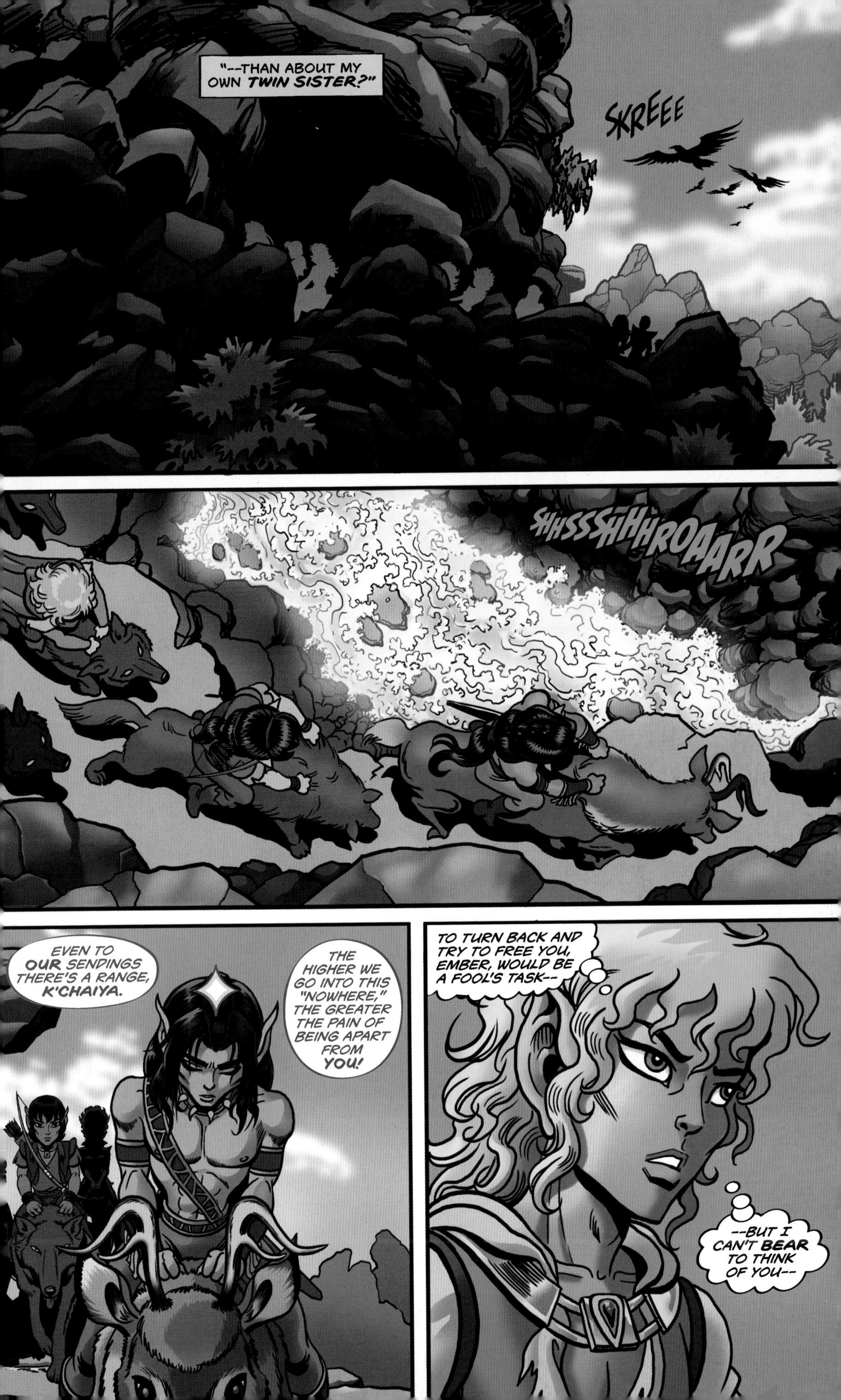
"--THAN ABOUT MY OWN TWIN SISTER?"
SKREEE
SHHSSHHHROAARR
EVEN TO OUR SENDINGS THERE'S A RANGE, K'CHAIYA.
THE HIGHER WE GO INTO THIS "NOWHERE," THE GREATER THE PAIN OF BEING APART FROM YOU!
TO TURN BACK AND TRY TO FREE YOU, EMBER, WOULD BE A FOOL'S TASK--
--BUT I CAN'T BEAR TO THINK OF YOU--

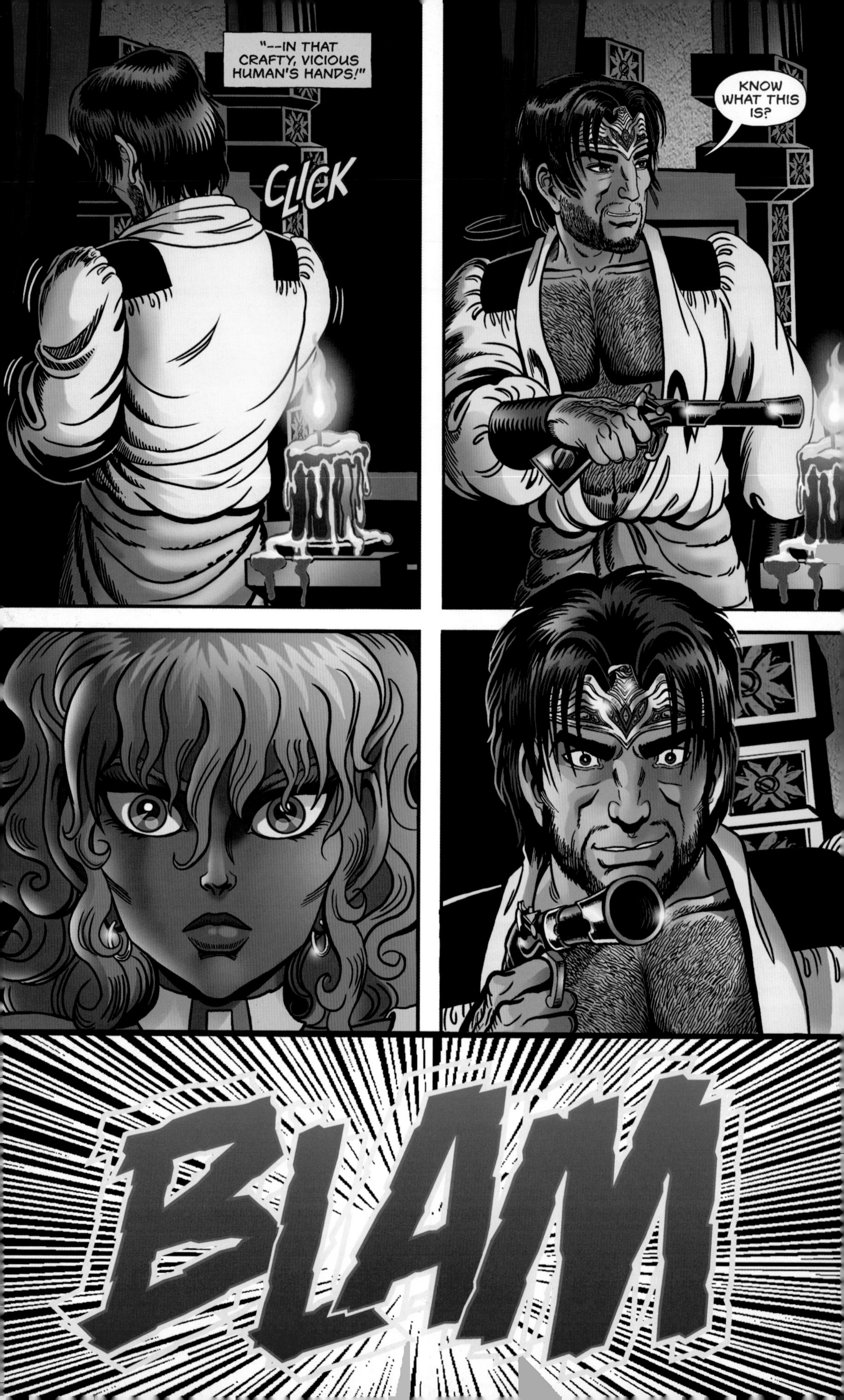
"--IN THAT CRAFTY, VICIOUS HUMAN'S HANDS!"
CLICK
KNOW WHAT THIS IS?
BLAM

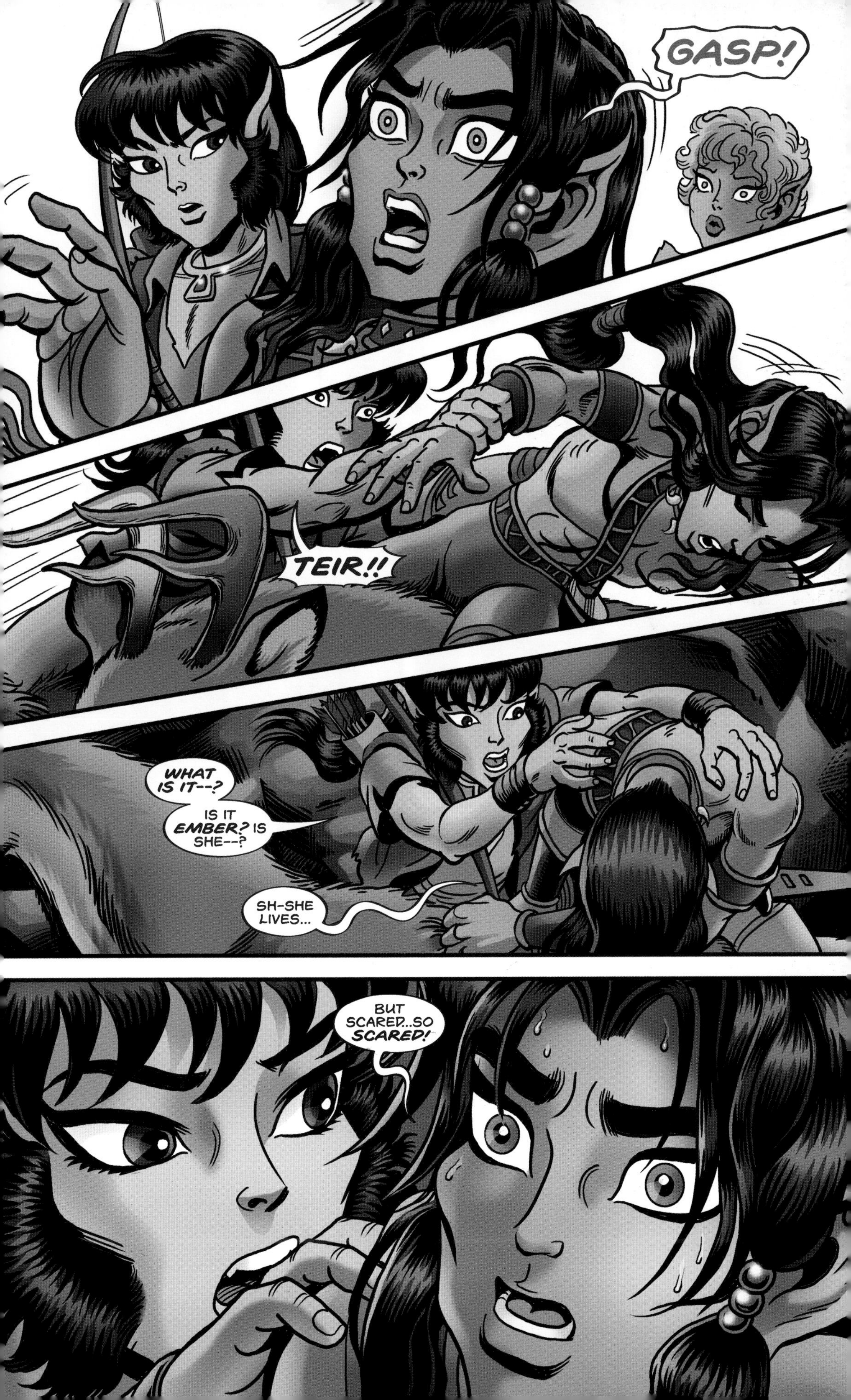
GASP!
TEIR!!
WHAT IS IT--?
IS IT EMBER? IS SHE--?
SH-SHE LIVES...
BUT SCARED...SO SCARED!

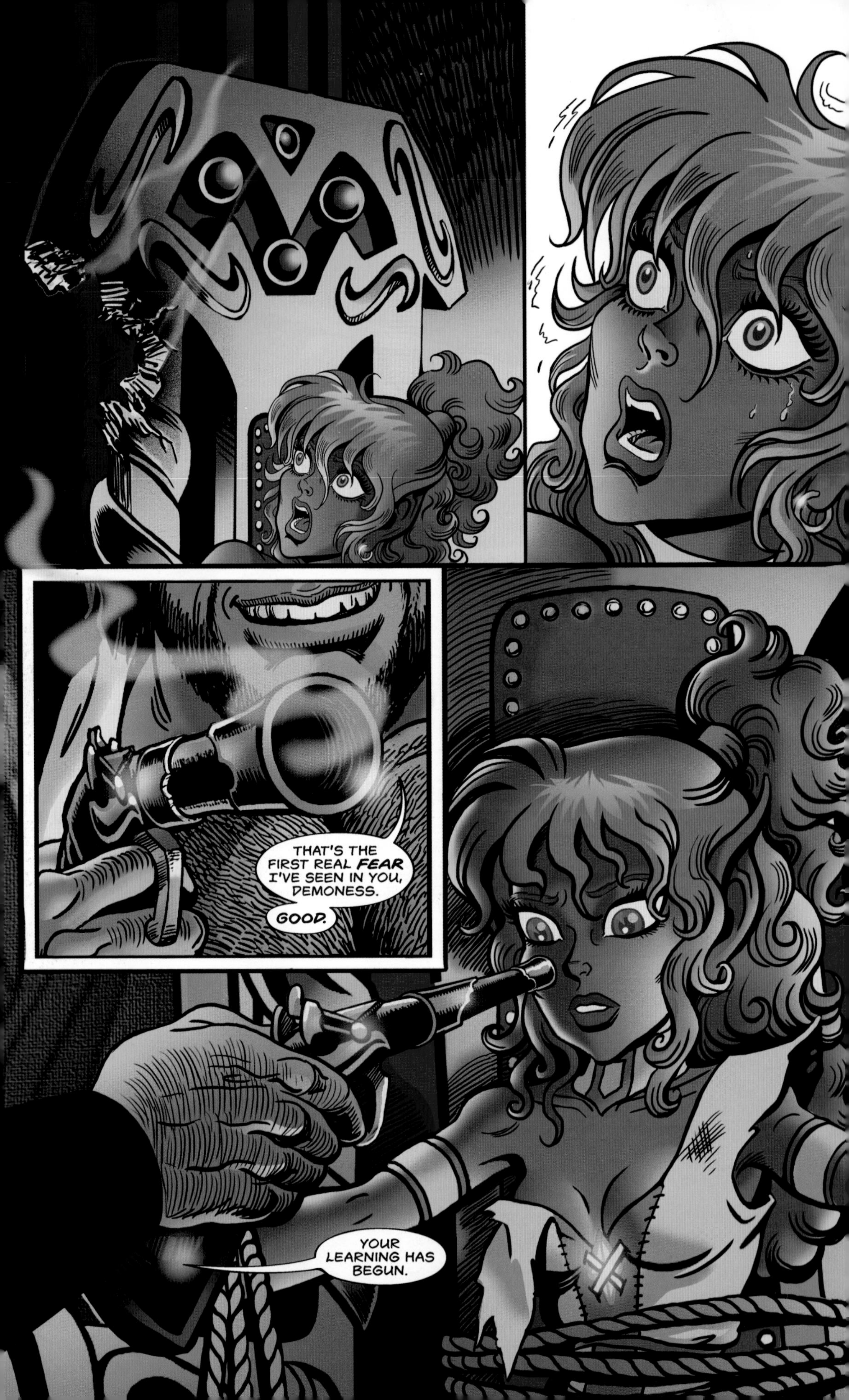
THAT'S THE FIRST REAL FEAR I'VE SEEN IN YOU, DEMONESS.
GOOD.
YOUR LEARNING HAS BEGUN.

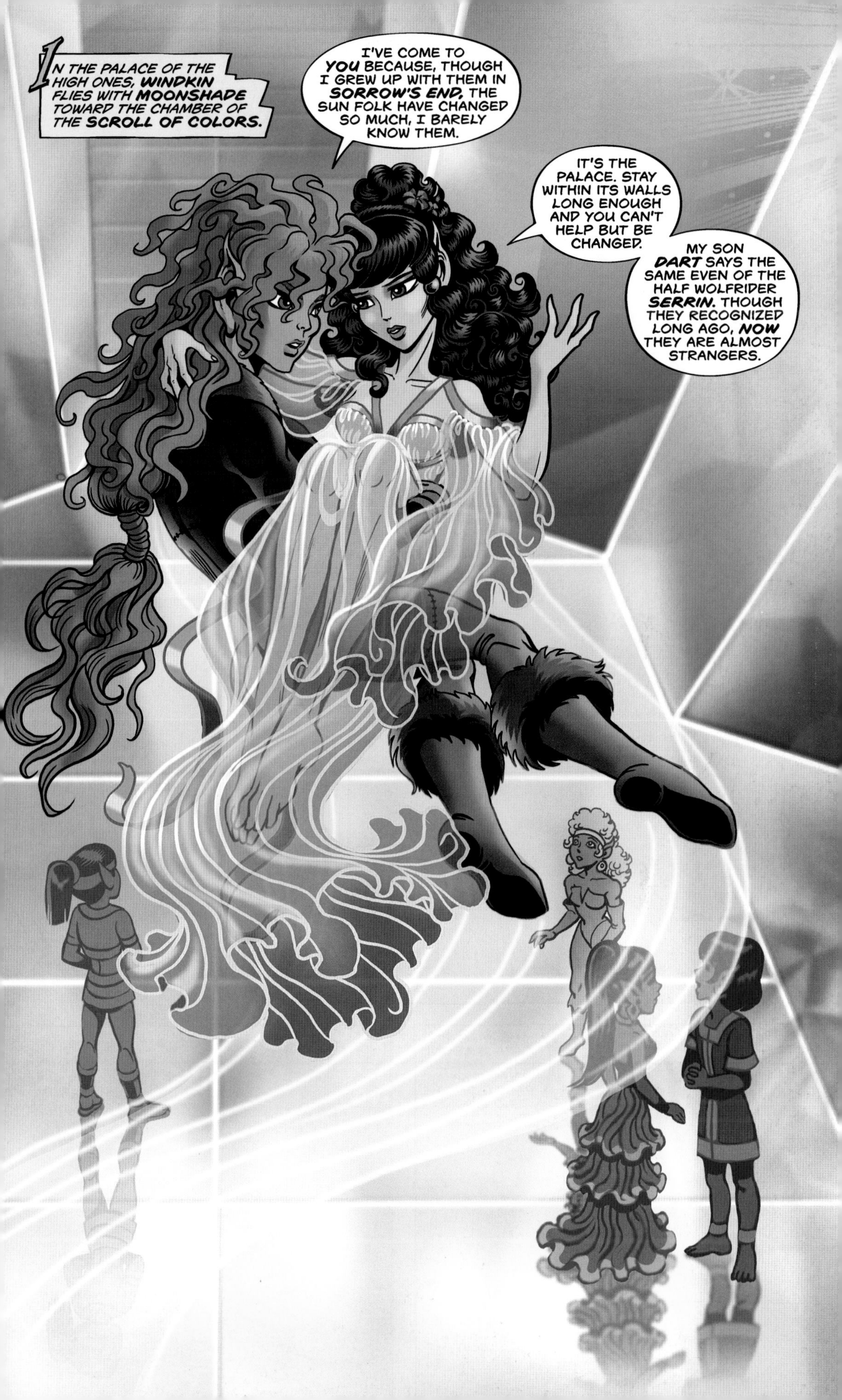
IN THE PALACE OF THE HIGH ONES, WINDKIN FLIES WITH MOONSHADE TOWARD THE CHAMBER OF THE SCROLL OF COLORS.
I'VE COME TO YOU BECAUSE, THOUGH I GREW UP WITH THEM IN SORROW'S END, THE SUN FOLK HAVE CHANGED SO MUCH, I BARELY KNOW THEM.
IT'S THE PALACE. STAY WITHIN ITS WALLS LONG ENOUGH AND YOU CAN'T HELP BUT BE CHANGED.
MY SON DART SAYS THE SAME EVEN OF THE HALF WOLFRIDER SERRIN. THOUGH THEY RECOGNIZED LONG AGO, NOW THEY ARE ALMOST STRANGERS.

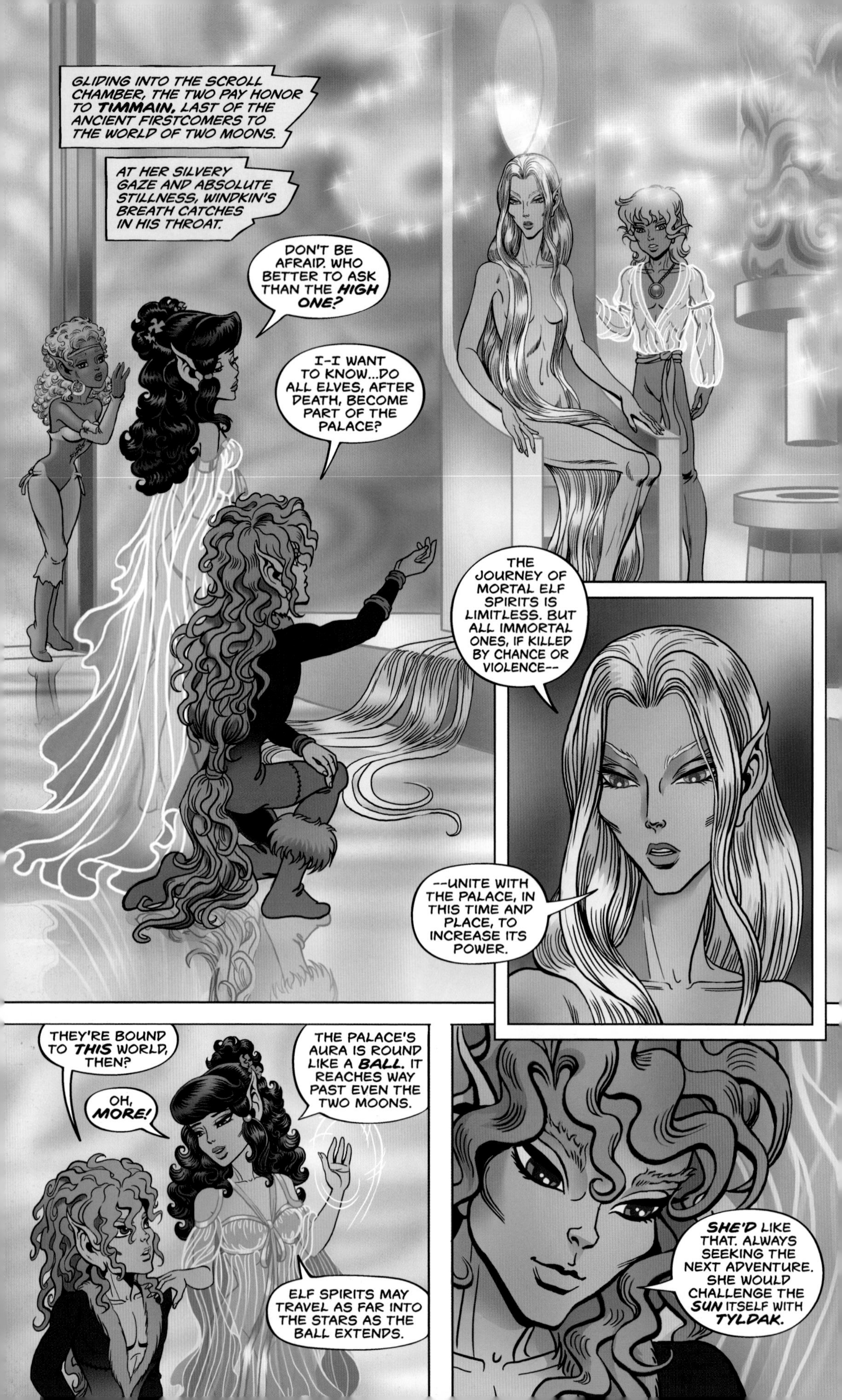
GLIDING INTO THE SCROLL CHAMBER, THE TWO PAY HONOR TO **TIMMAIN**, LAST OF THE ANCIENT FIRSTCOMERS TO THE WORLD OF TWO MOONS.
AT HER SILVERY GAZE AND ABSOLUTE STILLNESS, WINDKIN'S BREATH CATCHES IN HIS THROAT.
DON'T BE AFRAID. WHO BETTER TO ASK THAN THE **HIGH ONE**?
I-I WANT TO KNOW...DO ALL ELVES, AFTER DEATH, BECOME PART OF THE PALACE?
THE JOURNEY OF MORTAL ELF SPIRITS IS LIMITLESS. BUT ALL IMMORTAL ONES, IF KILLED BY CHANCE OR VIOLENCE--
--UNITE WITH THE PALACE, IN THIS TIME AND PLACE, TO INCREASE ITS POWER.
THEY'RE BOUND TO **THIS** WORLD, THEN?
OH, **MORE!**
THE PALACE'S AURA IS ROUND LIKE A **BALL**. IT REACHES WAY PAST EVEN THE TWO MOONS.
ELF SPIRITS MAY TRAVEL AS FAR INTO THE STARS AS THE BALL EXTENDS.
SHE'D LIKE THAT. ALWAYS SEEKING THE NEXT ADVENTURE. SHE WOULD CHALLENGE THE **SUN** ITSELF WITH **TYLDAK**.

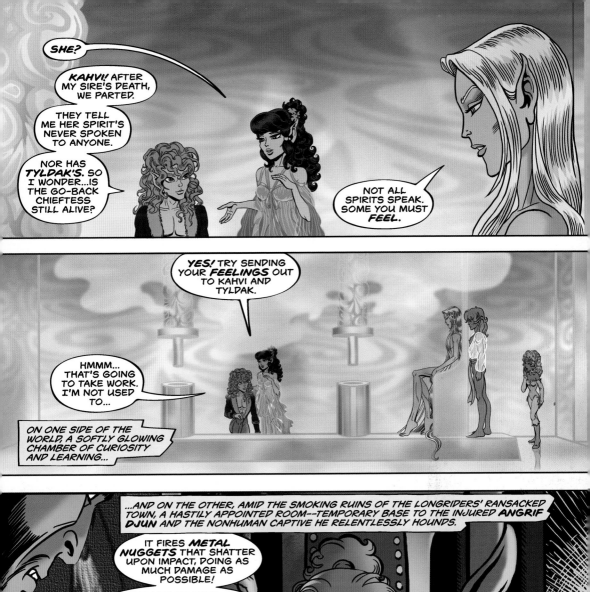

SHE?

KAHVI! AFTER MY SIRE'S DEATH, WE PARTED.

THEY TELL ME HER SPIRIT'S NEVER SPOKEN TO ANYONE.

NOR HAS TYLDAK'S. SO I WONDER...IS THE GO-BACK CHIEFTESS STILL ALIVE?

NOT ALL SPIRITS SPEAK. SOME YOU MUST FEEL.

YES! TRY SENDING YOUR FEELINGS OUT TO KAHVI AND TYLDAK.

HMMM... THAT'S GOING TO TAKE WORK. I'M NOT USED TO...

ON ONE SIDE OF THE WORLD, A SOFTLY GLOWING CHAMBER OF CURIOSITY AND LEARNING...

...AND ON THE OTHER, AMID THE SMOKING RUINS OF THE LONGRIDERS' RANSACKED TOWN, A HASTILY APPOINTED ROOM--TEMPORARY BASE TO THE INJURED ANGRIF DJUN AND THE NONHUMAN CAPTIVE HE RELENTLESSLY HOUNDS.

IT FIRES METAL NUGGETS THAT SHATTER UPON IMPACT, DOING AS MUCH DAMAGE AS POSSIBLE!

I'D LIKE TO HAVE ENDED DEAR PAPA'S REIGN WITH THIS, BUT HAD TO RESORT TO MORE...CONVENTIONAL MEANS.

THERE'S ONLY ONE, YOU SEE, MADE BY MY FATHER'S MASTER SMITH.

TWO-EDGE!

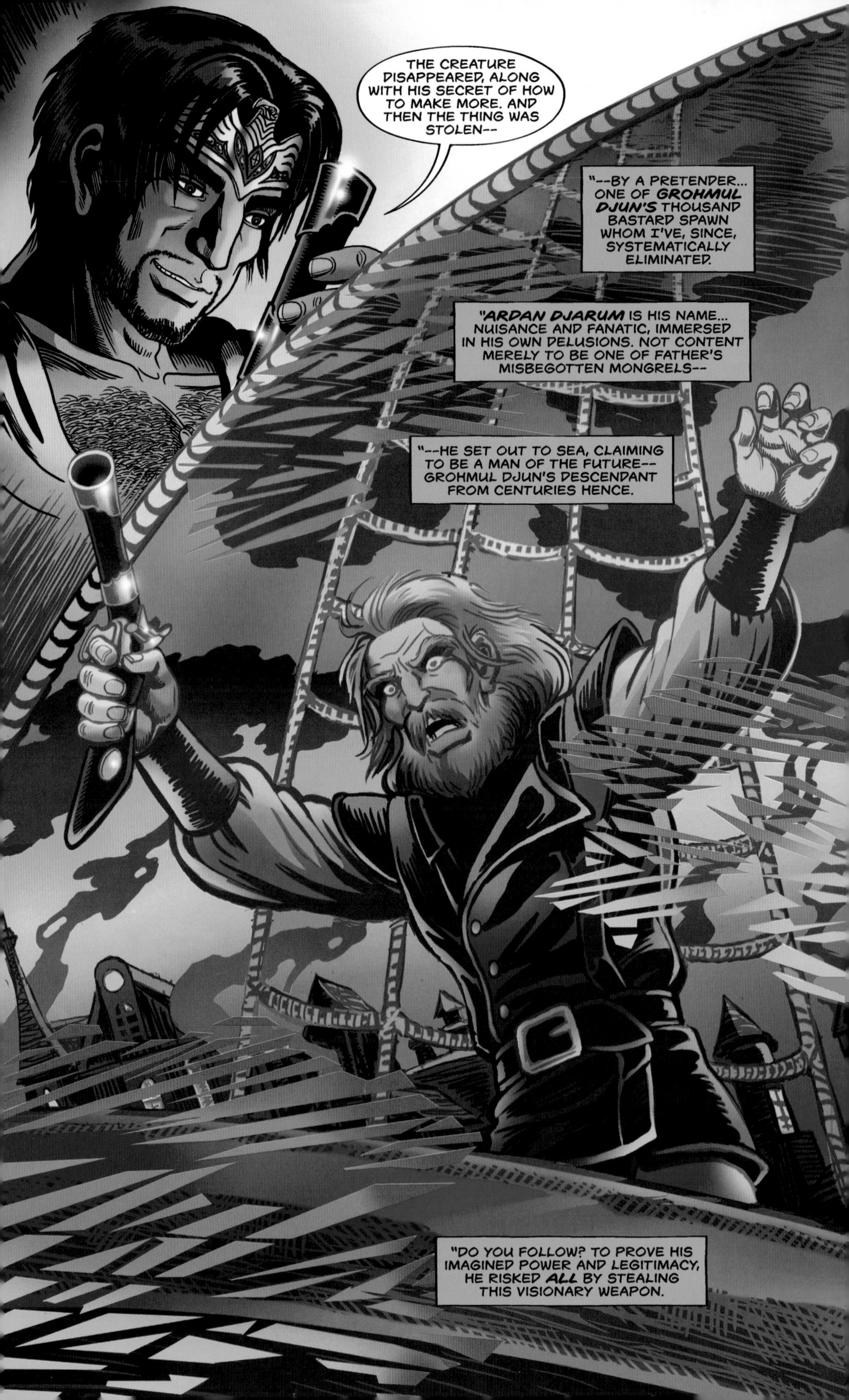
THE CREATURE DISAPPEARED, ALONG WITH HIS SECRET OF HOW TO MAKE MORE. AND THEN THE THING WAS STOLEN--
"--BY A PRETENDER... ONE OF GROHMUL DJUN'S THOUSAND BASTARD SPAWN WHOM I'VE, SINCE, SYSTEMATICALLY ELIMINATED.
"ARDAN DJARUM IS HIS NAME... NUISANCE AND FANATIC, IMMERSED IN HIS OWN DELUSIONS. NOT CONTENT MERELY TO BE ONE OF FATHER'S MISBEGOTTEN MONGRELS--
"--HE SET OUT TO SEA, CLAIMING TO BE A MAN OF THE FUTURE-- GROHMUL DJUN'S DESCENDANT FROM CENTURIES HENCE.
"DO YOU FOLLOW? TO PROVE HIS IMAGINED POWER AND LEGITIMACY, HE RISKED ALL BY STEALING THIS VISIONARY WEAPON.

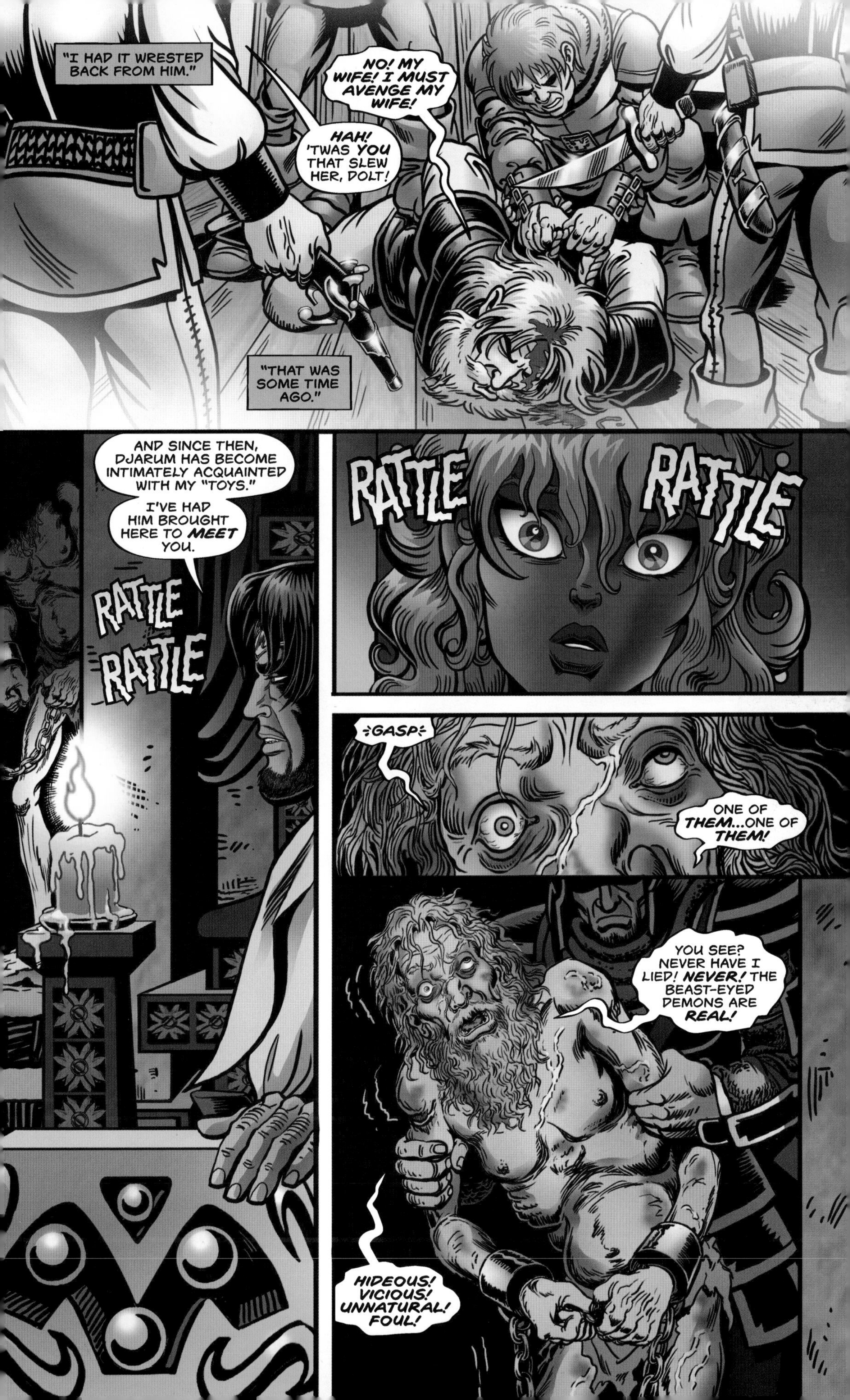
"I HAD IT WRESTED BACK FROM HIM."
NO! MY WIFE! I MUST AVENGE MY WIFE!
HAH! 'TWAS YOU THAT SLEW HER, DOLT!
"THAT WAS SOME TIME AGO."
AND SINCE THEN, DJARUM HAS BECOME INTIMATELY ACQUAINTED WITH MY "TOYS."
I'VE HAD HIM BROUGHT HERE TO MEET YOU.
RATTLE RATTLE
RATTLE RATTLE
GASP
ONE OF THEM...ONE OF THEM!
YOU SEE? NEVER HAVE I LIED! NEVER! THE BEAST-EYED DEMONS ARE REAL!
HIDEOUS! VICIOUS! UNNATURAL! FOUL!

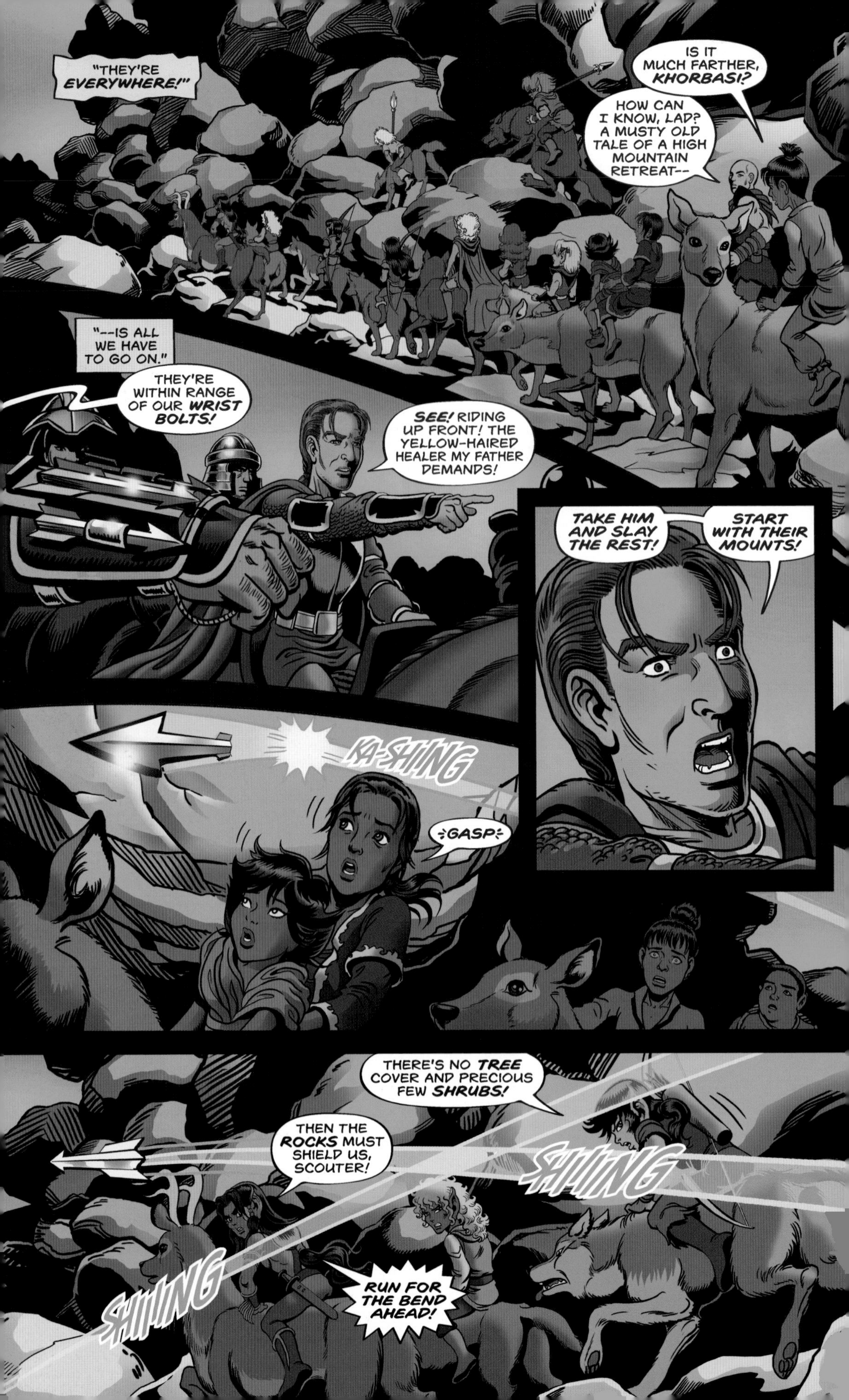
"THEY'RE EVERYWHERE!"
IS IT MUCH FARTHER, KHORBASI?
HOW CAN I KNOW, LAD? A MUSTY OLD TALE OF A HIGH MOUNTAIN RETREAT--
"--IS ALL WE HAVE TO GO ON."
THEY'RE WITHIN RANGE OF OUR WRIST BOLTS!
SEE! RIDING UP FRONT! THE YELLOW-HAIRED HEALER MY FATHER DEMANDS!
TAKE HIM AND SLAY THE REST!
START WITH THEIR MOUNTS!
KA-SHING
GASP
THERE'S NO TREE COVER AND PRECIOUS FEW SHRUBS!
THEN THE ROCKS MUST SHIELD US, SCOUTER!
SHIING
SHIING
RUN FOR THE BEND AHEAD!

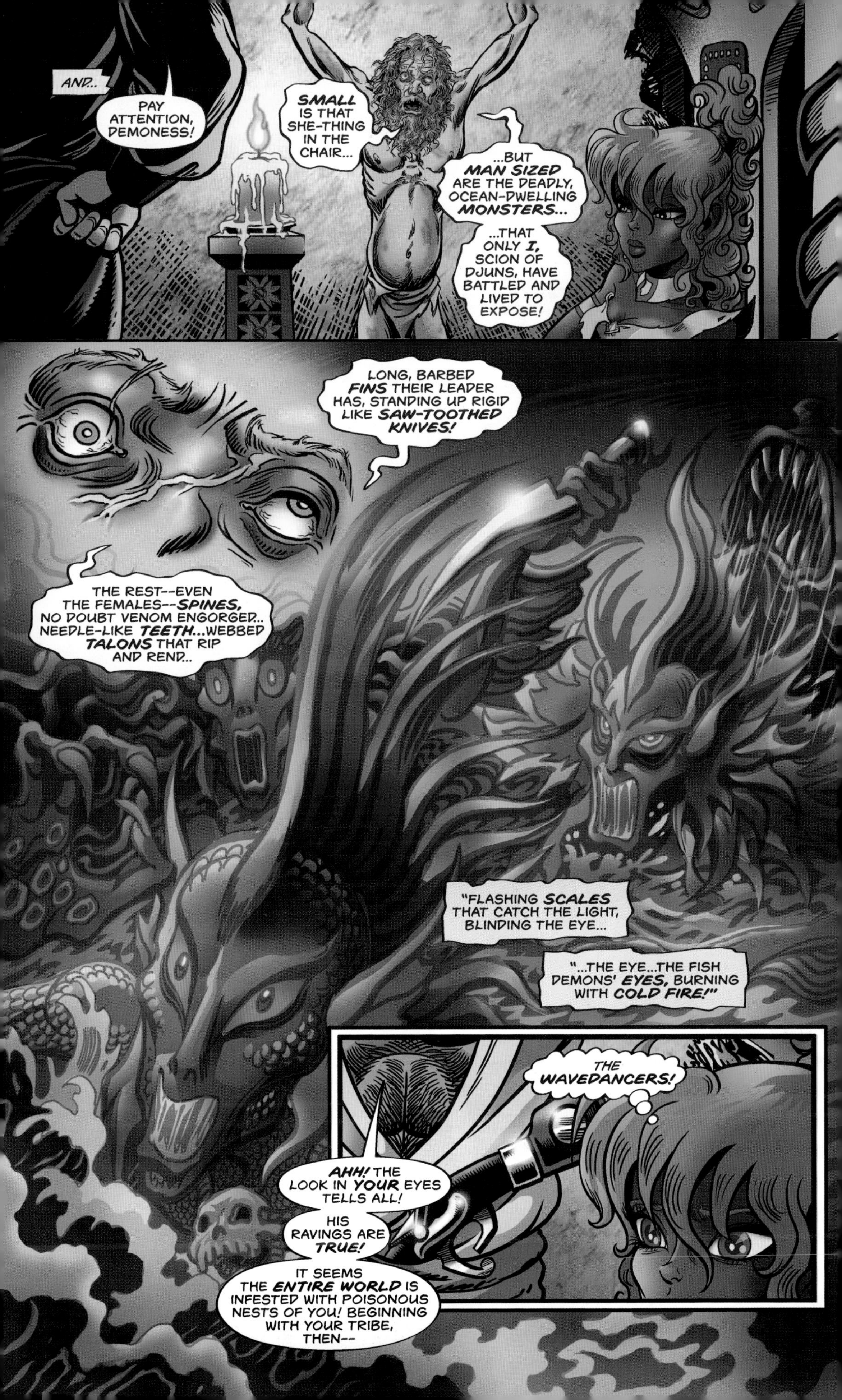
AND..
PAY ATTENTION, DEMONESS!
SMALL IS THAT SHE-THING IN THE CHAIR...
...BUT MAN SIZED ARE THE DEADLY, OCEAN-DWELLING MONSTERS...
...THAT ONLY I, SCION OF DJUNS, HAVE BATTLED AND LIVED TO EXPOSE!
LONG, BARBED FINS THEIR LEADER HAS, STANDING UP RIGID LIKE SAW-TOOTHED KNIVES!
THE REST--EVEN THE FEMALES--SPINES, NO DOUBT VENOM ENGORGED... NEEDLE-LIKE TEETH...WEBBED TALONS THAT RIP AND REND...
"FLASHING SCALES THAT CATCH THE LIGHT, BLINDING THE EYE...
"...THE EYE...THE FISH DEMONS' EYES, BURNING WITH COLD FIRE!"
THE WAVEDANCERS!
AHH! THE LOOK IN YOUR EYES TELLS ALL!
HIS RAVINGS ARE TRUE!
IT SEEMS THE ENTIRE WORLD IS INFESTED WITH POISONOUS NESTS OF YOU! BEGINNING WITH YOUR TRIBE, THEN--

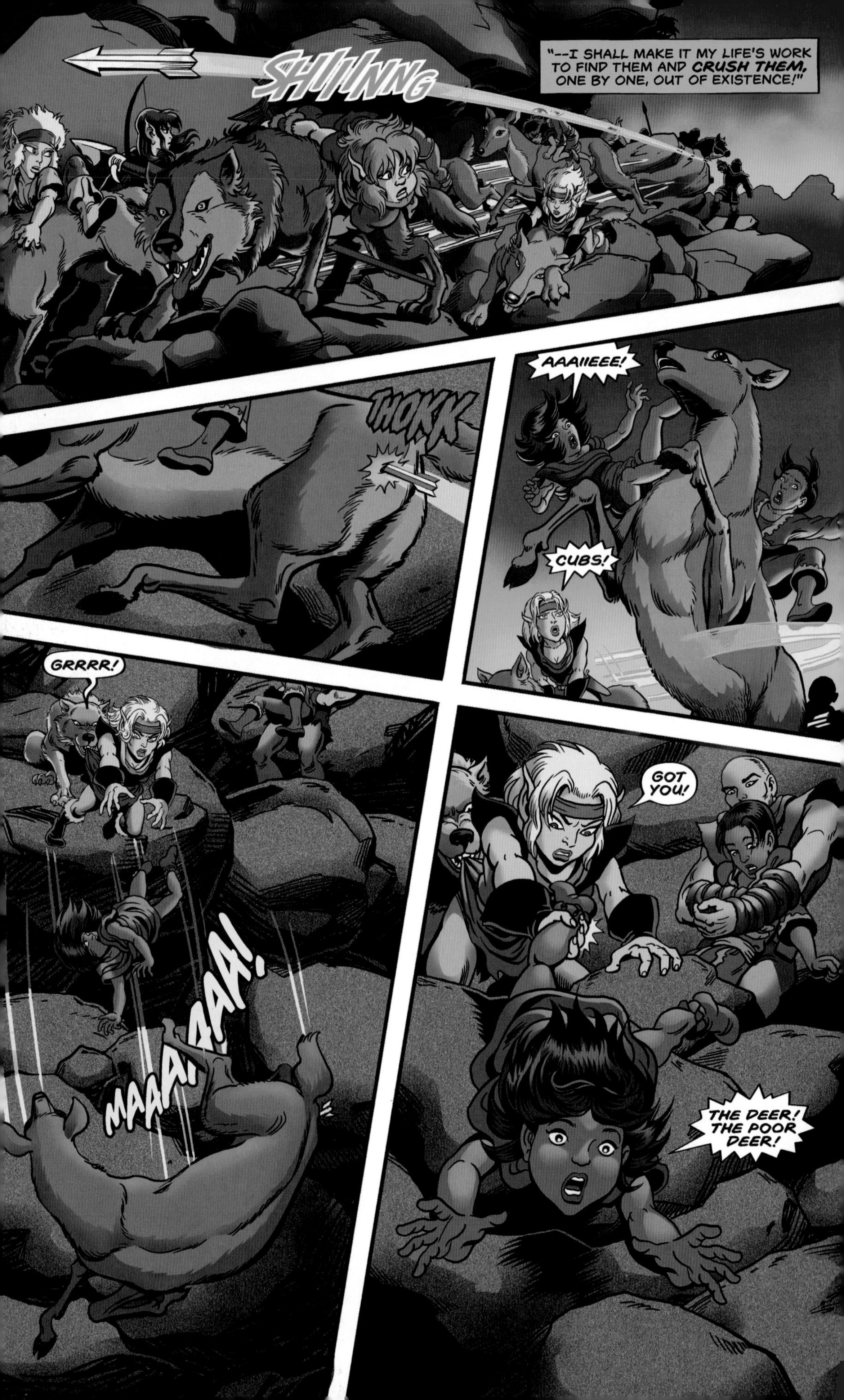
"--I SHALL MAKE IT MY LIFE'S WORK TO FIND THEM AND CRUSH THEM, ONE BY ONE, OUT OF EXISTENCE!"
SHIIINNG
THOKK
AAAIIEEE!
CUBS!
GRRRR!
MAAAAAA!
GOT YOU!
THE DEER! THE POOR DEER!

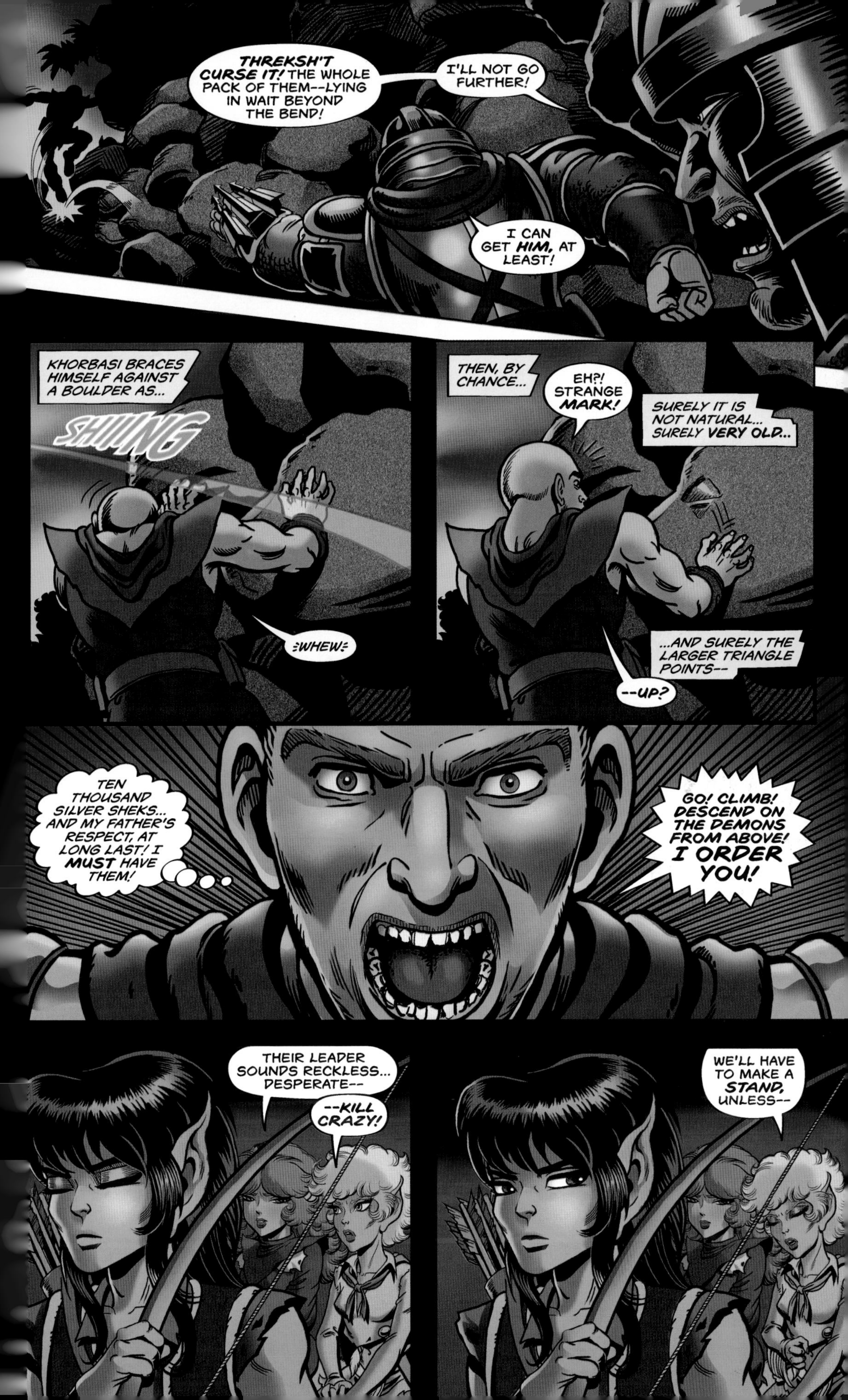
THREKSH'T CURSE IT! THE WHOLE PACK OF THEM--LYING IN WAIT BEYOND THE BEND!
I'LL NOT GO FURTHER!
I CAN GET HIM, AT LEAST!
KHORBASI BRACES HIMSELF AGAINST A BOULDER AS...
SHING
WHEW
THEN, BY CHANCE...
EH?! STRANGE MARK!
SURELY IT IS NOT NATURAL... SURELY VERY OLD...
...AND SURELY THE LARGER TRIANGLE POINTS--
--UP?
TEN THOUSAND SILVER SHEKS... AND MY FATHER'S RESPECT, AT LONG LAST! I MUST HAVE THEM!
GO! CLIMB! DESCEND ON THE DEMONS FROM ABOVE! I ORDER YOU!
THEIR LEADER SOUNDS RECKLESS... DESPERATE--
--KILL CRAZY!
WE'LL HAVE TO MAKE A STAND, UNLESS--

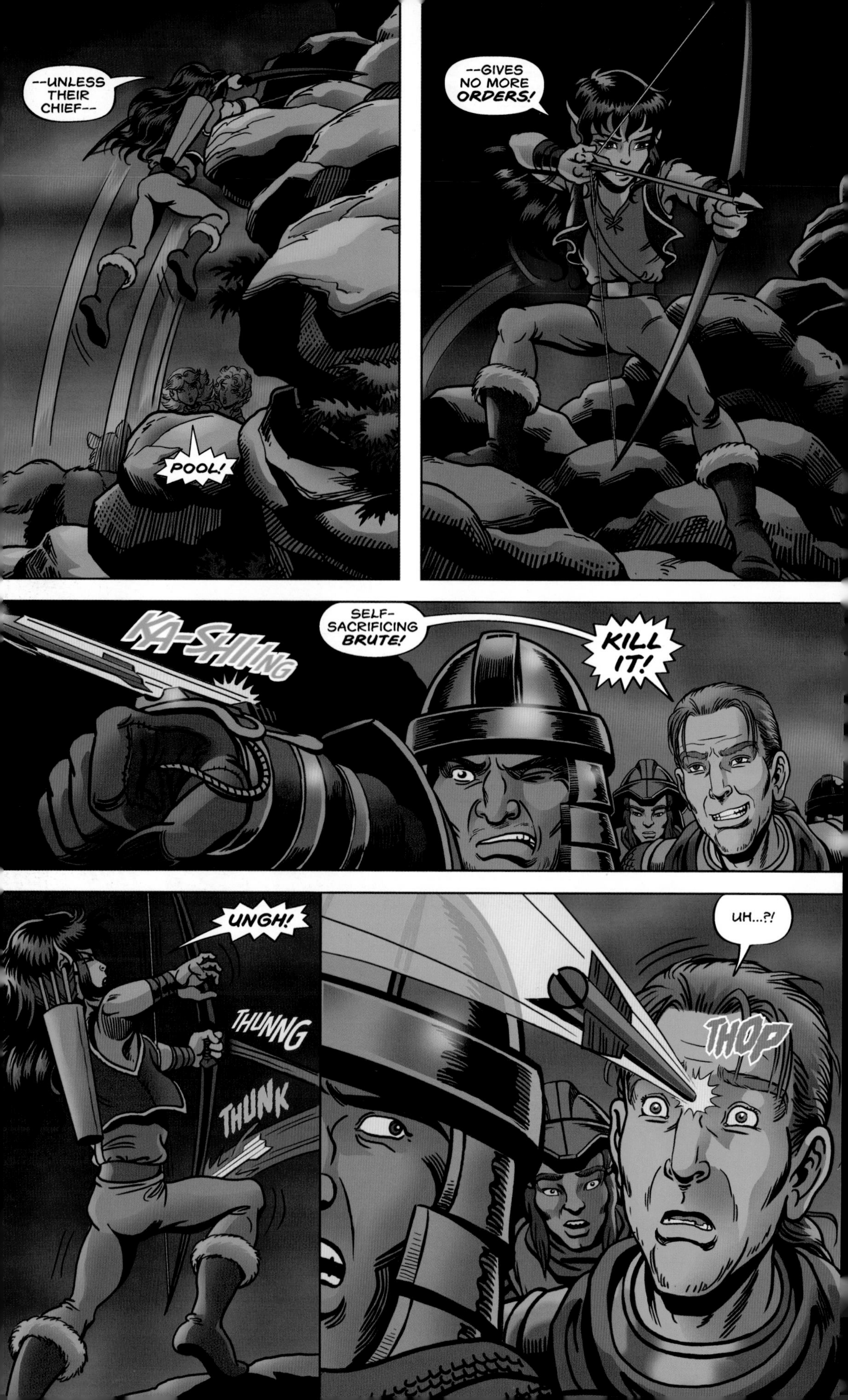
--UNLESS THEIR CHIEF--
POOL!
--GIVES NO MORE ORDERS!
KA-SHIIING
SELF-SACRIFICING BRUTE!
KILL IT!
UNGH!
THUNNG
THUNK
UH...?!
THOP

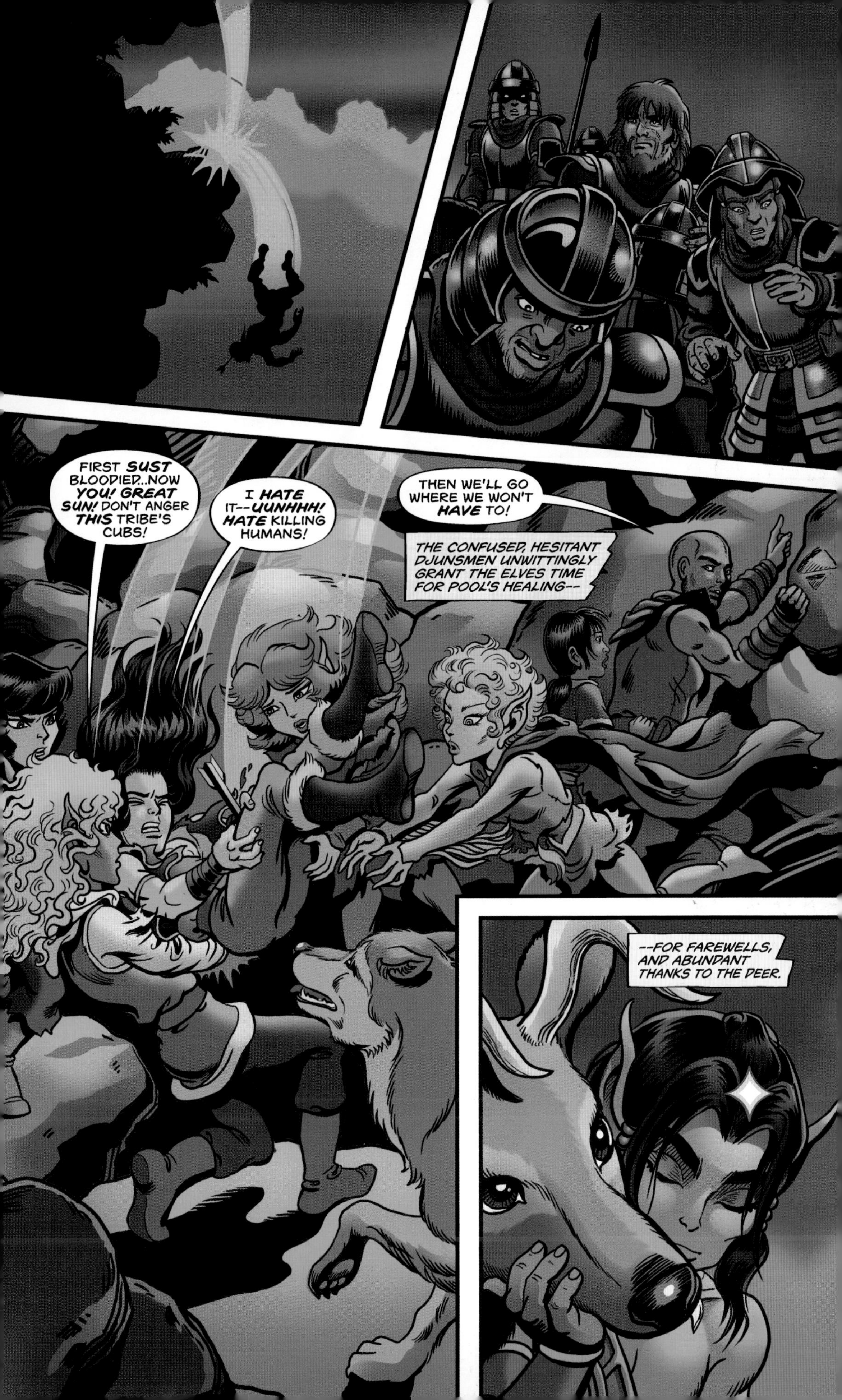

FIRST SUST BLOODIED...NOW YOU! GREAT SUN! DON'T ANGER THIS TRIBE'S CUBS!
I HATE IT--UUNHHH! HATE KILLING HUMANS!
THEN WE'LL GO WHERE WE WON'T HAVE TO!
THE CONFUSED, HESITANT DJUNSMEN UNWITTINGLY GRANT THE ELVES TIME FOR POOL'S HEALING--
--FOR FAREWELLS, AND ABUNDANT THANKS TO THE DEER.

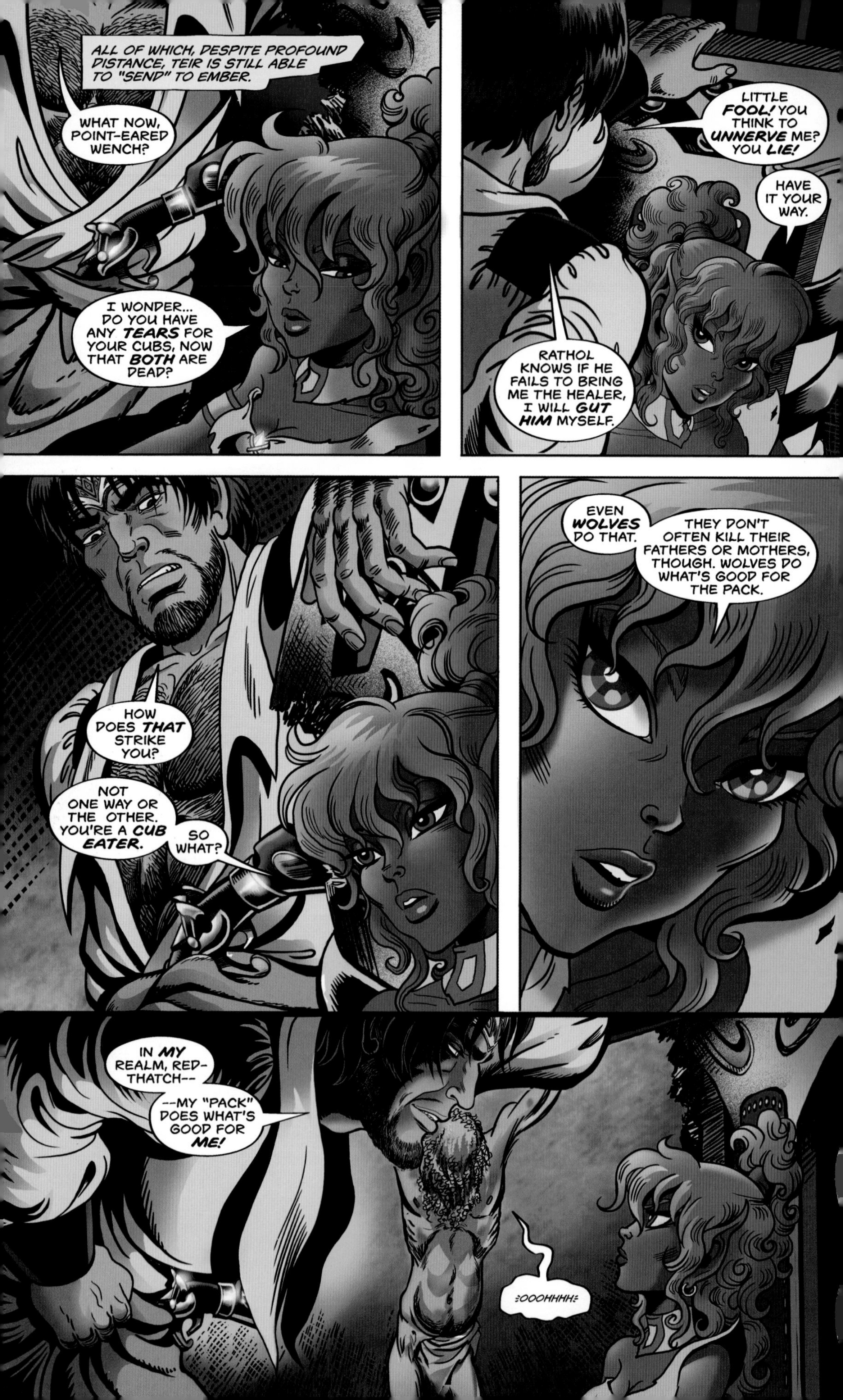
ALL OF WHICH, DESPITE PROFOUND DISTANCE, TEIR IS STILL ABLE TO "SEND" TO EMBER.
WHAT NOW, POINT-EARED WENCH?
I WONDER... DO YOU HAVE ANY TEARS FOR YOUR CUBS, NOW THAT BOTH ARE DEAD?
LITTLE FOOL! YOU THINK TO UNNERVE ME? YOU LIE!
HAVE IT YOUR WAY.
RATHOL KNOWS IF HE FAILS TO BRING ME THE HEALER, I WILL GUT HIM MYSELF.
HOW DOES THAT STRIKE YOU?
NOT ONE WAY OR THE OTHER. YOU'RE A CUB EATER.
SO WHAT?
EVEN WOLVES DO THAT.
THEY DON'T OFTEN KILL THEIR FATHERS OR MOTHERS, THOUGH. WOLVES DO WHAT'S GOOD FOR THE PACK.
IN MY REALM, RED-THATCH--
--MY "PACK" DOES WHAT'S GOOD FOR ME!
OOOHHHH

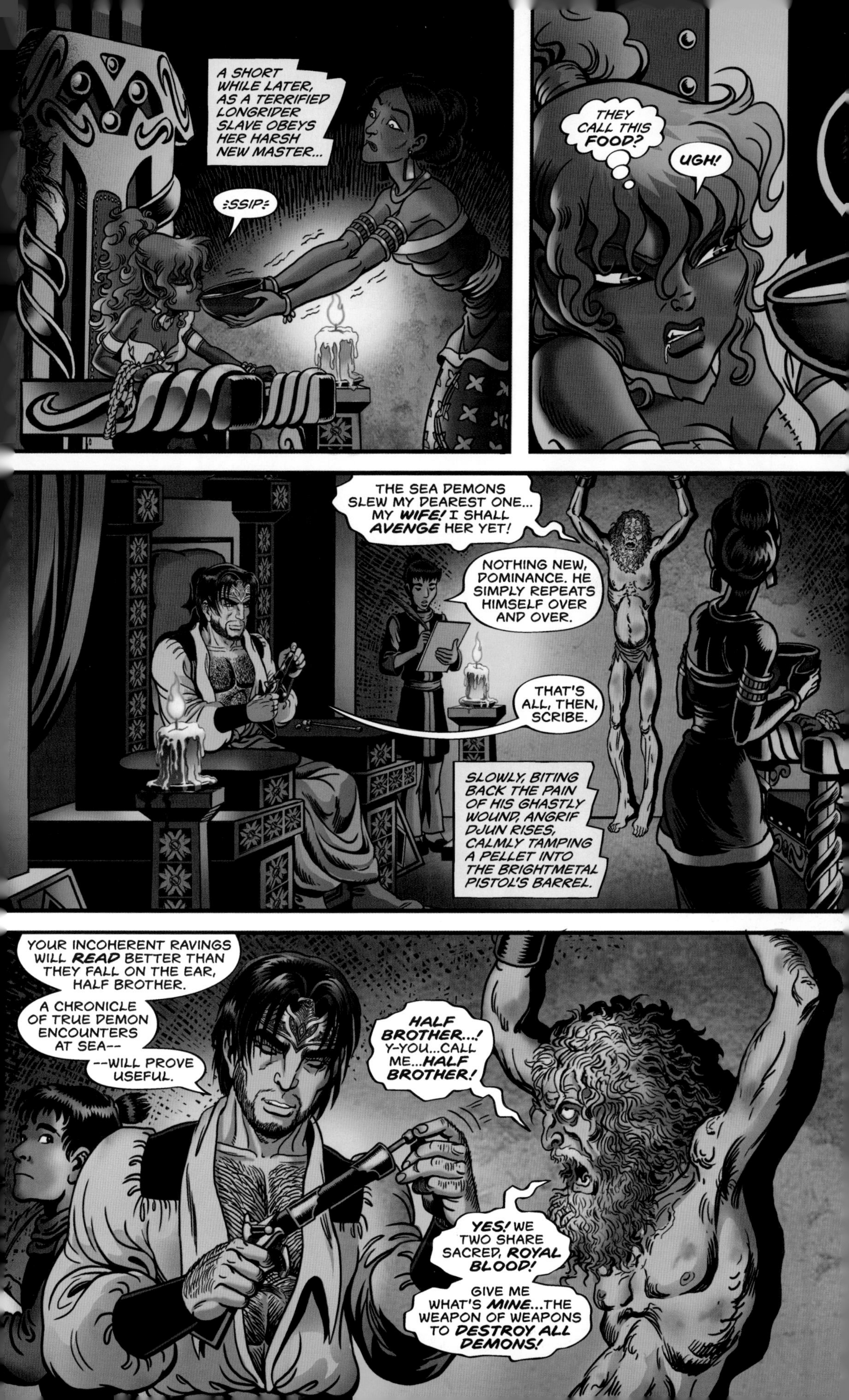
A SHORT WHILE LATER, AS A TERRIFIED LONGRIDER SLAVE OBEYS HER HARSH NEW MASTER...
:SSIP:
THEY CALL THIS FOOD?
UGH!
THE SEA DEMONS SLEW MY DEAREST ONE... MY WIFE! I SHALL AVENGE HER YET!
NOTHING NEW, DOMINANCE. HE SIMPLY REPEATS HIMSELF OVER AND OVER.
THAT'S ALL, THEN, SCRIBE.
SLOWLY, BITING BACK THE PAIN OF HIS GHASTLY WOUND, ANGRIF DJUN RISES, CALMLY TAMPING A PELLET INTO THE BRIGHTMETAL PISTOL'S BARREL.
YOUR INCOHERENT RAVINGS WILL READ BETTER THAN THEY FALL ON THE EAR, HALF BROTHER.
A CHRONICLE OF TRUE DEMON ENCOUNTERS AT SEA--
--WILL PROVE USEFUL.
HALF BROTHER...! Y-YOU...CALL ME...HALF BROTHER!
YES! WE TWO SHARE SACRED, ROYAL BLOOD!
GIVE ME WHAT'S MINE...THE WEAPON OF WEAPONS TO DESTROY ALL DEMONS!

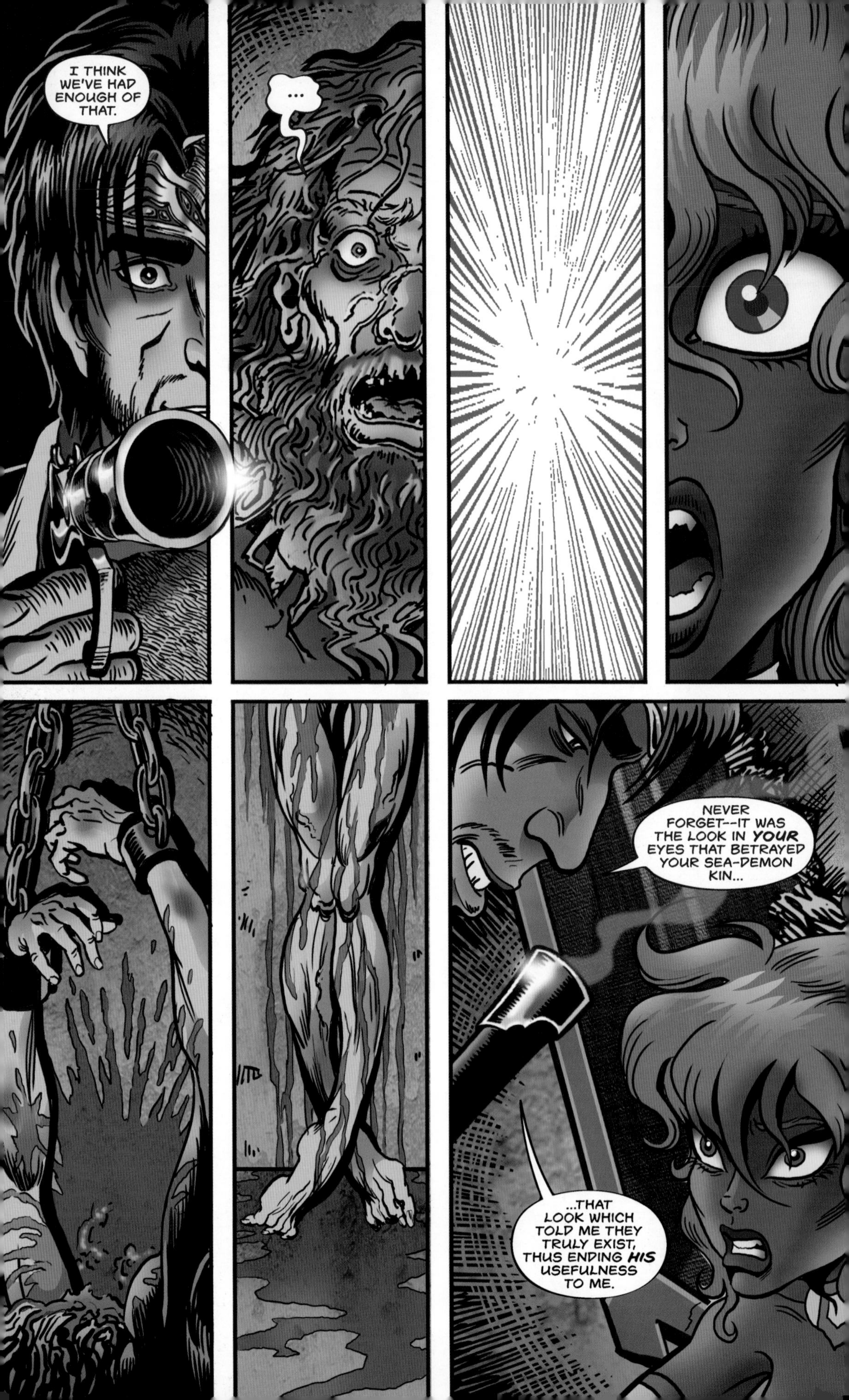
I THINK WE'VE HAD ENOUGH OF THAT.
...
NEVER FORGET--IT WAS THE LOOK IN **YOUR** EYES THAT BETRAYED YOUR SEA-DEMON KIN...
...THAT LOOK WHICH TOLD ME THEY TRULY EXIST, THUS ENDING **HIS** USEFULNESS TO ME.

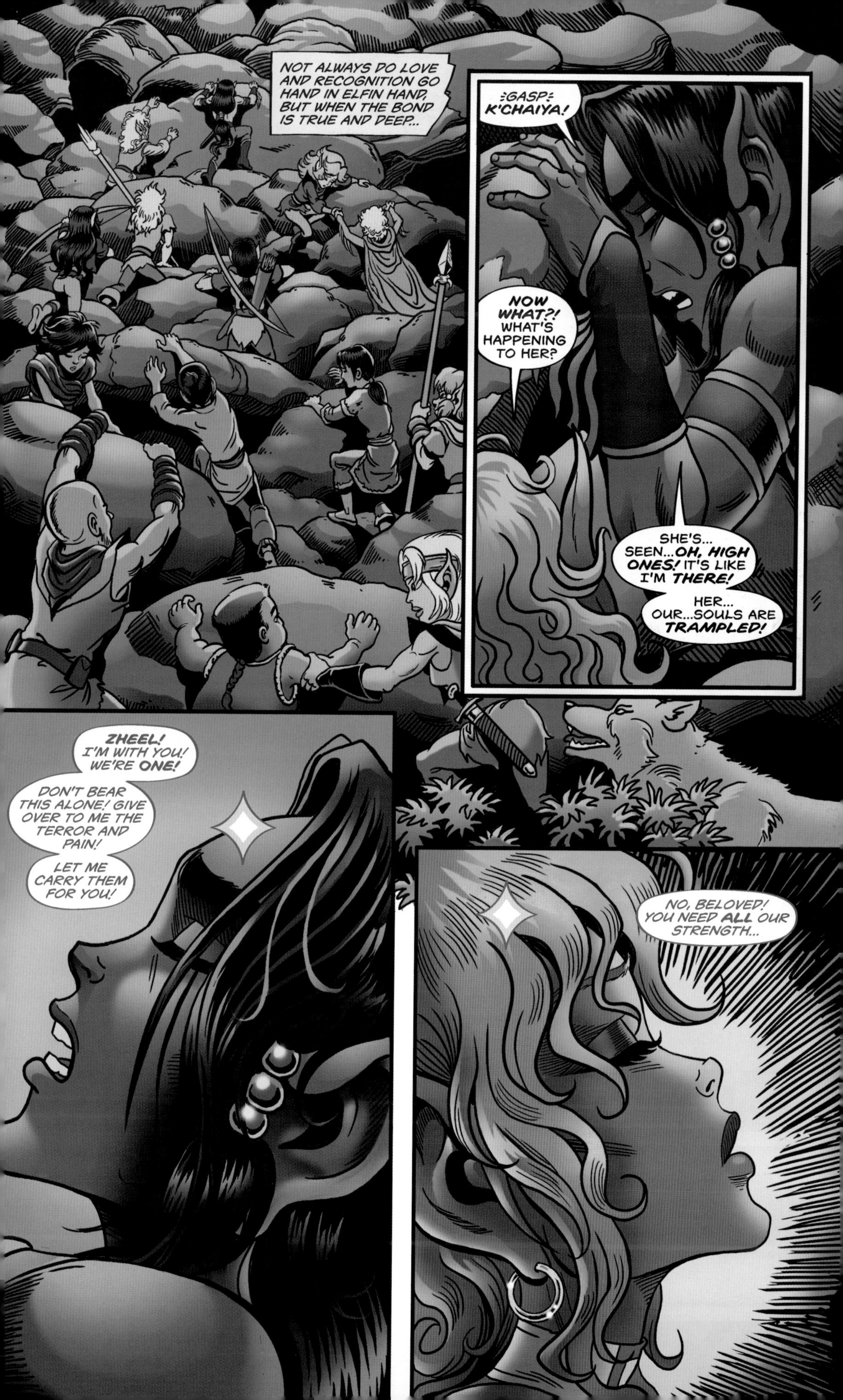
NOT ALWAYS DO LOVE AND RECOGNITION GO HAND IN ELFIN HAND, BUT WHEN THE BOND IS TRUE AND DEEP...
GASP K'CHAIYA!
NOW WHAT?! WHAT'S HAPPENING TO HER?
SHE'S... SEEN...OH, HIGH ONES! IT'S LIKE I'M THERE!
HER... OUR...SOULS ARE TRAMPLED!
ZHEEL! I'M WITH YOU! WE'RE ONE!
DON'T BEAR THIS ALONE! GIVE OVER TO ME THE TERROR AND PAIN!
LET ME CARRY THEM FOR YOU!
NO, BELOVED! YOU NEED ALL OUR STRENGTH...

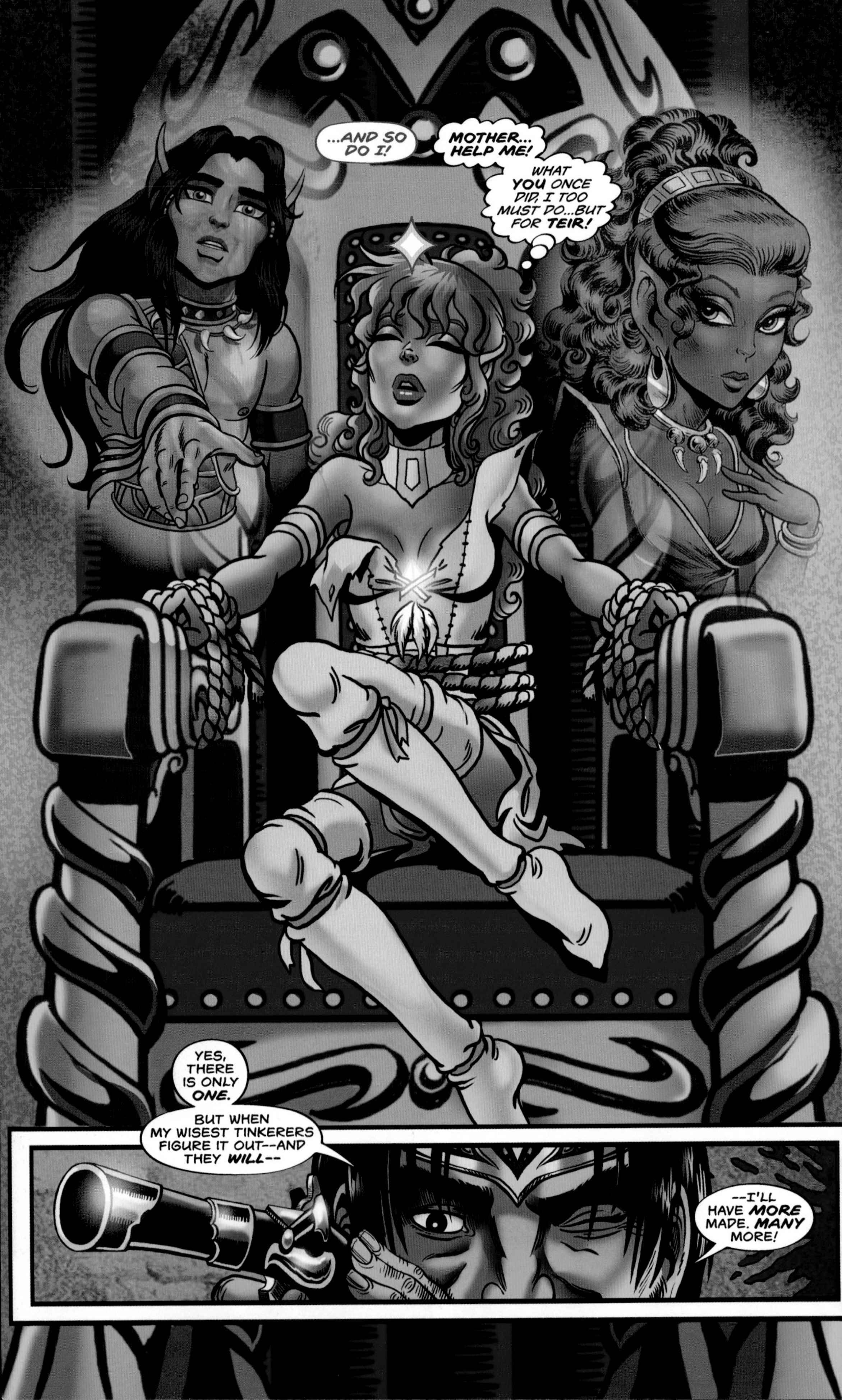
...AND SO DO I!
MOTHER... HELP ME!
WHAT YOU ONCE DID, I TOO MUST DO...BUT FOR TEIR!
YES, THERE IS ONLY ONE.
BUT WHEN MY WISEST TINKERERS FIGURE IT OUT--AND THEY WILL--
--I'LL HAVE MORE MADE. MANY MORE!

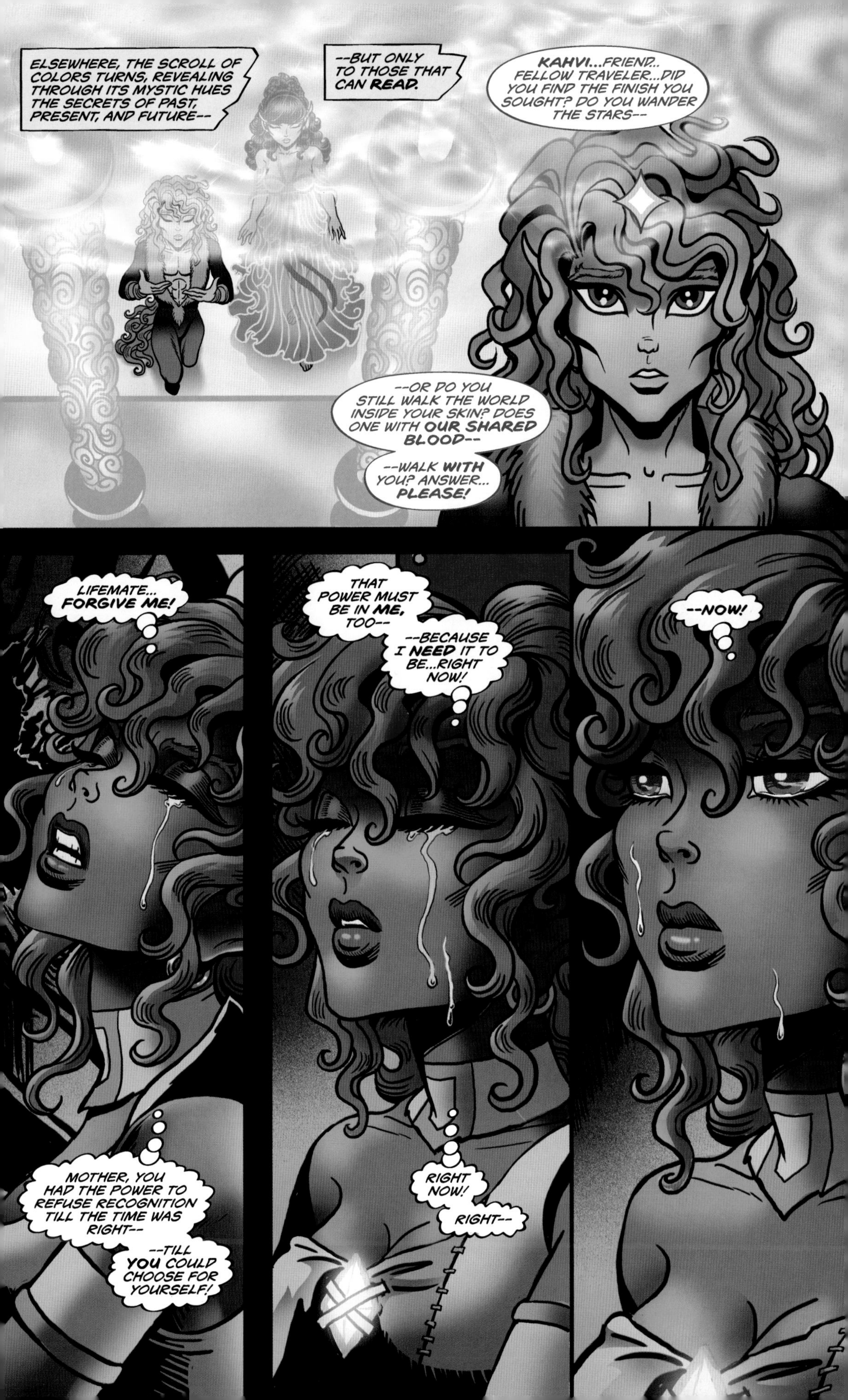

ELSEWHERE, THE SCROLL OF COLORS TURNS, REVEALING THROUGH ITS MYSTIC HUES THE SECRETS OF PAST, PRESENT, AND FUTURE--
--BUT ONLY TO THOSE THAT CAN READ.
KAHVI...FRIEND... FELLOW TRAVELER...DID YOU FIND THE FINISH YOU SOUGHT? DO YOU WANDER THE STARS--
--OR DO YOU STILL WALK THE WORLD INSIDE YOUR SKIN? DOES ONE WITH OUR SHARED BLOOD--
--WALK WITH YOU? ANSWER... PLEASE!
LIFEMATE... FORGIVE ME!
MOTHER, YOU HAD THE POWER TO REFUSE RECOGNITION TILL THE TIME WAS RIGHT--
--TILL YOU COULD CHOOSE FOR YOURSELF!
THAT POWER MUST BE IN ME, TOO--
--BECAUSE I NEED IT TO BE...RIGHT NOW!
RIGHT NOW!
RIGHT--
--NOW!

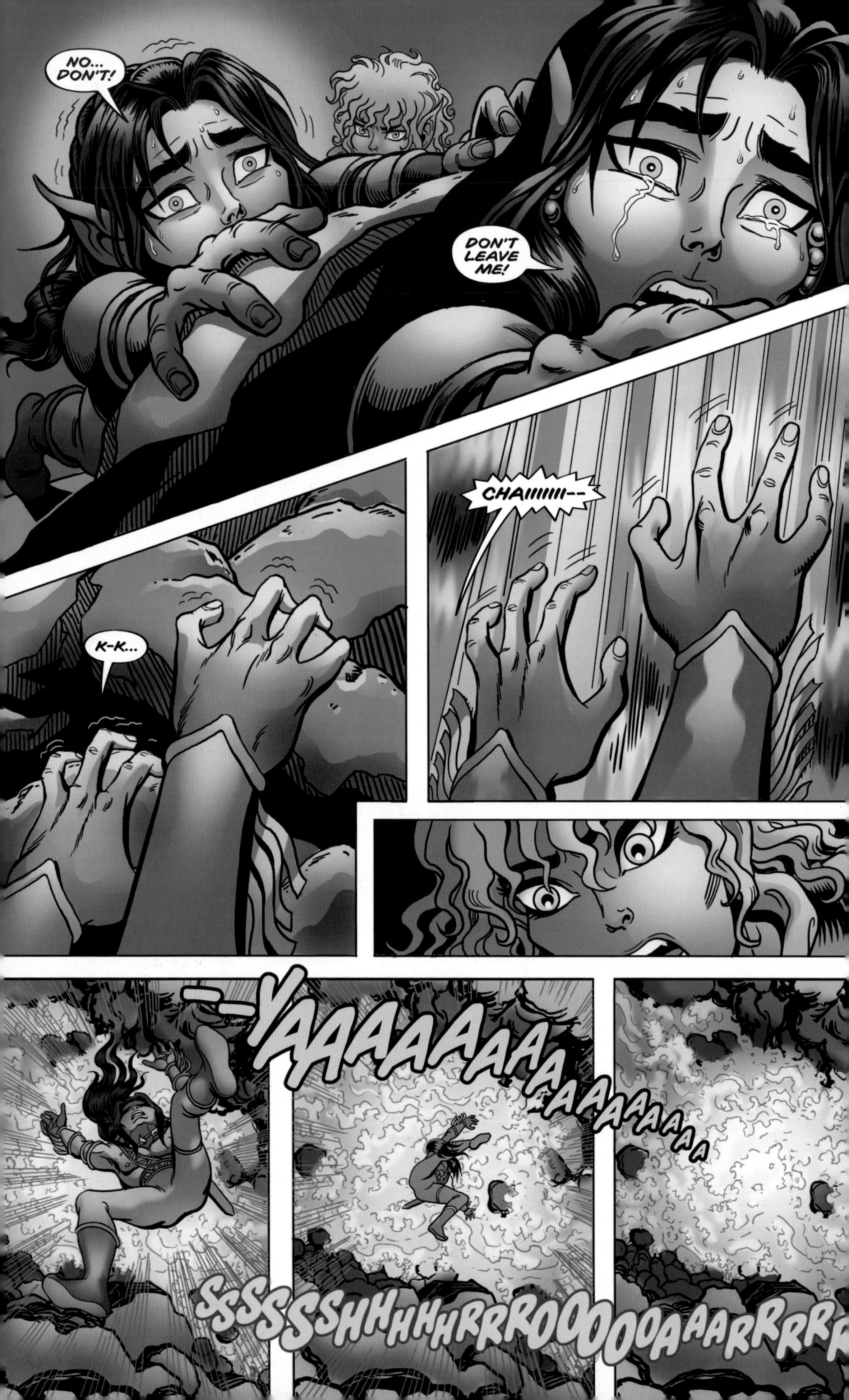
NO... DON'T!
DON'T LEAVE ME!
K-K...
CHAIIIIIII--
--YAAAAAAAAAAAAAAAAAA
SSSSSHHHHHHRRROOOOOOAAARRRRR

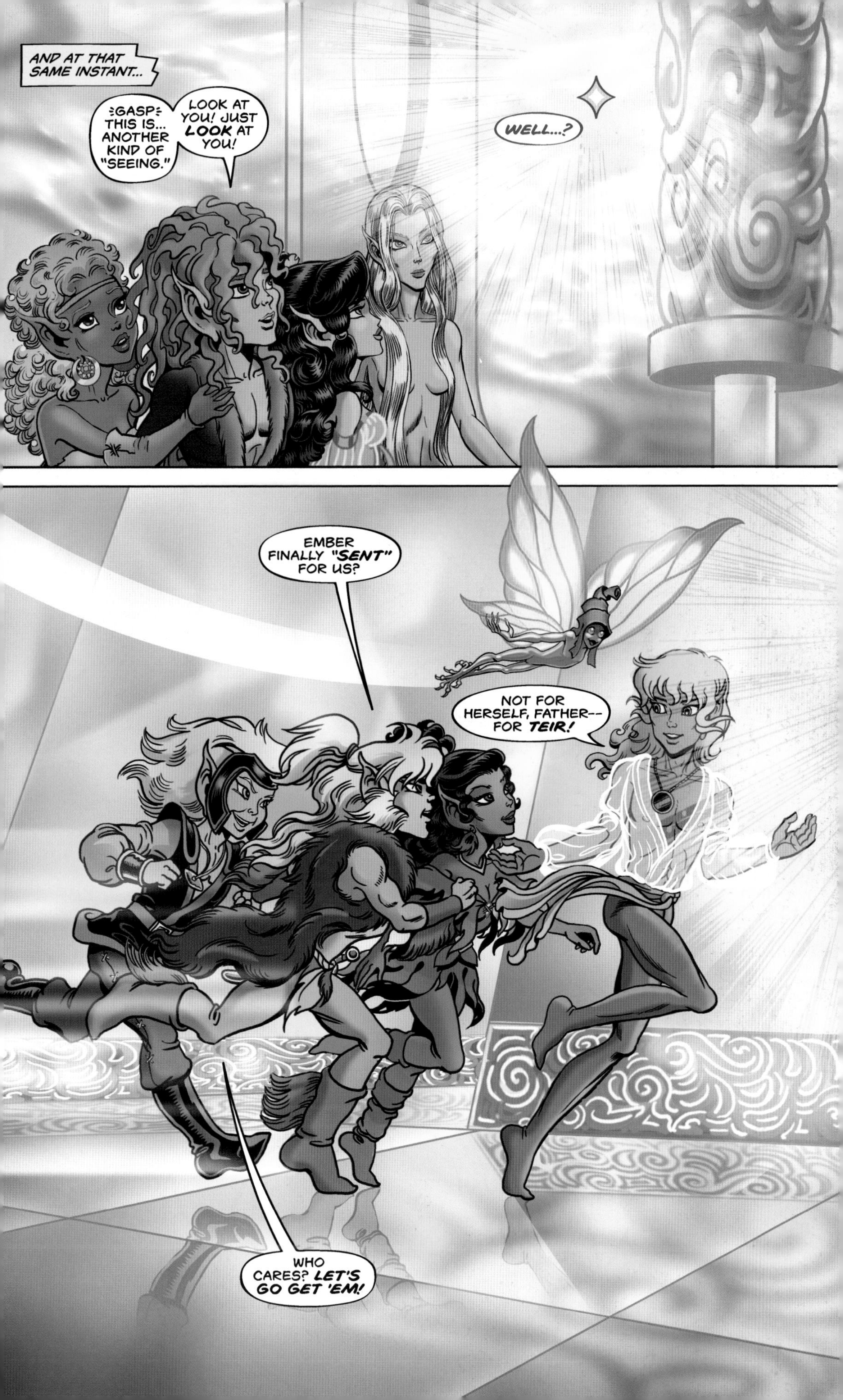
AND AT THAT SAME INSTANT...
:GASP: THIS IS... ANOTHER KIND OF "SEEING."
LOOK AT YOU! JUST LOOK AT YOU!
WELL...?
EMBER FINALLY "SENT" FOR US?
NOT FOR HERSELF, FATHER-- FOR TEIR!
WHO CARES? LET'S GO GET 'EM!

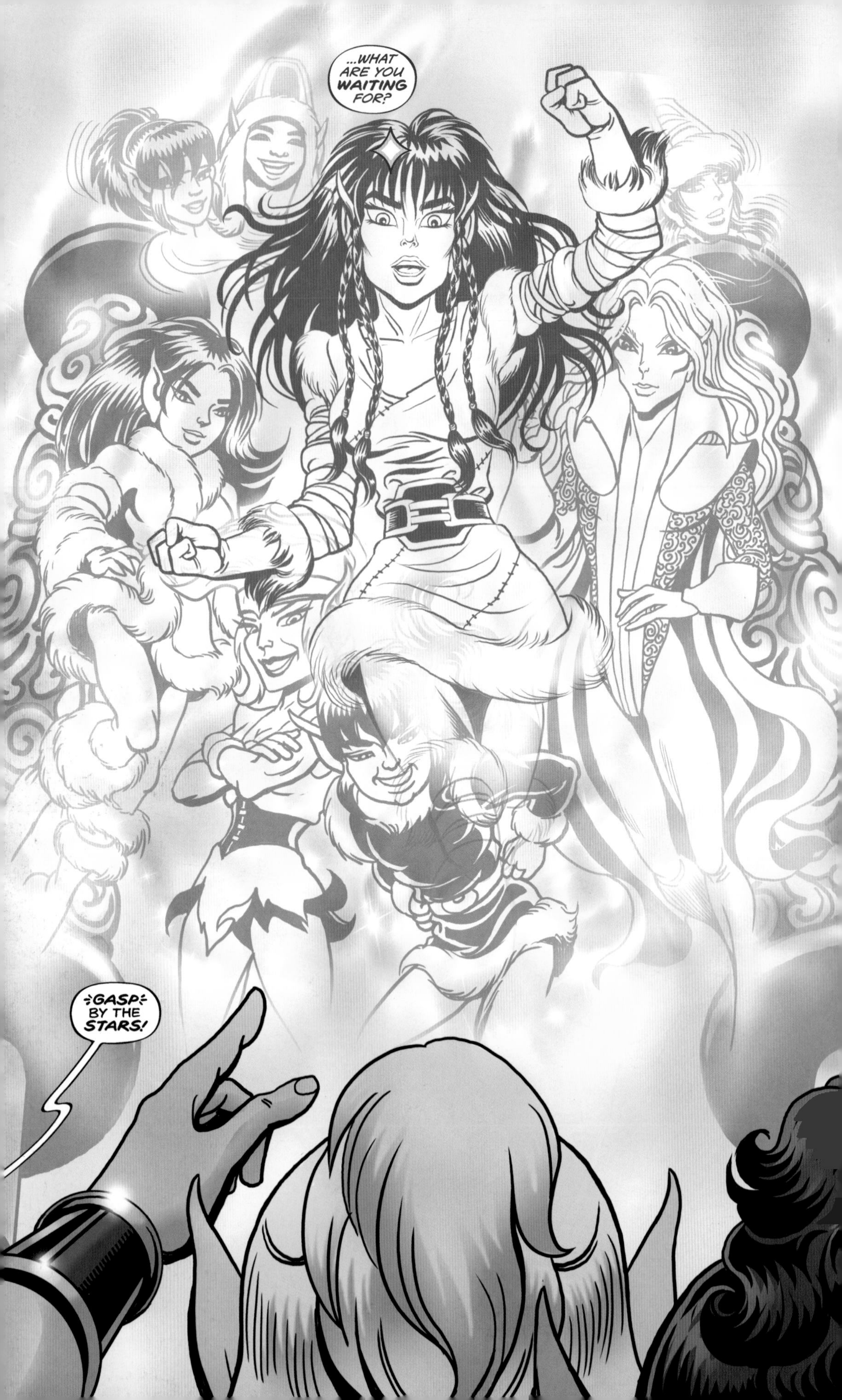
...WHAT ARE YOU WAITING FOR?
GASP BY THE STARS!

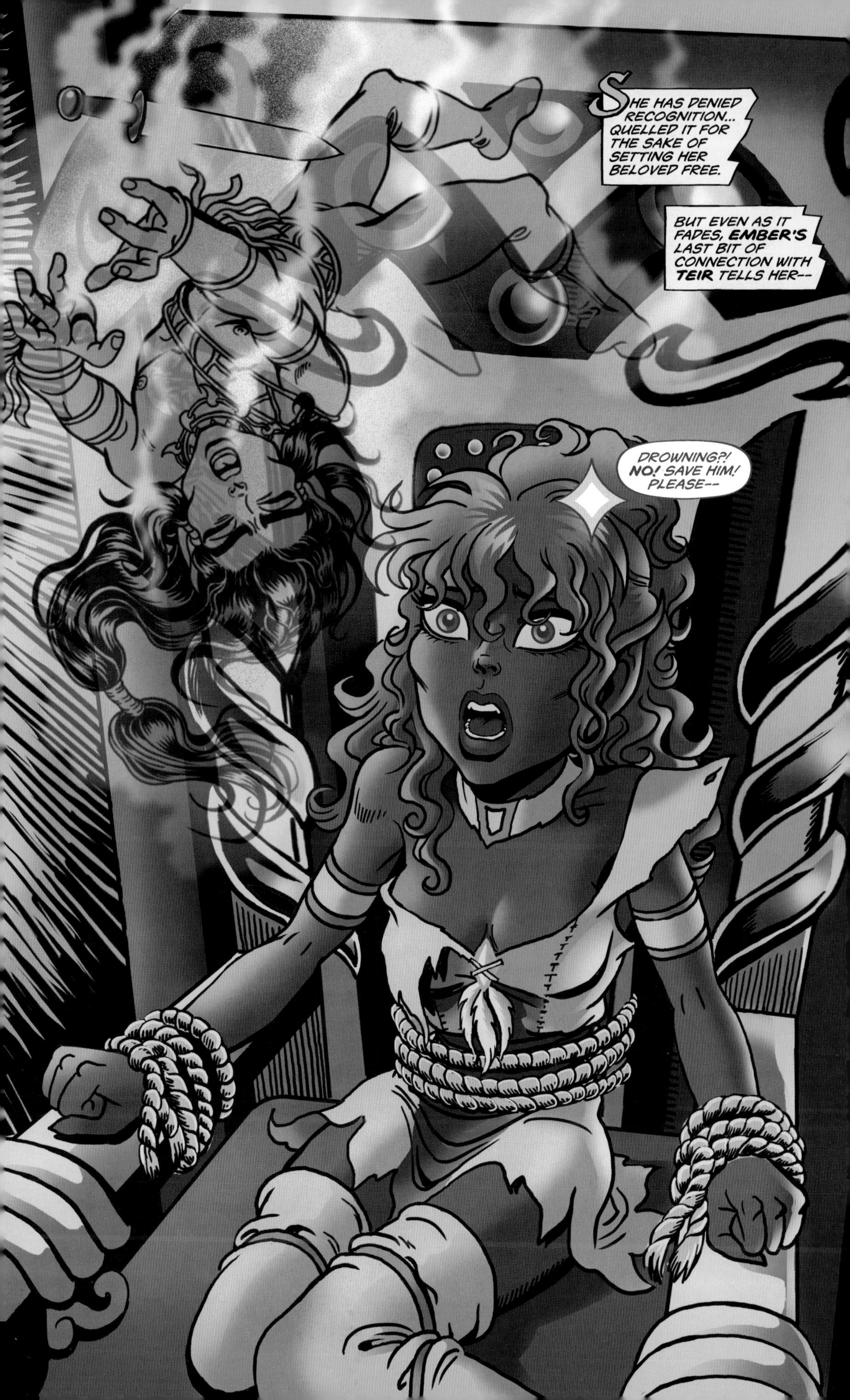

SHE HAS DENIED RECOGNITION... QUELLED IT FOR THE SAKE OF SETTING HER BELOVED FREE.
BUT EVEN AS IT FADES, EMBER'S LAST BIT OF CONNECTION WITH TEIR TELLS HER--
DROWNING?! NO! SAVE HIM! PLEASE--

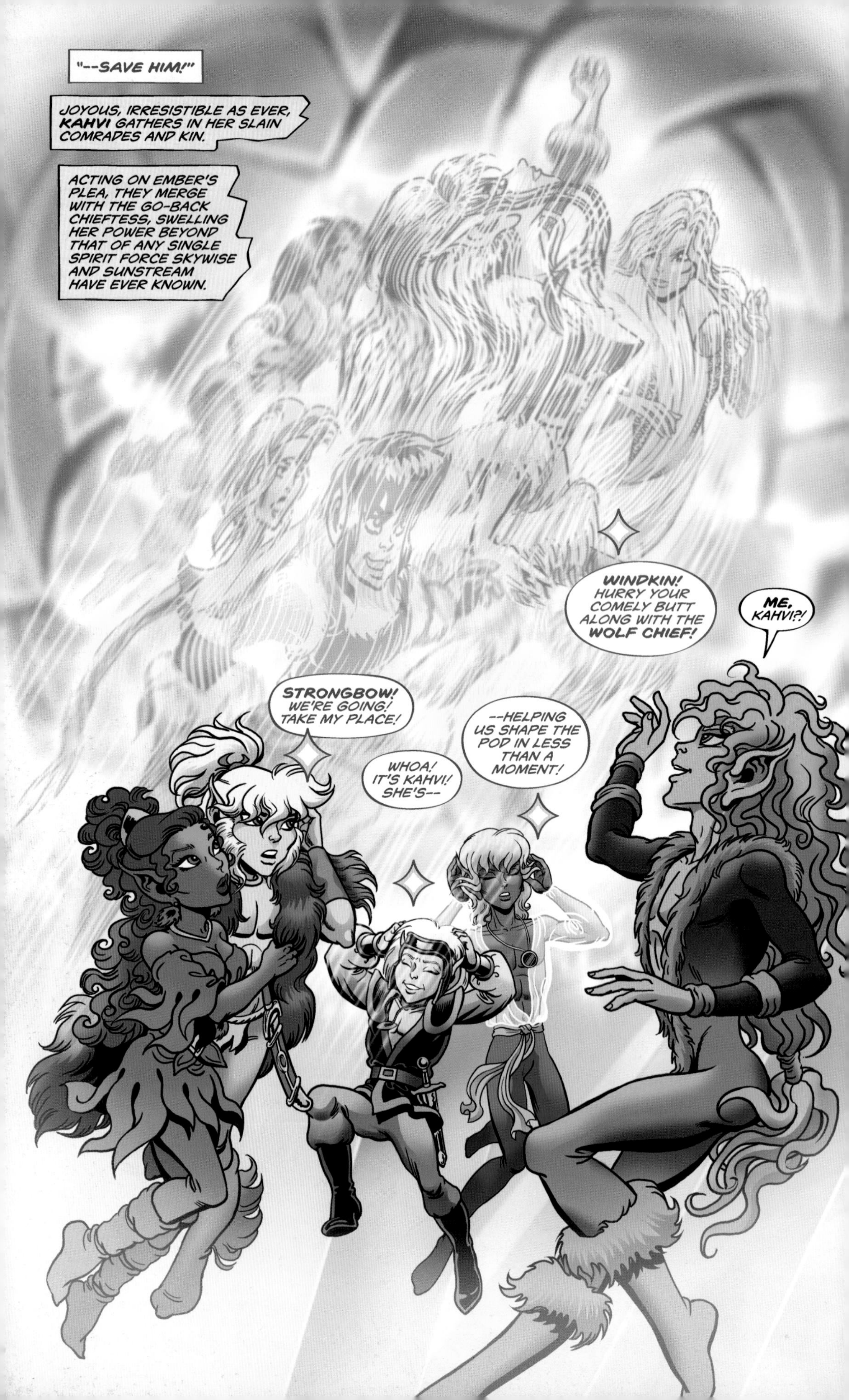
"--SAVE HIM!"
JOYOUS, IRRESISTIBLE AS EVER, KAHVI GATHERS IN HER SLAIN COMRADES AND KIN.
ACTING ON EMBER'S PLEA, THEY MERGE WITH THE GO-BACK CHIEFTESS, SWELLING HER POWER BEYOND THAT OF ANY SINGLE SPIRIT FORCE SKYWISE AND SUNSTREAM HAVE EVER KNOWN.
WINDKIN! HURRY YOUR COMELY BUTT ALONG WITH THE WOLF CHIEF!
ME, KAHVI?!
STRONGBOW! WE'RE GOING! TAKE MY PLACE!
WHOA! IT'S KAHVI! SHE'S--
--HELPING US SHAPE THE POD IN LESS THAN A MOMENT!

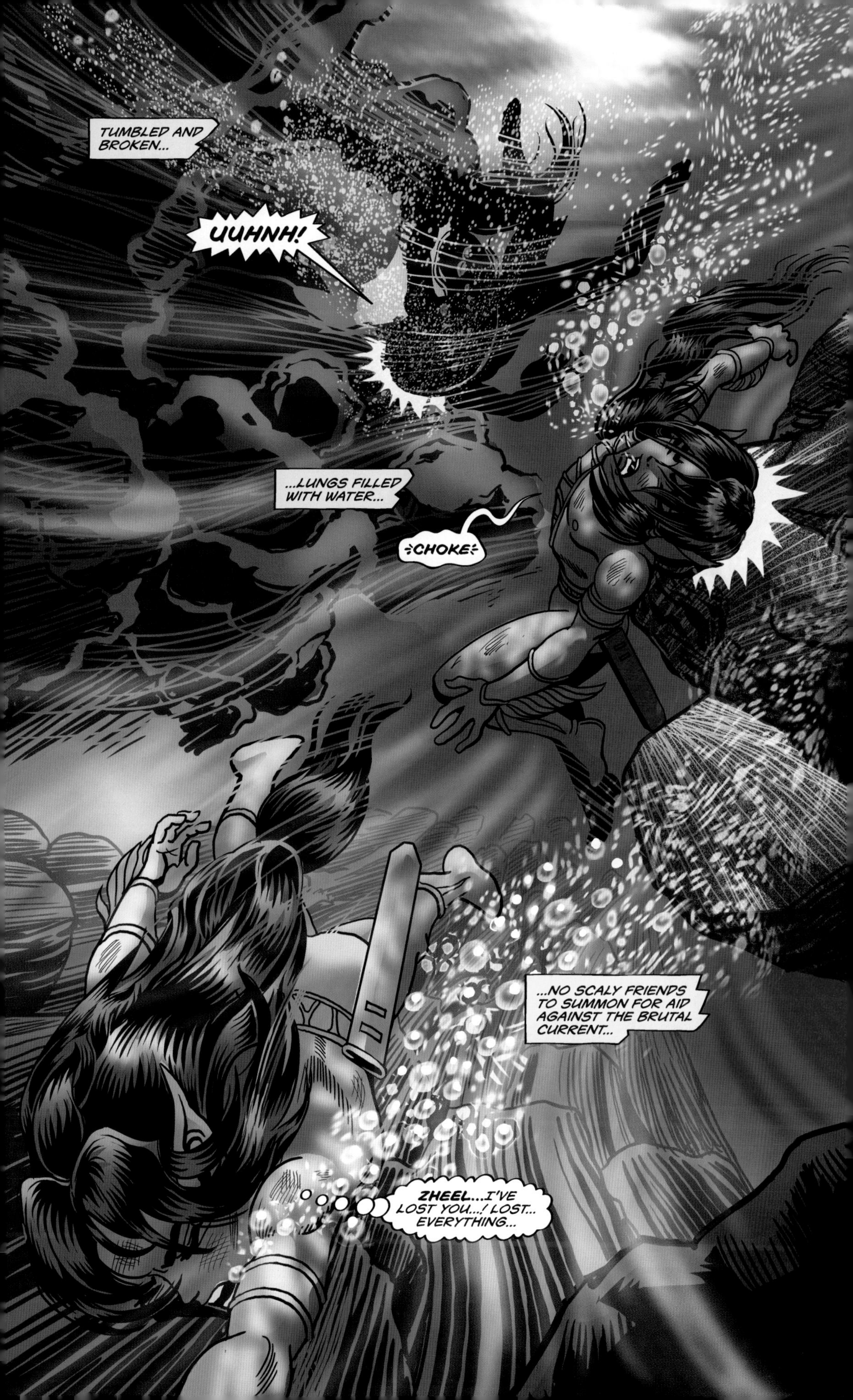

TUMBLED AND BROKEN...
UUHNH!
...LUNGS FILLED WITH WATER...
CHOKE
...NO SCALY FRIENDS TO SUMMON FOR AID AGAINST THE BRUTAL CURRENT...
ZHEEL...I'VE LOST YOU...! LOST... EVERYTHING...

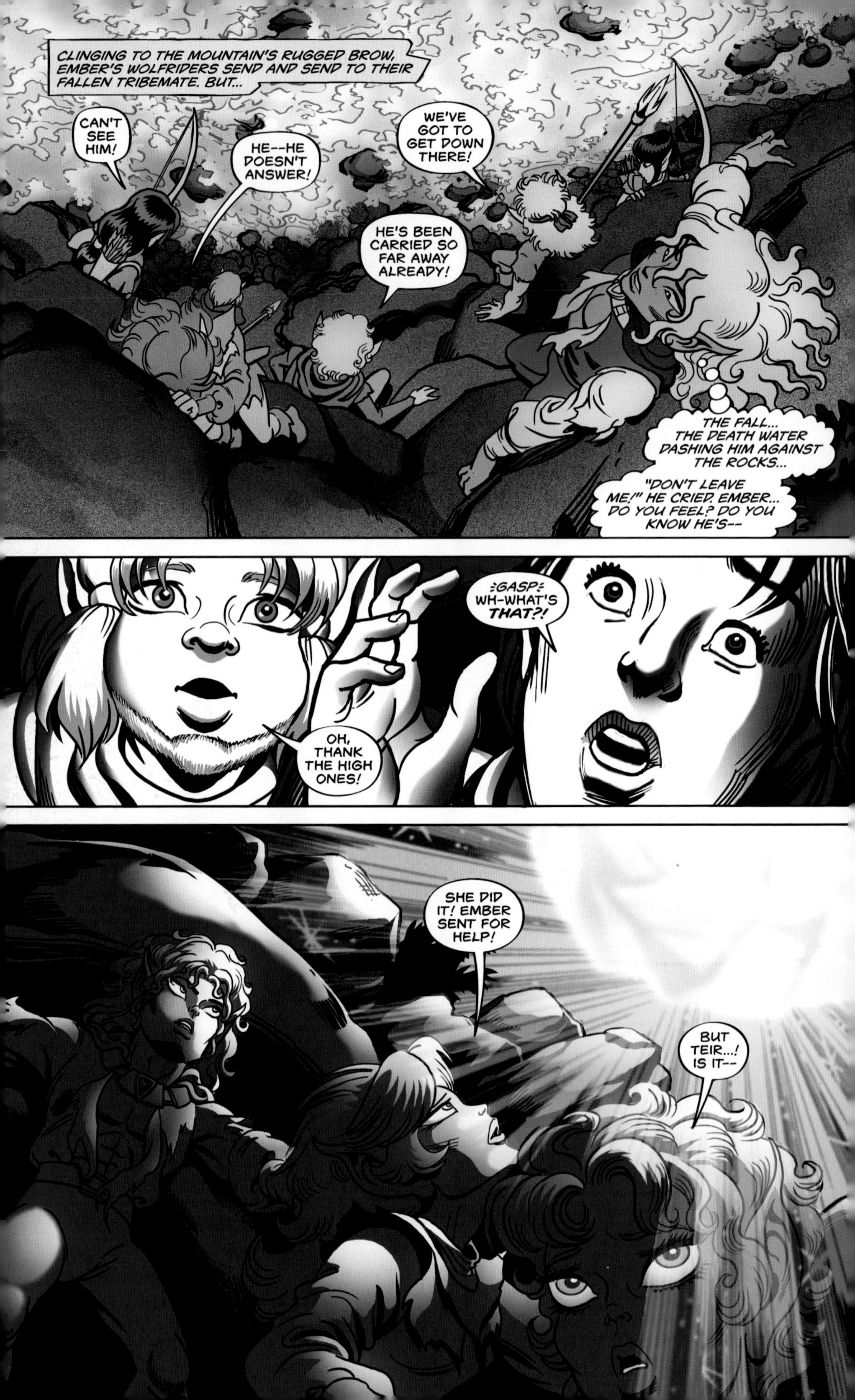
CLINGING TO THE MOUNTAIN'S RUGGED BROW, EMBER'S WOLFRIDERS SEND AND SEND TO THEIR FALLEN TRIBEMATE. BUT...
CAN'T SEE HIM!
HE--HE DOESN'T ANSWER!
WE'VE GOT TO GET DOWN THERE!
HE'S BEEN CARRIED SO FAR AWAY ALREADY!
THE FALL... THE DEATH WATER DASHING HIM AGAINST THE ROCKS...
"DON'T LEAVE ME!" HE CRIED. EMBER... DO YOU FEEL? DO YOU KNOW HE'S--
GASP WH-WHAT'S THAT?!
OH, THANK THE HIGH ONES!
SHE DID IT! EMBER SENT FOR HELP!
BUT TEIR...! IS IT--

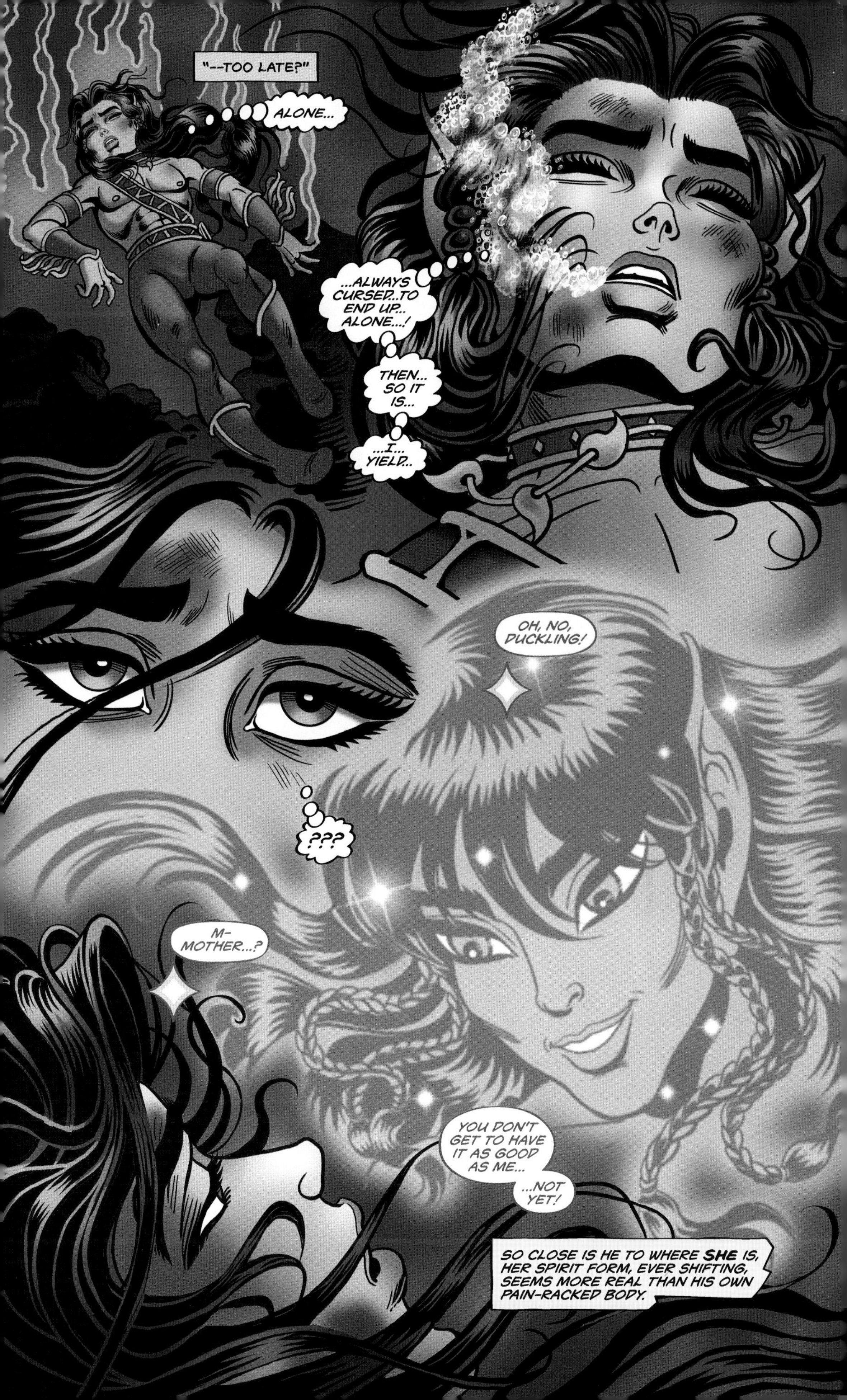
"--TOO LATE?"
ALONE...
...ALWAYS CURSED...TO END UP... ALONE...!
THEN... SO IT IS...
...I... YIELD...
OH, NO, DUCKLING!
???
M-MOTHER...?
YOU DON'T GET TO HAVE IT AS GOOD AS ME...
...NOT YET!
SO CLOSE IS HE TO WHERE SHE IS, HER SPIRIT FORM, EVER SHIFTING, SEEMS MORE REAL THAN HIS OWN PAIN-RACKED BODY.

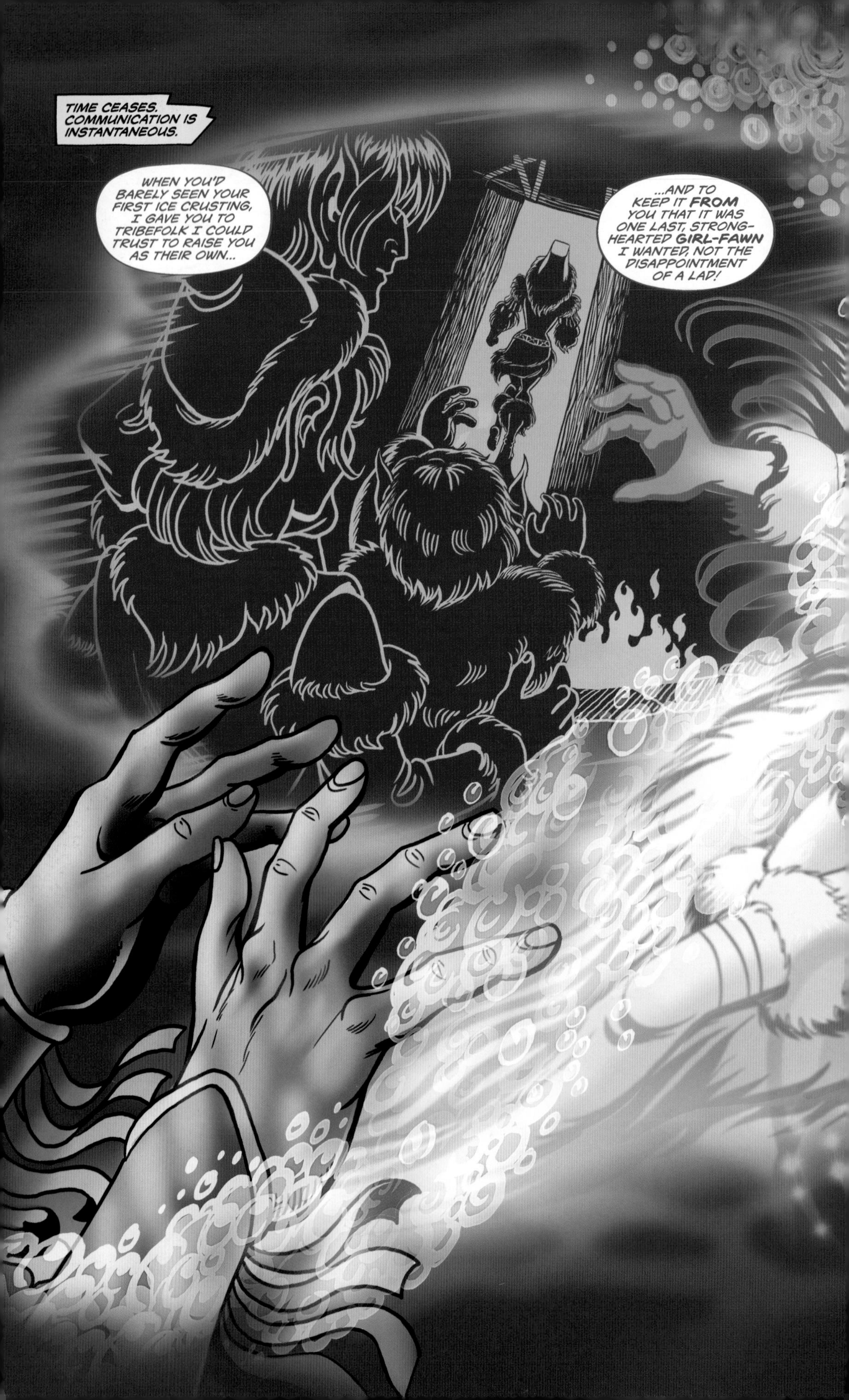
TIME CEASES. COMMUNICATION IS INSTANTANEOUS.
WHEN YOU'D BARELY SEEN YOUR FIRST ICE CRUSTING, I GAVE YOU TO TRIBEFOLK I COULD TRUST TO RAISE YOU AS THEIR OWN...
...AND TO KEEP IT **FROM** YOU THAT IT WAS ONE LAST, STRONG-HEARTED **GIRL-FAWN** I WANTED, NOT THE DISAPPOINTMENT OF A LAD!

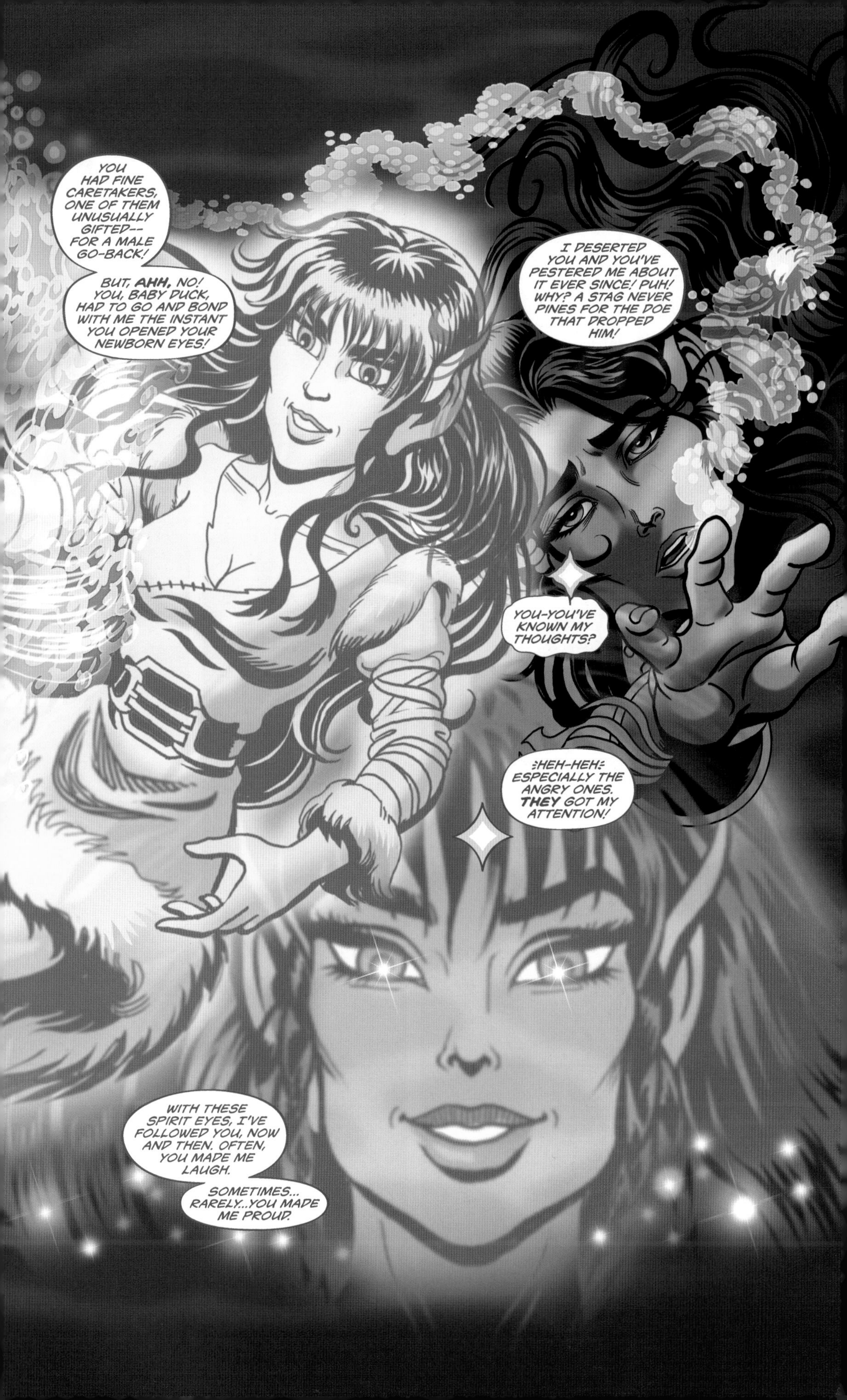
YOU HAD FINE CARETAKERS, ONE OF THEM UNUSUALLY GIFTED-- FOR A MALE GO-BACK!
BUT, AHH, NO! YOU, BABY DUCK, HAD TO GO AND BOND WITH ME THE INSTANT YOU OPENED YOUR NEWBORN EYES!
I DESERTED YOU AND YOU'VE PESTERED ME ABOUT IT EVER SINCE! PUH! WHY? A STAG NEVER PINES FOR THE DOE THAT DROPPED HIM!
YOU-YOU'VE KNOWN MY THOUGHTS?
HEH-HEH ESPECIALLY THE ANGRY ONES. THEY GOT MY ATTENTION!
WITH THESE SPIRIT EYES, I'VE FOLLOWED YOU, NOW AND THEN. OFTEN, YOU MADE ME LAUGH.
SOMETIMES... RARELY...YOU MADE ME PROUD.

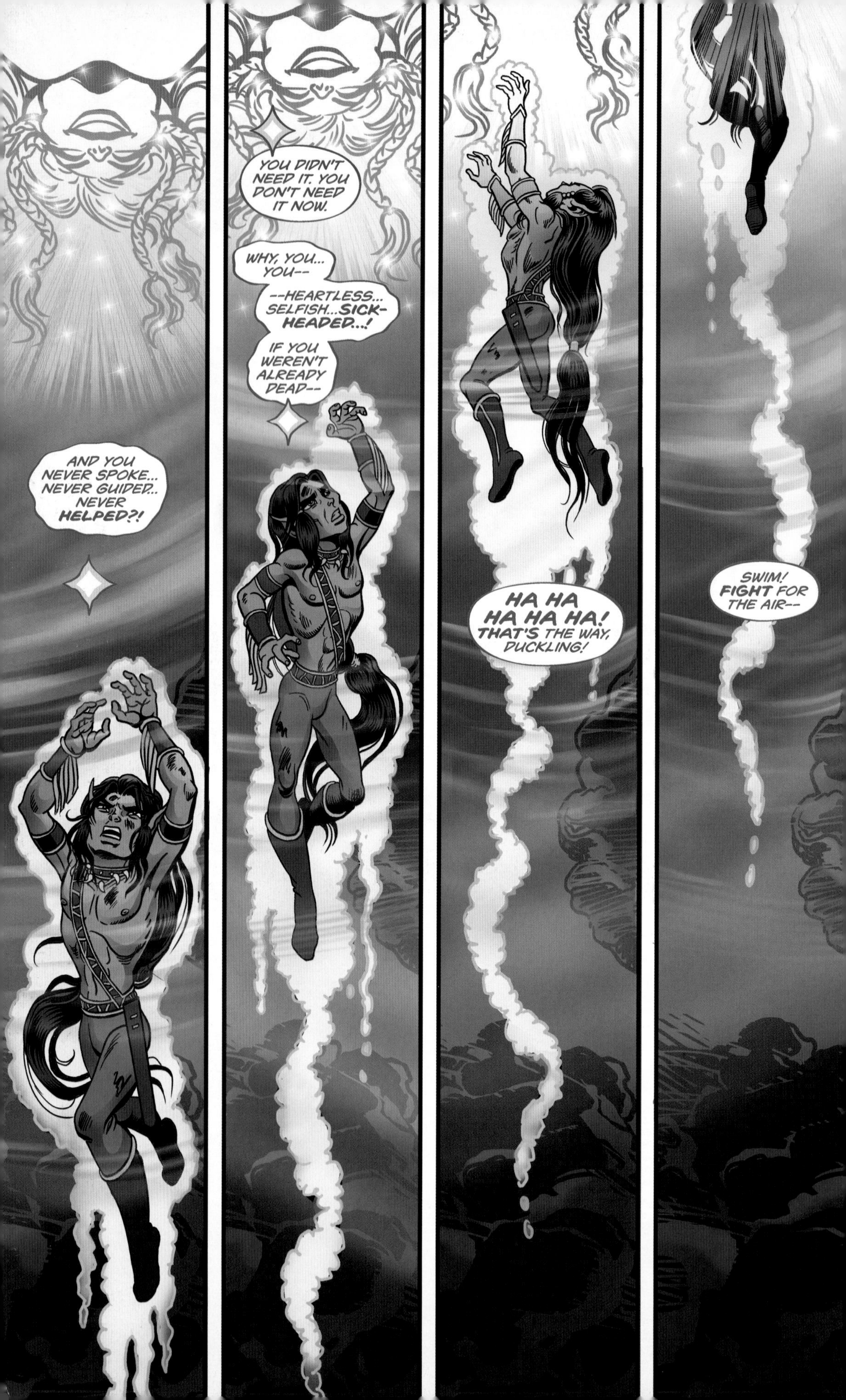
AND YOU NEVER SPOKE... NEVER GUIDED... NEVER HELPED?!
YOU DIDN'T NEED IT. YOU DON'T NEED IT NOW.
WHY, YOU... YOU--
--HEARTLESS... SELFISH...SICK-HEADED...!
IF YOU WEREN'T ALREADY DEAD--
HA HA HA HA HA! THAT'S THE WAY, DUCKLING!
SWIM! FIGHT FOR THE AIR--

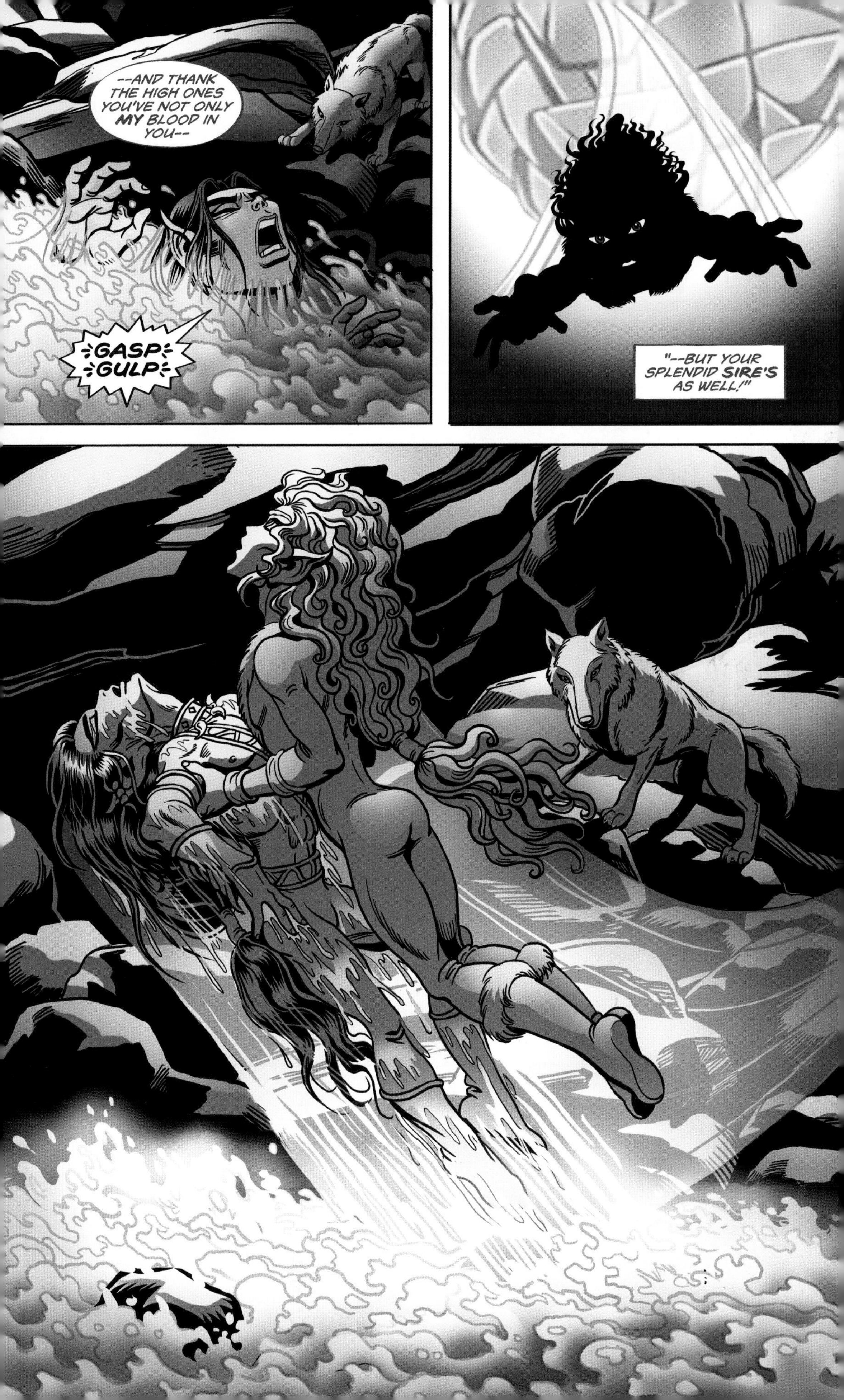
--AND THANK THE HIGH ONES YOU'VE NOT ONLY MY BLOOD IN YOU--
GASP GULP
"--BUT YOUR SPLENDID SIRE'S AS WELL!"

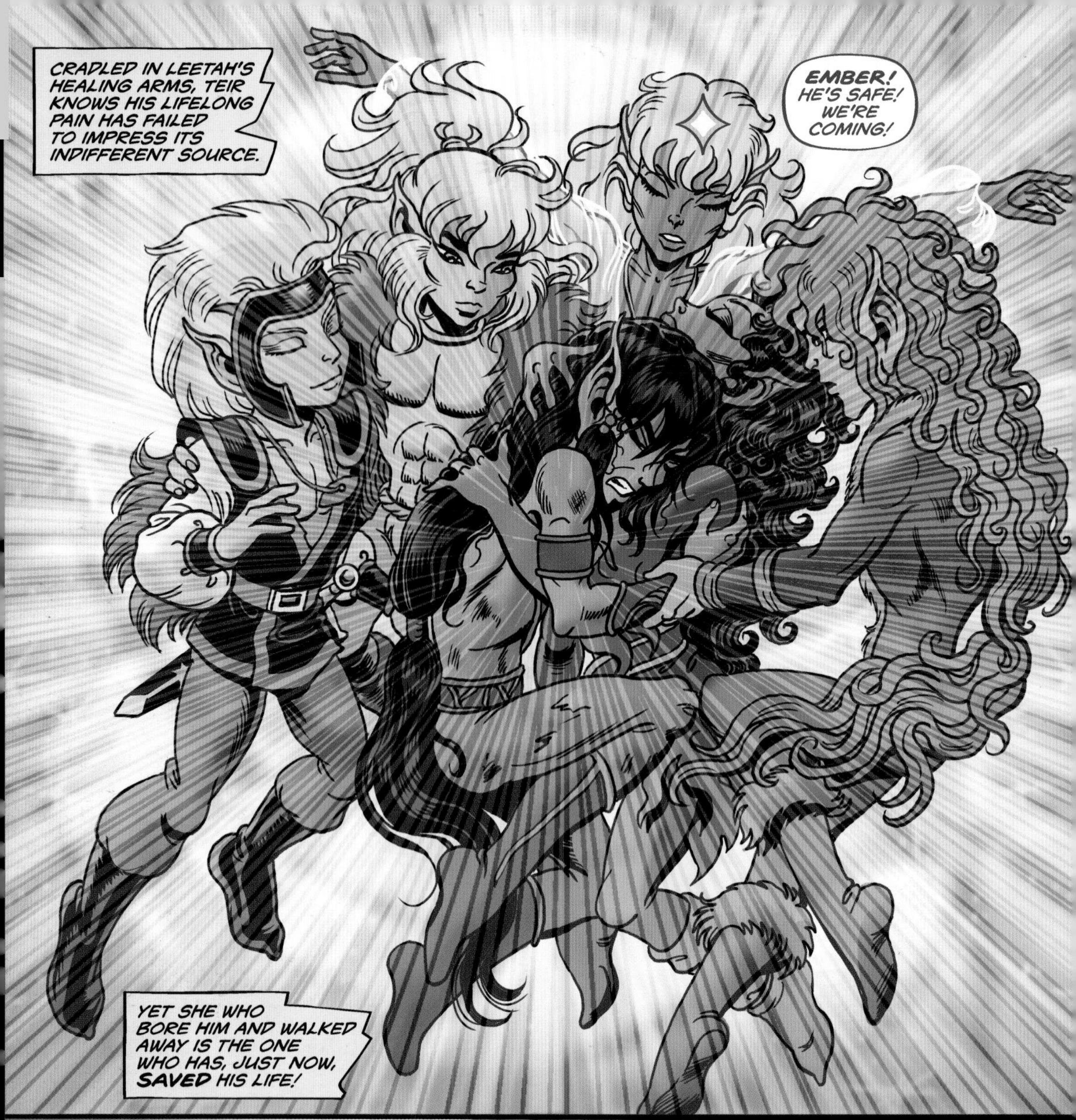
CRADLED IN LEETAH'S HEALING ARMS, TEIR KNOWS HIS LIFELONG PAIN HAS FAILED TO IMPRESS ITS INDIFFERENT SOURCE.
EMBER! HE'S SAFE! WE'RE COMING!
YET SHE WHO BORE HIM AND WALKED AWAY IS THE ONE WHO HAS, JUST NOW, SAVED HIS LIFE!

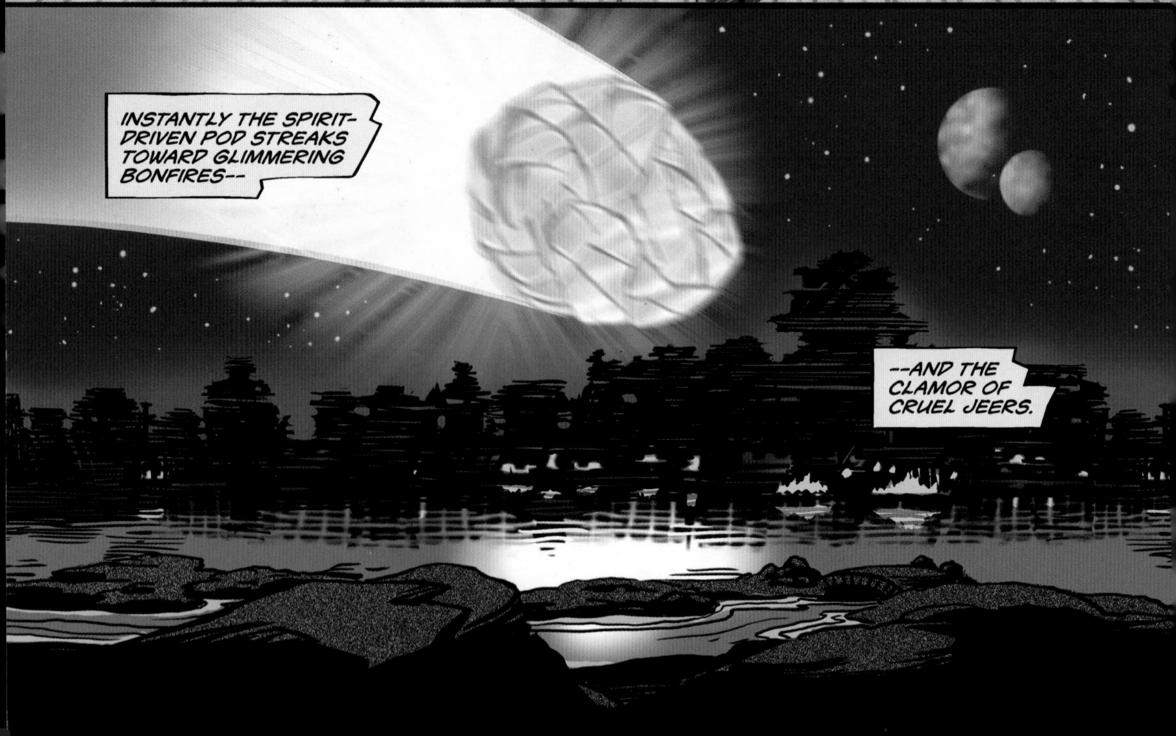
INSTANTLY THE SPIRIT-DRIVEN POD STREAKS TOWARD GLIMMERING BONFIRES--
--AND THE CLAMOR OF CRUEL JEERS.

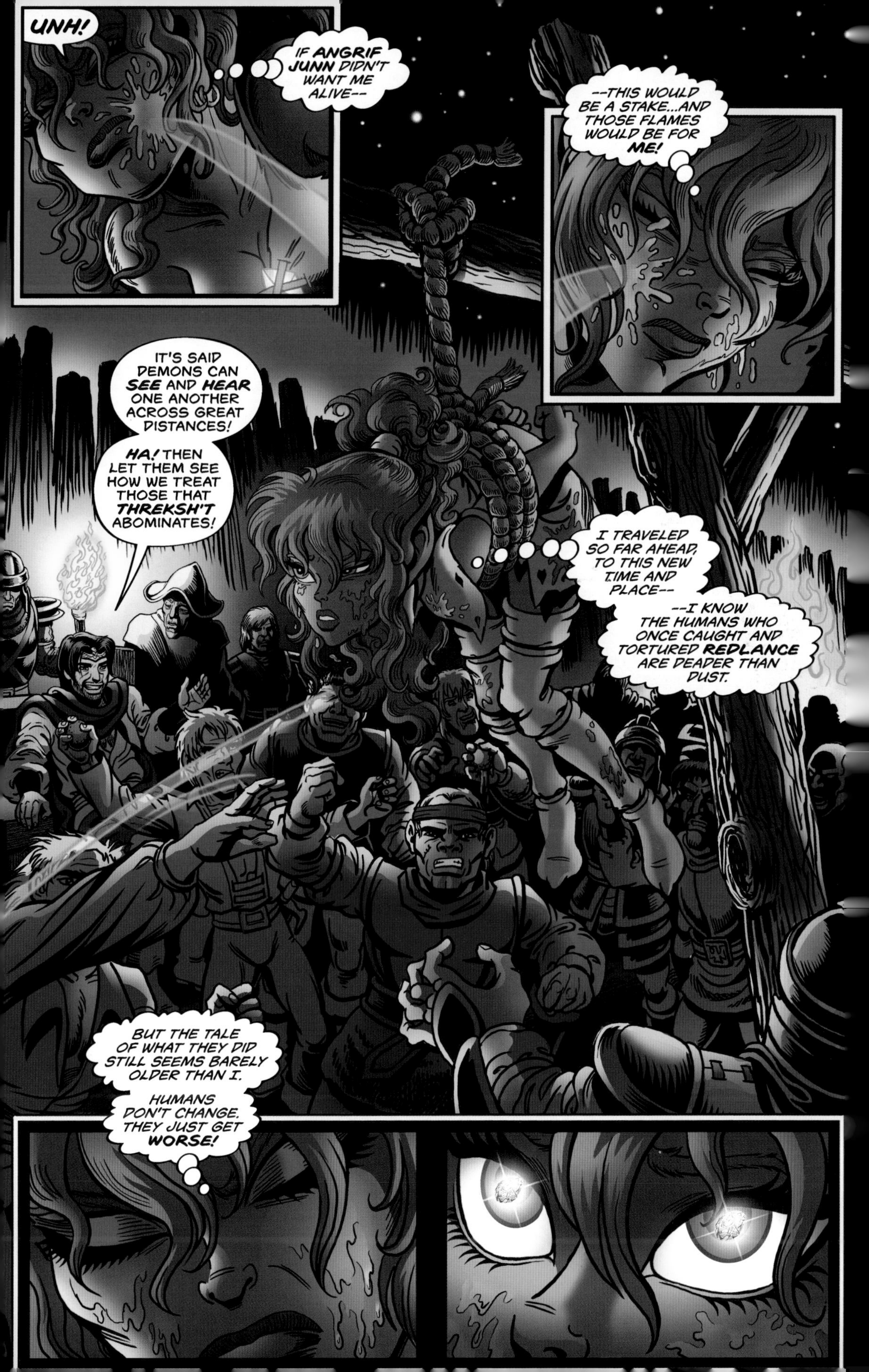
UNH!
IF ANGRIF JUNN DIDN'T WANT ME ALIVE--
--THIS WOULD BE A STAKE...AND THOSE FLAMES WOULD BE FOR ME!
IT'S SAID DEMONS CAN SEE AND HEAR ONE ANOTHER ACROSS GREAT DISTANCES!
HA! THEN LET THEM SEE HOW WE TREAT THOSE THAT THREKSH'T ABOMINATES!
I TRAVELED SO FAR AHEAD, TO THIS NEW TIME AND PLACE--
--I KNOW THE HUMANS WHO ONCE CAUGHT AND TORTURED REDLANCE ARE DEADER THAN DUST.
BUT THE TALE OF WHAT THEY DID STILL SEEMS BARELY OLDER THAN I.
HUMANS DON'T CHANGE. THEY JUST GET WORSE!

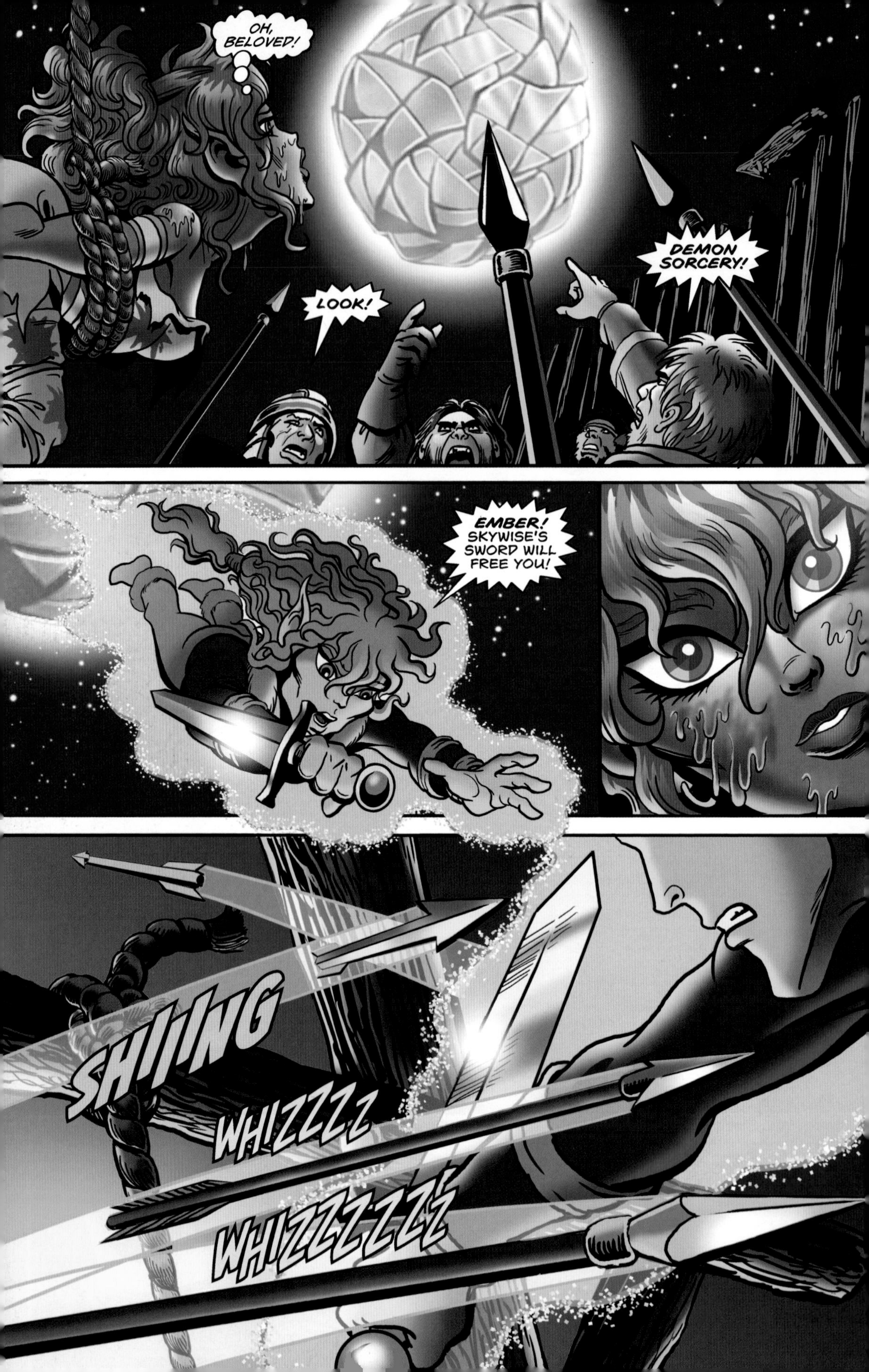
OH, BELOVED!
LOOK!
DEMON SORCERY!
EMBER! SKYWISE'S SWORD WILL FREE YOU!
SHIIING
WHIZZZZ
WHIZZZZZZ

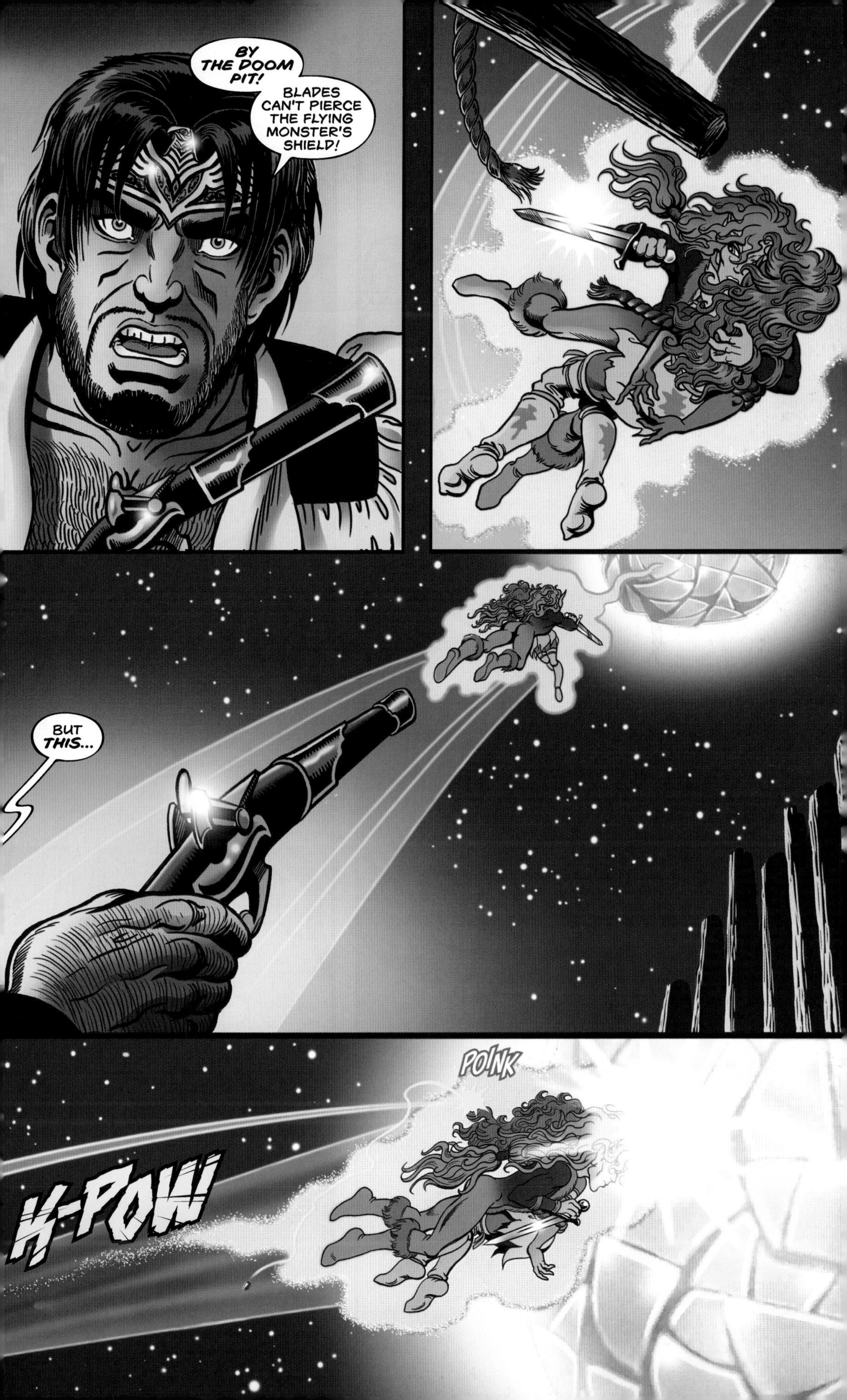
BY THE DOOM PIT!
BLADES CAN'T PIERCE THE FLYING MONSTER'S SHIELD!
BUT THIS...
POINK
K-POW

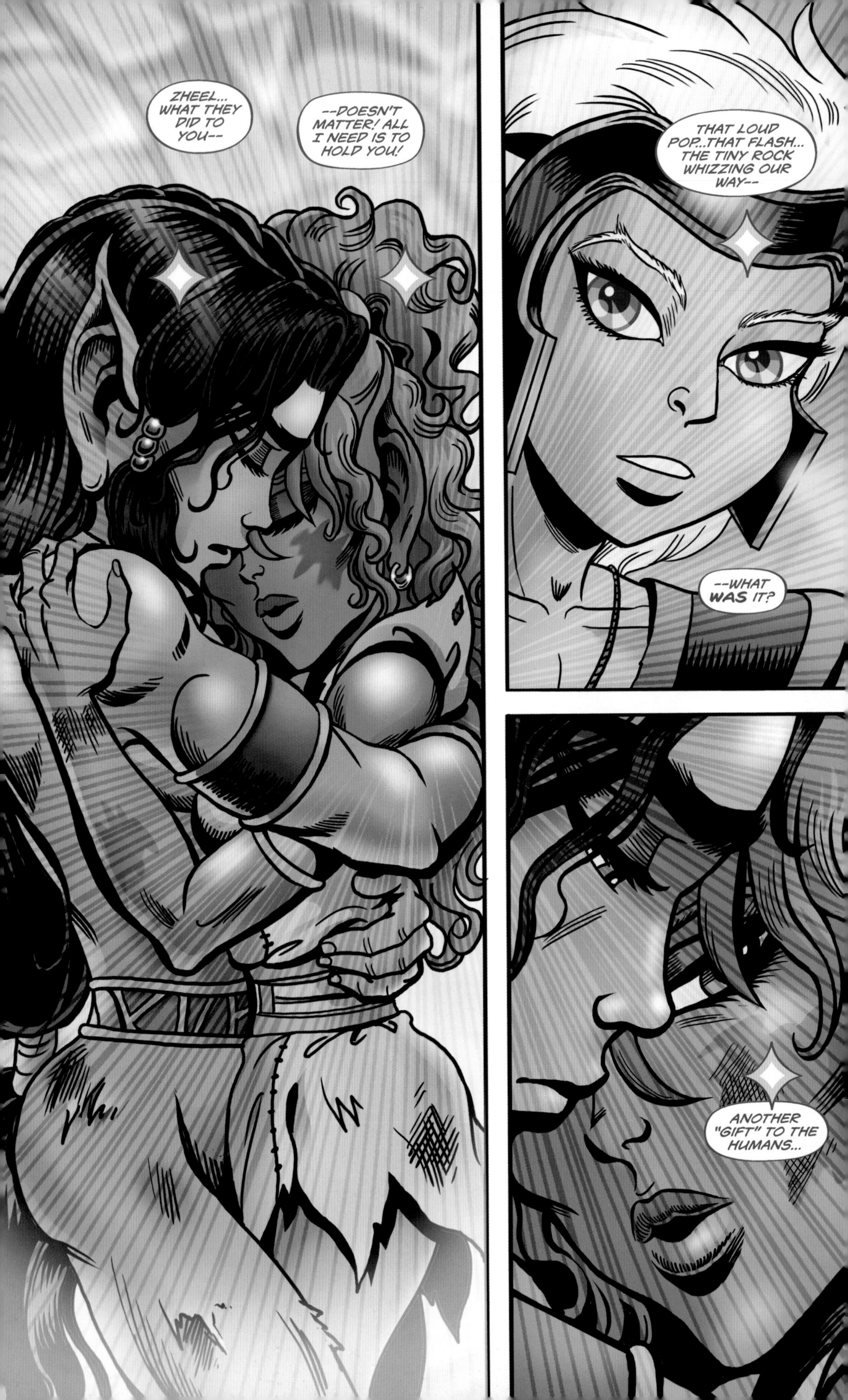
ZHEEL... WHAT THEY DID TO YOU--
--DOESN'T MATTER! ALL I NEED IS TO HOLD YOU!
THAT LOUD POP...THAT FLASH... THE TINY ROCK WHIZZING OUR WAY--
--WHAT **WAS** IT?
ANOTHER "GIFT" TO THE HUMANS...

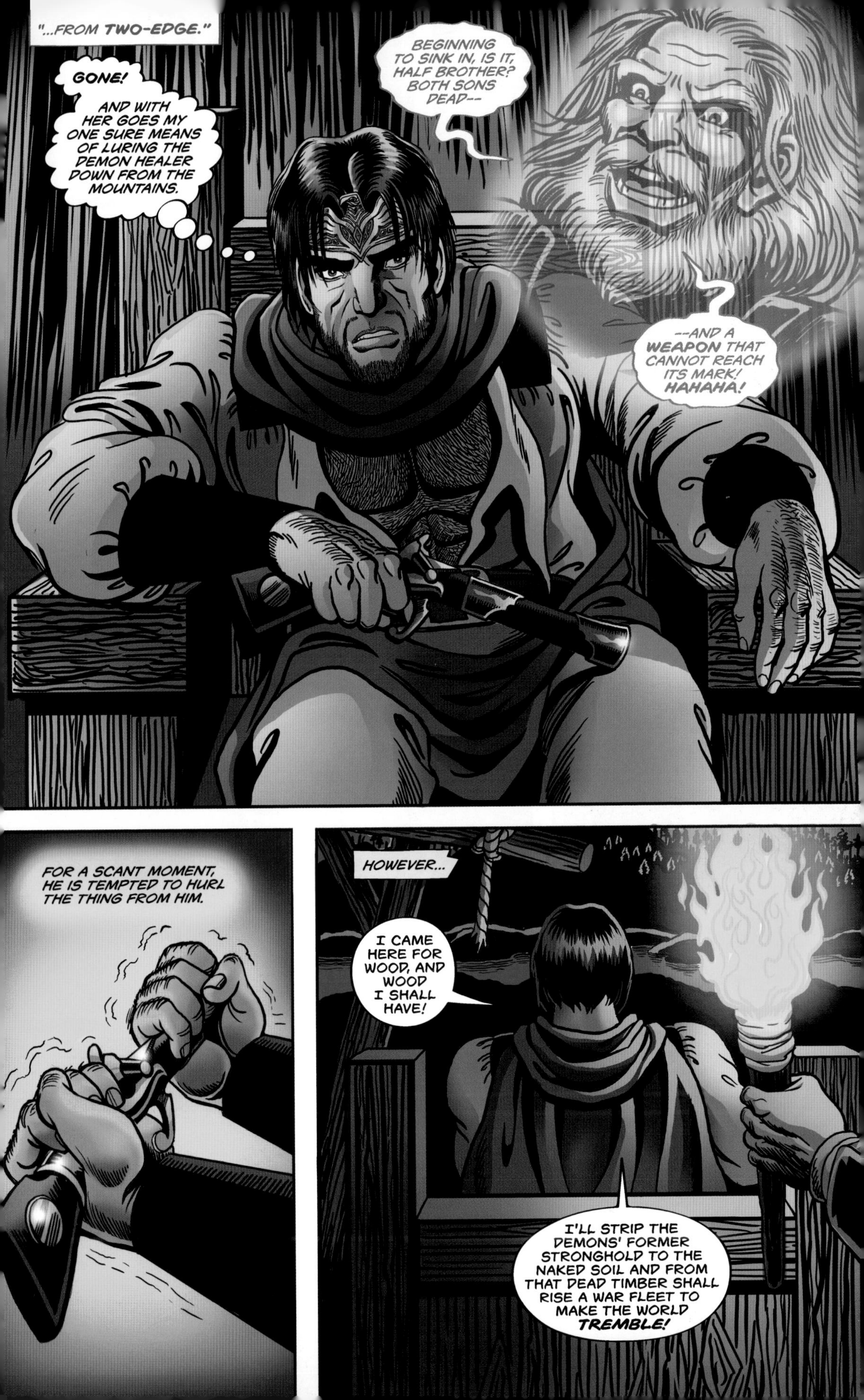
"...FROM TWO-EDGE."
GONE!
AND WITH HER GOES MY ONE SURE MEANS OF LURING THE DEMON HEALER DOWN FROM THE MOUNTAINS.
BEGINNING TO SINK IN, IS IT, HALF BROTHER? BOTH SONS DEAD--
--AND A WEAPON THAT CANNOT REACH ITS MARK! HAHAHA!
FOR A SCANT MOMENT, HE IS TEMPTED TO HURL THE THING FROM HIM.
HOWEVER...
I CAME HERE FOR WOOD, AND WOOD I SHALL HAVE!
I'LL STRIP THE DEMONS' FORMER STRONGHOLD TO THE NAKED SOIL AND FROM THAT DEAD TIMBER SHALL RISE A WAR FLEET TO MAKE THE WORLD TREMBLE!

EVEN AS THE WOUNDED DJUN GROWLS HIS OATH, THE MAGICAL VESSEL APPEARS IN THE MIDST OF EMBER'S THANKFUL TRIBEMATES.

:GASP: THEY DID IT!

AND ALL IN THREE BLINKS OF AN EYE!

AYOOOOAAAAHHH!

OOOOOOWWWOOOOOOO

...

WHAT ARE *THEY* DOING HERE, KHORBASI?

THEY--THEY'RE THE CHILDREN YOU GAVE ME PERMISSION TO RESCUE, CHIEFTESS.

HUMANS...

THOUGH WE SEE NO BLOOD, YOU'VE BEEN WOUNDED FOR CERTAIN, CUB.

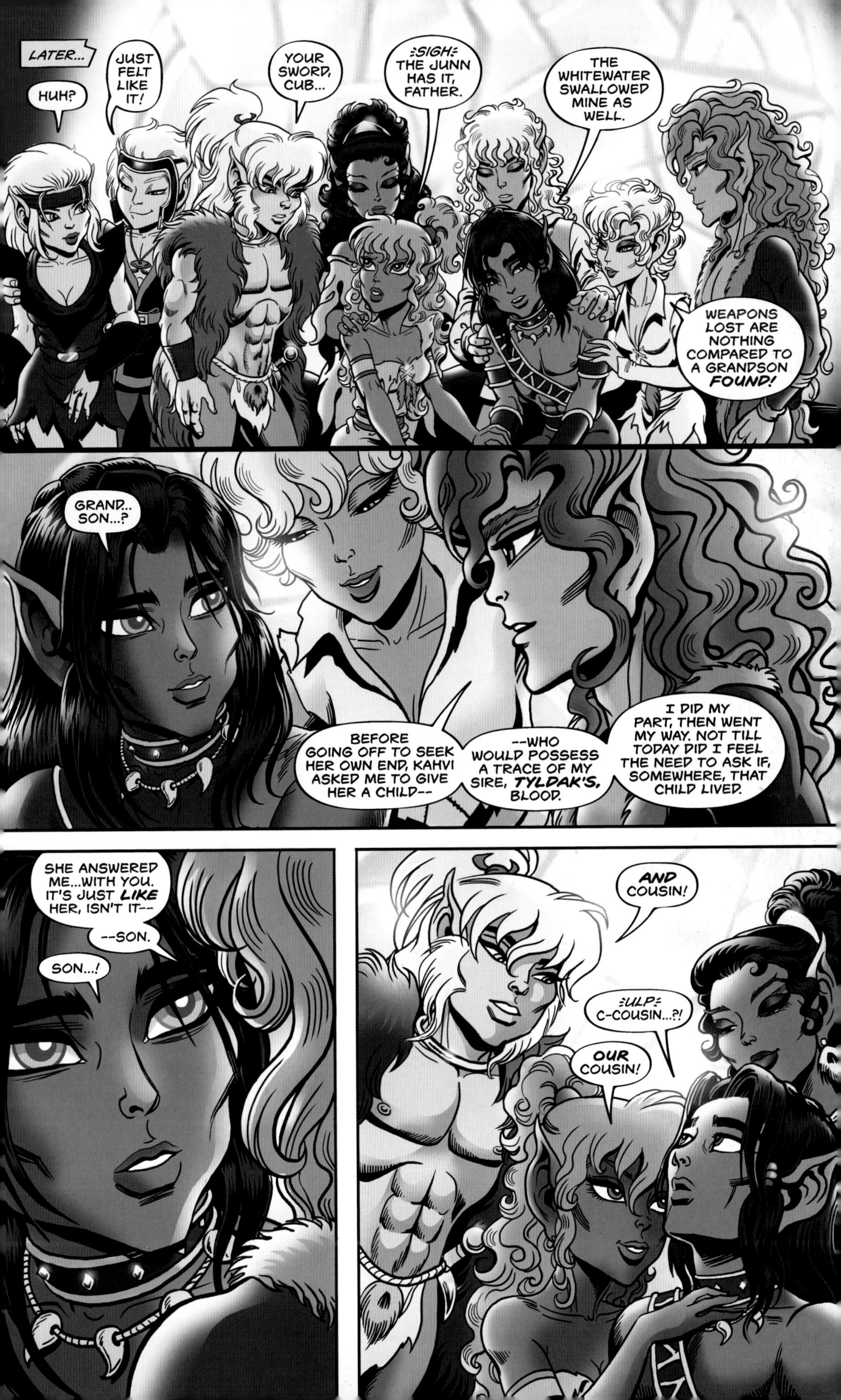
LATER...
HUH?
JUST FELT LIKE IT!
YOUR SWORD, CUB...
SIGH
THE JUNN HAS IT, FATHER.
THE WHITEWATER SWALLOWED MINE AS WELL.
WEAPONS LOST ARE NOTHING COMPARED TO A GRANDSON FOUND!
GRAND... SON...?
BEFORE GOING OFF TO SEEK HER OWN END, KAHVI ASKED ME TO GIVE HER A CHILD--
--WHO WOULD POSSESS A TRACE OF MY SIRE, TYLDAK'S, BLOOD.
I DID MY PART, THEN WENT MY WAY. NOT TILL TODAY DID I FEEL THE NEED TO ASK IF, SOMEWHERE, THAT CHILD LIVED.
SHE ANSWERED ME...WITH YOU. IT'S JUST LIKE HER, ISN'T IT--
--SON.
SON...!
AND COUSIN!
ULP
C-COUSIN...?!
OUR COUSIN!

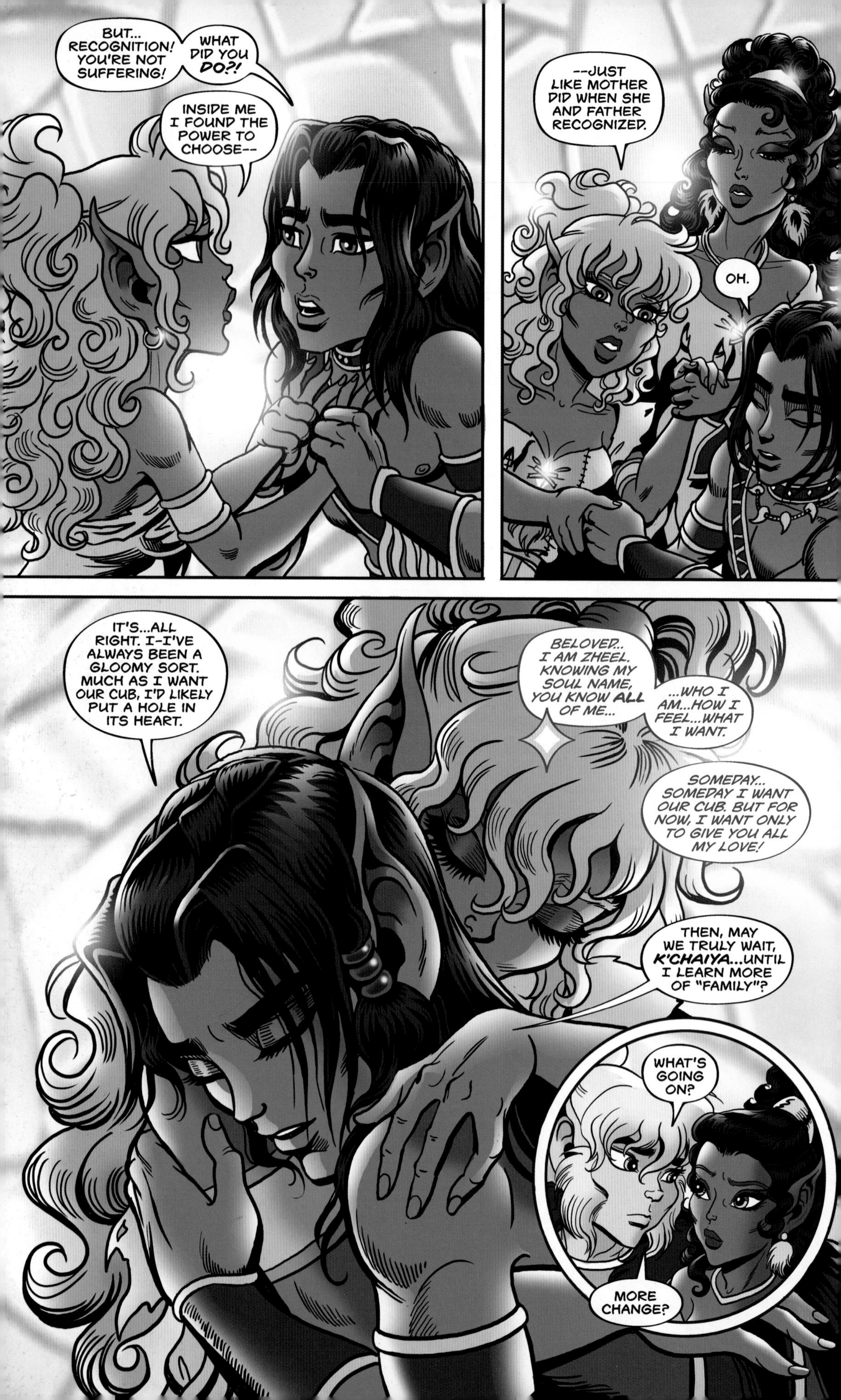

BUT... RECOGNITION! YOU'RE NOT SUFFERING!
WHAT DID YOU DO?!
INSIDE ME I FOUND THE POWER TO CHOOSE--
--JUST LIKE MOTHER DID WHEN SHE AND FATHER RECOGNIZED.
OH.
IT'S...ALL RIGHT. I-I'VE ALWAYS BEEN A GLOOMY SORT. MUCH AS I WANT OUR CUB, I'D LIKELY PUT A HOLE IN ITS HEART.
BELOVED... I AM ZHEEL. KNOWING MY SOUL NAME, YOU KNOW ALL OF ME...
...WHO I AM...HOW I FEEL...WHAT I WANT.
SOMEDAY... SOMEDAY I WANT OUR CUB. BUT FOR NOW, I WANT ONLY TO GIVE YOU ALL MY LOVE!
THEN, MAY WE TRULY WAIT, K'CHAIYA...UNTIL I LEARN MORE OF "FAMILY"?
WHAT'S GOING ON?
MORE CHANGE?

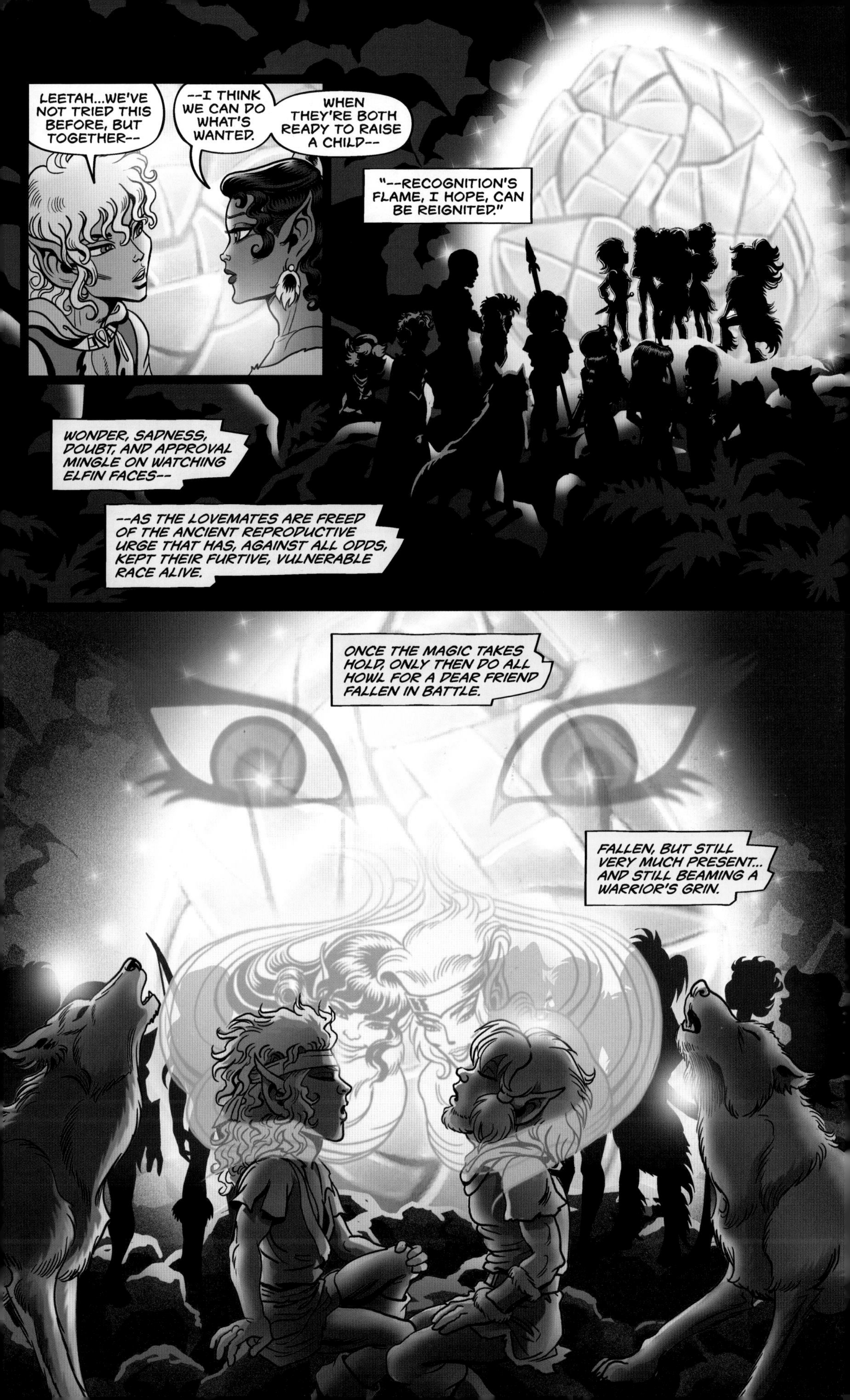

LEETAH...WE'VE NOT TRIED THIS BEFORE, BUT TOGETHER--
--I THINK WE CAN DO WHAT'S WANTED.
WHEN THEY'RE BOTH READY TO RAISE A CHILD--
"--RECOGNITION'S FLAME, I HOPE, CAN BE REIGNITED."
WONDER, SADNESS, DOUBT, AND APPROVAL MINGLE ON WATCHING ELFIN FACES--
--AS THE LOVEMATES ARE FREED OF THE ANCIENT REPRODUCTIVE URGE THAT HAS, AGAINST ALL ODDS, KEPT THEIR FURTIVE, VULNERABLE RACE ALIVE.
ONCE THE MAGIC TAKES HOLD, ONLY THEN DO ALL HOWL FOR A DEAR FRIEND FALLEN IN BATTLE.
FALLEN, BUT STILL VERY MUCH PRESENT... AND STILL BEAMING A WARRIOR'S GRIN.

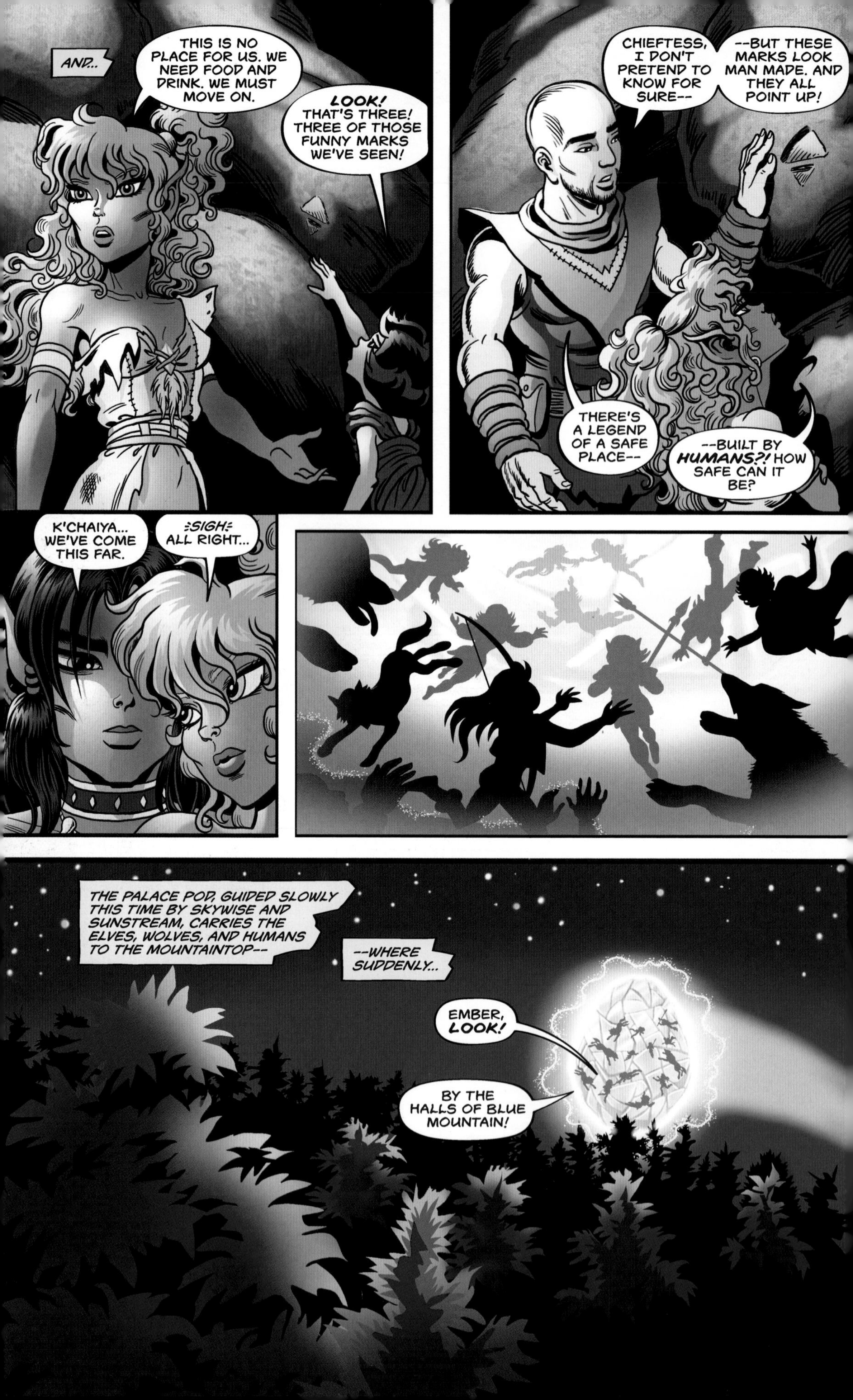
AND..
THIS IS NO PLACE FOR US. WE NEED FOOD AND DRINK. WE MUST MOVE ON.
LOOK! THAT'S THREE! THREE OF THOSE FUNNY MARKS WE'VE SEEN!
CHIEFTESS, I DON'T PRETEND TO KNOW FOR SURE--
--BUT THESE MARKS LOOK MAN MADE. AND THEY ALL POINT UP!
THERE'S A LEGEND OF A SAFE PLACE--
--BUILT BY HUMANS?! HOW SAFE CAN IT BE?
K'CHAIYA... WE'VE COME THIS FAR.
SIGH ALL RIGHT...
THE PALACE POD, GUIDED SLOWLY THIS TIME BY SKYWISE AND SUNSTREAM, CARRIES THE ELVES, WOLVES, AND HUMANS TO THE MOUNTAINTOP--
--WHERE SUDDENLY...
EMBER, LOOK!
BY THE HALLS OF BLUE MOUNTAIN!

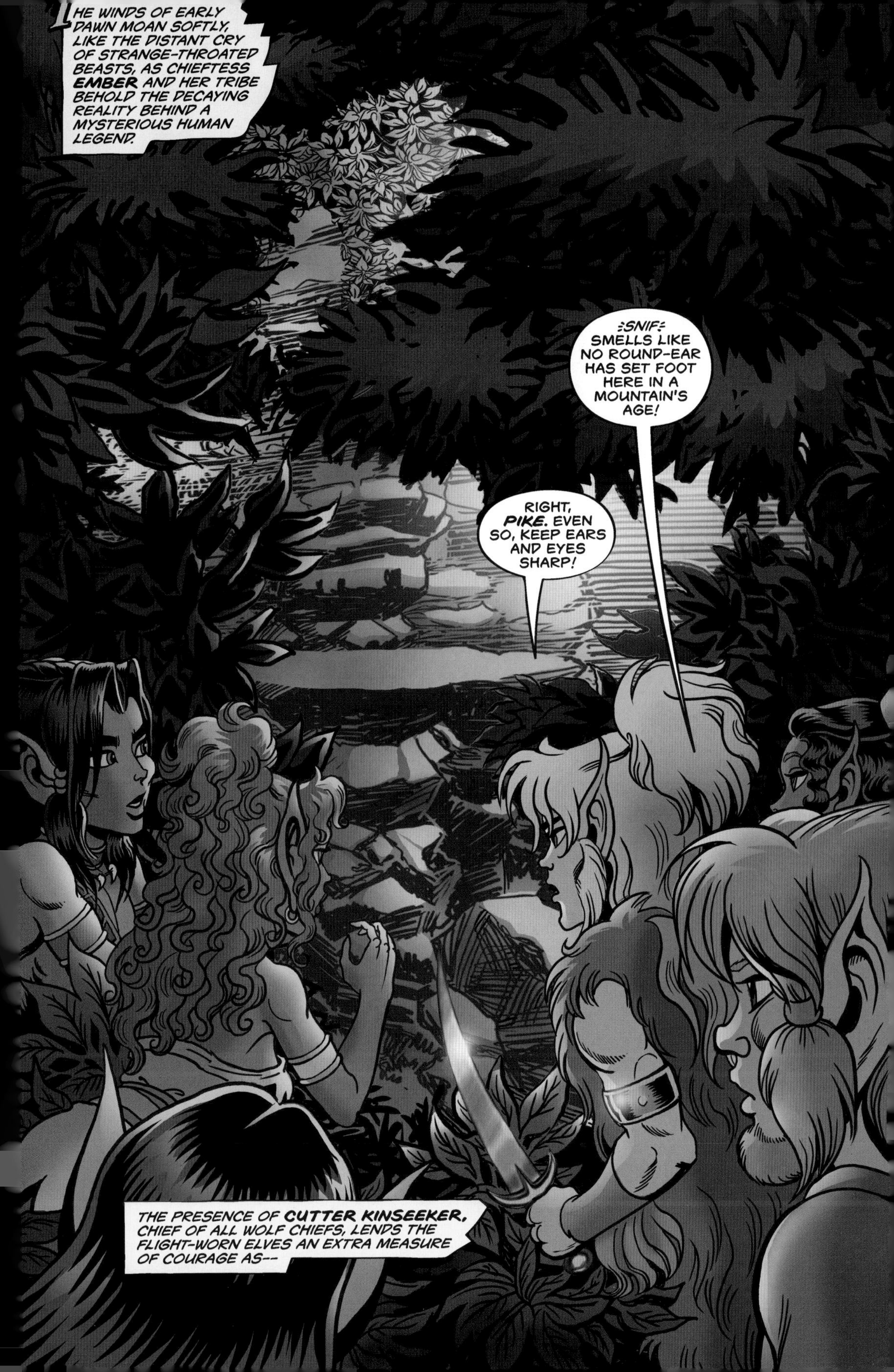
THE WINDS OF EARLY DAWN MOAN SOFTLY, LIKE THE DISTANT CRY OF STRANGE-THROATED BEASTS, AS CHIEFTESS EMBER AND HER TRIBE BEHOLD THE DECAYING REALITY BEHIND A MYSTERIOUS HUMAN LEGEND.
SNIF SMELLS LIKE NO ROUND-EAR HAS SET FOOT HERE IN A MOUNTAIN'S AGE!
RIGHT, PIKE. EVEN SO, KEEP EARS AND EYES SHARP!
THE PRESENCE OF CUTTER KINSEEKER, CHIEF OF ALL WOLF CHIEFS, LENDS THE FLIGHT-WORN ELVES AN EXTRA MEASURE OF COURAGE AS--

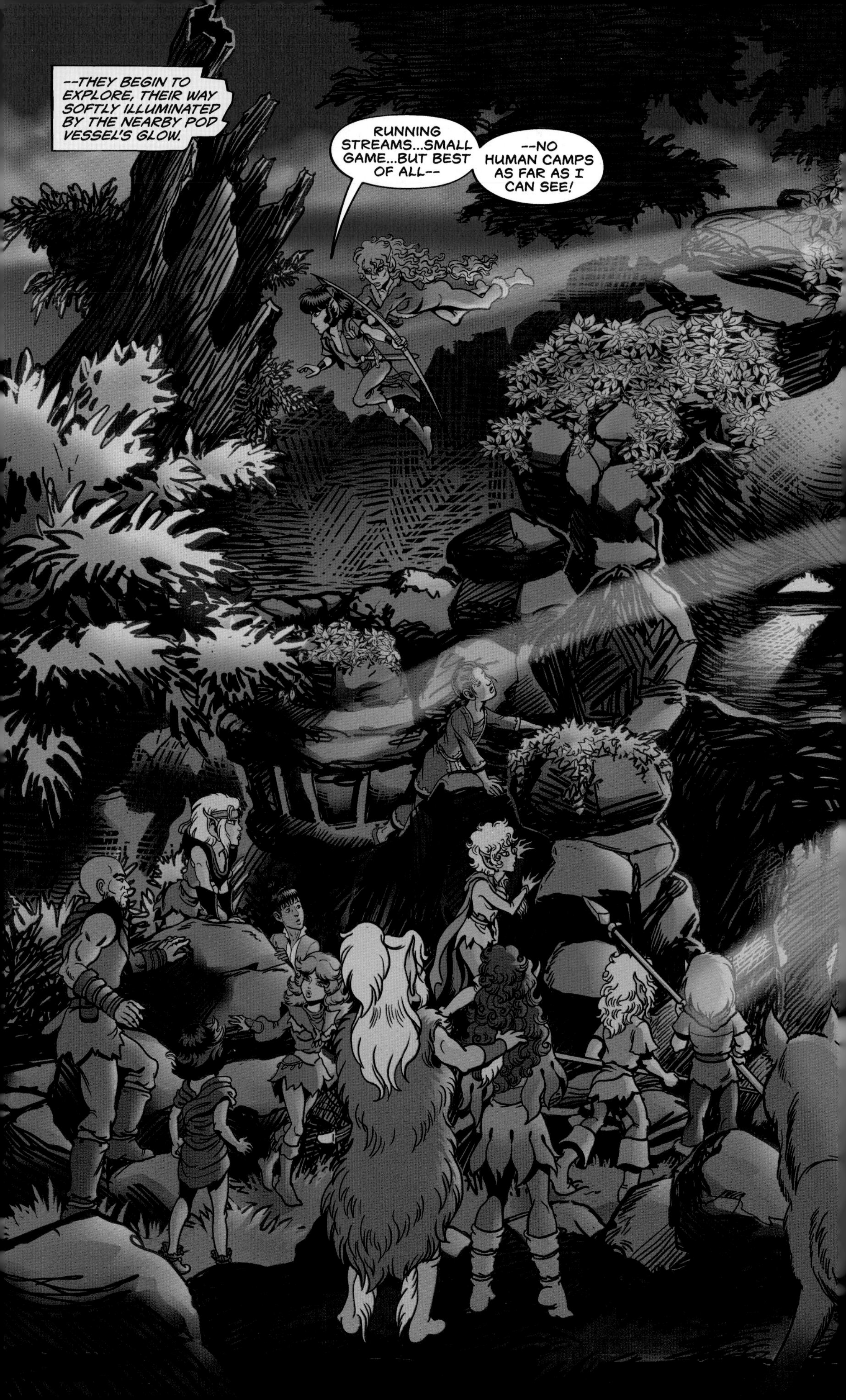
--THEY BEGIN TO EXPLORE, THEIR WAY SOFTLY ILLUMINATED BY THE NEARBY POD VESSEL'S GLOW.
RUNNING STREAMS...SMALL GAME...BUT BEST OF ALL--
--NO HUMAN CAMPS AS FAR AS I CAN SEE!

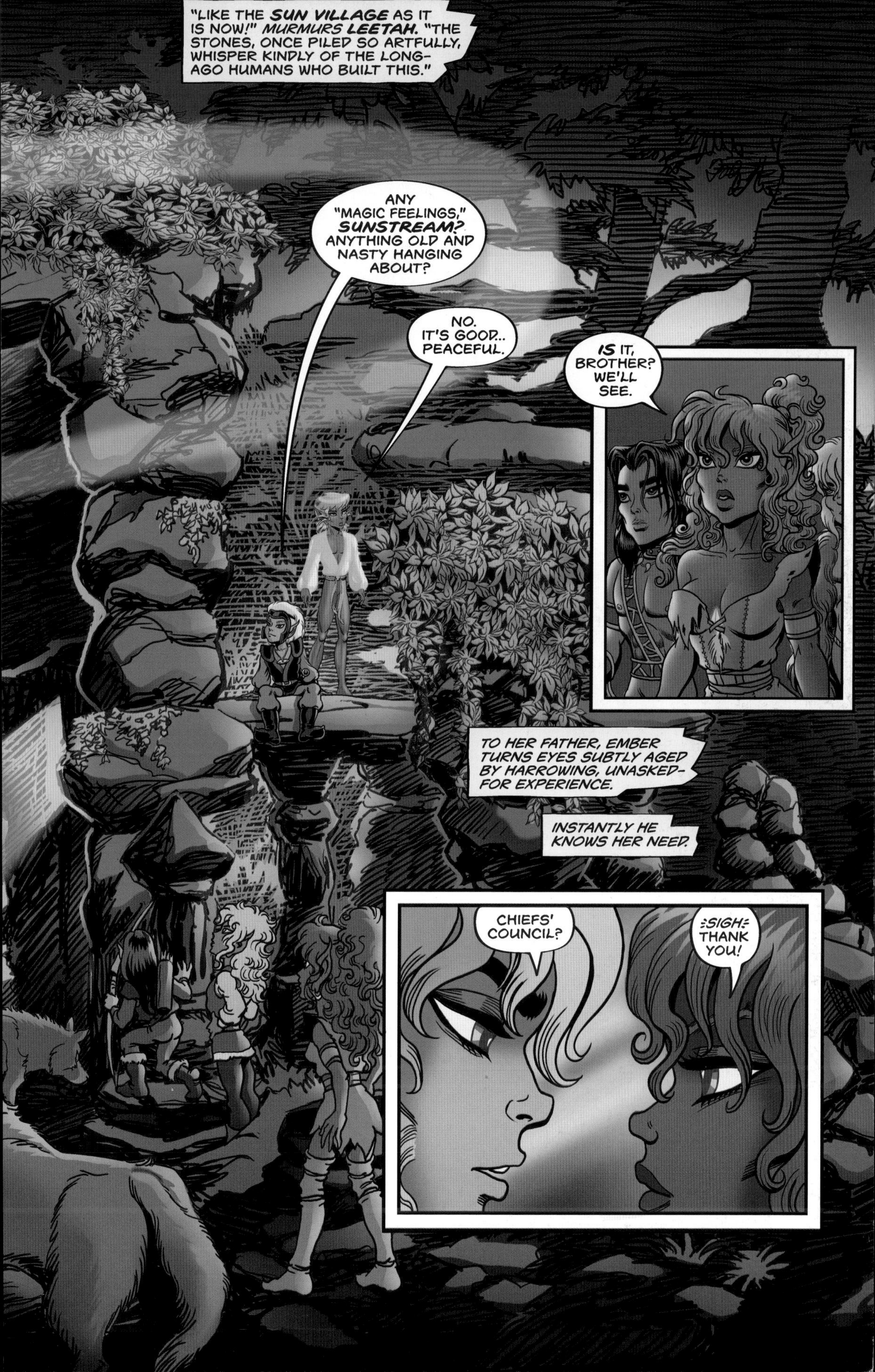
"LIKE THE SUN VILLAGE AS IT IS NOW!" MURMURS LEETAH. "THE STONES, ONCE PILED SO ARTFULLY, WHISPER KINDLY OF THE LONG-AGO HUMANS WHO BUILT THIS."
ANY "MAGIC FEELINGS," SUNSTREAM? ANYTHING OLD AND NASTY HANGING ABOUT?
NO. IT'S GOOD... PEACEFUL.
IS IT, BROTHER? WE'LL SEE.
TO HER FATHER, EMBER TURNS EYES SUBTLY AGED BY HARROWING, UNASKED-FOR EXPERIENCE.
INSTANTLY HE KNOWS HER NEED.
CHIEFS' COUNCIL?
SIGH THANK YOU!

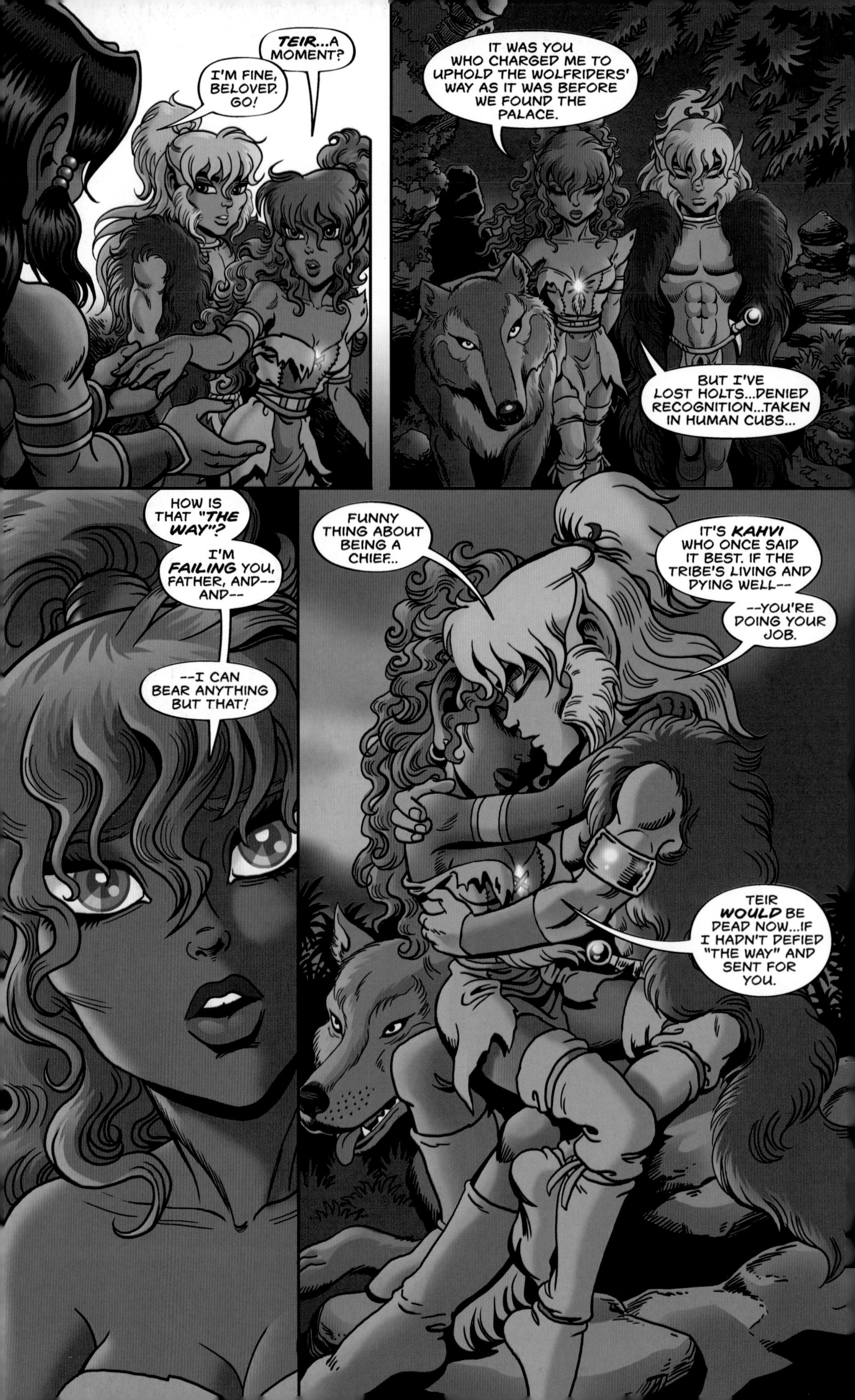
TEIR...A MOMENT?
I'M FINE, BELOVED. GO!
IT WAS YOU WHO CHARGED ME TO UPHOLD THE WOLFRIDERS' WAY AS IT WAS BEFORE WE FOUND THE PALACE.
BUT I'VE LOST HOLTS...DENIED RECOGNITION...TAKEN IN HUMAN CUBS...
HOW IS THAT "THE WAY"?
I'M FAILING YOU, FATHER, AND-- AND--
--I CAN BEAR ANYTHING BUT THAT!
FUNNY THING ABOUT BEING A CHIEF...
IT'S KAHVI WHO ONCE SAID IT BEST. IF THE TRIBE'S LIVING AND DYING WELL--
--YOU'RE DOING YOUR JOB.
TEIR WOULD BE DEAD NOW...IF I HADN'T DEFIED "THE WAY" AND SENT FOR YOU.

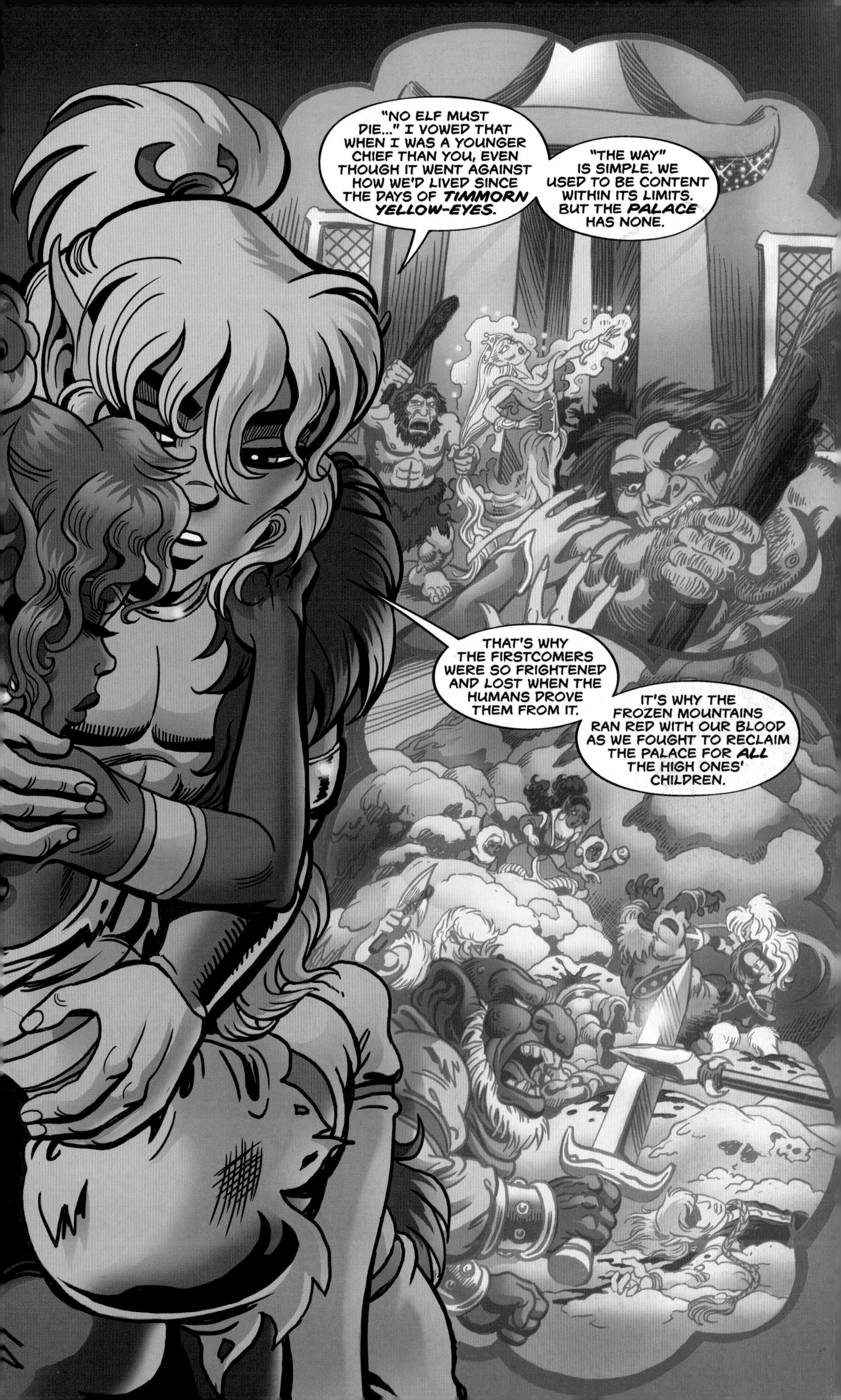
"NO ELF MUST DIE..." I VOWED THAT WHEN I WAS A YOUNGER CHIEF THAN YOU, EVEN THOUGH IT WENT AGAINST HOW WE'D LIVED SINCE THE DAYS OF **TIMMORN YELLOW-EYES**.
"THE WAY" IS SIMPLE. WE USED TO BE CONTENT WITHIN ITS LIMITS. BUT THE **PALACE** HAS NONE.
THAT'S WHY THE FIRSTCOMERS WERE SO FRIGHTENED AND LOST WHEN THE HUMANS DROVE THEM FROM IT.
IT'S WHY THE FROZEN MOUNTAINS RAN RED WITH OUR BLOOD AS WE FOUGHT TO RECLAIM THE PALACE FOR **ALL** THE HIGH ONES' CHILDREN.

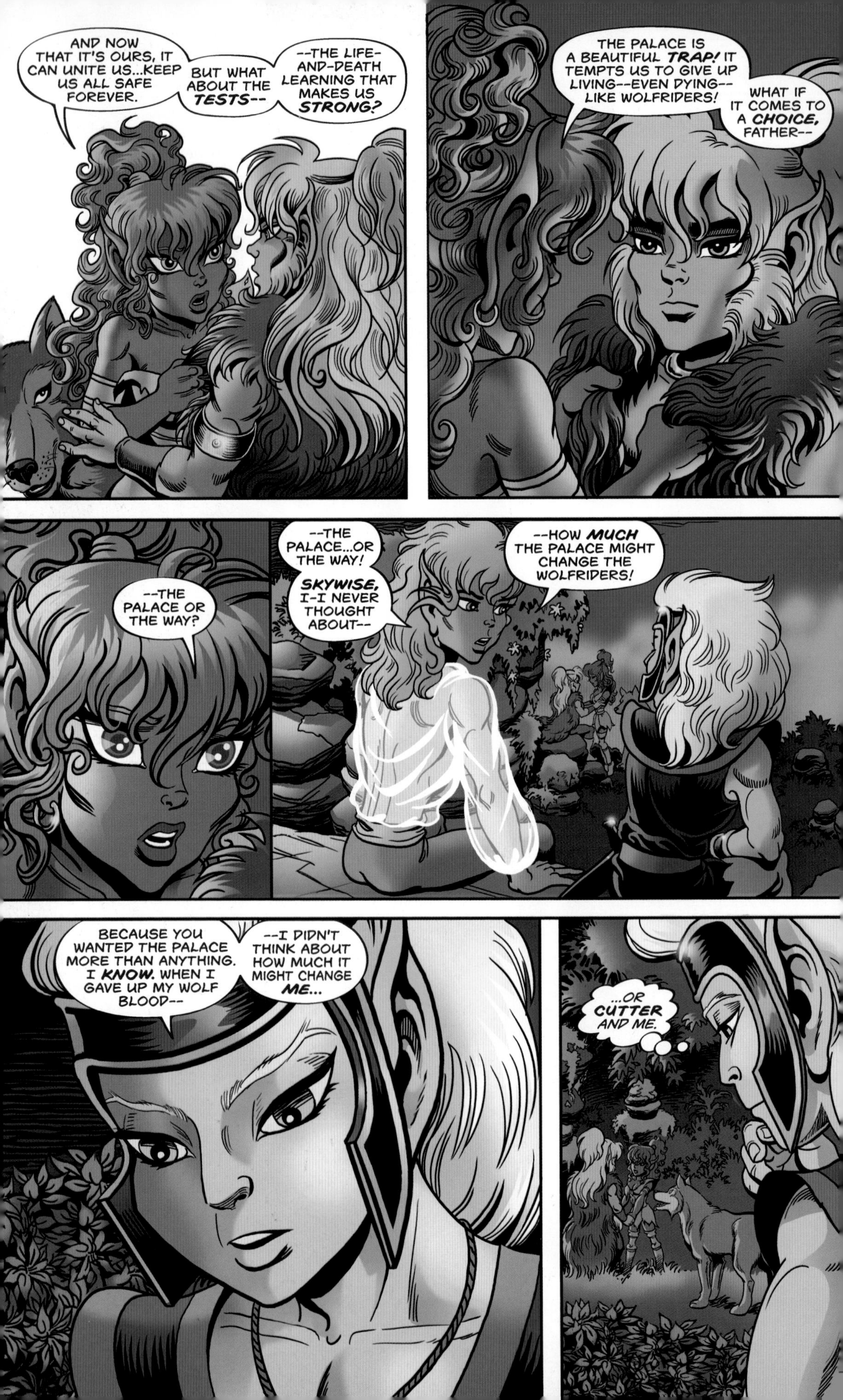
AND NOW THAT IT'S OURS, IT CAN UNITE US...KEEP US ALL SAFE FOREVER.
BUT WHAT ABOUT THE TESTS--
--THE LIFE-AND-DEATH LEARNING THAT MAKES US STRONG?
THE PALACE IS A BEAUTIFUL TRAP! IT TEMPTS US TO GIVE UP LIVING--EVEN DYING--LIKE WOLFRIDERS!
WHAT IF IT COMES TO A CHOICE, FATHER--
--THE PALACE OR THE WAY?
--THE PALACE...OR THE WAY!
SKYWISE, I-I NEVER THOUGHT ABOUT--
--HOW MUCH THE PALACE MIGHT CHANGE THE WOLFRIDERS!
BECAUSE YOU WANTED THE PALACE MORE THAN ANYTHING. I KNOW. WHEN I GAVE UP MY WOLF BLOOD--
--I DIDN'T THINK ABOUT HOW MUCH IT MIGHT CHANGE ME...
...OR CUTTER AND ME.

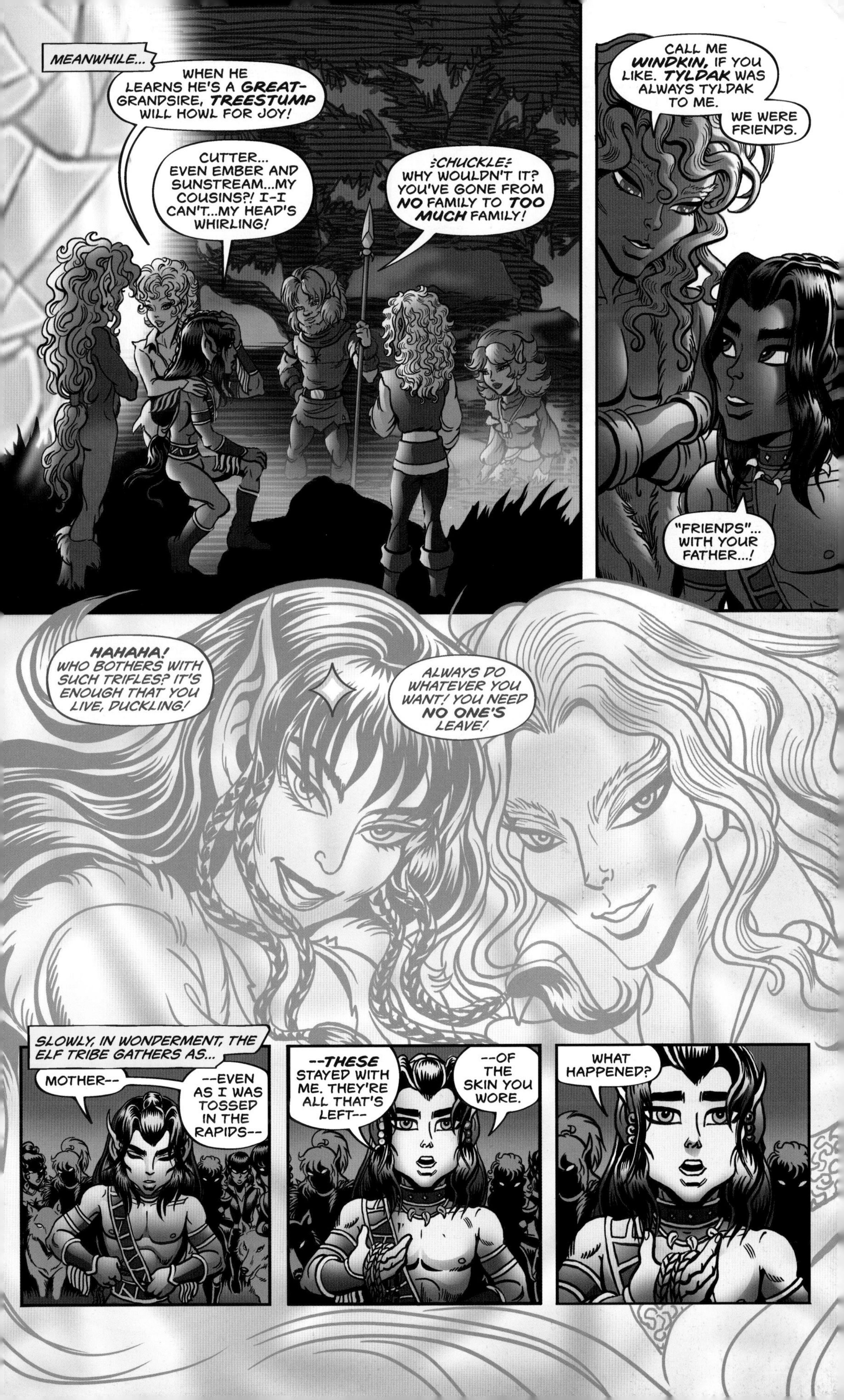
MEANWHILE...
WHEN HE LEARNS HE'S A GREAT-GRANDSIRE, TREESTUMP WILL HOWL FOR JOY!
CUTTER... EVEN EMBER AND SUNSTREAM...MY COUSINS?! I-I CAN'T...MY HEAD'S WHIRLING!
:CHUCKLE: WHY WOULDN'T IT? YOU'VE GONE FROM NO FAMILY TO TOO MUCH FAMILY!
CALL ME WINDKIN, IF YOU LIKE. TYLDAK WAS ALWAYS TYLDAK TO ME.
WE WERE FRIENDS.
"FRIENDS"... WITH YOUR FATHER...!
HAHAHA! WHO BOTHERS WITH SUCH TRIFLES? IT'S ENOUGH THAT YOU LIVE, DUCKLING!
ALWAYS DO WHATEVER YOU WANT! YOU NEED NO ONE'S LEAVE!
SLOWLY, IN WONDERMENT, THE ELF TRIBE GATHERS AS...
MOTHER--
--EVEN AS I WAS TOSSED IN THE RAPIDS--
--THESE STAYED WITH ME. THEY'RE ALL THAT'S LEFT--
--OF THE SKIN YOU WORE.
WHAT HAPPENED?

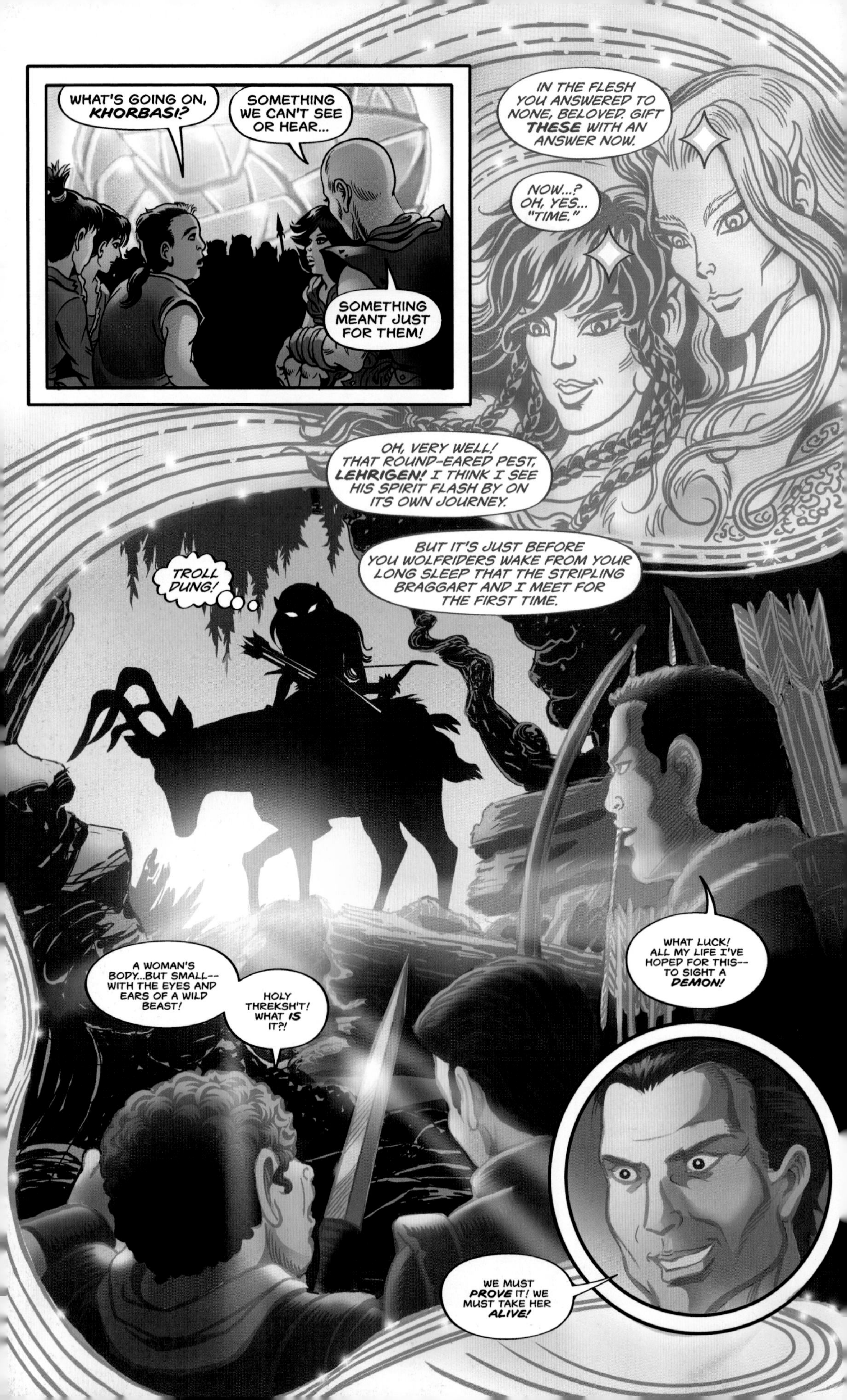
WHAT'S GOING ON, KHORBASI!?
SOMETHING WE CAN'T SEE OR HEAR...
SOMETHING MEANT JUST FOR THEM!
IN THE FLESH YOU ANSWERED TO NONE, BELOVED. GIFT THESE WITH AN ANSWER NOW.
NOW...? OH, YES... "TIME."
OH, VERY WELL! THAT ROUND-EARED PEST, LEHRIGEN! I THINK I SEE HIS SPIRIT FLASH BY ON ITS OWN JOURNEY.
BUT IT'S JUST BEFORE YOU WOLFRIDERS WAKE FROM YOUR LONG SLEEP THAT THE STRIPLING BRAGGART AND I MEET FOR THE FIRST TIME.
TROLL DUNG!
WHAT LUCK! ALL MY LIFE I'VE HOPED FOR THIS-- TO SIGHT A DEMON!
A WOMAN'S BODY...BUT SMALL-- WITH THE EYES AND EARS OF A WILD BEAST!
HOLY THREKSH'T! WHAT IS IT?!
WE MUST PROVE IT! WE MUST TAKE HER ALIVE!

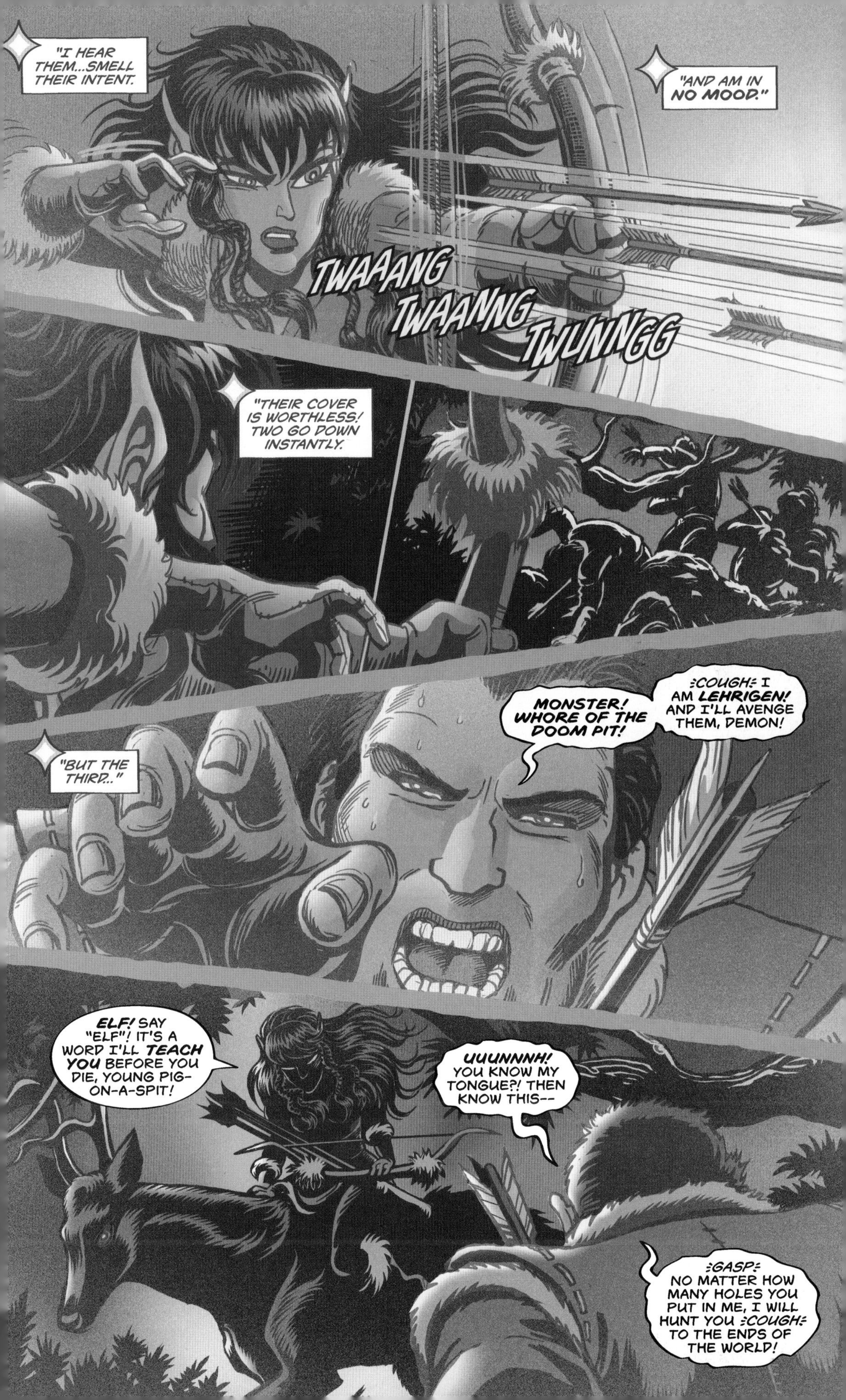
"I HEAR THEM...SMELL THEIR INTENT.
"AND AM IN NO MOOD."
TWAAANG
TWAANNG
TWUNNGG
"THEIR COVER IS WORTHLESS! TWO GO DOWN INSTANTLY.
"BUT THE THIRD..."
MONSTER! WHORE OF THE DOOM PIT!
:COUGH: I AM LEHRIGEN! AND I'LL AVENGE THEM, DEMON!
ELF! SAY "ELF"! IT'S A WORD I'LL TEACH YOU BEFORE YOU DIE, YOUNG PIG-ON-A-SPIT!
UUUNNNH! YOU KNOW MY TONGUE?! THEN KNOW THIS--
:GASP: NO MATTER HOW MANY HOLES YOU PUT IN ME, I WILL HUNT YOU :COUGH: TO THE ENDS OF THE WORLD!

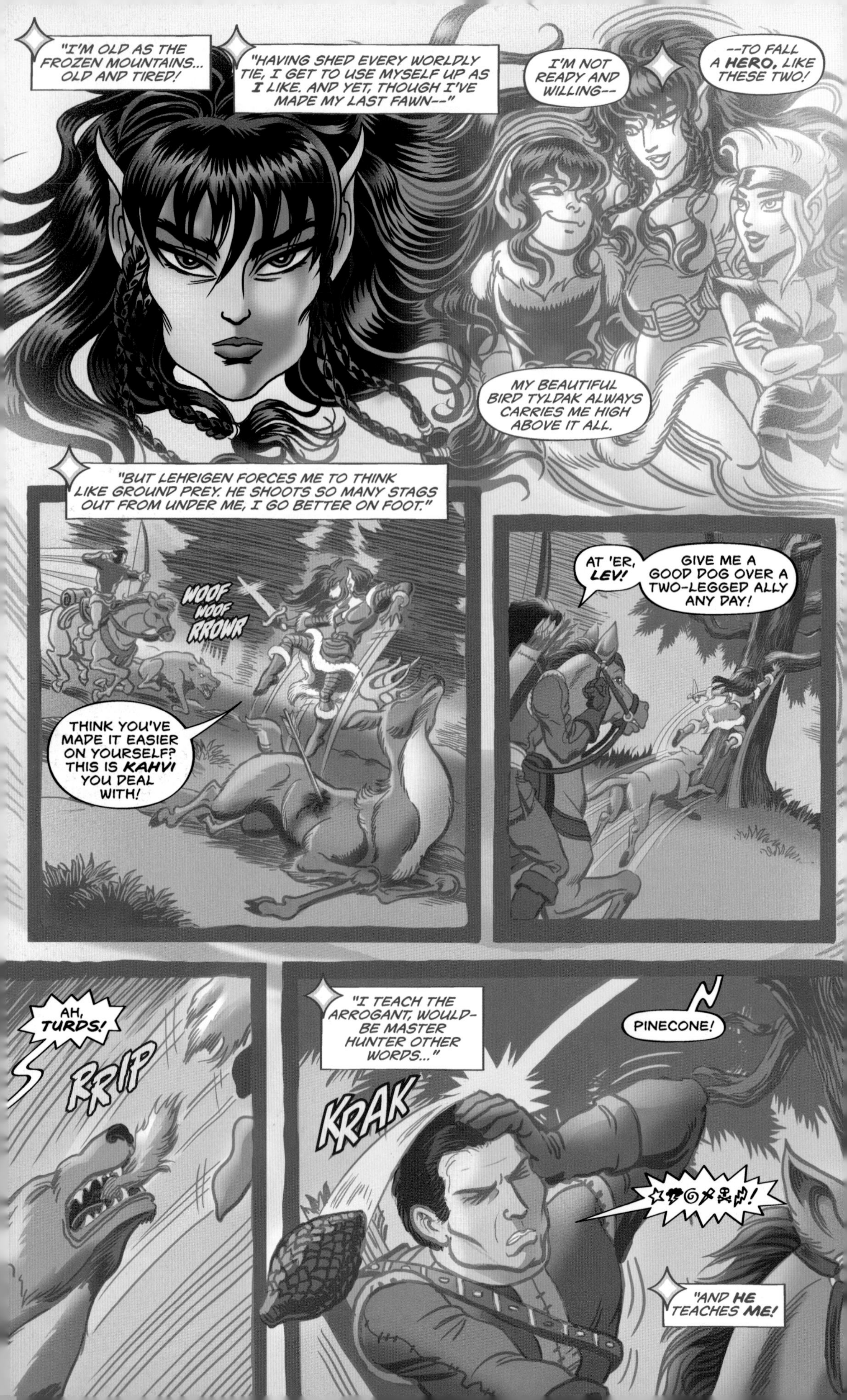
"I'M OLD AS THE FROZEN MOUNTAINS... OLD AND TIRED!
"HAVING SHED EVERY WORLDLY TIE, I GET TO USE MYSELF UP AS I LIKE. AND YET, THOUGH I'VE MADE MY LAST FAWN--"
I'M NOT READY AND WILLING--
--TO FALL A HERO, LIKE THESE TWO!
MY BEAUTIFUL BIRD TYLDAK ALWAYS CARRIES ME HIGH ABOVE IT ALL.
"BUT LEHRIGEN FORCES ME TO THINK LIKE GROUND PREY. HE SHOOTS SO MANY STAGS OUT FROM UNDER ME, I GO BETTER ON FOOT."
WOOF WOOF RROWR
THINK YOU'VE MADE IT EASIER ON YOURSELF? THIS IS KAHVI YOU DEAL WITH!
AT 'ER, LEV!
GIVE ME A GOOD DOG OVER A TWO-LEGGED ALLY ANY DAY!
AH, TURDS!
RRIP
"I TEACH THE ARROGANT, WOULD-BE MASTER HUNTER OTHER WORDS..."
PINECONE!
KRAK
"AND HE TEACHES ME!

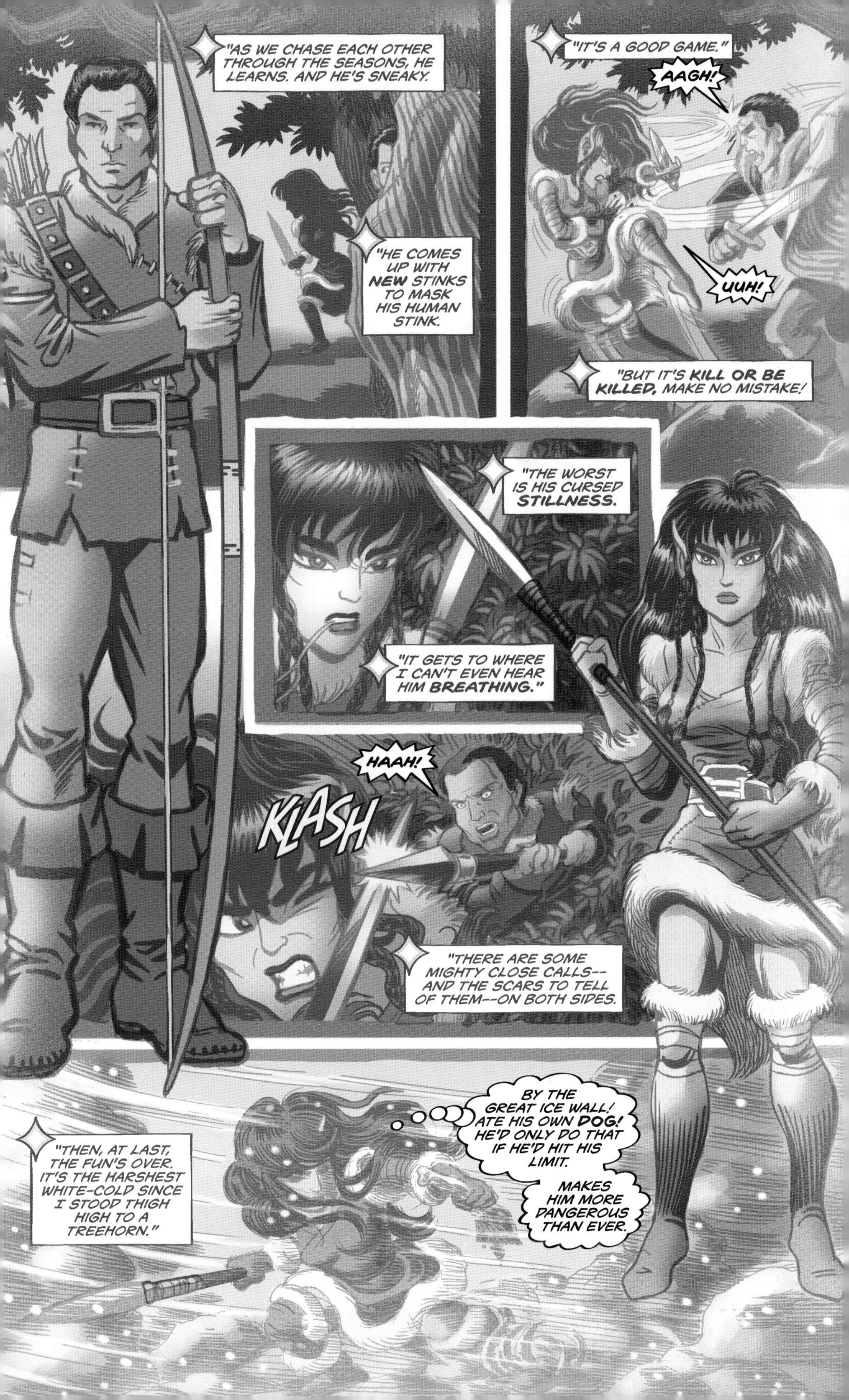
"AS WE CHASE EACH OTHER THROUGH THE SEASONS, HE LEARNS. AND HE'S SNEAKY.
"HE COMES UP WITH NEW STINKS TO MASK HIS HUMAN STINK.
"IT'S A GOOD GAME."
AAGH!
UUH!
"BUT IT'S KILL OR BE KILLED, MAKE NO MISTAKE!
"THE WORST IS HIS CURSED STILLNESS.
"IT GETS TO WHERE I CAN'T EVEN HEAR HIM BREATHING."
HAAH!
KLASH
"THERE ARE SOME MIGHTY CLOSE CALLS-- AND THE SCARS TO TELL OF THEM--ON BOTH SIDES.
"THEN, AT LAST, THE FUN'S OVER. IT'S THE HARSHEST WHITE-COLD SINCE I STOOD THIGH HIGH TO A TREEHORN."
BY THE GREAT ICE WALL! ATE HIS OWN DOG! HE'D ONLY DO THAT IF HE'D HIT HIS LIMIT.
MAKES HIM MORE DANGEROUS THAN EVER.

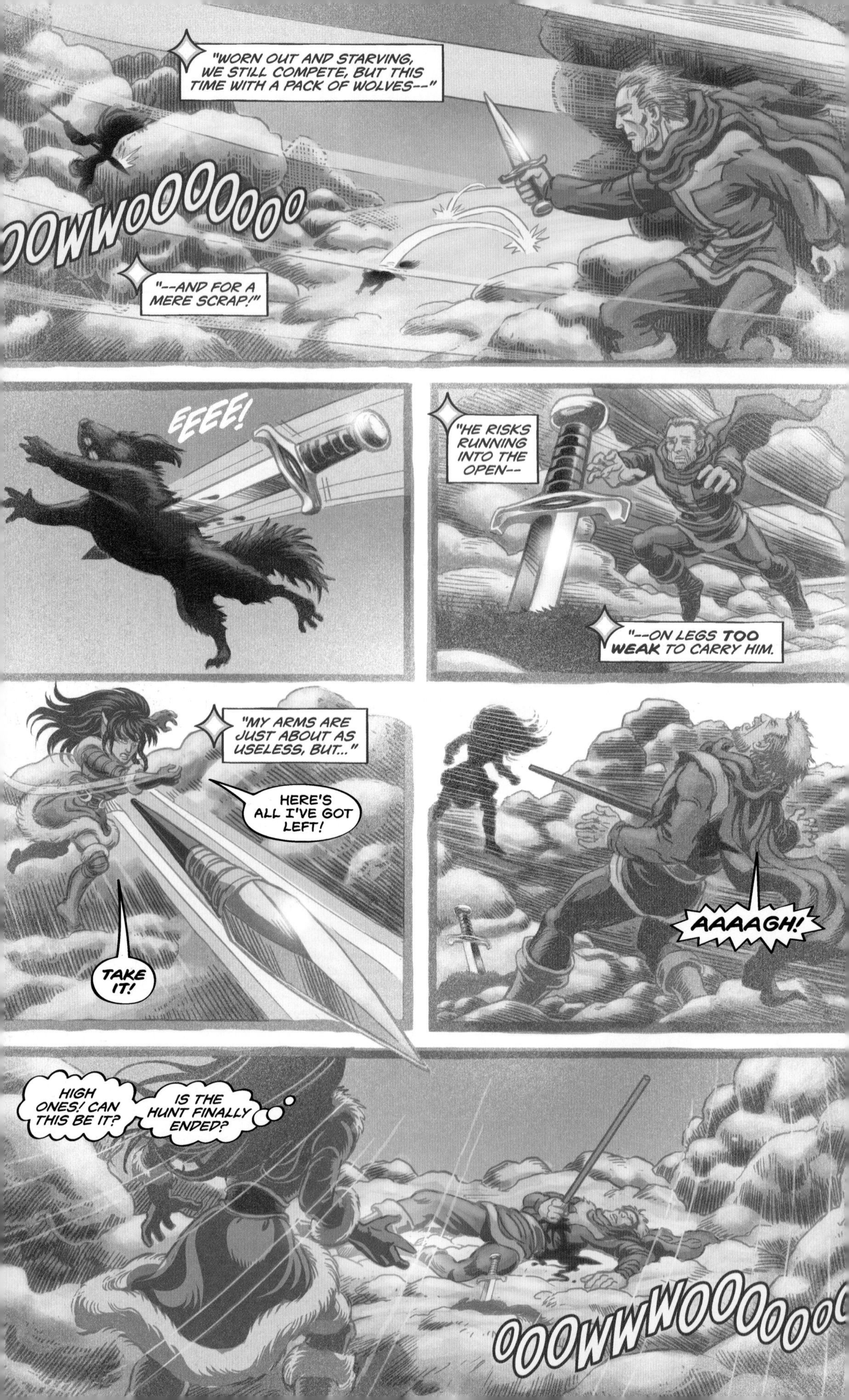
"WORN OUT AND STARVING, WE STILL COMPETE, BUT THIS TIME WITH A PACK OF WOLVES--"
OOWWOOOOOOOO
"--AND FOR A MERE SCRAP!"
EEEE!
"HE RISKS RUNNING INTO THE OPEN--
"--ON LEGS TOO WEAK TO CARRY HIM.
"MY ARMS ARE JUST ABOUT AS USELESS, BUT..."
HERE'S ALL I'VE GOT LEFT!
TAKE IT!
AAAAGH!
HIGH ONES! CAN THIS BE IT?
IS THE HUNT FINALLY ENDED?
OOOWWWOOOOOOO

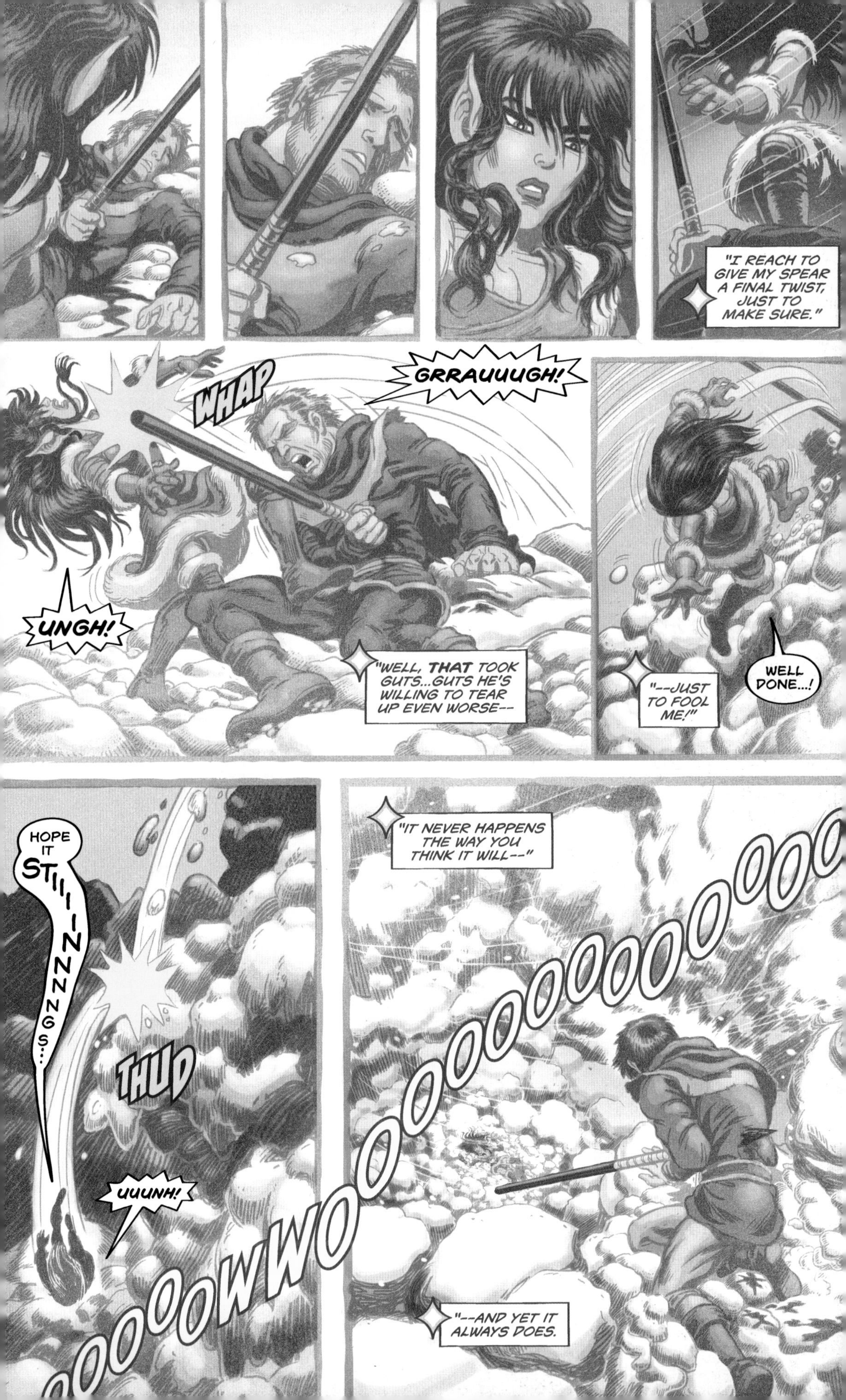
"I REACH TO GIVE MY SPEAR A FINAL TWIST, JUST TO MAKE SURE."
GRRAUUUGH!
WHAP
UNGH!
"WELL, THAT TOOK GUTS...GUTS HE'S WILLING TO TEAR UP EVEN WORSE--
"--JUST TO FOOL ME!"
WELL DONE...!
HOPE IT STIIIIINNNNNGS...
THUD
UUUNH!
"IT NEVER HAPPENS THE WAY YOU THINK IT WILL--"
OOOOOOWWOOOOOOOOOOOOOOOO
"--AND YET IT ALWAYS DOES.

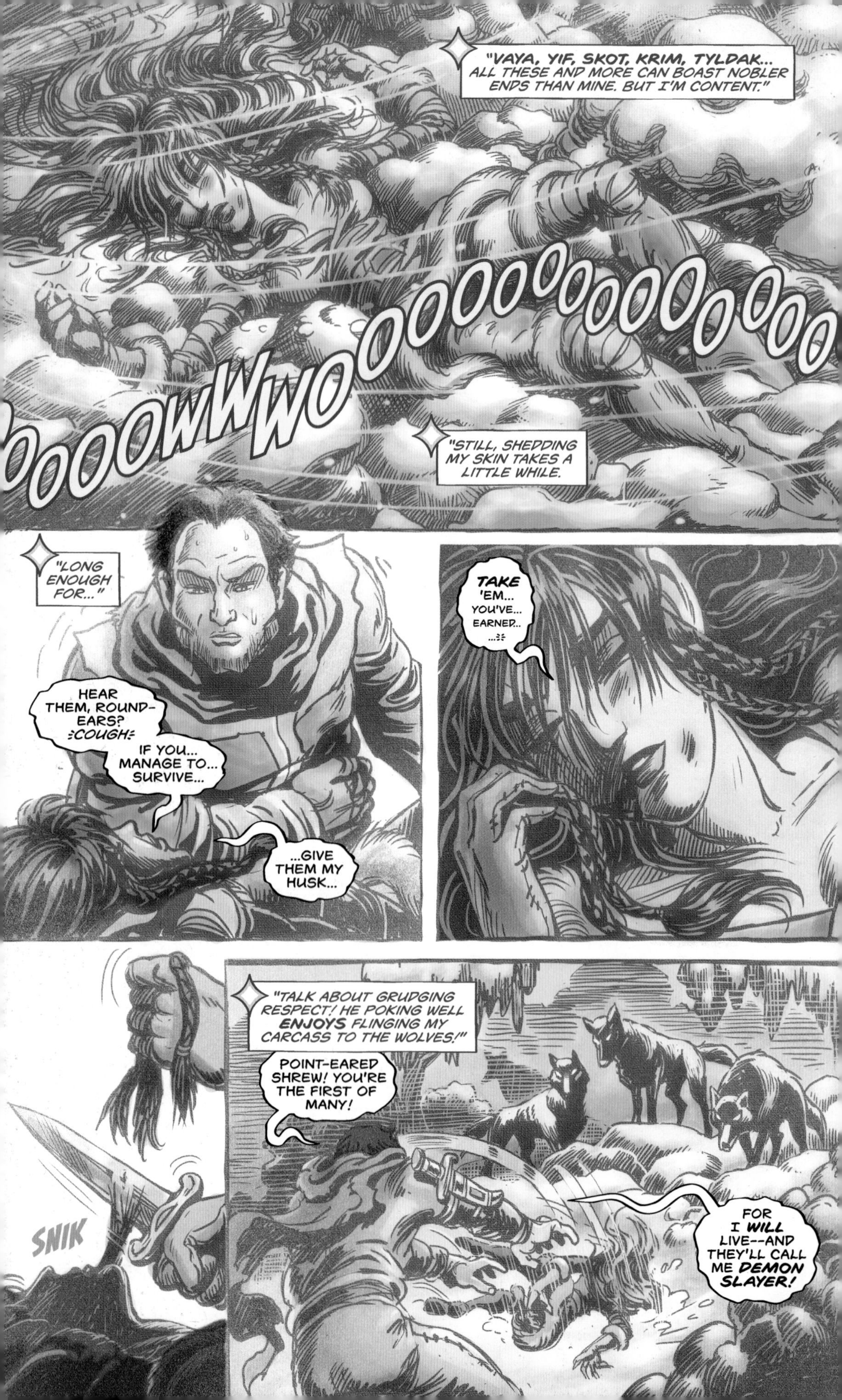
"VAYA, YIF, SKOT, KRIM, TYLDAK... ALL THESE AND MORE CAN BOAST NOBLER ENDS THAN MINE. BUT I'M CONTENT."
OOOOOWWWWOOOOOOOOOOOOOOOO
"STILL, SHEDDING MY SKIN TAKES A LITTLE WHILE.
"LONG ENOUGH FOR..."
HEAR THEM, ROUND-EARS? :COUGH:
IF YOU... MANAGE TO... SURVIVE...
...GIVE THEM MY HUSK...
TAKE 'EM... YOU'VE... EARNED... ...:::
"TALK ABOUT GRUDGING RESPECT! HE POKING WELL ENJOYS FLINGING MY CARCASS TO THE WOLVES!"
POINT-EARED SHREW! YOU'RE THE FIRST OF MANY!
SNIK
FOR I WILL LIVE--AND THEY'LL CALL ME DEMON SLAYER!

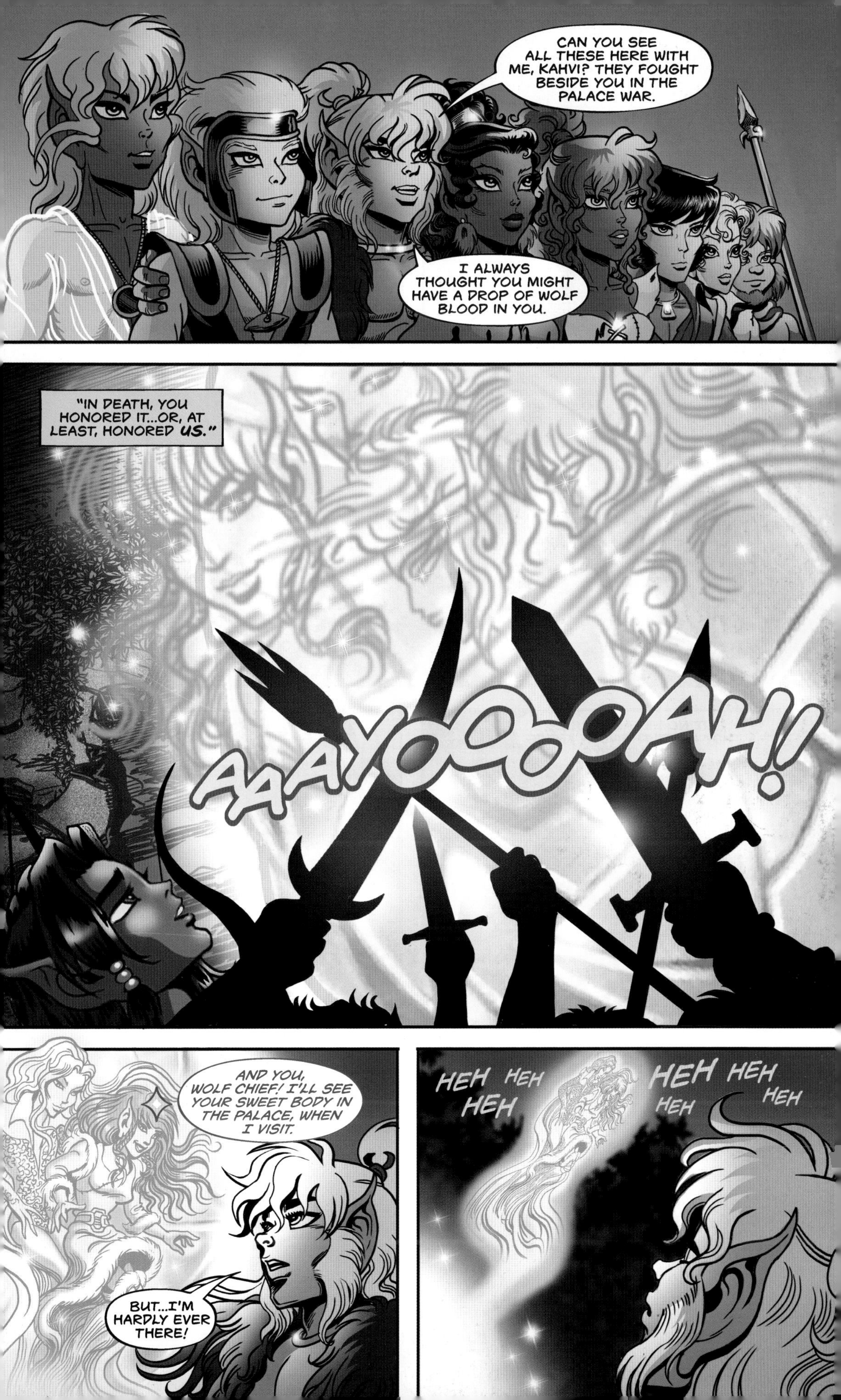
CAN YOU SEE ALL THESE HERE WITH ME, KAHVI? THEY FOUGHT BESIDE YOU IN THE PALACE WAR.
I ALWAYS THOUGHT YOU MIGHT HAVE A DROP OF WOLF BLOOD IN YOU.
"IN DEATH, YOU HONORED IT...OR, AT LEAST, HONORED US."
AAAYOOOOAH!
AND YOU, WOLF CHIEF! I'LL SEE YOUR SWEET BODY IN THE PALACE, WHEN I VISIT.
BUT...I'M HARDLY EVER THERE!
HEH HEH HEH
HEH HEH HEH HEH
HEH

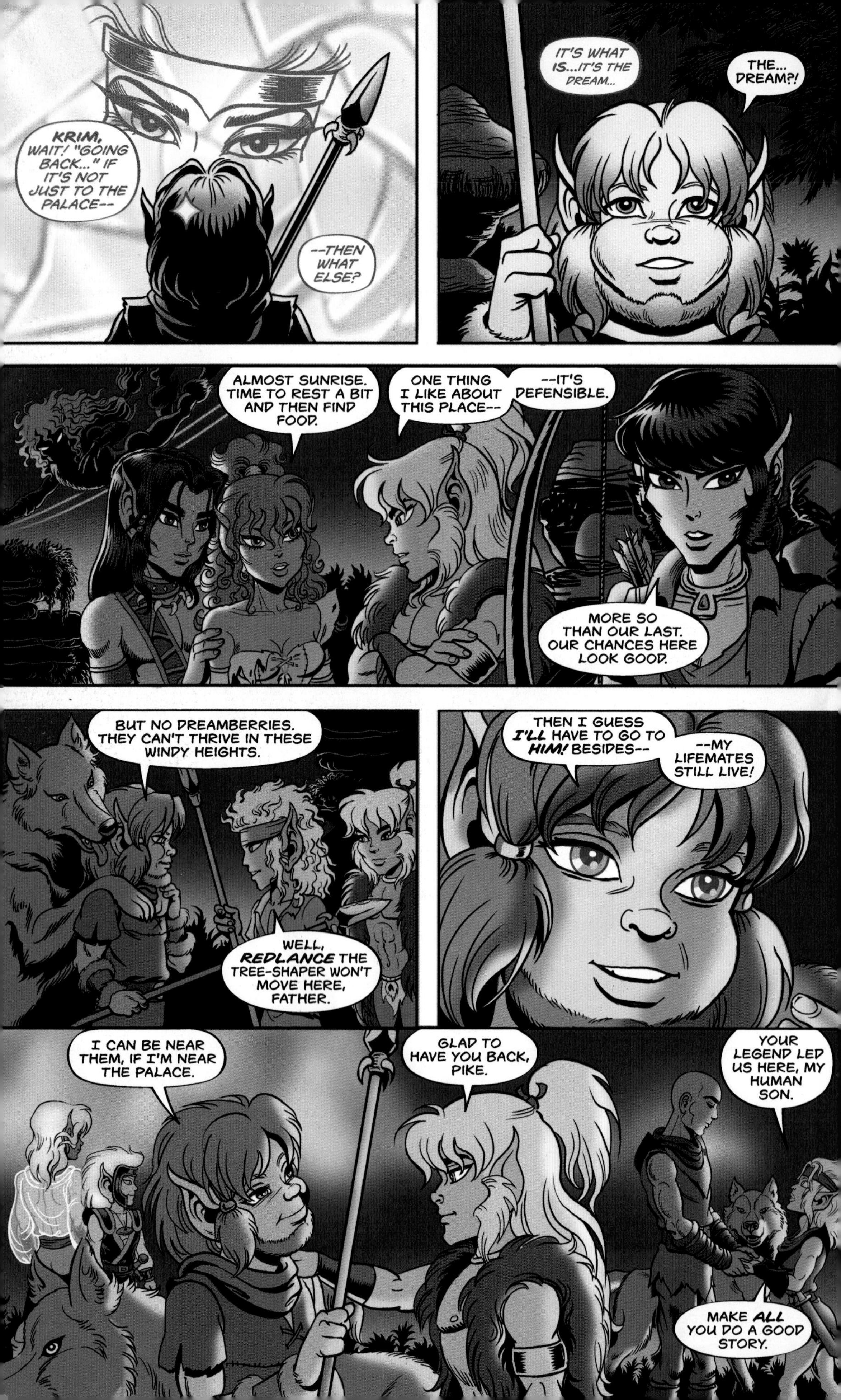
KRIM, WAIT! "GOING BACK..." IF IT'S NOT JUST TO THE PALACE--
--THEN WHAT ELSE?
IT'S WHAT IS...IT'S THE DREAM...
THE... DREAM?!
ALMOST SUNRISE. TIME TO REST A BIT AND THEN FIND FOOD.
ONE THING I LIKE ABOUT THIS PLACE--
--IT'S DEFENSIBLE.
MORE SO THAN OUR LAST. OUR CHANCES HERE LOOK GOOD.
BUT NO DREAMBERRIES. THEY CAN'T THRIVE IN THESE WINDY HEIGHTS.
WELL, REDLANCE THE TREE-SHAPER WON'T MOVE HERE, FATHER.
THEN I GUESS I'LL HAVE TO GO TO HIM! BESIDES--
--MY LIFEMATES STILL LIVE!
I CAN BE NEAR THEM, IF I'M NEAR THE PALACE.
GLAD TO HAVE YOU BACK, PIKE.
YOUR LEGEND LED US HERE, MY HUMAN SON.
MAKE ALL YOU DO A GOOD STORY.

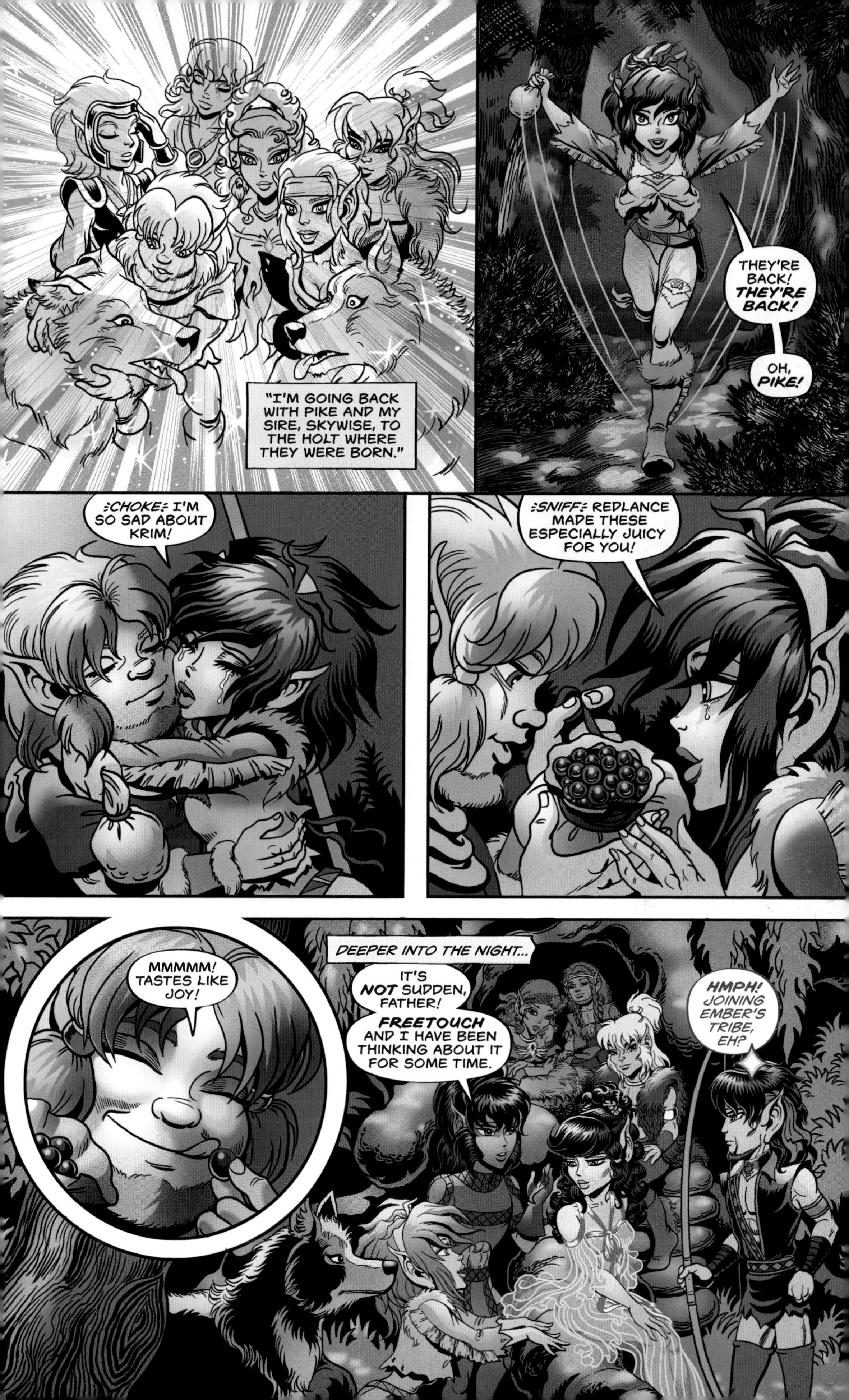
"I'M GOING BACK WITH PIKE AND MY SIRE, SKYWISE, TO THE HOLT WHERE THEY WERE BORN."
THEY'RE BACK! ***THEY'RE BACK!***
OH, ***PIKE!***
CHOKE I'M SO SAD ABOUT KRIM!
SNIFF REDLANCE MADE THESE ESPECIALLY JUICY FOR YOU!
MMMMM! TASTES LIKE JOY!
DEEPER INTO THE NIGHT...
IT'S ***NOT*** SUDDEN, FATHER!
FREETOUCH AND I HAVE BEEN THINKING ABOUT IT FOR SOME TIME.
HMPH! *JOINING EMBER'S TRIBE, EH?*

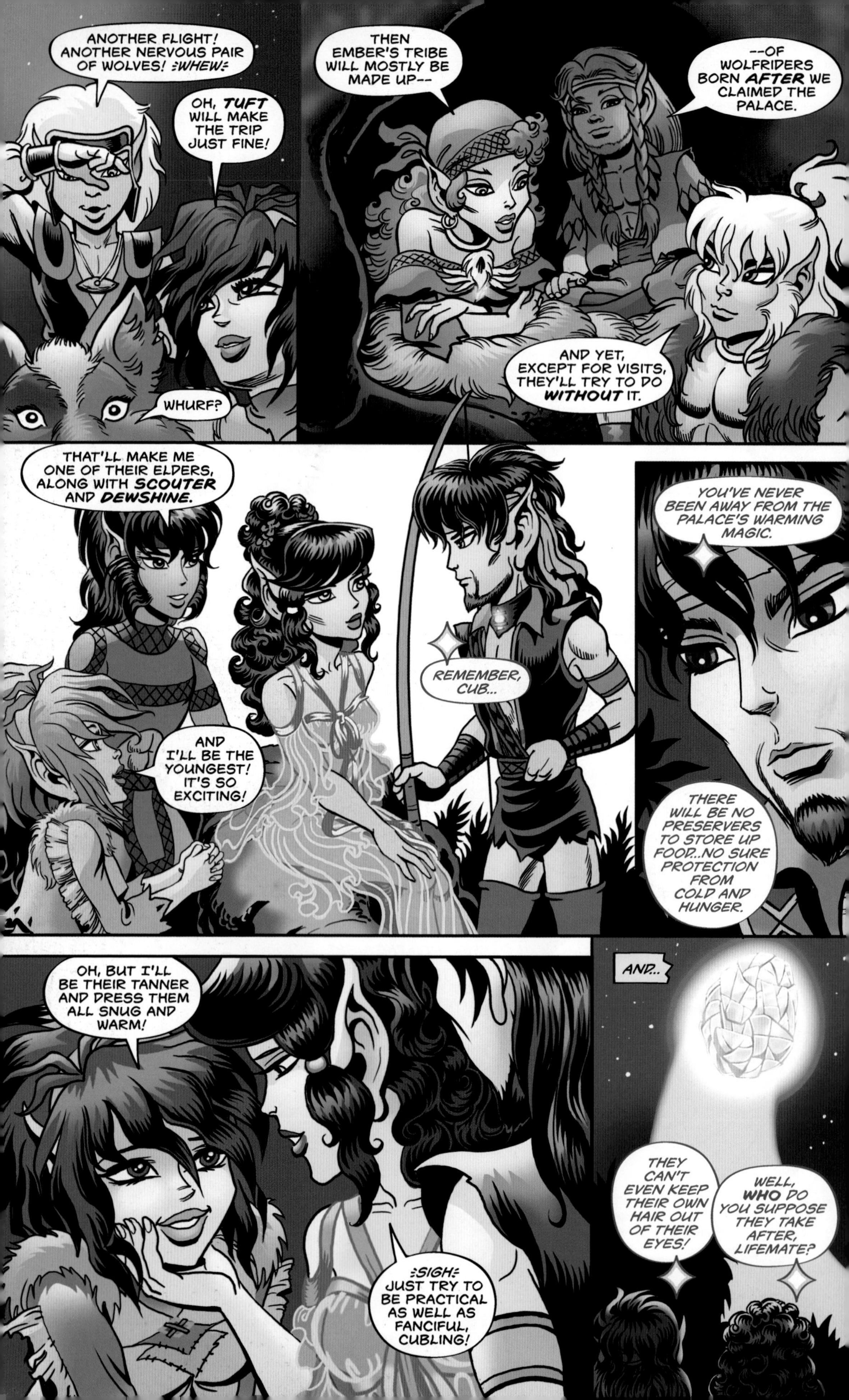
ANOTHER FLIGHT! ANOTHER NERVOUS PAIR OF WOLVES! :WHEW:
OH, TUFT WILL MAKE THE TRIP JUST FINE!
WHURF?
THEN EMBER'S TRIBE WILL MOSTLY BE MADE UP--
--OF WOLFRIDERS BORN AFTER WE CLAIMED THE PALACE.
AND YET, EXCEPT FOR VISITS, THEY'LL TRY TO DO WITHOUT IT.
THAT'LL MAKE ME ONE OF THEIR ELDERS, ALONG WITH SCOUTER AND DEWSHINE.
AND I'LL BE THE YOUNGEST! IT'S SO EXCITING!
REMEMBER, CUB...
YOU'VE NEVER BEEN AWAY FROM THE PALACE'S WARMING MAGIC.
THERE WILL BE NO PRESERVERS TO STORE UP FOOD...NO SURE PROTECTION FROM COLD AND HUNGER.
OH, BUT I'LL BE THEIR TANNER AND DRESS THEM ALL SNUG AND WARM!
:SIGH: JUST TRY TO BE PRACTICAL AS WELL AS FANCIFUL, CUBLING!
AND...
THEY CAN'T EVEN KEEP THEIR OWN HAIR OUT OF THEIR EYES!
WELL, WHO DO YOU SUPPOSE THEY TAKE AFTER, LIFEMATE?

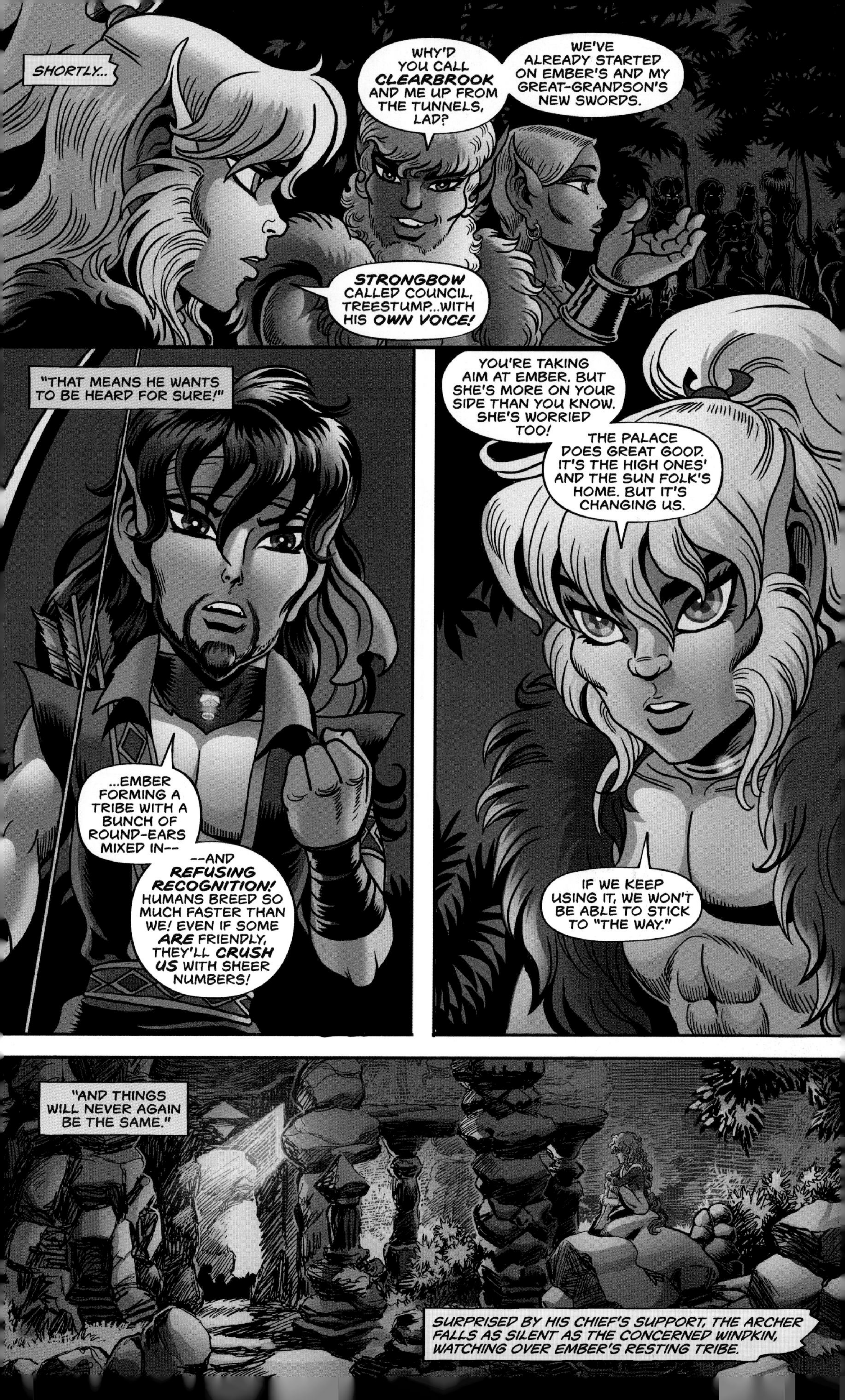

SHORTLY...
WHY'D YOU CALL CLEARBROOK AND ME UP FROM THE TUNNELS, LAD?
WE'VE ALREADY STARTED ON EMBER'S AND MY GREAT-GRANDSON'S NEW SWORDS.
STRONGBOW CALLED COUNCIL, TREESTUMP...WITH HIS OWN VOICE!
"THAT MEANS HE WANTS TO BE HEARD FOR SURE!"
...EMBER FORMING A TRIBE WITH A BUNCH OF ROUND-EARS MIXED IN--
--AND REFUSING RECOGNITION! HUMANS BREED SO MUCH FASTER THAN WE! EVEN IF SOME ARE FRIENDLY, THEY'LL CRUSH US WITH SHEER NUMBERS!
YOU'RE TAKING AIM AT EMBER. BUT SHE'S MORE ON YOUR SIDE THAN YOU KNOW. SHE'S WORRIED TOO!
THE PALACE DOES GREAT GOOD. IT'S THE HIGH ONES' AND THE SUN FOLK'S HOME. BUT IT'S CHANGING US.
IF WE KEEP USING IT, WE WON'T BE ABLE TO STICK TO "THE WAY."
"AND THINGS WILL NEVER AGAIN BE THE SAME."
SURPRISED BY HIS CHIEF'S SUPPORT, THE ARCHER FALLS AS SILENT AS THE CONCERNED WINDKIN, WATCHING OVER EMBER'S RESTING TRIBE.

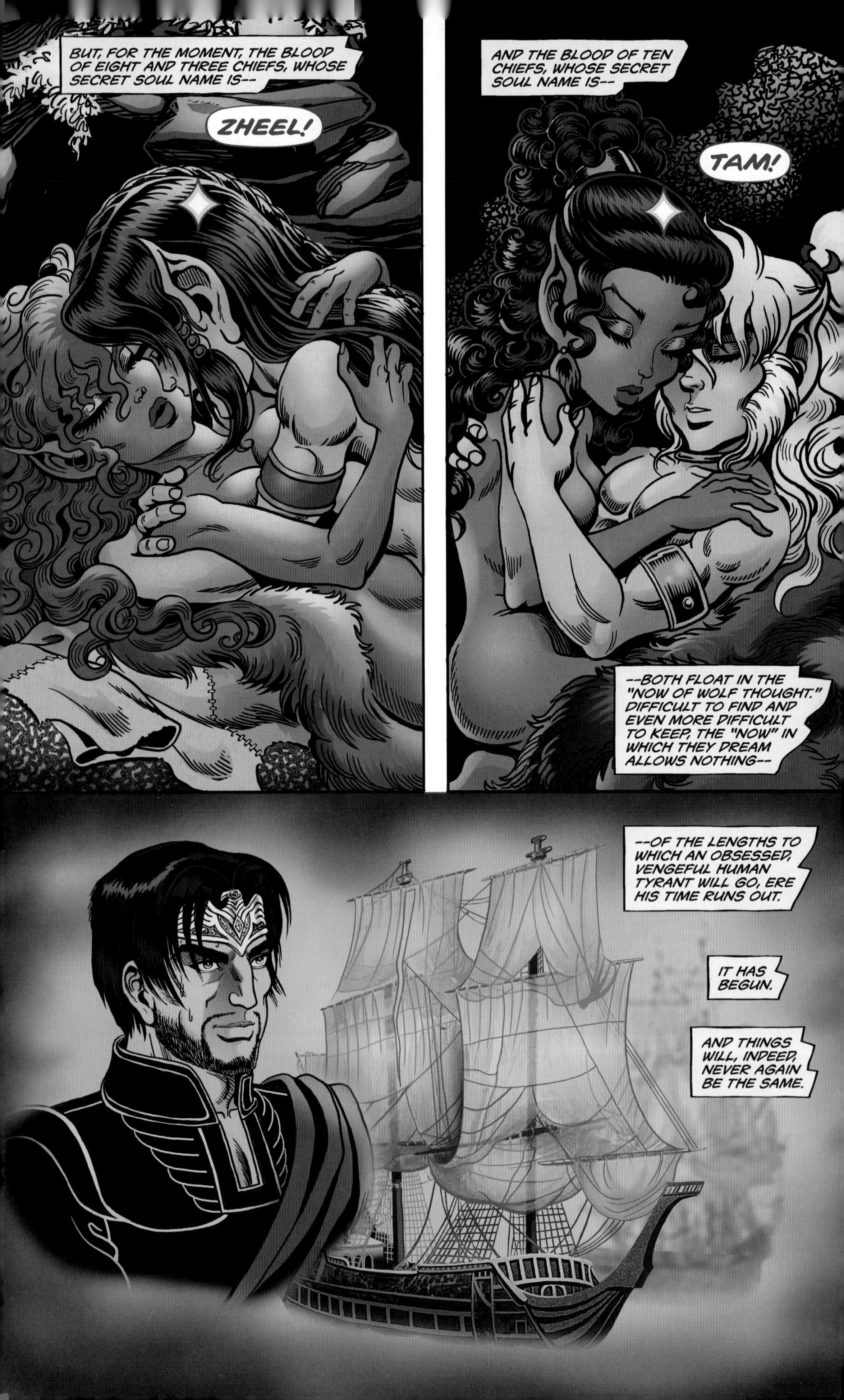
BUT, FOR THE MOMENT, THE BLOOD OF EIGHT AND THREE CHIEFS, WHOSE SECRET SOUL NAME IS--
ZHEEL!
AND THE BLOOD OF TEN CHIEFS, WHOSE SECRET SOUL NAME IS--
TAM!
--BOTH FLOAT IN THE "NOW OF WOLF THOUGHT." DIFFICULT TO FIND AND EVEN MORE DIFFICULT TO KEEP, THE "NOW" IN WHICH THEY DREAM ALLOWS NOTHING--
--OF THE LENGTHS TO WHICH AN OBSESSED, VENGEFUL HUMAN TYRANT WILL GO, ERE HIS TIME RUNS OUT.
IT HAS BEGUN.
AND THINGS WILL, INDEED, NEVER AGAIN BE THE SAME.

COVER GALLERY

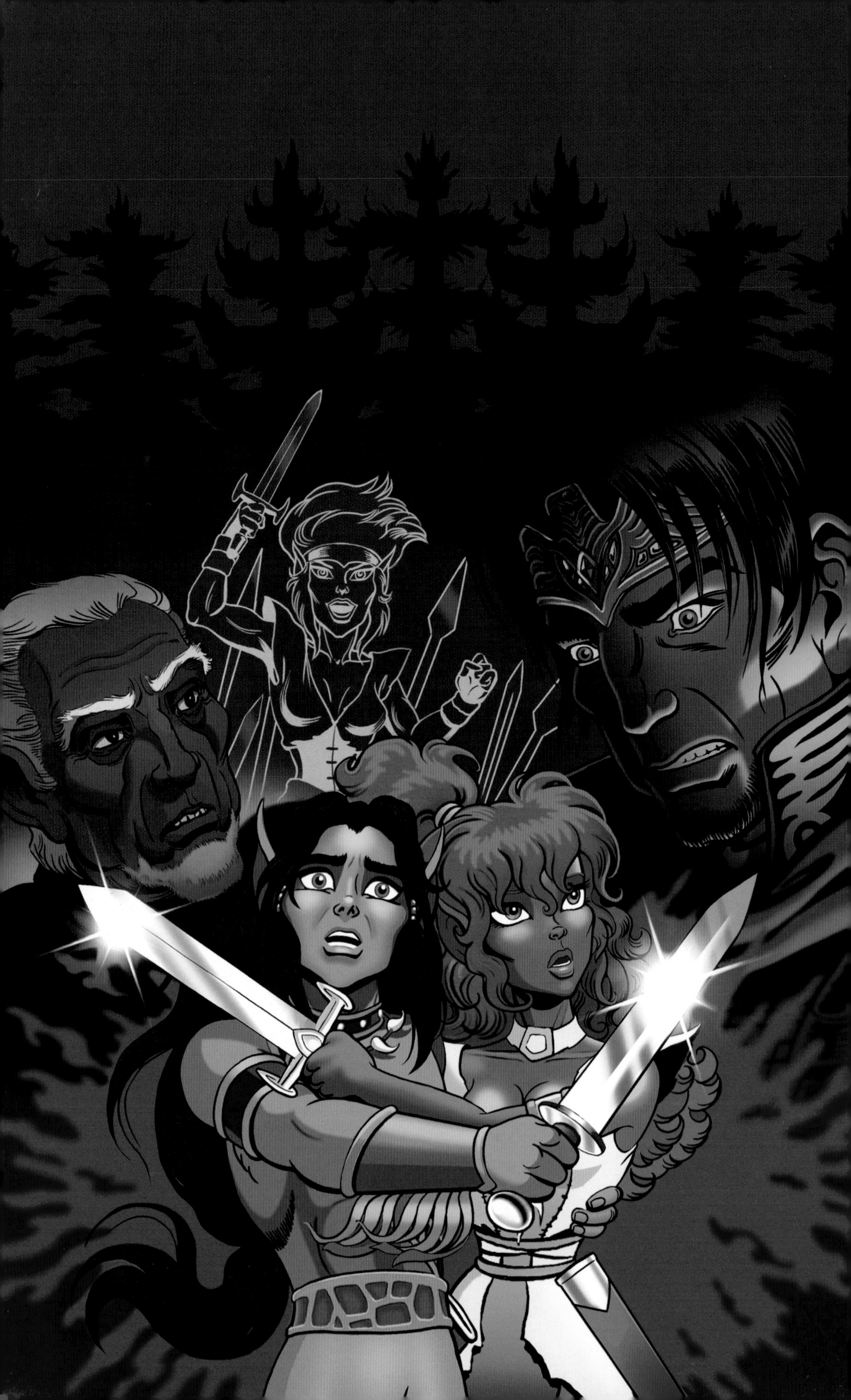

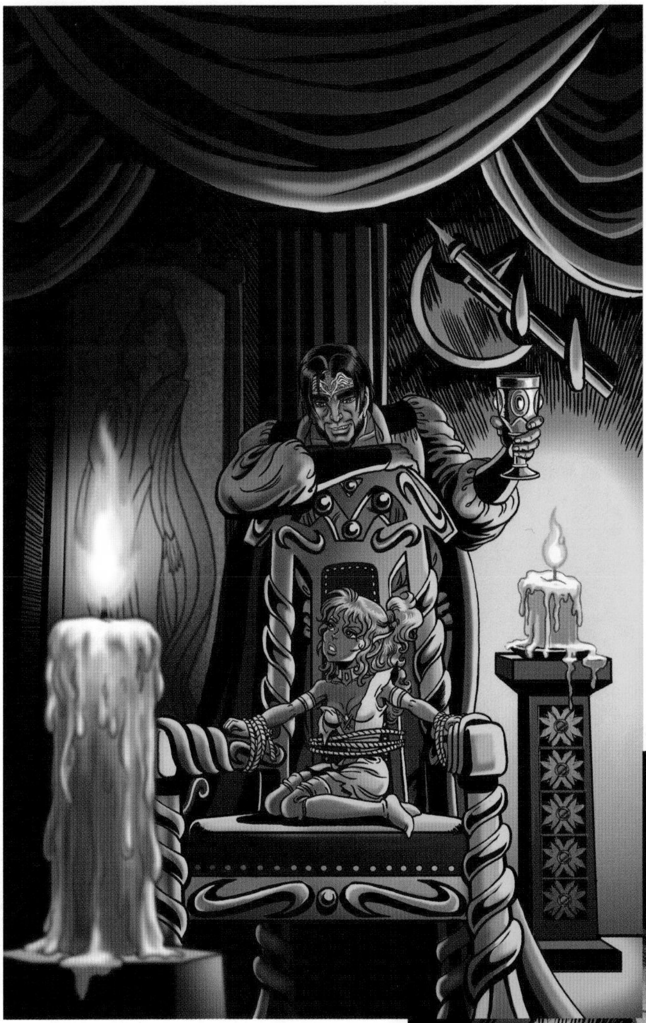

Every Final Quest cover is symbolic. For Final Quest Special (page 6), Wendy used the classic trio design, set against the shimmering Palace of the High Ones, but also hinted via the broken Bridge of Destiny that things could start falling apart. Issue #1 (frontispiece) puts Ember front and center. She's strong, she's the pivotal character, and she makes no apologies! In issue #2 (opposite), Ember and Teir finally experience Recognition, but the normally happy event is assaulted from all sides as the lovers seek to protect each other.

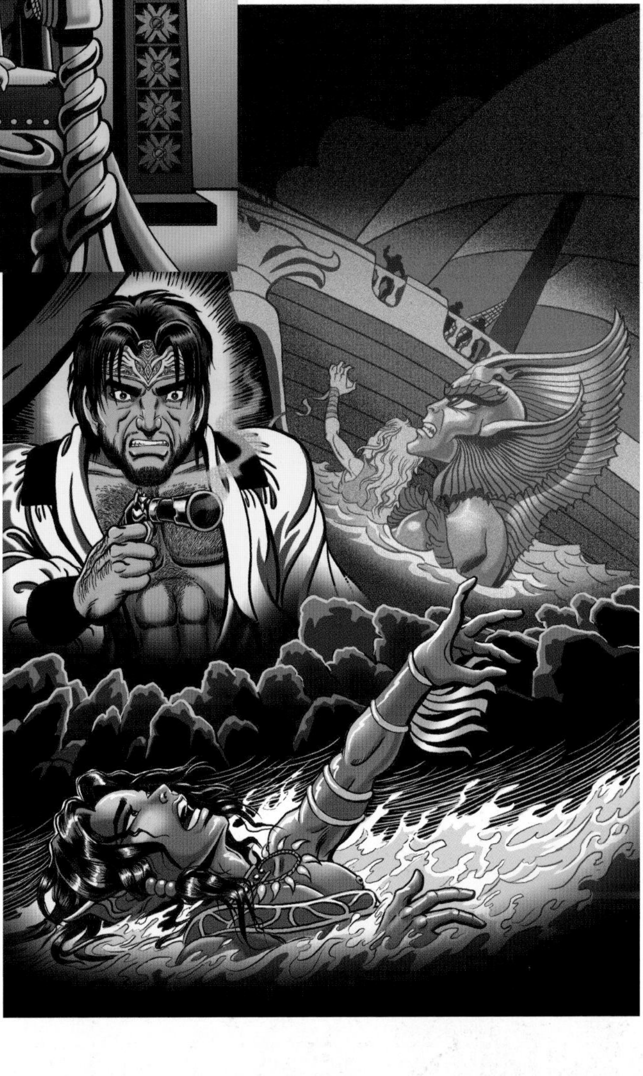

We don't often realize how diminutive the elves are, compared to humans. The cover to issue #3 (above) brings the disparity home, as Ember is dwarfed by the Djun's massive chair. Final Quest #4's cover (right) paints the issue's main story elements in bold colors to create visual tension and excitement. Issue #5's cover (next page) was the most difficult for Wendy. She hates the very idea of bondage yet dug deep to show Ember in that awful state. Finally, the cover to issue #6 (page 191) features two swords that were lost, symbolizing the losses Ember and Teir have both had to make.

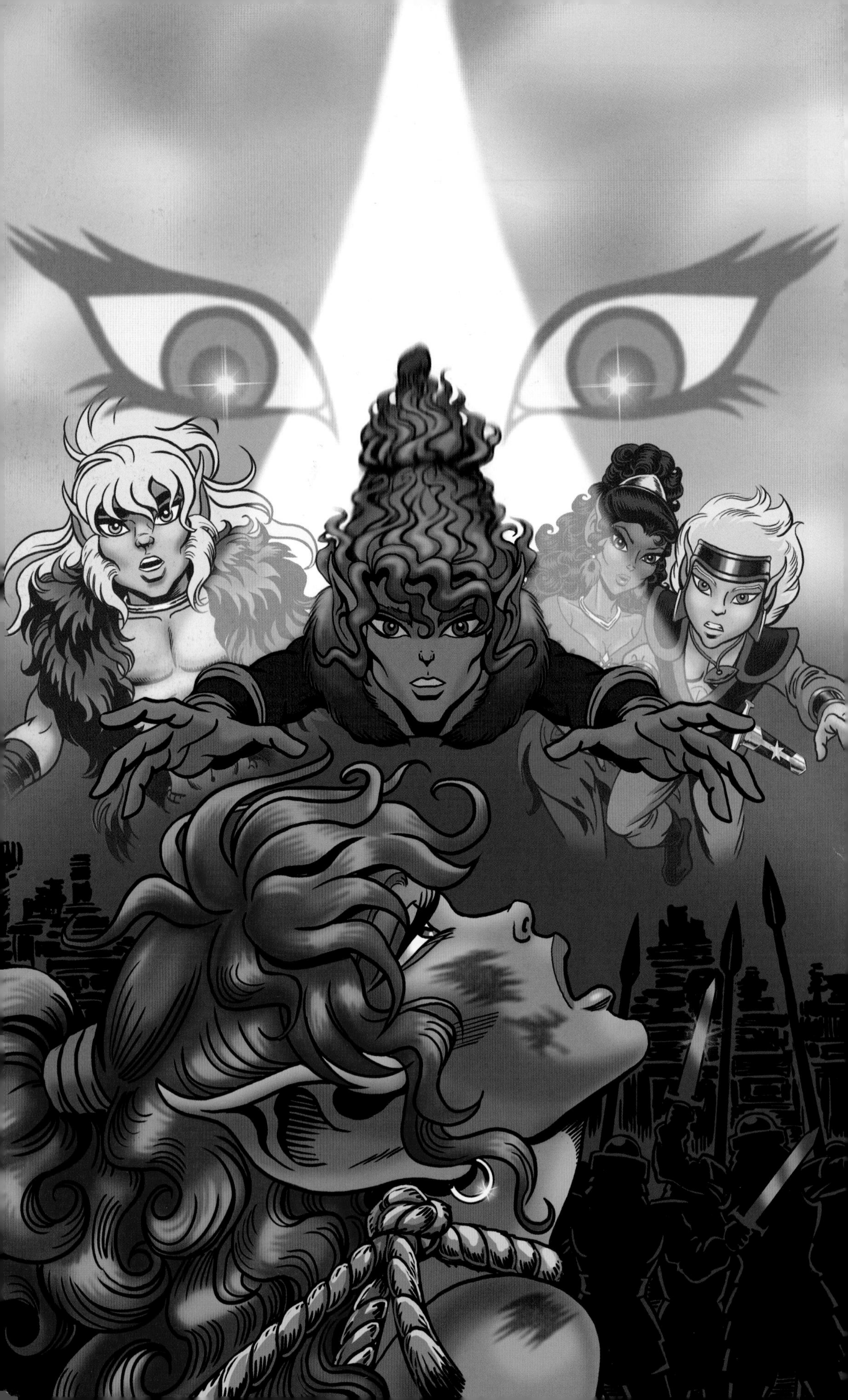

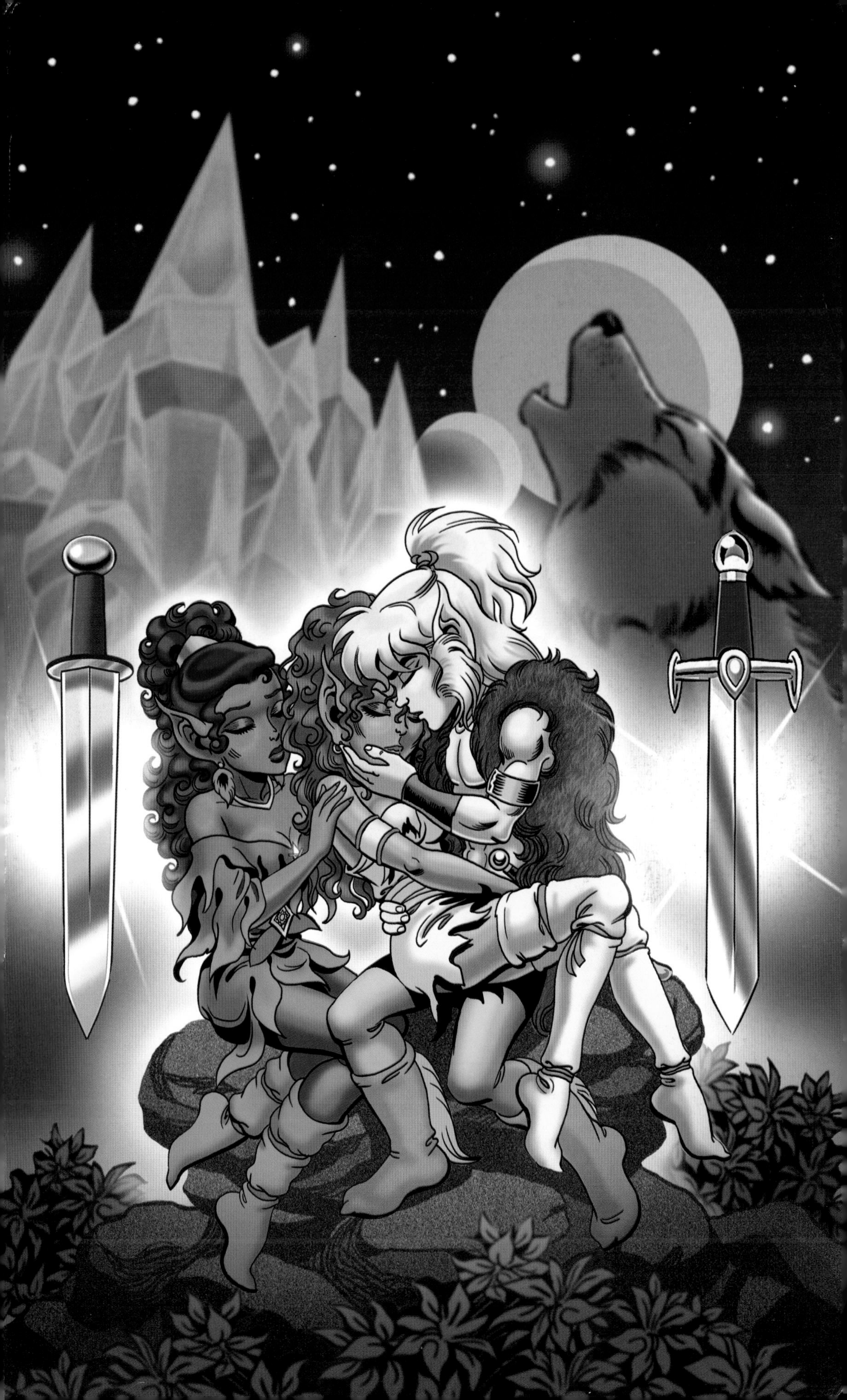

ElfQuest®

DISCOVER THE LEGEND OF *ELFQUEST*! ALLIANCES ARE FORGED, ENEMIES DISCOVERED, AND SAVAGE BATTLES FOUGHT IN THIS EPIC FANTASY ADVENTURE, HANDSOMELY PRESENTED BY DARK HORSE BOOKS!

THE COMPLETE ELFQUEST
Volume 1: The Original Quest
978-1-61655-407-1 | $24.99

Volume 2
978-1-61655-408-8 | $24.99

ELFQUEST: THE ORIGINAL QUEST GALLERY EDITION
978-1-61655-411-8 | $125.00

ELFQUEST: THE FINAL QUEST
Volume 1
978-1-61655-409-5 | $17.99

Volume 2
978-1-61655-410-1 | $17.99
Coming in 2016!